THE COMPANY OF ADVENTURERS

THE AUTHOR "TAGGED," JUNE, 1913, BY LADY
COLLECTORS FOR NINETTE SANITARIUM,

THE COMPANY OF ADVENTURERS

A NARRATIVE OF SEVEN YEARS IN THE SERVICE OF THE
HUDSON'S BAY COMPANY DURING 1867-1874

ON THE GREAT BUFFALO PLAINS

WITH HISTORICAL AND BIOGRAPHICAL NOTES AND COMMENTS

BY

ISAAC COWIE

Introduction to the Bison Book Edition
by David Reed Miller

Illustrated by Black and White Copies of Water-color Sketches made by a Swiss Settler
on his journey from Europe, via Hudson Bay, to Red River Settlement
in 1821, through the courtesy of Dr. Doughty, C.M.G., Dominion
Archivist, and other hitherto unpublished pictures

University of Nebraska Press
Lincoln and London

First Bison Book printing: 1993
Most recent printing indicated by the last digit below:
10   9   8   7   6   5   4   3   2   1

Library of Congress Cataloging-in-Publication Data
Cowie, Isaac, b. 1848.
The company of adventurers: a narrative of seven years in the service of the Hudson's Bay Company during 1867–1874 on the great buffalo plains . . . / by Isaac Cowie; introduction to the Bison book edition by David Reed Miller.
p.   cm.
Originally published: Toronto: William Briggs, 1913.
"Bison book."
ISBN 0-8032-1464-2
ISBN 0-8032-6350-3 (pbk.).
1. Northwest, Canadian—Description and travel—1867–1950.
2. Cowie, Isaac, b. 1848. 3. Hudson's Bay Company. 4. Fur trade—Northwest, Canadian—History—19th century. I. Title.
F1060.9.C87   1993
917.19'2041—dc20
92-37703
CIP

Reprinted from the original edition published by William Briggs, Toronto, in 1913. The University of Nebraska Press is indebted to Isaac Cowie's granddaughter, Barbara Johnstone, for supplying a copy of that edition for reproduction. In order to accommodate a new introduction and avoid repagination of the entire volume, arabic page numbering in this Bison Book edition begins with the dedication.

∞

CONTENTS

APPENDIX A.

APPENDIX B.

APPENDIX C.

LIST OF ILLUSTRATIONS

LIST OF ILLUSTRATIONS

8

Introduction to the Bison Book Edition

By David Reed Miller

In the 1860s young Isaac Cowie went to the Canadian North-west as an employee of the Hudson's Bay Company. Luckily for us, he kept a vivid journal of his voyage through Hudson Bay and his years as a fur trader at Fort Qu'Appelle, located on the Qu'Appelle River, a tributary of the Assiniboine River.

Arriving just prior to a time of treaty-making with Indian groups on the prairies, Cowie was able to record a number of observations before their eventual forced relocation to reserves. He also witnessed the rising frustration of Métis seeking to define a place within the changing frontier environment of Red River and the adjacent prairies. His remarkable description, for example, of Indian groups and their encampments in the Qu'Appelle Valley is the most definitive of the few that exist for the Canadian prairies of this period.[1]

Many years later, Cowie embellished his journal, offering his reflections and opinions in hindsight. The chapters of these reminiscences of an old frontiersman and settler were first serialized in columns of the *Manitoba Free Press,* and published in book form as *The Company of Adventurers* in 1913.

The arrival of eighteen-year-old Isaac Cowie in the Qu'Appelle River Valley in 1867 occurred during an important shift in the economic and social role of the fur trade in Canada. The Hudson's Bay Company was confronting the industrial age as the buffalo hide and provisions trades were declining. The stockholders' economic interests had shifted to opening settlement through land sales, developing mineral resources, and fostering new forms of transportation.[2]

The British government did not encroach jurisdictionally into the Red River country until 1857, with its Board of Trade amendment to the Company's charter "granting the Crown authority to annex any portion of the Company's chartered territories for the purpose of establishing a Crown colony."[3] When the

Company's exclusive license to trade in the Northwest Territory and the Pacific Coast was about to expire, a select committee of the House of Commons sought to determine the character of the Company's progress, the regions in which it conducted business, the suitability of activities beyond the fur trade, and the opportunities for agricultural settlement. The HBC governor Sir George Simpson wanted another full-term extension, claiming that the Northwest was fit only for the trade. The committee recommended that the Company's monopoly be continued in the Far North where there was little chance of settlement, but that Crown colonies be allowed on Vancouver Island and the Pacific slope, and that "the way be left open for acquisition of the valleys of the Red and Saskatchewan by Canada."[4] The Dawson-Hind and Palliser explorations of the Canadian prairies in 1857 gave an impression of open country with little game, especially buffalo, left, and economically declining societies of Indians and Métis.[5]

During Simpson's governorship in the first part of the nineteenth century, an employment preference for Orkneymen as "European" clerks was established, often to the disadvantage of Métis or mixed-blood descendants of trade personnel of previous generations. A contemporary historian observed, "The islanders' hardihood, docility, and diligence, as well as their obvious poverty, were likely to make them good servants." With Stromness often being the last port of call for most HBC ships heading to the bay, they were readily available. The last recorded group of islanders came in the year 1891.[6] Another disposition for adaptability that made islanders preferred as employees was the ease with which they intermarried with Cree and other Indian women. Earlier generations of Orkneymen had intermarried with Swampy Cree women. Many of these men retired with their families to the Red River settlement. Frequently their sons assumed various positions in the trade, and many daughters became the wives of successive generations of newcomers to the country.[7]

Isaac Cowie was born 18 November 1848 in Lerwick, Shetland Islands, the second child of Dr. John Cowie, who had served as HBC ship's surgeon on a trip to the Bay in 1849, and later as an HBC recruiting officer in Shetland and Orkney. Isaac Cowie's mother was Margaret Heddell Greig, daughter of the procurator fiscal for Shetland. Isaac had three brothers: Robert, who followed his father into medicine; James, who followed Isaac into the trade as a clerk; and Archibald, who became a journalist in London. Isaac was educated in grammar schools in Lerwick and Aberdeen, and worked in a lawyer's office as a clerk for twenty-one months between 1864 and 1866. In August 1866 he made his first application to the HBC, shortly before his father's death. During the winter of 1867, while awaiting his acceptance, he completed two sessions of medical courses at Edinburgh University. He also served three years as a part-time militiaman in the 1st Zetland Rifles. With a broad range of experience, Isaac entered into contract with the HBC as an apprentice clerk, leaving in July 1867, and was assigned to Fort Qu'Appelle, where he served until 1874.[8] One of his remarkable achievements during this time was his vaccinating of the Qu'Appelle area Indians during a smallpox epidemic the autumn of 1869 (see pages 381–82). In 1870–71, he wintered at Last Mountain Lake (located forty-three kilometres northwest from present-day Regina, Saskatchewan), and in 1871–72 at the Cypress Hills (located near present-day Maple Creek, Saskatchewan).[9] He was promoted to clerk and given charge of Fort Qu'Appelle in 1872. The story of his trip to Canada and this initial period of employment are the subject of *The Company of Adventurers*.

Cowie's employment with the Hudson's Bay Company continued beyond the time described in his book. He was assigned to Manitobah House, 1874–79; Ile a la Crosse/Portage La Loche, 1879–80; Fort McMurray, 1880–88 (furlough in 1884 for his honeymoon to Britain); furlough 1888–89; Norway House/Ile a la Crosse, 1889–90/1890–91, and retired, according to his service card, with the rank of junior chief trader in September 1891.[10]

On 29 March 1884 Isaac Cowie married Margaret Jane Sinclair of St. Andrew's parish, made up of fur-trade families located twenty miles north of present-day Winnipeg. Her parents were HBC clerk William Sinclair and Jane MacDonald, daughter of a HBC Blackfoot interpreter/York boat steersman, "Big" Donald MacDonald. Cowie's wife was educated and understood the demands of the trade upon the families of Company employees. Five of their eight children reached adulthood.[11]

Cowie did not leave his employment with the Company entirely on amicable terms. He had been lured by the romanticism of the trade and the Canadian West, but his initial enthusiasm waned as years passed and as he found himself receiving what he regarded as insufficient recognition for his record of faithful service. Shortly before Christmas 1889, while in charge of the English River District Ile a la Crosse post, he exchanged blows with his subordinate, Colin McIntyre. Not long after having arrived in the English River District, Cowie was joined by his wife; both of them were grieving over the recent death of their three-year-old daughter, Effie. Early in the new year the local Oblate priest, Father Rapet, conveyed to Bishop Grandin reports of "drunken and threatened violence" having occurred in the post at Ile a la Crosse. The bishop's subsequent complaint was relayed to Commissioner Wrigley in Winnipeg, who dispatched J. McDougall to investigate the rumored incidents.[12] McDougall forwarded his inspection report on 1 May, including testimony of several clerks. Making no definite recommendations, he noted that "a very unfriendly feeling appears to have existed between Messrs. Cowie and McIntyre from the time of the former's arrival in the district. Former managers of the district appear to have had perfect confidence in Mr. McIntyre and he was spoken of as a capable and reliable officer."[13]

McIntyre, a clerk, was resentful of Cowie's apparent favoritism toward another clerk, McDermot, who was seeking to be posted to Green Lake, a position that McIntyre also sought. He appeared to be jealous because Cowie was expressing his gratitude "that Mr. McDermot's sister who is a hospital nurse was so kind to his little girl when she was sick."[14] McIntyre conspired to undermine a portion of the trade to make Cowie look bad, communicating surreptitiously with Chief Samuel of the Ile a la Crosse Chipewyans. This letter was suppressed by Father Rapet because he knew "it might injure the Company's business."[15] However, Father Rapet was more concerned about the example the HBC men were demonstrating for the Native peoples he was attempting to missionize. He was horrified when, after getting to know Cowie and his wife, he realized that the allegations against Cowie were mostly unsubstantiated. Chief Samuel Egou of the Chipewyans also attempted to retract his previous statement, solicited by McIntyre, and to express his new-found confidence in Cowie, but to no avail. The damage had been done in the form of negative impressions promoted about Cowie and his competence.[16]

In the midst of this controversy, Cowie sought a promotion or additional compensation, explaining that he was deeply in debt. He hoped to clear the debt over a period of three years, but recognized that it would be difficult on the salary of a junior trader. The special demands of travel and boarding expenses with the position of junior trader also posed extreme hardship without additional compensation. Cowie responsibly had secured his loan with a life insurance policy that was in the possession of the Northern Department office. He explained that illness in his family had caused him to be on furlough from Athabasca in Outfit 1888. The expense of travel and board in Manitoba for three months in connection with this and the final burden of medical and funeral expenses—all resulted in his increased personal debt.[17] The correspondence about his request recognized his value to the Company in his particular position, and recommended meeting his terms.[18] Cowie's, or the Company's, decision not to continue his employment was undoubtedly influenced by a combination of factors, but foremost may have been the extent of his indebtedness and the regulations concerning the promotion he sought. Cowie blamed HBC Governor Donald Smith for turning loose many career men prior to their term of eligibility for pension.[19] The tone of his comments about the HBC in some of his later columns and in places in *The Company of Adventurers* reflected his increasingly critical attitude and his sense of personal injustice.

Cowie moved his family to Edmonton, where, between 1892 and 1901, he was involved in real estate and insurance businesses; was a founder, secretary, and president of the Edmonton Board of Trade; and began the intermittent practice of writing promotional pamphlets.[20]

In 1892 the anthropologist Franz Boas, working for the World's Columbian Exposition in Chicago, engaged Cowie to prepare a collection of Plains Cree material culture, to include as complete an inventory of objects as possible. The collection, apparently collected from the Battle River areas near Edmonton, numbered 110 objects, including a hide tipi. It was displayed in the ethnological exhibitions of the Exposition. Cowie was awarded a certificate of merit and a medal in a competition for collections contributed by amateur ethnologists. The ethnographic value of his collection, which was later incorporated into those of the Field Museum of Natural History, has been recognized in several publications.[21] Cowie may have assisted Boas with some anthropometry fieldwork, but the only record that exists outside of family recollections is one article by Cowie.[22]

The Northwest was rough and tumble in many ways, and the economics of survival were often arduous. Cowie, who was filled with many ideas for developing the region, was drawn to Edmonton because of its expanding economic climate. At that time, with perseverance, gold could be panned from the Saskatchewan River near Edmonton, and Cowie considered major dredge-mining operations. Searching for backers, he even traveled to England to attract investors. He arranged for the Earl of Minto, Governor-General of Canada, to be present for the christening of one of his barges on the Saskatchewan River, seeking all the publicity he could in the promotion of this venture. Eventually, however, the shares for gold-dredging operations became worthless, as the venture was not successful on the scale Cowie had imagined.

Cowie also had an idea, which he outlined in a booklet, "The All Red Route to the Arctic," for utilizing waterways to connect Edmonton via the MacKenzie River system and around Alaska to the Pacific. This scheme drew upon his own experience of supervising the HBC York boat brigade transport in the Athabasca District and his role in putting the first steamboats on the northern waters.[23] Confronted with the necessity of supporting a family, Cowie fell in with the promoters. However, in his granddaughter's opinion, he was never really one with them because he lacked both the personal capital and the disposition to take advantage of others for personal profit.[24] Although his responsibilities in real-estate transactions included the buying and selling of Métis scrip, he became increasingly sympathetic to the contemporary plight of the Métis and the ways in which they as a group were being denied a land base.[25]

In the spring of 1901 Cowie's wife died suddenly of peritonitis at the age of thirty-seven. She had left the children with her mother in Winnipeg, going to Chicago for the necessary surgery. Returning to his children in Winnipeg, Cowie was taken off the train in Calgary with typhoid fever, and could not go on until he had partially recovered. Another daughter, Jessie, died in 1912 at age seventeen of meningitis, and his eleven-and-a-half-year-old daughter Ruby assumed the mother role for the family.[26]

In Winnipeg, Cowie was again an agent for a land company and soon became a free-lance writer, lobbyist and promoter of old settlers' land claims, researcher, amateur historian and copyist. From 1901 until his death in 1917, Winnipeg was his home.

Cowie's business activities included affiliation with his late wife's uncle by marriage, John B. Allan, in the Canada West Land Company, which continued to involve him in real estate. Soon after arriving in Winnipeg, Cowie was befriended by John W. Dafoe, publisher of the *Manitoba Free Press,* who asked him to contribute a weekly column on historical topics. Motivated to seek ideas and research subjects for his column, Cowie looked for individuals with an interest in the history of the Canadian West and with experiences similar to his own.

Drawing upon his background in real estate, and especially in the handling of the various forms of scrip, Cowie was instrumental in the forming of organizations that also sought special issuances of scrip for land arrangements. Four of these groups were the Winnipeg Old Times Association, the Hudson's Bay Colonists of Assiniboia, the Veterans of the Fur Trade Association (led by the Rev. Mr. Taylor of Prince Albert, Saskatchewan), and the Pioneers of Rupert's Land, the last of which he served for many years as executive secretary. For these groups he was both an important researcher and a lobbyist in the pursuit of their specific land claims. Cowie was among the retired fur-trade employees who joined with the descendants of the earliest settlers in the region to protest unfair treatment in access to lands that were being made available to recent immigrants but not to those who felt they had built the country in its early stages. In the course of preparing arguments for such protests, Cowie was drawn into historical research, where he began to recognize the importance of historical documents. For example, his assistance in publishing details of the Rev. Mr. Taylor's discovery of an early register of all the settlers on Red River lands (between the time of the Selkirk colonization efforts and the 1860s) allowed specific individual claims to be validated.[27] Several times he journeyed to Ottawa to lobby and took these opportunities to pursue historical research in libraries and archival collections. These were times of revelation and joy to him.[28]

His vocation fed a growing avocation as an amateur historian. His fascination with historical documents led to his locating HBC and other fur trade or regional historical documents—such as post journals, correspondence, and ledgers—that had, for one reason or another, ended up in the possession of individuals rather than the Company. Cowie learned that documents that had been in buildings at old Fort Qu'Appelle were still in the hands of a local neighbor. Cowie was able to borrow these and make complete copies before returning them, his usual practice when he located new items. Seeking resources to keep up his searches and to defray the costs of reproduction, he would contact individuals, archives, or libraries he thought would be interested in buying copies. In one case, his copies of some of these documents were published under his name as editor in the *Collections of the State Historical Society of North Dakota*.[29] Other collections with Cowie typescripts included the Arthur S. Morton Papers at the University of Saskatchewan and those in the Saskatchewan Provincial Archives, British Columbia Provincial Archives, Alberta Provincial Archives, Minnesota Historical Society, and the Manitoba Provincial Archives. He was an early promoter for the founding of the Manitoba Provincial Archives. Initially, the recipients of his copies were grateful to receive them, given the value of the historical information, but some archivists became concerned to have original typescript copies rather than carbon copies. Several archivists began to compare notes and were distressed to find Cowie in the business of selling these copies to multiple public repositories. Cowie, not a professional historical documentary editor, appears, in good faith, to have perceived himself to be providing information important to preserve for future researchers.[30]

At the urging of a number of people, Cowie arranged to have his serialization for the *Manitoba Free Press* published in book form. Much of the preparation of *The Company of Adventurers* for publication, including the excellent indexing, which was rare for histories of this time, was done in collaboration with his daughter, Ruby Johnstone, who during the years in Winnipeg was his assistant and typist. The publisher, William Briggs, stipulated that Cowie had to secure three hundred advance subscribers before printing the approximately five hundred copies, since he felt that only western Canadians would be interested readers. The promotion for the book was also left to Cowie, and, according to his descendants, he realized no direct financial gain from its publication.[31]

Although *The Company of Adventurers* was well received by the initial subscribers, and reviewed in the major Canadian prairie newspapers, its success was limited. Cowie began thinking of other book-length projects—one about his accomplishments in Edmonton and another that would pick up in 1874 and continue documenting the second part of his HBC career. He began manuscripts, but none of these has survived among his papers.[32] Because of his busy lobbying, the collapse of his health, and the coming of the First World War (which put an end to the federal government's consideration of additional land claims through scrip proposals), neither of these book projects was completed.

This book is a major testament to Cowie, who had experienced the fur trade as it was waning in an increasingly industrialized world. The significance of *The Company of Adventurers* rests on the quality of Cowie's observations and individual perspectives. It is particularly important that he was positioned to observe cultural and social dynamics among northern Plains Indians in their relations with traders and missionaries at a time when few availed themselves of such an opportunity.

NOTES

1. Cowie's original journal from which this book was written is not located in his papers in the Hudson's Bay Company Archives (HBCA), housed in the Manitoba Provincial Archives, Winnipeg, E.86/1-65. Cowie's manuscript HBC journal of daily occurrences for his winter at Last Mountain House is part of a collection sold to W. R. Coe for the Coe Collection of Western Americana of Yale University in 1958, collection description and accompanying notation supplied by W. Kaye Lamb from a letter of 2 March 1958, Fort Qu'Appelle Search File, HBCA.

Other accounts for the Canadian Prairies that treat the vicinity of the Qu'Appelle River valley for this same period include: W. F. Butler, *The Great Lone Land: A Narrative of Travel and Adventurer in the*

Northwest of America (London: Sampson, Low, Marston, Low, and Searle, 1872), travels in 1870–1871; Henry Youle Hind, *North-west Territory. Reports of Progress; Together with a Preliminary and General Report on the Assiniboine and Saskatchewan Exploring Expedition, Made Under Instructions from the Provincial Secretary, Canada* (Toronto: J. Lovell, 1859); John Palliser, *The Papers of the Palliser Expedition 1857–1860*, edited by Irene Spry, *Publications of the Champlain Society* Vol. 44 (Toronto: Champlain Society, 1968), travels in 1857–1860; and James Carnegie, Ninth Earl of Southesk, *Saskatchewan and the Rocky Mountains* (Edinburgh: Edmonston and Douglas, 1875), travels in 1859–1860.

2. Arthur J. Ray, *The Canadian Fur Trade in the Industrial Age* (Toronto: University of Toronto Press, 1989), 1–48.

3. George F. G. Stanley, *The Birth of Western Canada: A History of the Riel Rebellions* (Toronto: University of Toronto Press, 1960), 21.

4. W. L. Morton, *Manitoba: A History* (Toronto: University of Toronto Press, 1957), 95.

5. Ibid., 96–97.

6. Elaine Allan Mitchell, "The Scot in the Fur Trade," in *The Scottish Tradition in Canada,* ed. W. Stanford Reid (Toronto: McClelland and Stewart, 1976), 40–41. The demand for islanders is discussed in Philip Goldring, "Lewis and the Hudson's Bay Company in the Nineteenth Century," *Scottish Studies* 24 (1980): 23–42. The climate and cultural geography of the Shetlands, Cowie's homeland, are described in detail in Alexander Fenton, *The Northern Isles: Orkney and Shetland* (Edinburgh: John Donald Publishers Ltd., 1978), and in Cowie's brother's book, Robert Cowie, *Shetland, Descriptive and Historical, and a Topographical Description of That Country* (Aberdeen, 1871).

7. See discussions by Jennifer S. H. Brown, *Strangers in Blood: Fur Trade Company Families in Indian Country* (Vancouver: University of British Columbia Press, 1980); Irene M. Spry, "The Métis and Mixed-blood of Rupert's Land before 1870," in Jacqueline Peterson and Jennifer S. H. Brown, editors, *The New People: Being and Becoming Métis in North America* (Winnipeg: University of Manitoba Press and Lincoln: University of Nebraska Press, 1985), 95–118; and Sylvia Van Kirk, *"Many Tender Ties": Women in Fur-Trade Society, 1670–1870* (Winnipeg: Watson & Dwyer and Norman: University of Oklahoma Press, 1980). These examine the emerging racialism of nineteenth century fur trade society which further reflected the rigidity of Victorian-era social mores of race and class.

8. Letter of Isaac Cowie, Lerwick, Shetland Isles, to Nicol Finlayson, late Chief Factor, HBC, August 1866, copy supplied to the author by Professor Victor Cowie, a great nephew. Considerable biographical information is provided in a letter to the author from Barbara A. John-

stone (granddaughter of Isaac Cowie), 6 March 1981. Ms. Johnstone is a former custodian (1953–58) and curator (1958–61) of the HBC Museum in Winnipeg and superintendent of Lower Fort Garry National Historic Park (1961–67).

9. The Last Mountain House post site, a Saskatchewan Provincial Historic Park, was excavated in the mid-1960s by the Regina Archaeological Society; see the site report, Olga Klimko and John Hodges, *Last Mountain House: A Hudson's Bay Company Outpost in the Qu'Appelle Valley* (in press). Reconstructed buildings and displays of selected artifacts were completed in the 1970s and opened to the public during the summer months (*Last Mountain House Provincial Historic Park,* Saskatchewan Parks and Renewable Resources, brochure, n.d.). The location of Cowie's Cypress Hills post is thought to be in the vicinity of the Chimney Coulee, at the east end of the Cypress Hills (*Guide to Historic Sites and Points of Interest,* Regina: Saskatchewan Diamond Jubilee & Canada Centennial Corporation, 1965, 19).

10. Barbara Johnstone letter to author, 6 March 1981.

11. Ibid.

12. See Commissioner Wrigley's Correspondence Inward, HBCA D.20/60/1a, fols. 15–25: McDougall to Wrigley, 1 May 1890; Rapet to Wrigley, 20 March 1890; S. L. Parsons to Wrigley, 5 May 1890; Cowie to Wrigley, 8 May 1890; copy of Cowie to William Armit, London, 8 May 1890 (fol. 73); Parson to Wrigley, 12 May 1890. The author acknowledges the contribution of John Hample's unpublished paper "A Preliminary Sounding of Isaac Cowie's Papers" (1986) in locating these sources and providing an initial interpretive reconstruction of these events.

13. McDougall to Wrigley, 1 May 1890, HBCA D.20/60/1a, fol. 15.

14. McIntyre to Wrigley, 12 January 1890, HBCA D.20/60/1a, fol. 21.

15. McDougall to Wrigley, 1 May 1890, HBCA D.20/60/1a, fol. 16.

16. Rapet to Wrigley, 28 March 1890, HBCA D.20/60/1a, fol. 25–28; and Rapet to Honorable Sir (probably Commissioner Wrigley in Winnipeg), 9 June 1890, HBCA D.20/60/2a, fol. 291–92.

17. Cowie to William Armit, London, 8 May 1890, HBCA D.20/60/1a, fol. 73.

18. S. H. Parson, Montreal, to Joseph Wrigley, Winnipeg, 5 May 1890, HBCA D.20/60/1a, fol. 55–56; and ibid, 12 May 1890, HBCA D.20/60/1a, fol. 104–5.

19. For a discussion of the career of Donald A. Smith and his influence in the HBC, see Arthur J. Ray, *The Canadian Fur Trade in the Industrial Age,* 12–16, 18–19.

20. Pamphlets listed in HBCA Guide to Cowie Papers, Correspondence for E.86/21 include such titles as: *The Agricultural & Mineral Resources of the Edmonton Country Alberta Canada* (1897; rev. ed.

1901, 55 pp.); *"To the Klondyke" Pocket Edition: La Rue & Picard's Guide to the Goldfields viz Edmonton* (n.d., 14 pp.); *The Western Plains of Canada Rediscovered, 1903,* by Isaac Cowie, author of "The Grass, Grain and Goldfields of Western Canada," etc. (n.d., 40 pp.); *Information for Intending Settlers Concerning Edmonton and District,* 1 fol., page proof, "one hundred questions and answers; *Edmonton: The Agricultural Possibilities and Resources of the Surrounding District: Information Issued by the Edmonton Board of Trade, 1908,* for the use of those intending to follow agricultural pursuits (1908, 26pp.).

21. Gretchen Beardsley, "Notes on Cree Medicines, Based on a collection Made by I. Cowie in 1892," *Papers of the Michigan Academy of Science, Arts, and Letters,* 27 (1941):483–96; and James W. VanStone, "The Isaac Cowie Collection of Plains Cree Material Culture from Central Alberta," *Fieldiana: Anthropology,* New Series, Number 17 (30 September 1991):1–56.

22. Barbara Johnstone letter to author, 6 March 1981; Isaac Cowie, "The Half-Blood Indian—An Anthropomorphic Study," *Manitoba Free Press,* 14 August 1915, 11 and 15.

23. Ibid.

24. Interview, Barbara Johnstone with the author, 24 August 1991.

25. Cowie's circular describing "the (three) different kinds of scrip in which I deal." HBCA E.86/3 Cowie Papers. For details about the Half Breed Scrip, its origin, administration, and the traffic in its sale, see discussions in Paul L. A. H. Chartrand, *Manitoba's Métis Settlement Scheme of 1870* (Saskatoon: Native Law Centre, University of Saskatchewan, 1991); Gerhard Ens, "Métis Lands in Manitoba," *Manitoba History* 5 (1983) : 2–11, and "Dispossession or Adaptation? Migration and Persistence of the Red River Métis, 1835–1890," *Historical Papers 1988* (Ottawa: Canadian Historical Association, 1988), pp. 120–144; Thomas E. Flanagan, "The History of Métis Aboriginal Rights: Politics, Principle, and Policy," *Canadian Journal of Law and Society* 5 (1990): 71–94, and *Métis Lands in Manitoba* (Calgary: University of Calgary Press, 1991); Joe Sawchuk, Patricia Sawchuk, and Theresa Ferguson, *Métis Land Rights in Alberta: A Political History* (Edmonton: Métis Association of Alberta, 1981); and D. N. Sprague, "Government Lawlessness in the Administration of Manitoba Land Claims, 1870–1887," *Manitoba Law Journal* 10 (1980) : 415–41, "The Manitoba Land Question, 1870–1882," *Journal of Canadian Studies* 15 (1980) : 3: 74–84, and *Canada and the Métis, 1869–1885* (Waterloo: Wilfrid Laurier University Press, 1988). Cowie's recognition of "French halfbreed" "legal" rights was connected to his own sense of injustice being done to the pioneers of Rupert's Land; see this book, 450–51.

26. Barbara Johnstone letter to author, 19 September 1991; and interview, 24 August 1991.

27. See Scrapbook of the Pioneers of Rupert's Land, 1908–1915 and other files in Cowie Papers, HBCA E.86/8-15.

28. Barbara Johnston letter to author, 6 March 1981.

29. Isaac Cowie, editor, "The Minutes of the Council of the Northern Department of Rupert's Land 1830 to 1843," *Collections of the State Historical Society of North Dakota,* Vol. 4 (Bismarck: State Historical Society of North Dakota, 1913), pp. 694–865. Dr. Orin G. Libby, Superintendent of the State Historical Society of North Dakota, was a correspondent of Cowie, and purchased a number of typescript copies of documents.

30. See correspondence in the Cowie Papers concerning the copying of Minutes of Council for the Northern Department (1912–1913), and regarding the copying of Fort Ellice Journals (1916), HBCA E. 86/6-7.

31. Briggs did not bind the whole print run; the remainder were only bound by Ryerson Press sometime after 1930, a number of years after the latter bought the Briggs' backlist. Ryerson put them on sale with the HBC's book department in Winnipeg. The later binding is green with black lettering, which distinguishes it from the blue with gold embossed seal of the HBC that was the initial binding; Ryerson Press to Miss[*sic*] Ruby B. Johnstone, 8 May 1924 (with more recent annotations by Barbara Johnstone), HBCA Cowie Papers E.86/2.

32. Barbara Johnstone letter to author, 6 March 1981.

PREFACE

To preserve in print some of the recollections of personal experiences and oral history of the West, which are so quickly perishing by the departure of old pioneers and frontiersmen on the last lone trail, I was asked by Mr. W. Sanford Evans, Editor of *The Winnipeg Telegram,* in 1902, and by Mr. J. W. Dafoe, Editor of *The Manitoba Free Press,* in 1912, to contribute a series of articles to their Saturday issues. As other older-timers, who were much better qualified, refrained from taking up their pens in the good cause, I was happy to avail myself of the opportunities so liberally accorded me by these influential periodicals. While I felt sure of finding, for my simple narrative of things as they were, indulgent appreciation by the old-timers generally, I was not prepared for the interest shown in the parts already published by so many of the newcomers, who are the pioneers of the present in this land of yet untouched—perhaps undreamt—natural resources. To meet a demand, often kindly expressed to me by those interested in the past, to have these published articles put in a collected form, and to bring down my recollections to a definite period, arrangements were made to bring out this book, ending with the time I left Fort Qu'Appelle, before the Mounted Police took effective possession of the plains, in June, 1874.

Herein are republished from *The Manitoba Free Press,* with slight corrections, mainly of typographical errors, the articles which I proposed in the Foreword thereto, down to " Summer Journey to Cypress Hills, 1868." Then, the estimated space for the whole of the proposed series of articles having been exceeded, further publication ceased. When Dr. William Briggs undertook to bring out this book it was estimated that one of 316 pages would cover the period from the summer of 1868 to the spring of 1874, it being impossible to include in a book of ordinary size as well what might have been written of Lake Manitoba, Ile à la Crosse, Portage la Loche and Athabasca; but the 316 pages have been exceeded beyond expectation, and I have learned the wisdom of first completing the manuscript of a book ere making a contract for its publication. As a consequence of this and the rush of other work on the publisher, the issue of the book has been delayed far beyond the time at which I hoped it might appear.

The arrangement with the publisher having been contingent upon my obtaining a sufficient number of subscribers, I now have the pleasure of thanking those whose kindness enabled me to guarantee him against loss; and I take pride in appending the list, which contains so many eminent and respected names.

For the illustrations I here record my grateful obligations to Dr. Doughty, Dominion Archivist, for the sketches by a Swiss Selkirk settler in 1821-2; to Mrs. Cowan, the widow of Dr. William Cowan (who was in charge of Fort Garry when it was seized by Riel in 1869), for many photographs of Hudson's Bay officials; to Mr. J. G. M. Christie for the picture of his grandfather, Governor Christie; to Mr. W. J. McLean for that of York Factory, by his father-in-law, Chief Trader Murray; and to retired Chief Factor William Clark for the view of Norway House so beautifully taken by Chief Factor James McDougall. My special acknowledgments are due to Mr. Edward Lawson, artist on the staff of *The Manitoba Free Press,* for touching up the Swiss artist's sketches for printing, and for drawing from my rude diagrams the bird's-eye view of Fort Qu'Appelle in 1867.

The country in which the Qu'Appelle Indians hunted and fought lay south and west from the great Saskatchewan trail which, passing north of Touchwood Hills to the North Saskatchewan at Carlton, followed the course of that river to Edmonton and terminated in pack trails through the Rocky Mountains. Distinguished travellers took that route, and wrote about the Saskatchewan country as the scene of their hunting exploits. The British and Canadian exploring expeditions of 1858-9, under Captain Palliser and Professor Hind, respectively, failed to cross the Couteau de Missouri to the south-west, and their farthest point west was only a few miles along the South Saskatchewan beyond the Elbow. Beyond the Couteau and the Elbow their native guides and men refused to proceed; for these marked, at that period, the limit of the hunting-grounds won by the Crees and their allies from the Blackfeet and other hostile tribes. To reach the Cyprè (erroneously now called " Cypress ") Hills, Palliser was obliged to go round by Edmonton, where he obtained Blackfoot guides and men acquainted with that tribe to accompany him in sufficient force to ensure tolerance on the journey south to the hills. Even under these circumstances his followers made the journey with fear and reluctance.

In 1859 the Right Honourable Henry Chaplin and the late Sir Frederick Johnstone made a buffalo-hunting dash across the Couteau to the Old Wives' Lakes, to which Mr. Archibald McDonald gave their names, that now appear on maps; but they published no record of their intrusion into the country lying west of the Couteau and stretching to the Cyprè Hills, which continued to be the battleground between the Qu'Appelle Indians and the Blackfoot Confederacy during my seven years on the plains. The scene of my story is largely in this region, whose records, up to the spring of 1874, have never before been written.

The limits of an ordinary book have rendered the mention of many interesting persons and incidents impossible, but, I hope, the facts herein derived from my own experience and from the credible information of others may prove of some historical value in the future and also be of interest to people of the present day. The only apology I have to make for " rushing into print " is already given in the Foreword—none of those who were better qualified seemed willing to take up the task. These, however, may have the goodness to correct and amplify the statements herein contained. Indeed, I hope, in view of a possible second edition, that anyone noting any error or omission will have the kindness to point it out to me; for I am anxious that the book may furnish reliable data of history for future reference.

Isaac Cowie.

Winnipeg,
Thanksgiving Day, 20th October, 1913.

FOREWORD

TO THE ARTICLES WHICH WERE PUBLISHED IN SATURDAY
ISSUES OF THE *MANITOBA FREE PRESS* FROM
FEBRUARY 17TH TO DECEMBER 14TH, 1912.

LISTENING to many a splendid story of adventure in the wilderness, around camp fires, and during the long winter nights before a blazing open chimney of the quarters in an isolated post, I have often urged the narrators to preserve in writing such interesting and valuable material. A few said they might take that trouble if it did not look like boasting, and others, who could tell the best of stories, were incapable of putting them on paper. But nearly all thought that there was nothing in their lives and adventures of interest to any-one outside of the Company's people and their friends and companions—the missionaries in the wilds. There was also an understanding, amounting to the effect of an unwritten law, that the Company's employees should publish nothing, and above all, when they occasionally visited parts civilized enough to have newspapers, to avoid reporters as they would his satanic majesty himself, lest some of the trade secrets of the solitudes might be revealed to rivals and other possible invaders of the fur preserves.

Since I ceased to be connected with the Company all this old policy of secrecy as to the Indian country has become a thing of the past in those parts in which I was stationed; and as those much better able and experienced than myself still refrain from recording their memories of life in the Hudson's Bay service, under many conditions which have passed away, never to return, and the few survivors of those participants in the past are rapidly, one by one, leaving on the last lone trail,

I shall attempt in the papers which follow to record such typical experiences and incidents as may serve to give new-comers to this country some idea of the life of their pre-decessors—the pioneers of Rupert's Land.

At the time of my coming to the country, in 1867, it was as much in the state of nature, outside the Red River Settle-ment and the pickets of the posts and mission stations, as it was when originally discovered and explored. Only nature's highways through the webs of interlocking waterways were in use, except where the Red River cart roved complainingly o'er the plains. But great changes to come were already cast-ing their shadows before, and eighteen years after my arrival the prairies had been swept of their buffalo, and the great transcontinental railway had invaded the domain of the cart and cayuse, leaving only picturesque memories of a wild and romantic past. The prairie Indians, when I first saw them, were monarchs of all they surveyed, living like princes on the fat of abundant game, hunting their sport, and war their glorious pastime; for they were

> "Free as the day when nature first made man,
> Ere the base laws of servitude began,
> When wild in woods the noble savage ran."

No more pitiful result of the coming of civilization into the North-West can be seen than the contrast between "the chief his warriors leading," in barbaric splendor arrayed, when buffalo covered the plains, and the poor, ragged outcasts who now pick up the leavings of the people who are now lords of the land. To a less unfortunate extent have the circumstances of the bold and the free Metis hunters, the freighters of the plains and the traders been affected, but they, too, when all things became new, found their old happy days were over, and many of them were too old ever to become reconciled to the civilization which had eclipsed the things of the past. Yet these are the men who were the forerunners of and blazed the trail and beat the path for the newcomers, and who, recommending them to the friendship of the Indians, gave freely also the benefit of their long experience and acquaintance of the country. Their successors owe them a debt which can never be repaid; but at least we should try to keep their memory green, and this writing is my mite towards that object.

The space, so kindly accorded me by the *Free Press,* will permit only of such matters as may serve as samples of things as they were in the days when the silent West had neither newspapers (except one in Red River) nor telegraphs nor railways; before the buffalo king of the prairies had been superseded by the cereal king, No. 1 hard. These papers will allude to the long and intimate connection of the men of the Orkney Islands with the Hudson's Bay Company and territories; the recruits annually engaged in the northern and western isles of Scotland for the service, and the terms of their contracts; the voyage from Orkney to Hudson Bay; York Factory, the seaport of Rupert's Land; the boat voyage from York Factory to Red River; the Red River Settlement; journey to Fort Qu'Appelle; Swan River district; winter trip to Wood Mountain; summer journey to Cypress Hills, 1868; the Red River troubles of 1869-70; smallpox on the plains; winter, 1871-2, at Cypress Hills; American whiskey traders, and plotted Indian raid on Manitoba, 1873; Lake Manitoba; Ile à la Crosse; Portage la Loche; and the opening of the Edmonton route to Athabasca. The articles, under some such headings, will appear serially in weekly instalments of two or three columns until completed.

Some ten years ago I wrote for the Winnipeg *Telegram,* from memory only, without the aid of the few notes which I have lately found in an old cassette, an account of my journey through Hudson Bay and Red River to Qu'Appelle. Part of these papers will present the same facts in different manner, which I hope may prove as true to life as my former effort, which was pronounced by many who had gone through similar experiences to be a faithfully simple record of things as they were in the old days. With the addition of some rather thrilling experiences among the wild Indians of the prairies, these papers may prove interesting to anyone connected with the " days of auld lang syne " in Western Canada, and perhaps to a few of the numerous newcomers who have come to build an empire of infinite possibilities therein.

ISAAC COWIE.

Winnipeg, February 1, 1912.

INTRODUCTION

A COMPREHENSIVE, ancient and modern history of the Hudson's Bay Company has yet to be written. It will probably be the work of many minds, each dealing with different aspects of its vast and varied operations, and tinged with the personality and prejudices of each writer. In the Dominion of the Fur Trade, extending far beyond the far-flung frontiers of the present Dominion of Canada, the fur-traders were the pioneers of the British Empire, and, if that Empire to-day does not include all the regions they explored and exploited in the grand old days of yore, the glory of their deeds of daring should not be forgotten, nor should it be diminished, because the British Government and the Company's directors from time to time suffered the North-Western States, Oregon and California and the interior of Alaska, to fall into the hands of American rivals.

In a vast territory where history was made at every important fur-trading post, by men who seldom attempted to leave written records which have been allowed to see the light of day in print, it is to-day a task of as great difficulty to exhume the buried remains of the human and personal history of individual pioneers as it is to find in the buried cities of the ancient Orient the material by which men of science of the present day try to interpret the past and depict it. True, many, in fact a surprisingly great number of books have been written by eminent explorers of the highest merits, as well as many by very able authors as the result of their studies of books and documents to which they had access—often denied the public; but these latter writers are all more or less special pleaders for views, more or less distorted by race and religion, and other circumstances over which they had as little control.

Every one of the books written has recorded occurrences and the names of those who participated in these events, which,

3   31

by the master hand of the great historian, who may yet arise, will be gathered and assorted and reconstructed into a properly proportioned historical body inspired by the soul of the past. Gathering together the dead bones of history, he will clothe them with flesh, infuse blood into the flesh, and into the reincarnation breathe the breath of life. But we may have long to wait for the advent of this great historian, and within the compass of a short sketch it is impossible to give even a list of the probable titles of the volumes upon volumes which such a history would fill. However, what follows is an attempt to give some data of the history of the Hudson's Bay Company from the fur-traders' point of view.

A French Idea Adopted by Prince Rupert.

In Old Quebec, even as in the old Red River Settlement later, while a few small farmers had been established and found a market in the home consumption for their produce, the trading and trapping in furs afforded the first and chief motives of the early French, their source of personal profit and sole source of public revenue. That revenue had not only to provide for local expenditures but also tribute to the French Crown or its resident or non-resident favorites. Heavy license fees and duties were levied for permission to trade in furs and on the furs themselves, which, as in the case of the Hudson's Bay Territories later, were the only articles exportable with profit from the colony.

The laborious occupation of farming was regarded with contempt by the gentlemen of old feudal France who had come to try their fortune in the new country and to fight for it in their genteel profession of arms. They had souls above any kind of trade—except that in furs, which afforded rich prizes in profits, and demanded in the wilds the best qualities of the courageous soldier in its prosecution.

The results of the adventures of these daring soldier fur-traders were enviably lucrative, as a monopoly guarded by licenses only given to favorites. Hence there arose " free

traders" even in those days, who took the liberty, without
having the license, to try their fortunes in the alluring depths
of the unexplored forests of New France and the regions unknown beyond. And two of these "free traders," who were
detested by the colonial governors as smugglers and criminals
as such, became, through the persecutions to which they were
subjected in that regard, the founders of that "Last Great
Monopoly"—"The Governor and Company of Adventurers
of England trading into Hudson's Bay."

RADISSON AND GROSEILLERS.

These two great worthies were Pierre Esprit Radisson and
Medard Chouart Groseillers, both of whom were born in
France. The latter was first married to a daughter of Abraham Martin, who gave his name to the historic Plains of
Abraham, the field of Wolfe's conquest and death, and whose
second wife was Radisson's sister. Groseillers had been a lay
helper to the Jesuit missionaries while a youth, but Radisson
appears to have never allowed any religious leanings to interfere with his secular objects, and is sometimes said to have
incurred animosity on the part of the priests for his suspected
Protestantism. The yoke of his allegiance to France, and
when he changed it to England, sat as lightly on Radisson as
did the ties of religion.

The histories of Radisson and the diverse estimates of his
almost incomprehensible character and almost incredible
adventures and achievements have been told in many books,
which, with others, no doubt to follow, will be read with
intense interest in this truly remarkable man, and with
admiration of his unique exploits, if not of the methods he
often adopted to achieve them. In this place, however, only
a brief synopsis of his romantic career may be given, principally taken from Miss Laut's fascinating book, "The Pathfinders of the West."

Radisson was born at St. Malo, in Normandy, in 1632. At
the age of seventeen he sallied out from the shelter of the

settlement of Three Rivers, Quebec, for sport in the woods, and was captured by the Iroquois Indians. With characteristic adaptability he took to the Indian life and was adopted into the tribe, from whom he escaped to the Dutch Fort Orange, and found his way by sea, *via* Europe, back to Three Rivers, in 1654, after two years' absence, and was welcomed home as one back from the dead. Three years afterwards he joined the Onondaga expedition, was besieged with it and saved it from the Iroquois. In 1658 he started on a trapping and exploring expedition, and passing by Lakes Nipissing and Huron wintered at Green Bay; then by way of modern Wisconsin he reached and discovered the Upper Mississippi, and explored in the present Minnesota and Manitoba. On his return he had an encounter with the Iroquois on the Ottawa, and arrived at Montreal in 1660. Next year, eluding the authorities, he set out with Groseillers again, hoping to reach Hudson Bay, and built a wintering post near the present Duluth, from which he visited the Sioux camps, and is supposed to have reached Lake Winnipeg. From this expedition he returned to Quebec in 1663. Says Miss Laut: " England and France alike conspired to crush the man while he lived; and when he died they quarrelled over the glory of his discoveries." The point is not whether he reached Hudson or James Bay or not, but that he found where the bay lay and the watershed sloping towards it. The cargo of furs brought back, from the wilderness they had discovered, was worth $300,000 in modern money. Of this, after being mulcted by the governor of New France for leaving without his permission, and for royalties and revenue, Radisson and Groseillers had less than $20,000 left.

The Tipping of the Scales—From New France to Old England.

" Had the governors of New France encouraged instead of persecuted the discoverers," says Miss Laut, " France could have claimed all North America but the narrow strip of New

England on the east and the Spanish settlements on the south. Having repudiated Radisson and Groseillers, France could not claim the fruits of deeds which she punished."

Groseillers spent his time and money in a vain attempt to obtain justice and restitution in Paris. The influence of the licensed trading company, to whom the monopoly in fur trade was given as favorites at court, was too strong against him. Radisson and he then determined to find their way into Hudson Bay by sea, without asking French leave, but by taking it from Canada. In Boston they met Captain Zechariah Gillam, and set out in his ship for the voyage, but had to turn back owing to the lateness of the season. Next spring, 1665, one of the two ships contracted for with their owners in Boston was wrecked on Sable Island, which resulted in a lawsuit which exhausted all their resources, but brought their exploits to the ear of a British Commissioner in New England, who urged them to renounce their allegiance to ungrateful France and go to England, where they arrived in 1666. The plague was then raging in London, and there was war with the Dutch during which nothing could be done. But the court favored the plan to trade in Hudson Bay laid before King Charles II., who meanwhile allowed the adventurers forty shillings per week.

Prince Rupert.

" A fellow-feeling makes one wondrous kind." To the equally adventurous, dashing cavalry leader and free rover of the seas, Prince Rupert, these free rovers of the wilds appealed as kindred spirits. His own needs as well as his quick intelligence also urged his sympathies into taking up their promising project as his own. So, the Dutch war being over, in the spring of 1668, two vessels were despatched with the first trading outfit for Hudson Bay. The *Eagle,* in which went Radisson, was driven back to London, badly damaged, but the *Nonsuch,* Captain Gillam, with Groseillers on board, anchored at the mouth of Rupert's River on the 29th of September, after a voyage of three months from Gravesend, of which two were occupied in reaching Resolution Island at the mouth of Hudson Straits.

THE FIRST HUDSON'S BAY COMPANY'S FORT.

Near the mouth of Rupert's River Groseillers built a palisaded fort which was named by him after King Charles (but the modern successor has long been called Rupert's House instead), and in the summer of 1669 the *Nonsuch* returned to London with a full cargo of furs, and Groseillers received honor and reward.

THE ROYAL CHARTER.

Although Radisson had been baffled in making the voyage in the *Eagle,* like a good general he turned the defeat into victory; for on his return to London he allied himself to the daughter of Sir John Kirke and assisted Prince Rupert in organizing the fur company, to which the success of the voyage of the *Nonsuch* assured the royal charter granted in May, 1670, to Prince Rupert, as Governor, and his Company of Adventurers of England, consisting of a duke, an earl, two barons, three baronets, four knights, five esquires, " and John Portman, citizen and goldsmith of London."

Prince Rupert actively directed the operations of the Company till the time of his death. Had he lived longer no doubt his schemes of activity and enterprise would have been carried out and left as a legacy of success for his successors to follow. He was succeeded by the Duke of York, afterwards James II, the last of the Stuart kings. The great general, John Churchill, Duke of Marlborough, followed the Duke of York as governor; and the office and that of director has ever after been filled by men of title and station, with strong influence at court and with the government of the day, as well as others of established business ability and standing.

INTRODUCTION

A Century on the Coast.

Till 1674 the two great French explorers and traders remained on the Bay, having, in addition to Fort Charles, established a post at Moose, in 1671, and made a trading voyage to the mouth of the Nelson. After the first three years of most successful trade with the Indians at Fort Charles it began to fall off on account of the increased activity of the French from the south. Groseillers counselled moving inland and driving off such competition, but the English factor (Bailey) objected, and proposed moving to the west coast of the Bay, where there would be no rivalry. Divided counsels, intensified by the Englishman's suspicion of foreigners and his ignorance of a trade in which his French associates were past masters, led to quarrels, and Radisson was recalled home by the ship in 1674. After six years, which he spent in the service of France, from which he had received pardon and a commission in the navy, Radisson returned to Quebec in 1681, and set out with his nephew, Baptiste Groseillers, in two small vessels, which entered Hayes River, and, ascending it fifteen miles from salt water, anchored. While Groseillers built a trading post, Radisson paddled up stream towards Lake Winnipeg to notify the Indians of their presence. The post was named Fort Bourbon and the river was named Ste. Therese, and York Fort, which became the great emporium of the Hudson's Bay Company, was afterwards established in the vicinity, within easier reach of the sea.

It is impossible to follow the romantic and varied career of this prince of explorers further than to say that a ship under Captain Gillam's son from Boston and a Hudson's Bay ship from London both entered the Nelson River while the French were on the Hayes, that Radisson outwitted and captured both, and on returning to Quebec was again assailed with similar ill-treatment by his fellow-countrymen there. Again he was driven by French injustice to the English side, and, returning with the Company's ship to Hayes River, in 1684, he secured from his nephew the transfer of his fort and his furs to the English, between whom and the Indians he then arranged a peace treaty, which has endured to this day. It will well repay all interested readers to look up his detailed history in " The Pathfinders of the West " and other books. The last trace of this wonderful man, the actual originator of the great Company, is to be found merely in the final entry of the payment of an annual allowance of £50 in their books in 1710.

Space also forbids anything but a mere mention of the capture by the French of the posts on the Bay, and their restoration, generally by negotiation in treaties between the two countries on the termination of their frequently recurring wars. The necessity of attempting to defend the Bay posts while they remained in their own hands, and the impossibility of attempting to extend their trade into the interior when these were in the hands of the French, are very good reasons why the Company made no very great effort to reach the interior. Again, it was much more profitable to allow the Indians to bring the furs to the Bay than for the traders to go to the expense and privation, not to speak of the risk, of penetrating into the vast unknown regions of the interior. Neither was the class of officers and men of the English company suitable, or rendered suitable by training, to encounter the dexterous and daring *coureur de bois* in his chosen ground and occupation. It was not until the cession of Canada by France in 1763 that it became possible for British fur-traders to employ the French-Canadians, with complete confidence in their reliability, in the fur-trading operations in the Indian countries for which they were so admirably adapted by nature and training, qualities of which the North-West Company made such great use subsequently.

In spite of these adverse considerations, the directors in London frequently urged their factors on the Bay to at least send men to the up-country to attract new tribes to resort to

the factories of the coast. Beckles Wilson, in his book on
"The Great Company," after dwelling upon the unsuitable
character of the servants for such service, says that the factors
dreaded equally the prospect of leading an expedition into the
interior themselves, and the prestige which might be gained
by a subordinate in doing so. The inducements offered by
the Company do not appear either to have been adequate to
induce men to volunteer for such unusual and dangerous
service, and Mr. Wilson only mentions three young men as
exceptions to the general rule. These were William Bond,
who was drowned in the Bay some years later, and Thomas
Moore and George Geyer, who continued for some years to
set an example which was not followed by others, and of
which they finally got tired, before subsequently attaining the
rank of governors.

Forty Years Before Verandrye.

"Indeed," says Mr. Wilson, "almost without exception,
once a fort was built the servants seem to have clung closely
to it, and it was not till the year 1688 that a really brave,
adventurous figure, bearing considerable resemblance to the
bushrangers of the past and the explorers of the future,
emerges into the light of history. Henry Kelsey, a lad of
barely eighteen years of age, was the forerunner of all the
hardy British pioneers of the ensuing century. He is described
as active, ' delighting much in Indians' company, being never
better pleased than when he is travelling among them.' Young
as he was, Kelsey volunteered to find out a site for a fort on
Churchill River. No record exists of this voyage; but a
couple of years later he repeated it, and himself kept a diary
of his tour."

He set out in July, 1691, and penetrated to the country of
the Assiniboines, the buffalo and the grizzly bear, forty years
before Verandrye's voyages of discovery; "and in behalf of
the Hudson's Bay Company had taken possession of the
lands he traversed, and had secured for his masters the trade

of Indians hitherto considered hostile." That the success of Kelsey was as much due to his adapting himself to ways suited to the circumstances of the country at that time, and long afterwards, as well as to his other qualities, is shown by this next quotation: "He returned to York Factory after this first expedition, apparelled after the manner of his Indian companions, while at his side trudged a young woman with whom he had gone through the ceremony of marriage after the Indian fashion. It was his desire that Mistress Kelsey should enter with her husband into the court, but this desire quickly found an opponent in the Governor, whose scruples, however, were soon undermined when the explorer flatly declined to resume his place and duties in the establishment unless his Indian wife were admitted with him."

HEARNE, THE GREAT EXPLORER.

While the exploits of Radisson, and those less dazzling of Kelsey, may be comparatively unknown to the general public, the name of Samuel Hearne, the discoverer of the Coppermine River to the Arctic Ocean and the Athabasca Lake in his voyages alone with Indians, which ended successfully in 1772, those who have studied geography have often read. In the Athabasca he preceded the grand explorers of the North-West Company, who completed the work on the Mackenzie which he had begun to the eastward.

That Hearne was a man of intrepid courage his wonderful journeys testify. His horror at the massacre of the poor Esquimaux by his Indians at the Bloody Fall of the Coppermine also bore witness to his humanity, and he showed moral courage of the highest order when, to prevent the needless slaughter of his garrison of forty men in Fort Prince of Wales, he surrendered that great stronghold—impregnable had it been manned by its complement of four hundred men—to the overwhelming force of the famous French admiral, La Perouse, in three great ships of war, by whom he was surprised.

Hearne was originally of the Company's sea service and had taken part in several of the many expeditions fitted out by the Company for the discovery of the North-West Passage from Hudson Bay, to which this passing allusion only can be made here.

The Daring Enterprise of the North-West Company.

The very important fact may be news to many that the present Hudson's Bay Company is the lineal successor to the honor and glory acquired by the old North-West Company of Montreal, in its discoveries in and occupation of the countries which are now Saskatchewan, Alberta and British Columbia. It is well to recall to the recollection of Canadians that the union of the North-West with the old Hudson's Bay Company was effected upon equal terms, each supplying an equal amount of capital and the Canadian company putting in their rights of discovery and occupancy of the country as a set-off to the claims of the English company under their royal charter, to retain the benefit of which the proud Nor'-Westers consented to the elimination of their name in the united concern.

Not only did the Nor'-Westers merge their claims and their capital with those of the old Hudson's Bay Company, but they also furnished the coalition with the men and methods by whose means their business had been conducted with such marvellous success and enterprise.

But before this mutually beneficial arrangement had been arrived at the old English company had been roused from its passive policy of waiting on the coast for its customers to come down from the far interior, by the traders from Canada cutting the line of communications and intercepting the Indians in the interior on their way to the Bay. New blood was introduced in the class of employees at the same time as the new policy of adopting that of its competitors. Hearne was sent up and chose as the site of the central inland establishment the passage between the main Saskatchewan and the

Upper Churchill River, near which, at Portage la Traite, Frobisher had intercepted the Chipewyans bound for the bay with such a quantity of furs as to render him independent for life by the profit thereon.

Many of the North-West officers were Highland Jacobites themselves or sons of those who had fought at Culloden, or were related by blood to those who had been defeated and butchered after the fight by the orders of the Duke of Cumberland. So when Hearne, in 1774, gave to the new Hudson's Bay house at this strategic point on the route of the Nor'-Westers the detested name of "Cumberland," the English company appeared to intend to add insult as well as injury to the clansmen.

The Struggle Between the Rival Companies Begins.

The gage of battle was thus thrown down by the Hudson's Bay Company by the planting of "that settlement which Mr. Hearne hath called Cumberland House, which is twenty-six feet broad, thirty-eight feet long and twenty-one and one-half feet in height," says Mr. H. Marten, chief of York Fort, in a letter to Mr. William Falconer, master of Severn House, January 1st, 1776. The Hudson's Bay Company in any big enterprise has always been slow to begin, but once started, its determination and enterprise in pursuing the path set before it have usually aroused alarm in the camp of its opponents and the admiration of its friends.

The pin-pricks inflicted by the cursory excursions of the petty traders from New France inland on its trade coming to the coast, while annoying to Moose and Albany, had not been sufficiently injurious to cause any general movement to establish posts in the up-country, except one on the Moose and several on the Albany River. But the great bulk of the furs came to York and Churchill, and were brought down from the far interior by the Indians themselves, and the cutting of this line of communication by the British Canadian traders, after the conquest of Canada, was a tail-twisting exploit which roused the British lion from his slumbers in security on the sea-coast.

Like a lion in his wrath the Bay Company took the field aggressively and reached the Indians of the interior, from their coign of vantage on the coast of the Bay long before the earliest canoes of the Canadians could arrive from Montreal. The Englishmen brought, too, a superior quality of goods (a traditional policy continued to this day) ; fixed prices—the same to chief or child—for goods and furs; and inflexible honesty in word and deed in their dealings with the Indians. Their goods were not only better in general quality, but they also took in exchange the heavier and less valuable furs, while the canoemen from Montreal only wanted the lighter and more valuable peltries owing to the handicap of their long and difficult journey to the base at Montreal. Moreover, the familiar and friendly French employees of the Canadian traders, while they might be better liked by the natives, did not command the same respect and trust which the English and Orkney servants of the Hudson's Bay Company received from the Indians.

The North-West Company Formed.

To meet the policy of the Hudson's Bay Company, no longer defensive but offensive, the private unassociated Montreal traders banded together and in 1783 united in the splendid organization of the North-West Company. Many books have been written of the deeds of the daring officers and men of this wonderful company, and probably many more will be written ere the fascination and historical interest of the subject are exhausted. Briefly as it must be merely mentioned herein, the personnel in officers and men was a rare combination of the most efficient races. The officers were chiefly men of Scottish Highland blood and of the lineage of the chiefs of their clans, who had come to Canada as soldiers of fortune to retrieve fortunes shattered by espousing the cause of the Stuart kings. The men were of a race renowned in old

France for its warlike virtues, which coming to Canada and taking to the woods as hunters and to the waters as voyageurs had become pre-eminently the best qualified for service in the fur trade. Behind this fighting force were the brains and the money of far-seeing, shrewd merchants in Montreal, who on the cession of Canada had come to exploit its resources, and its chief resource up to that time, and long after, was the richness of the country in furs.

Strong as was this combination of forces the company was also bound together and vivified by the co-operative alliance between capital and labor, in which the youngest apprentice clerk in the wilds was animated to feats of zeal and devotion to the interests of the company by the assured prospect of promotion to the rank of wintering partner in a business of which the profits were immense. In a vast wilderness where employees could neither be reached by swift commands nor watched by the eye of a master, every partner and every subordinate aspiring to such office gave every energy to the benefit of the business which they regarded as their own. And when in the fulness of time the company with the Royal Charter and that with the co-operative principle laid down their arms through exhaustion, and coalesced in the union under the chartered company's name, this principle, essential to preserve the *esprit de corps* which had distinguished the operations of the North-West Company, was retained as part and parcel of the terms of union. This was the more readily arranged because the Hudson's Bay Company had been accustomed to allow their factors and captains a certain bonus on the profits of individual commands, and the system of the Nor'-Westers was an amplified and extended improvement thereon.

In the year after the establishment of Cumberland House by the Hudson's Bay Company, the Canadian traders, who were later to form the North-West Company, proceeded to connect the discoveries of the early French explorers on the Saskatchewan with that of the Hudson's Bay discoverer,

Hearne, on Lake Athabasca, and in doing so established a chain of posts by the Upper Churchill—called by them the English River—Portage la Loche, and the Clearwater and Athabasca Rivers. On Lake Athabasca was founded Fort Chipewyan, which, as the centre of waterways radiating therefrom to every point of the compass, remains to this day the fur capital of the Great North Land.

From this strategic base Alexander Mackenzie started on his magnificent career by discovering the mighty river which bears his name, and following it to the Arctic Ocean. Next, departing from Fort Chipewyan, he ascended the Peace River to McLeod's Fort, in the vicinity of the present Dunvegan, and plunged into the great unknown Peace River gorge of the Rocky Mountains, and the land of the mountain and the flood—well named New Caledonia—to emerge triumphant over every danger and distress on the shore of the vast Pacific —the first civilized man to cross by land, 22nd of July, 1783, the country which is now Canada. These marvellous voyages were made possible by Mackenzie's French-Canadian voyageurs, who were there at the finish of the course set by Cartier, La Salle and La Verandrye to La Chine, although between them and China there rolled the immensity of the waterway across the Pacific.

The lead given by Mackenzie was followed by the establishment of posts along the routes explored by him, and, on the Pacific slope, by his fellow companymen and countrymen, Stuart, Fraser and Thompson, on the Fraser and the Columbia and their feeders to the sea.

The Commercial War in the Wilderness.

From the time of the cession of Canada down to the treaty of peace and union between the rival fur traders in 1821, a period of some sixty years, a war in trade and traffic continued with increasing intensity between the British subjects from Canada and those from Hudson Bay in the fur country. While the Nor'-Westers increased their traffic by ever fresh discoveries, the men from the Bay followed the paths so opened up, always excepting those beyond the Rocky Mountains, into which country their royal charter was not claimed to extend. Neither did it, contended the Nor'-Westers—even if it might be valid,—extend to the Athabasca and Mackenzie country, which drained into the Arctic Ocean, unlike the country of Rupert's Land which sent its waters into Hudson Bay according to the wording of the gift of King Charles II., to his entirely-beloved cousin, Prince Rupert, and his Adventurers of England.

The scope of this book does not allow any attempt at detail of the intricate and innumerable petty feuds and forays between the rival fur-traders, which enlivened the otherwise dull monotony of their existence. These were perhaps provoked more frequently and even joyfully by the brave dunniewassal from Scotland and the fighting French of the Nor'-Westers than by the staider Englishmen and Orkneymen of the Hudson's Bay service.

These minor collisions were very frequently caused by the Indians, outfitted by the Nor'-Westers, giving the furs secured by their means and at their risk of loss, to their opponents. As an Indian could no more produce furs in any quantity without the equipment, which, by the necessities of his improvident nature, had to be advanced by a trader, than the unsown field of a farmer a crop, it was very annoying for the trader who had taken the risk to see his opponent reap where he had not sown. From my own more modern experience in this way with "free traders" I can fully sympathize with the Nor'-Westers, who, exasperated in that way, used force to right the wrong, in a wilderness where writs did not run and

> " The good old rule, the simple plan
> That those should take who have the power,
> And those should keep who can "

prevailed, and was practised by the stronger trading party, whether its flag flew on its fly the letters " N.W.C." or "H.B.C."

Those Canadians, who had succeeded to the rights of discovery, exploration and trade acquired by the early French pioneers, and who, not content with following paths previously made plain by these, had made the furthest points reached by their predecessors their own points of fresh departure for the discovery of the richer fur countries which lay beyond the basin draining into the Hudson Bay, to be followed and harassed by traders who had "slumbered on the Bay" till this great and notable work had been accomplished, would not have been ordinary men had they not deeply resented the intrusion of the Hudson's Bay Company to reap where they had not sown. But the Nor'-Westers were extraordinary men, both in brawn and brain, and they fought with both, and would have beaten the Bay Company, too, had it not been a Company with a convenient base on Hudson Bay, whilst that of the North-West Company was at the end of the long canoe route at the distant port of Montreal.

THE SCHEMES OF SELKIRK.

The causes and the class of the minor troubles between the rival traders resided in the nature of the business, and they prevailed between the Canadian individual traders and different companies before they united as a measure of defence against the common foe—the Hudson's Bay Company. The causes of conflict were not, therefore, between the Hudson's Bay Company as an old country concern and the North-West Company as a colonial combination. In fact, despite the natural resentment of the Canadians against the intruding English, for mutual comfort and protection their posts were often placed side by side in dangerous Indian districts. Probably they disliked each other less, being whites in a savage country, than rival storekeepers in Winnipeg do to-day—only the old fur trader had to administer the law himself, according to his light and power, and the city merchant is constrained to resort to the "courts of justice."

Matters were in this state when the then Earl of Selkirk

4   47

conceived the idea of forming an utterly isolated settlement on the Red River. In this invasion of the wilds he went contrary to the teaching of all ancient and modern military art as well as the dictates of common sense, which, had the latter been used, would have clearly shown him that the invasion of a country to be permanent and successful must be sustained by an easily travelled line of communication with its base. This the old sailing craft coming once a year to Hudson Bay did not provide, much less the route for row boats and over rapids and portages which had been used by the boatmen of the fur traders, inured to superhuman toil, but was in the state in which the hand of nature had left it.

It is but fair to say, however, that he had seen the need of a port on the Bay and of the right to improve the route between it and his projected colony, which the grant he secured from the Hudson's Bay Company provided for. But instead of first protecting his line of communication—to still use the military terms—he hurled a flying column of his invading colonists into the heart of an Indian country, without the consent of the natives, and against the advice of the only whites who knew the territory. Neither were these settlers, who had thus been thrust into danger, in sufficient numbers to have been capable of self-defence against the warlike tribes of the Red River valley. The vanguard should have been a sufficient force of soldiers—not untrained settlers with helpless and innocent women and children alike to be defended and to hamper the defence.

Selkirk had been for years meditating this project, and had ample control over the Hudson's Bay Company to have seen that such food as the country afforded and some shelter should have been provided in advance for his settlers. The want of these drove them into the degradation and danger of having to find them, away from the site of proposed farming operations, amongst the Indians on the buffalo plains. In a country where the safety of the whites, among an overwhelming number of natives, depended so much on their racial prestige, this was a fatal error. Even an experienced fur trader, left by himself in most friendly Indian camps on the plains, and unhampered by wife or child of his race, had an unenviable duty which could only be performed if he were nerved by "courage and fidelity." Fortunately the Indians treated the unfortunate refugees with kindness and humanity; but amongst Indians as well as in every other community there are always "bad men" who must have been an ever-present cause of anxiety to the settlers and their families.

If a monument is to be erected to Lord Selkirk, another one one hundred times as impressive should be made to the memory of the brave white women who came with their menfolk to undergo all the dangers and hardships both inherent in the adventure and others to which they were subjected through the incomprehensible and censurable want of foresight of the originator and managers of the scheme.

The Nor'-Westers could not consistently pretend that the country had no agricultural possibilities; for indeed it was through their own eulogies of these, as the result of the cultivation round many of their posts to eke out food supplies, that the Earl of Selkirk had his attention drawn thereto. But the fur traders contended, with reason, that until civilized means of commercial communication could be established, the attempt to establish an agricultural community was premature, and it was also dangerous alike to the settlers and the fur trade, of which the light and valuable product alone could stand the enormous cost of export to outside markets.

Conscientiously entertaining these convictions, inspired with sympathetic good feeling towards the settlers of their own Scottish race, as undoubtedly the Highlanders of the North-West Company were as individuals, it is slanderous to accuse them of being actuated by merely mercenary motives and the protection of the fur trade, and to say that they seduced and intentionally deceived more than half of their countrymen into deserting the colony, and from only selfish motives provided them with a free passage to Canadian settlements.

INTRODUCTION

The Earl's Gamekeepers vs. The Native and North-West Poachers.

However sympathetic the Nor'-Westers might feel towards the actual settlers themselves, their leaders had from the very first more than suspected that Selkirk, who had acquired a controlling interest in the Hudson's Bay Company's shares, intended to use his scheme of settlement as a means to, or a mere blind for, the destruction of their hitherto enormously profitable trade. If the settlers could be coerced into becoming soldiers, and the Hudson's Bay Company be supplied by Selkirk's undertaking to furnish them with a suitable class of servants in sufficient numbers to overawe the force of the Canadian company at Red River, the long line of communication between Montreal and Athabasca might be cut at that vital point—vital to the route itself as well as for providing the preserved provisions from the prairies required by the canoemen passing to and from the north and Fort William.

On January the 8th, 1814, Lord Selkirk's agent, Miles McDonnell, under his commission from the Hudson's Bay Company, as Governor of Assiniboia, issued a proclamation prohibiting the export of all such provisions, stating all these were required by the settlers. An edict was also issued commanding the natives to cease hunting buffalo on horseback, as the animals were thereby scared away from the Settlement.

Not content with putting these rules on paper, Selkirk's agents proceded to put them in practice by seizing pemmican belonging to the North-West Company in transit, and by breaking into their posts, while the guns of Fort Douglas commanded the route on the river so that boats might not pass.

The Tragedy of Seven Oaks.

On June 19th, 1816, a party of North-West Company's men, numbering sixty-five, and composed of French-Canadian, English, Scotch and Metis engaged servants, besides a larger number of Metis and Indians hired for the occasion, while conveying provisions from a point above the fort to one below it on the river, in making this portage, out on the prairie to avoid the cannon of Fort Douglas, were pursued by Governor Semple, with a following of twenty men. The historian of Red River, Hargrave, says (page 487) : " The party, under Governor Semple, were provided with guns, but they were in an unserviceable state, some being destitute of locks and all more or less useless." (It is also said by another authority that they went without any ammunition to recharge their guns.) " This fact," continues Hargrave, " was, of course, unknown to their opponents, who were apparently sincere in the belief that the governor was prepared to offer serious resistance to them before the carnage commenced, after which their entire want of order and discipline rendered them incapable of reason or consideration. The infatuation which led the governor's party to attempt by a vain exhibition of useless weapons to intimidate nearly three times their number of men to whom the saddle and their gun were instruments of their daily occupation, is almost incomprehensible."

The native levies of the Nor'-Westers had a superstitious horror of cannon. But as soon as they had drawn their pursuers out of range of the fort, choosing their own time and ground, they faced about. Opening out into skirmishing order, at which they were experts, they then confronted the compact body under Semple, with an equally strong opposing force, and threatened his flanks simultaneously with treble his numbers.

While thus outnumbered and unsupported and nearly surrounded by his already incensed adversaries, the unfortunate governor lost his temper with the North-West clerk, Mr. Boucher, who had advanced to parley, and seized the bridle of the latter's horse. On this, the first shot was fired on the governor's side, by a woeful accident, it is said, and was followed by an exchange of volleys. One account says that on delivering their fire the natives threw themselves backwards on the ground to reload, which was mistaken by the governor's men as the deadly result of their fire, and they raised a cheer of triumph, bringing their opponents quickly to their feet with recharged weapons, which poured in a volley and converted the cheer into the shrieks of the dying and the groans of the wounded.

Up to this point the affair had been a fight, forced upon a well-armed, skilful and superior body by a very inferior force, which can scarcely be said to have been armed, blindly led into the jaws of death by their incompetent governor. But from this point on it became a brutal butchery of the wounded and a fiendish mutilation of the dead also, which revealed in all its horrors the danger of employing savages in disputes between the whites.

The Surrender of Fort Douglas.

Months before, the veteran Colin Robertson had received warning of the preparations being made in the west by the Nor'-Westers to avenge the pillage and capture of their property and posts by the Hudson's Bay people. Robertson, as an experienced fur-trader, had been appointed chief adviser to the inexperienced governor, and he was a man of tested courage. When his solemn counsel and advice was rejected by Semple, Robertson washed his hands of the business in indignation and betook himself to the Bay. Other warnings of the storm brewing in the west were given to the governor, and so unheeded that he did not even see that the flintlocks of his men were in order.

When natives brought sure news of the near approach of the North-West brigade, if his desire were to protect the settlers he had ample time to bring them into the fort, and, with their aid, hold it secure from attack, for the settlers numbered, at that time, two hundred, including their families. He might then have relied on their fighting in their own defence in the fort; although the policy of the settlers, living on their defenceless farms, had always been one of non-intervention in the conflicts between the rival fur traders, and

Colonists on the Red River in North America.

1, 2. A Swiss colonist with wife and children from the Canton of Berne. 3. A German colonist from the disbanded De Meuron Regt. 4. A Scottish Highland colonist. 5. An immigrant colonist from French Canada.

TYPES OF LORD SELKIRK'S SETTLERS IN 1822.

From a photo of black and white drawing of a Swiss Colonist, touched up by Mr. Lawson, artist of the *Manitoba Free Press.*

Courtesy of Dr. Doughty, Dominion Archivist.

they wisely desired to give the wild partisans of the Canadian company no additional cause for animosity and incur their vengeance by taking part in quarrels of which they had been, and were likely to be, the innocent and greatest sufferers. But after the defeat and slaughter of Semple and his followers had inspired their opponents with victory, and had had the reverse effect upon the settlers, who had by that time taken refuge in the fort, Mr. John Pritchard (the only one of Semple's followers who had been given quarter and taken prisoner) was sent by the North-West warriors to inform the settlers that they must save themselves from their fury by immediate surrender, and, if so, a safe escort to Lake Winnipeg would be given them, and they would be allowed to take with them all their personal effects. "At first," says Mr. Beckles Wilson, "the colonists refused to listen to those terms. Sheriff Mc-Donnell, who was now in charge of the settlement, resolved to hold the fort as long as there were men to guard it. But they were not long of this courageous temper. After fully considering the situation the settlers concluded to depart, and after several conferences between the sheriff and Cuthbert Grant, a capitulation was arranged."

THE NAMELESS BRAVE.

The lives thus uselessly sacrificed by Semple's unmitigated mismanagement were his own, those of his officers—Doctor White, Secretary Wilkinson, Captain Rodgers and Lieutenant Holte, and the only comparatively wealthy colonist, Mr. Alexander McLean, besides those of three other colonists and fifteen Hudson's Bay servants, whose names are not to be found in any of the histories mentioning the massacre. Only one of the North-West levies, Batoche, was killed, and one, Trottier, wounded. Could not the names of those who perished with him be discovered and graven with that of Governor Semple on the monument which has been erected at Seven Oaks? That neat, but inconspicuous, monument is about a

quarter of a mile outside the city limits on the east side of
the old "King's Road," between old Fort Garry and the
existing Lower Fort Garry—in fact on Main Street North.
It is just south of Inkster's Creek, and reads thus:

SEVEN OAKS.

Erected in 1891 by

THE MANITOBA HISTORICAL SOCIETY

Through the generosity of

THE COUNTESS OF SELKIRK

On the site of Seven Oaks,

where fell

GOVERNOR ROBERT SEMPLE

and

TWENTY OF HIS OFFICERS AND MEN,

June 19, 1816.

The simple monument marks the site of the shambles into
which the Governor of Rupert's Land led the Hudson's Bay
Company's officers and men, who followed him to death and
butchery " with courage and fidelity." Small as were they in
numbers and so lowly in rank that their names have not even
found a place on the inscription, their blood was not shed in
vain. For their slaughter aroused the British and the Canadian Governments to intervene and enforce the policy which
caused the union of the rival fur companies, and thereby
made possible the permanent and peaceful establishment of
the Red River Settlement.

Upon the monument proposed to be erected to the memory
of the fifth Earl of Selkirk, as the " Founder of the Colony of
Assiniboia," might most appropriately be inscribed with his

name and titles the names of the noble little army of martyrs whose death gave life to the Red River Settlement.

No punishment was meted out to those engaged in the affair by the courts of justice in Canada before which they were tried; but Mr. Alexander Ross, in his "Red River Settlement," records that the ends of poetic justice were fulfilled by the violent or sudden deaths which befel the twenty-six of the North-West party who alone took part in the massacre of the wounded.

War Still in the North.

Although, at Fort William, and on the Red River, the Commissioner appointed by the British and Canadian Governments, Colonel Coltman, had restored peace and property, the war in the interior still went on. In 1818, under Colin Robertson and another former North-West officer, Mr. Clarke, a big expedition of canoes, manned by Canadian voyageurs, had carried the strife for trade into the Nor'-Westers' great preserve on the Peace River and Athabasca. This was defeated and its leader made prisoner, all of which will be found in "The Conquest of the Great North-West." In 1819 Mr. Williams, the fur trader, who had succeeded the unfortunate Semple as Governor of Rupert's Land, however, with the Hudson's Bay Company's armed schooner *Cathulin,* on Lake Winnipeg, had transported a force of the De Meuron soldiers to Grand Rapids portage at the outlet of the Saskatchewan River. There he laid in wait for the fur brigades of the Nor'-Westers, and as each arrived, all unconscious of danger, their officers were taken by surprise and made prisoners, and their furs seized. In the Athabasca brigade Colin Robertson had been brought out, still a prisoner, but effected his escape at Cumberland House before reaching the Grand Rapids, where Governor Williams was waiting to rescue him. Williams took his prisoners to Norway House, and sent them on to York Factory. This was the last of what may be called the military contests of the sixty years' war for the fur trade.

THE UNION OF THE COMPANIES.

The contests between the partisans of the contending traders had been conducted in the remote obscurity of the wilderness, and this state of things might have continued much longer without the rumors and reports, more or less unreliable, which reached the Canadian and British Governments, rousing them into action. But from the moment that Lord Selkirk had secured the grant, which he had engineered from the Hudson's Bay Company, giving him " an empire of infinite possibilities," and he attempted aggressively to take possession of it and exploit it, whether he designed it or was merely the unconscious instrument, building better than he knew, it was inevitable that a contest would arise on a scale big and important enough to force itself on the notice of both governments. The fur traders of both companies could no longer, in their mutual interest to envelop their trade in the secrecy of solitude, " wash their dirty linen at home." To the eyes of prudes and puritans, whose actions and vices were masked and cloaked by the concealment of cities and civilized society much more effectively than were the lives of men who lived in the open on the rivers and lakes, the forests and prairies, of the wilderness, whenever the doings in that wilderness should be reported officially and put in print, the state of affairs so revealed of the fur countries may have appeared appalling and something to hold up their hands at in holy horror.

In England the sympathies of such were with those devout officers of the " castles, forts and fortifications, settlements, and plantations," on the coasts of Hudson Bay, who gathered the monk-like members of their garrisons to " perform the service of Almighty God " every Sunday and holy day, in the wanton attacks made upon them by the fierce and licen-

RED RIVER SETTLERS' DWELLINGS NEAR FORT DOUGLAS
IN 1822.

From a reproduction in black and white, by Mr. Lawson, artist of the *Manitoba Free Press,* of a water-color by a Swiss Colonist, in the Dominion Archives, Ottawa.

EARL GREY ON THE NELSON RIVER EN
ROUTE FOR HUDSON BAY.

tious freebooters and free-traders from Canada, led by escaped rebel Highlanders from Scotland.

In Canada the *pays d'en haut,* discovered and exploited by their voyageurs under renowned leaders, who carried the Cross as well as commerce into the territories of the heathen, was considered the patrimony and heritage of their French-Canadian representatives and descendants, who were glad to find congenial employment with a company largely officered by their Gaelic kindred and co-religionists from Scotland, who were engaged in defending their territorial rights against the greedy and unjust invasion of the perfidious English of the Bay of Hudson.

But neither the British nor the Canadian Government had any wish to assume the expensive task of establishing, under the protection of scattered and expensive military forces, a government independent of the fur traders to preserve the peace between them only; for the fur traders had proved themselves fully competent—by art when not by force—to protect themselves among Indians and in their invasion of their hunting grounds. The policy of planting such garrisons of troops instead of traders amongst the warlike tribes of the prairies would probably lead to interminable wars, and, in the vindication of British honor, to endless expense, for which the exportable resources of the country, in its trackless condition and in its " splendid isolation " at that period, could provide no adequate return.

Only Lord Selkirk professed, at that day and date, to predict the great future of the country for agricultural colonization. But his predictions, when they were not considered those of a philanthropic dreamer or the optimistic promises of the proprietor of an estate he wished to dispose of, were regarded as a mere veil to conceal the real and ultimate end he had in view, which was, in the opinion of Canadians, the destruction of the fur trade of the North-West Company in order to monopolize it himself. Be that as it may, the British Government preferred, for a more opportune time to come, that British interests and possession should be left to be maintained by the fur traders, their only subjects who could make profitable use of it, in that part of the interior of North America which was described by Jeremy Bentham to consist of "frightful solitude, impenetrable forests or barren tracts. . . . The barbarous hordes who traverse those deserts, without fixed habitation, always occupied with pursuit of their prey, and always filled with implacable rivalry, only meet to attack and destroy each other; so that the wild beast is not so dangerous to man as man himself."

The Far-Reaching Effect of the Union.

How in compliance with the wise advice of the Government—amounting to a warning, if not a command—Messrs. William McGillivray and Edward Ellice, the capitalists and agents of the North-West Company, managed to reconcile their fiery and indignant " wintering partners " and employees to the coalition, in which the proud name of their company was submerged, would require a tome to itself. They acted with wonderful wisdom and diplomacy, and the genius of the man, called forth by the occasion, who presided over the council of old warriors of the belligerent companies to make arrangements for conducting the trade of the united company, must have been tasked to the utmost to maintain even the semblance of peace and concord. But George Simpson was of the kind of which great generals, ambassadors and courtiers, and captains of industry are made, and he succeeded. He has never had a successor fit to fill the place he left vacant forty years after.

The great and notable effect of the union has been that peaceable possession and occupancy of the whole of the chartered territory of the Hudson's Bay Company (officially called Rupert's Land) and the Indian Territories beyond in the north and the Pacific slope under royal license, by the Company's resident officers and men, which held them for the British Crown against foreign encroachment, until they were

united to the Dominion of Canada. It was these pioneers and
frontiersmen in the wilderness—not the gentlemen of England
who lived at home in ease and drew profits on the trade conducted by their resident officers and men—who performed this
immense service to the Crown and to Canada. For their par-
ticipation in finding the money (for which they received full
return in profits of trade) the shareholders in London received
one-twentieth of the arable lands of the prairie provinces. But
the officers and the men who actually held the country by possession have never received one acre either from the Crown or
the Company. It is said that the Company's men received
their pay, which, like that of a soldier, was a paltry pittance,
but, unlike the volunteer soldiers, who received grants for a
few months' duty, the men who spent the best of their lives in
the wilderness have received neither thanks nor any such
acknowledgment of their services to this day.

The Red River Settlement Rendered Permanent.

The union also had a secondary consequence, but it was of
vital importance to the oft-harassed Selkirk colonists, for it
secured peace between the rival traders, between whom they
had become as pawns in the warlike game they had been playing. And it not only gave them peace, but protection also
through the forces, disbanded as supernumeraries by the two
companies on their coalition, coming in numbers ten times as
great as that of all Lord Selkirk's settlers. Sir George Simpson says: "Red River Settlement, therefore, ought really to
date its origin from 1821, the year in which the coalition
. . . left only physical impediments to be surmounted."

No longer was the colony looked upon as the vanguard of
an invading enemy by the fur traders; it became instead a
quiet haven in which the wanderers, weary with the wilderness, might find rest in the evening of their days, surrounded
by their children of native blood and birth, who, amid congenial society, would receive the advantage of churches and

INTRODUCTION

schools, denied to them in the lonely places of their birth. With the number of accessible books and the general information existing of the early history of Manitoba it would be mere repetition to attempt to give here such a summary of the history of Red River Colony as I have attempted to give, in these introductory remarks, of the less accessible and quite generally misunderstood history of the North-West and Hudson's Bay Companies, which were so wisely and advantageously united in 1821.

THE COMPANY OF ADVENTURERS.

CHAPTER I.

THE ORKNEY ISLANDERS AND RUPERT'S LAND— THE HALF CASTES.

> " And much of wild and wonderful
> In these rude isles might fancy cull,
> For thither came in times afar
> Stern Lochlin's sons of roving war—
> Kings of the main, their leaders brave,
> Their barks, the dragons of the wave."
> —*Sir Walter Scott.*

THE Orkney Islands, lying off the north of Scotland, have a romantic history of great antiquity. Peopled originally by the Picts, who have left in their Standing Stones of Stennis and their Brochs, scattered over the islands, evidence of their primeval occupation, the islands were conquered by the Norsemen, who made them the base of their forays by sea on the coasts of Britain and Ireland. From Orkney sallied forth Rollo to the conquest of Normandy; and the Earl of Orkney, though under the nominal sovereignty of the king of Norway, became, as lord of the northern and western isles, by virtue of his sea power, a greater lord than the king of Scotland.

According to tradition, the Picts were exterminated by these rovers of the seas, and in the eighteenth century although the islands had long before passed as a dowry of a Norse princess to the king of Scotland, the inhabitants still remained of purely Norse blood, taking naturally by instinct and environment to a life on the ocean wave.

During the continually recurring wars with France, British shipping bound for North America from all ports on the east coast avoided the English Channel, infested at such times by the cruisers and privateers of the enemy, and took their course north through the German Ocean, and west through the Pentland Firth to the North Atlantic. Lying north of the Pentland Firth, protected by sheltering islands, the Cairstone Roads afford fine anchorage off the town of Stromness, between which and the grand Hills of Hoy runs the Sound of that name—a gate to the west. In times of war fleets of merchantmen would assemble in Stromness Harbor and Cairstone Roads to be taken in convoy by the Royal Navy. At Stromness, too, whalers and sealers on the way to Greenland gathered to complete their crews with Orkneymen and together take their departure. So did many arctic exploring expeditions, including the *Erebus* and *Terror* of Sir John Franklin's last voyage.

The first record we have of the long connection which has existed to this day between the English Hudson's Bay Company and the men of Orkney occurred in 1707, and again in 1712, when fourteen and forty able-bodied seamen respectively were engaged by special agents sent from London, for service in the Bay. But it was not till 1740 that the Hudson's Bay ships began to make Stromness regularly their last port of call and rendezvous for the outward voyage—a practice which they continued for over a century and a half.

The Orkney seamen proved themselves handy men ashore as well as at sea. They were good fishermen, splendid boatmen, strong, hardy and obedient, and models of fidelity to the Company. So they came to be sought for not only for sea service, but for that ashore and inland. The pay given looks ridiculously small compared with the nominal wages of the present day, if the relative purchasing power of a pound then and now be not considered. Small as the wages appear, they soon accumulated, for there were no ways of spending them in the wilds; and often these men, after a

"THE OLD MAN OF HOY," 1813.

few years' service, returned home with savings sufficient to
buy a small croft, and settle down as independent crofters
and fishermen, to be envied and emulated by less fortunate
neighbors. In the island of Harray a number of these returned fur traders formed a large colony, known as the
" Peerie (little) lairds o' Harray," whose comparative opulence
induced many a young Orcadian to enlist for a long exile in
the Bay to attain the same happy result.

Life in the Company's service was stern and wild in any
case; and it became more dangerous during the wars with
France; and still more adventurous and exciting on occasional
expeditions sent into the interior to prevent the depredations
of the French-Canadian wood runners from cutting off their
trade with the Indians, who were wont to come down to the
coast with their furs.

Upon the formation of the British Canadian fur companies,
the Hudson's Bay Company was compelled to establish regular posts in the interior, where their men, adopting the
habit of the French in this respect, to foster more friendly
intercourse with the Indians, and to supply some solace in the
solitudes, took to themselves the daughters of the land. Many
of the offspring of these connections were sent home to Orkney
to be educated. A splendid school was endowed at St. Margaret's Hope, in South Ronaldshay, by a Hudson's Bay officer
for the sons of his fellows, to which many other Orkney gentlemen's sons were sent, turning out such pupils as the
Sinclairs, Isbisters, Kennedys, Cloustons, Ballendens and
Raes, and others of well-known repute.

The Orkney Pioneers of Red River.

Prior to the firm establishment of the Red River Settlement
on the union of the rival companies, in 1821, many of the
Orkneymen, retiring from the Company's service, took their
native wives and offspring home with them to Orkney. But
after the union these and their fellow employees from the
Highlands were encouraged to resort to the Red River, where

in numbers they soon exceeded all Lord Selkirk's own settlers. And many of these old fur traders, while seamen and fishermen by profession, had also some knowledge of tilling the soil, both as practised in their native islands and in the gardens and fields attached, wherever practicable, to the trading posts, to eke out the uncertain supply of food from forest and fishery. And it was these Orkneymen, with other veterans of the fur trade from their neighboring highlands and islands, and the French-Canadians of the North-West Company, who, coming in sufficient numbers to defend it, made permanent the settlement on the Red River, and permitted the long harassed settlers brought out by Lord Selkirk to abide in peace.

YORK FACTORY *versus* MONTREAL.

While the discovery of the interior was due to the dexterous and daring French-Canadian canoemen, and that ancestor of our present railways, the venerable Red River cart, was evolved by the North-Westers at Pembina in 1801, the greatest improvement in transportation, namely, that from the Bay to the interior, was effected by the inland " York " boats. These were designed on the model of the ancient Norse galley, manned by Orkney boatmen, and by their greater freight-carrying capacity, with smaller crews, enabled the Hudson's Bay Company to take such full advantage of the Hudson Bay route as to compete advantageously with their abler and more energetic rivals of the North-West, handicapped as these were by the distance from their base at Montreal, and the small cargo capacity of their heavily manned canoes.

THE ORIGINS OF THE HALFBREEDS.*

The so-called " English halfbreeds " of Rupert's Land are very largely of Orkney and Swampy Cree origin. The

* The North-West offers a rich and important yet unexplored field for the Ethnologist. The pedigrees of many families of mixed origin may still be traced; but the opportunity will not long remain.

Swampies were the first Indians with whom the Hudson's Bay people came in contact on the coast of the Bay. They are described by an authority who knew every tribe in the territory—Sir George Simpson—as a people the most comely in appearance and most amenable to civilization of all the natives in it. Years of friendly intercourse on the coast of Hudson Bay had loyally inclined them to the English, and when the Company's men began to take and keep permanently their daughters as wives, a friendship was established which has remained unbroken to this day. New-coming recruits from Scotland intermarried with the mixed offspring of their predecessors, and the prepotency of the strong Scottish strain soon tended to make the term "halfbreed" a misnomer in the case of those who were chiefly of British extraction. In the case of the French Metis, although the French original discoverers, who visited the country and left woodrangers and traders in it, had freely mingled their blood with the Indians, after the union of the Hudson's Bay and North-West companies, and the trade was diverted from Montreal to York Factory exclusively, there was much less fresh French blood brought in, and their Indian ancestry was composed of many varieties of Indians, much less susceptible of being influenced by the whites than the Swampies had been.

Under these stronger Indian influences the descendants of the insouciant French-Canadian voyageurs and rovers of the woods and prairies became further removed from their European ancestry; while the steadier "English halfbreeds" reverted more and more to the British type, and so became a power for peace and progress in the land of their birth. Rupert's Land owes much to these English natives, as they properly prefer to be called. In common with the better class of their countrymen of French extraction they have been the mediators, peacemakers, interpreters, and guides in the opening up of the country. Those educated in the good old Red River schools and in Britain have taken good place in all trades and professions. They became most eminent and successful missionaries; they have supplied many of the best officers and men the Hudson's Bay Company ever had; and a long list of eminent names might be made of such talented native gentlemen of Rupert's Land. Still it is due to this class and to their progenitors to make this passing mention, for little has been written about them, while the literature of the North-West abounds with the records of the daring French explorers, and full meed of praise has been published regarding the Selkirk settlers, neither of which classes, meritorious as they undoubtedly are, have exercised so large and beneficial an influence over the North-West as a whole as the settlers who came from the British Isles as fur traders and their descendants of partly Indian ancestry. Occasional unions were formed between the British and those of French descent, resulting in a progeny distinguished by the number of magnificently formed men and lovely women among them.

CHAPTER II.

THE PRINCE RUPERT—HER CREW, CARGO AND PASSENGERS.

> " Old Blowhard was our captain's name,
>   Our ship the *Lion Bold*,
> And we were bound for the northern main
>   To face the frost and cold."

ON a bright afternoon in the end of June, 1867, three barque-rigged vessels were riding at anchor in Cairstone Roads. At a distance the barques appeared like ordinary sailing-ships of their kind, but upon nearer approach their iron-plated bows and oak-sheathed water-lines showed that they were fortified for encountering the ice of the northern seas, like those in the whaling and sealing trade. But the string of whaleboats, from foreshrouds to stern, carried by whalers, did not hang from the davits of these three barques, which carried only two quarter-boats and dinghies at the stern, while the longboats rested on chucks on deck between the main and foremasts.

The smallest of the three vessels was the Moravian missionary barque *Harmony,* bound for mission stations on the bleak coast of Labrador with supplies, and to return with a cargo of furs and skins which the missionaries had traded from their native proselytes during the previous year. Such a mixture of trade and religion being viewed with displeasure by the Hudson's Bay Company, to whom the other two ships belonged, there was no exchange of such courtesies as are customary between ships meeting in the same port outward-bound. In fact, the stout old Hudson's Bay captains—Bishop of the *Prince Rupert* and James of the *Lady Head*—seemed to regard

67

the missionary barque as a pirate, which by rights ought to be blown out of the water; but that being impracticable, the fur-trade skippers ignored and had no dealings with the fur-trading missionaries.

A great event in social and business circles at Stromness was the annual visit of the Hudson's Bay Company's ships. The highly respected agent of the Company there for half a century had been Mr. Edward Clouston, a fine old gentleman of the Orkneys, who annually picked out good men for the service, and had given two of his own sons as officers to it. Full of years and with a highly honored record, he had shortly before retired from the agency, leaving the prestige of the Company higher than ever in Orkney.

While the merchants were selling outfits of clothing to the recruits and filling orders for people already at the far-off posts of Rupert's Land, friends came in to send parcels away on the ships to their kinsmen across the sea, and others had come to the old town to see their relatives off on their long journey to exile.

The event was celebrated by the gentry and the officers of the ships in dinners and dances ashore and afloat, and every kindly attention was paid by the hospitable and kind ladies of Stromness to the young lads who, like many a young Orcadian before, were going out as gentlemen apprentices to the fur trade.

Fresh provisions of all kinds were taken aboard. Huge quarters of prime Orkney beef were lashed up at the topmost shrouds, where, under a surface hardened by exposure to wind and sun, the meat kept perfectly fresh throughout the voyage. Live pigs, sheep and fowls, also for cabin use, were lodged in pens and coops under the longboat.

As the detachments of recruits from Stornoway, in the Hebrides, and Lerwick, in the Shetlands, and other parts of Orkney arrived, they were immediately sent aboard the ships and given no leave to visit the shore again. For they had received a half year's pay in advance, and had embarked at the landing amid the howls of lamentation of groups of old wives, weeping and wailing over the departure of a set of bonnie young lads who, they prophesied, would meet nought but frost and cold and starvation and "black women" in the wilderness and return no more to the land of their birth. The majority of the old wives making this outcry probably had never seen any of the young men before; but they uproared on general principles, and possibly as much with the object of attracting notice to themselves as of being in any actual distress over the lads going away. The real mourners —the mothers, wives, sisters and sweethearts—wept and sighed less obtrusively; and many a longing glance was cast over the bulwarks of the *Prince Rupert* towards the shore, while the ships lay waiting for the last letters from London by mail, and for a fair wind out of Hoy Sound to the Atlantic.

Form of Contract Between the Employees and the Company.

Each of these recruits for service in North America had signed the following form:

"An agremeent made this .... day of .... in the year of our Lord, one thousand eight hundred and sixty-seven, between .... of the parish of .... in the county of .... in Scotland, of the one part, and Governor and Company of Adventurers of England, trading into Hudson Bay, by .... their agent, of the other part, as follows:

Five Year Term.

"The said .... hereby contracts and agrees to enter into the service and employment of the said Company in North America, in the capacity of .... and that he will embark when thereunto required on board such ship or vessel as shall be appointed by or on behalf of the said Company and proceed to Hudson Bay, and for the term of five years to be computed from the said embarkation, and for such term as hereinafter mentioned and faithfully serve the said Company as their hired servant in the capacity of ....

DUTY BY DAY OR NIGHT.

and devote the whole of his time and labor in their service and
for their sole benefit, and that he will do his duty as such and
perform all such work and service by day or by night for the
said Company as he shall be required to do and obey all the orders
which he shall receive from the Governors of the Company in
North America, or others their officers or agents for the time
being.

MILITARY DUTIES.

and that he will with courage and fidelity in his said station in
the said service defend the property of the said Company, their
factories and territories, and will not absent himself from the
said service nor engage or be concerned in any trade or employment whatsoever, except for the benefit of the said Company, and
according to their orders.

FURS SACRED.

"And that all goods obtained by barter with the Indians, or
otherwise, which shall come to the hands or possession of the
said .... shall be held by him for the said Company only,
and shall be duly delivered up to the said Governors or other
officers at their factory or trading post, without any waste, spoil,
or injury thereto. And in case of any wilful neglect or default
herein he shall make good to the said Company all such loss as
they shall sustain thereby to be deducted out of his wages.

TO WORK PASSAGE.

"And the said .... further agrees that he is to work
his passage or passages when proceeding to his destination, and
from post to post in the event of its being found necessary to
move him in the country.

ABSOLUTE OBEDIENCE.

and that the said .... will faithfully obey all laws,
orders and regulations established or made by the Company for
good government of their settlements and territories, and at all
times during the residence of the said .... in North
America he will defend the rights and privileges of the said
Company and aid and support their officers and agents to the
utmost of his power.

FORM OF CONTRACT

A Year's Notice to Quit.

" And the said .... further engages and agrees that in case he should omit to give notice to the Governor or officers of the said Company in North America one year or upwards before the expiration of the said term of .... years, of his intention to quit their service and return to Europe, then he hereby promises and agrees to remain one year longer and also until the next ship in the service of the said Company shall sail from thence to Europe as their hired servant in North America, upon the like terms as are contained in this contract.

And the said .... also engages and agrees that in case the said Company shall not have any ship which will sail from North America for Europe immeditely after the expiration of the said term of .... years, or of such further term as hereinbefore mentioned, then he hereby promises and engages to remain in the service as a hired servant of the said Company in North America until the next ship of the said Company or some ship provided by them shall sail from thence to Europe upon the like terms as are contained in this contract.

To Work Way on Ship.

" Provided always that the said .... further agrees to keep watch and ward and perform such other work in the navigation of the ship of the said Company in which he shall be embarked on the outward and homeward voyages as he shall be required to perform by the commanding officer of the said vessel.

The Company's Only Liability.

" And the said .... on behalf of the said Company hereby engages that upon condition of the due and faithful service of the said............in like manner as aforesaid but not otherwise the said............shall receive from the said Company after the rate of............pounds per annum to commence on the day of his embarkation for Hudson Bay as aforesaid, and up to the day of his embarkation from thence to Europe on one of the ships of the said Company's service, or in any ship provided by them, or in the event of his determining to settle in the country up to the day of his quitting the service.

Summary Dismissal.

" Provided always and it is hereby expressly agreed between the said parties thereto that it shall be lawful for the Governor

71

or Governors or other officers of the said Company in North America at any time during the said term of .... years or such additional term as aforesaid to dismiss the said......... from their service and direct his return from thence to Europe in one of the ships in their employment or in some ship provided by them; and in such case his wages are to cease from the day of his embarkation for Europe.

FORFEITURE OF WAGES.

" And further, that in the case the said .... shall at any time during this contract desert the service of the said Company or otherwise neglect or refuse duly to discharge his duty as such hired servant as aforesaid then he shall forfeit and lose all his wages, for the recovery whereof there shall be no relief either in law or equity, and shall pay for his passage to Europe in one of the Company's ships the rate of passage money usually charged by the Company to persons who have not been in their service.

" In witness whereof the said parties have hereunto set their hands.

" Signed in the presence of ...."

Such were the rather one-sided terms of contract of the " recruits from Europe " on board the *Prince Rupert* and *Lady Head*. Therein the Company had fully guarded themselves against every contingency which might give the right to legal action against them. The sub-headings, of course, do not appear in the lithographed written forms.

NEITHER BOARD NOR LODGING.

Owing to the nature of their service in the wilds, the Company neither could nor would make any promises of board and lodging to their servants; for after leaving the chief factories and " The Settlement " the men would often be merely employed in providing themselves with food and shelter according to circumstances, and would have to rustle for themselves, the spacious heavens for their canopy, and mother earth for their couch. In lieu of rations they might be served out with powder and shot to hunt, twine to snare and fish, and some seed and a hoe to provide food for the present and future. But besides the wages specified in their contracts (£22 for laborers, £24 for sloopers, £35 for mechanics per annum), each was entitled to receive a " gratuity " of £2 a year in lieu of rations of tea and sugar.

LAND GRANTS PROMISED.

Many years before, the contracts had also entitled such servants as did not avail themselves of the privilege of the return passage to Europe, and desired to remain in the country after gaining their freedom, to a land grant up to one hundred acres out of the Company's possessions in North America, the precise locality not being given in the document, but later, in order to augment Lord Selkirk's Settlement, the land was given in the Red River Settlement. Some time after the above stipulation ceased to appear in the regular contracts, but about 1858, when the London board seemed anxious to appear active in colonizing, and up to, I think, 1862, mechanics and laborers electing to remain in the territories were guaranteed free grants of land in the Red River Settlement of fifty and twenty-five acres respectively, instead of their passage to Europe.

MANY GRANTS STILL WITHHELD.

I am credibly informed that a number of these retired servants, last mentioned, having lost, in their many journeys in the wilderness, their copies of the contract, have been unable to obtain these grants from the Company, although, the contracts having been all in triplicate, they must have either the two copies retained by them or registers thereof in their archives.

THE " PRINCE RUPERT " DESCRIBED.

The barque *Prince Rupert* was about five hundred tons burden. She had double, patent-reefing topsails, which had at that time not come into general use, but were such an obvious improvement and such a saving to life and limb as to be universally approved of by seamen, who, as a class, scorned all innovations. But here the march of improvement ceased, for, unlike the whalers and sealers going to Greenland, which some years before had adopted auxiliary steam propellers, to enable them to thread the winding openings in the ice and make headway against head winds, the *Prince Rupert* still depended on her sails alone.

She had a raised poop aft and a topgallant forecastle forward, where the officers aft and the boatswain and carpenter forward were accommodated. There were also berths for the second mate, a midshipman, and a passenger in the " half deck," immediately in front of the poop, while the crew and steerage passengers had quarters in the steerage forward. The cook's galley was a little deckhouse before the mainmast.

THE CREW.

The vessel was commanded by a splendid British sailor, who had made as mate and master over twenty voyages to the Bay—Captain Henry Bishop. The chief mate was Mr. MacPherson, who afterwards made many voyages as captain to the Bay. Mr. Campbell was the second mate. The boatswain, named Aitchison, was a fine old tar, and, next to the captain, the best seaman on board. He, too, had made many voyages in the Company's ships, besides all over the globe. The carpenter was an Orkneyman called Eunson, a fine, quiet and intelligent man. The apprentice or midshipman was Sidney Reynell, a refined English youth, who had already voyaged round the world on the Green Company's ships out of London. A cook and a steward and twelve able seamen completed the crew. Of these latter one was a Corsican and another a deserter from the French navy. This crew was ample to bring the ship from London to Stromness, and for the rest of the voyage all the steerage passengers were bound to assist on deck, while those engaged as " sloopers "—seamen —for the service on the Bay, and the Shetlanders, who are supposed to be born sailors, were, as a matter of course, berthed with the crew and sent aloft.

PASSENGERS.

That year all the " sloopers," twelve fine-looking young Shetland seamen, had been drafted for service at Moose Factory, and embarked on the *Lady Head* for the southern department. For service in the northern department bound for York Factory on the *Prince Rupert,* there were two blacksmiths, a boatbuilder, and a cooper—nominated " tradesmen " —and twenty-four laborers, the majority of the latter coming from the Hebrides; and a fine, healthy, hardy set of men they were. The recruits for service in the wilds had no weaklings among them, all such being at once rejected by the medical examiners; and only applicants having certificates of good character from the ministers of their church were accepted.

The cabin passengers were Miss Mason and maid, and three apprentice clerks, Alexander Christie, David Armit and myself. Miss Mason was returning home to her father, the Reverend William Mason, of the English Church Missionary Society, at York Factory. After receiving a good education in Scotland, to which his grandfather, Chief Factor Alexander Christie, twice Governor of Assiniboia, had retired, Christie was also returning to his native land, where his father was a chief trader and his uncle, William Christie, was the leading chief factor. Maternally, also, he was well connected, for his mother was sister of the distinguished scholar and patriotic native of Rupert's Land, Dr. A. K. Isbister. Armit was the grandson of a minister of Kirkwall, and son of a gentleman farmer near that place, the family being connections of Mr. William Armit, of the Hudson's Bay office in London, and afterwards secretary. My own connection with the Company arose through my father, Dr. John Cowie,* of Lerwick, having made several voyages as surgeon to Hudson Bay, and afterwards becoming the Company's agent in Shetland. We three had been taken out of a long list of applicants, mostly English lads inspired by such books as R. M. Ballantyne's "Young Fur Traders," to seek sport and travel in the wilds of North America. But very few such applicants were accepted, and the appointments were generally given those who had some connection already with the Company, and to the protégés of its directors, such as Mr. Edward Ellice and Mr. Matheson, of Ardross, who found the patronage useful in the constituencies which they represented in Parliament.

THE CARGO.

The cargo of the ship consisted of sixty tons of gunpowder, necessitating great caution against fire, with bullets and shot in proportion for large and small game; hundreds of cases of flintlock Indian guns, with a few hundred flintlock single and double-barreled guns of better quality, and only a small number, comparatively, of percussion guns—all being muzzle loaders. The next most important article was twine for fishing nets, upon which the food supply of most of the people of the country depended; for no food for daily consumption was imported, such as flour, biscuit and salt meats, except for occasional use at the posts on the coast, and a small annual allowance of flour for those in the interior. The annual allowance of flour† being three hundredweight for chief factors and traders, two hundredweight for clerks, one hundredweight for postmasters, one-half hundredweight for interpre-

* He was M.D. of St. Andrews and Licentiate of the Royal College of Surgeons of Edinburgh; and held besides other public appointments those of Admiralty Surgeon and Agent, and Surgeon to the Royal Naval Reserve.

† Owing to the generally poor quality of Red River flour at that time the quantity required for those small "winter allowances" to officers and men was imported by the ship. The Red River article was used by the boatmen plying between the settlement and York Factory.

ters and mechanics, and one-quarter hundredweight for the other yearly servants. There was also a large quantity of tea and tobacco, but never enough of the former to supply all the natives would consume. Sugar was another limited luxury in the interior. Other luxuries of civilization were a number of puncheons of rum, and smaller quantities of brandy and wines, forming altogether a considerable portion of the freight.

In hardware, axes, files, traps, knives, needles and awls, frying-pans, pots and copper kettles, flints and fire-steels, were all essentials. Blankets and clothing came in huge bales, but while desirable, their place could be taken by furs and skins, and they therefore could not be considered absolute necessities.

A good proportion of the cargo consisted of supplies being imported by the Red River settlers and the missionaries throughout the country; and a few cases, many containing books, and parcels of home-made clothing for individual officers and men, who were allowed so to import special articles for their own use. Some of the clerks stationed at the factory, to the envy of their brethren in the interior, availed themselves of this privilege by importing barrels of beer and preserved dainties for supper parties in the long winter nights.

CABIN FARE AND THE MATE.

The *Prince Rupert* was well found in food and grog for crew and passengers, also in lime juice to guard against scurvy. The cabin was supplied from the same source, with the addition of the live stock before mentioned, and beer, stout, and wine. So in the cabin we fared sumptuously every day, and the sea air increased our relish for these good things, which the ship's officers were fond of telling us would be the last chance of getting civilized food until we again took ship from Hudson Bay. In the wilds our fare would be bear and blubber, fish without bread or salt or vegetables in times of plenty, and leather and lichen off the rocks in time of want.

The mate, MacPherson, was the chief prophet of the evils we were going to encounter, becoming more particularly pessimistic whenever we got hold of his entries in the logbook and made fun of his writing, spelling and grammar. In the course of his sailings over many seas he had acquired tales of horror of all descriptions, the scenes of which he tried to adapt to the Hudson Bay territories, with the most laughable results. The Indian, according to him, was a cannibal who preferred tender young clerks to buffalo boss; lions and tigers hunted in packs with the timber wolves; crocodiles would devour us, serpents would add their stings to those of the mosquitoes, and if we ever reached the coast again we would take the first ship home and be glad to get salt junk instead of the dainty cabin fare upon which we were being pampered.

Although not much of a penman, and, as we afterwards saw, a poor hand at conning the ship through the ice, he was a smart man going aloft to reef topsails in a storm when his help was needed; but, with a terrific squint, he certainly did not seem to be quite the ladies' man he used to brag that he was. His attempts to catch the eye of the lady's-maid as she passed through the cabin, while they filled us, before whom he was showing off, with laughter, brought forth only a frown on the countenance of that demure and seasick damsel; but to make up for his failure in this case he went on to boast of the number of women who had fallen in love with him at first sight in every port he visited. Be that as it may, MacPherson provided us with plenty of merriment during the wearisome voyage, and I am sure that besides amusing himself he also desired to amuse us, and really pitied us as " young bears with all our troubles before us "—a favorite expression of his.

LAUNCHING A YORK BOAT AT PORTAGE ON NELSON RIVER.

A SAILING RACE OF YORK BOATS.

Courtesy of Hudson Bay Railway.

CHAPTER III.

ACROSS THE WESTERN OCEAN.

" We seek a wild and distant shore
Beyond the Atlantic main;
We leave thee to return no more
Nor view thy cliffs again."
—*The Emigrants' Farewell.*

ALL ABOARD.

EVERYTHING being now ready, the ships only waiting for a
fair wind to carry them through Hoy Sound to an offing at
sea, on June 28th Christie and I, who had been making the
best of the hospitalities and attractions of Stromness, were
ordered to embark. Our fine-looking chum, Reynell, who with
his attractive address and midshipmite's uniform, had become
a general favorite while on shore leave, went aboard that evening, and next morning at 5.30, after bidding a long farewell
to my brothers, Robert and James, * and my cousin, Gordon
Heddell, who had come from Lerwick to see me off, I got on
a small sailboat with Christie, and a gale from the west soon
put us alongside the *Prince Rupert*. It was only then I
seemed to feel the wrench of parting from home and friends
in all its intensity, and realized that I was bound for a long
exile from all one holds most dear. But we set to work to fix
up our stateroom for the voyage, hoping to get ashore for
church next day, which was Sunday.

* Robert Cowie, M.A. of Aberdeen, M.D. of Edinburgh, who
succeeded to my father in Lerwick, and died in 1874; and James,
who, after sailing the seven seas, entered the H.B.C. as clerk in
1876, and after serving in the Northern, Southern and Western
Departments, retired with a pension in 1911.

However, no one was allowed to go ashore on Sunday, but in the evening the Rev. Mr. Brand (brother-in-law of the Bishop of Rupert's Land), and Dr. Ballenden came aboard, the former holding service and the latter looking into the bill of health. The wind continuing unfavorable, though the weather was beautiful, we still lay at anchor in Cairstone Roads on Monday, and Captain Herd, a veteran dandy, and Hudson Bay skipper, who acted as " ship's husband " in London for the Company's Bay and Columbia ships, came off with a party of ladies and gentlemen. In such company we soon cheered up; and Captain Herd, as an old shipmate of my father, did me the special honor of parading the quarterdeck with me, giving good advice and best wishes for my welfare. At the same time he duly impressed me with his importance by snubbing Captain Bishop and expatiating on his titled acquaintances in London.

In the evening, the wind being now favorable, though light, from the north, the Moravian missionary barque *Harmony,* bound for Labrador, set all sail from royals down, presenting a beautiful sight as she weighed anchor and glided out past the rugged hills of Hoy, firing a salute of six guns as she went, which, however, was not returned by the battery of Stromness on the Sound.

Hoist " Blue-Peter."

On Tuesday, July 2nd, at eight bells in the morning watch, our consort, the *Lady Head,* fired a gun and ran up " Blue-Peter " to her foremast head as the signal to sail. Immediately the *Prince Rupert* followed suit, both ships also flying the British red ensign at the mizzen peak and the Company's arms—" the house flag "—at the mainmast head. The friends we had made at Stromness were kind and mindful to the last. While canvas was being loosened and the cable hove short, a pretty cutter with a party of gay picnickers passed us on their way to a neighboring islet. The ladies of the party fluttered their handkerchiefs and the men their hats in farewell, and

STROMNESS, WITH FISHING BOATS.

Courtesy of Mr. G. W. Baker, Barrister, Winnipeg.

LERWICK, FROM NORTH NESS.

Courtesy of Mr. G. W. Baker, Barrister, Winnipeg.

raising their voices in a melody wafted over the waters sang,
" Will ye no come back again," succeeded, as they sailed away
in the distance, by " Auld Lang Syne," of which faint and
intermittent strains were borne o'er the breeze till they faintly
died away.

Then, immediately after breakfast, to the inspiring strain
of the chanties, " Haul Away the Bowline " and " Across the
Western Ocean," the crew, led by the bosun, sheeted home
the canvas and tripped anchor, and the ships headed for
Hoy Sound. The *Lady Head* led and saluted the battery
with five guns, which were replied to as the *Prince Rupert*
ran by, and we answered with another five. Then we dipped
our ensign in good-bye to Scotland, from which a fine east
wind swiftly bore us away at the rate of nine and one-half
knots.

Next day the fair wind moderated, lessening the rate to
about seven knots. On the 4th, in the morning, a whale
showed himself near us, during a calm with a heavy swell.
By midday a gale from the north with a heavy sea arose, and
the water got into our bunks.

Upon the Atlantic.

During the night the gale abated, and next morning the
Lady Head was on our lee bow, within half a mile. She
signalled that Captain James was ill and had not been on
deck for two days. Having assisted my father and brother
in their practice and taken a session at the Edinburgh University and Royal Infirmary, Captain Bishop told me to be
ready to do what I could for our jovial friend, Captain James,
as soon as the sea went down enough to allow a boat to board
his ship. The occasion and necessity did not arise, but that
day I commenced my " experientia medica" in the service, by
prescribing pills composed of cayenne pepper and bread for
the seasickness of the lady's maid, who derived some physical
and, probably, more mental relief therefrom. On July 6th
there was a fine breeze from the east, the ship going eight

knots. The *Lady Head* was on our starboard quarter, hull down. Captain Bishop said we were about quarter of the way to York Factory now, and he had never before been so far on the way at this date. The 7th being Sunday was signalized only by a much better dinner than usual for all on board, and no unnecessary work. The weather was soft and calm, and our consort was seen ahead for the last time on the voyage, much to our regret, for she was something to look at on this otherwise tenantless ocean, and there was always the element of interest as to which ship were the better sailer in different winds and on various courses. Besides it was desirable, for mutual assistance, that the vessels should keep company till their ways diverged on Hudson Bay for Moose and York Factories respectively.

During the next three days we slipped along slowly with light beam and fair winds, enjoying fine weather, which encouraged all hands forward, off duty in the dog watch, to divert themselves by skylarking, dancing and music on deck.

THE DOG WATCH ENTERTAINMENTS.

The three leading characters in these diversions were a young Orkney recruit, who played on a fiddle, by ear, almost anything asked for; Jean, the French naval deserter; and Aitchison, the bold bosun, who was the manager of the show.

The professor of the violin was always ready to oblige; Jean was a tall, strapping and agile Frenchman, with a handsome, jovial and expressive countenance, black eyes, hair and moustache, always neat and tidy in dress. He was the boss dancer, executing *pas seul,* besides many acrobatic tricks and feats. His *vis-a-vis* in the hornpipe or break-down jig was the painted wooden figure of a nigger with jointed legs and arms, carved by the boatswain and operated by him by drumming in time to the fiddle on a thin springy board, over which " Sambo " was suspended so that his feet barely touched it. The skilful tapping of the boatswain on this board threw " Sambo " into gentle or rapid motion, or violent contortion at will. Opposite Sambo, Jean would perform, mimicking his steps, antics and contortions, always commencing to do so with the highest good humor, but as the fun grew fast and furious and Sambo became inimitable Jean would get excited and frantically furious, both physically and vocally. This was the climax to which the fiddler and boatswain led up, and it was ever tumultuously applauded. Jean could sing, too, in French, but the Marseillaise was the only song which was much appreciated.

Then one of the Highlanders from the Hebrides would be called upon, and render a song that reached the hearts of those who knew Gaelic. The bosun's mate, Agnew, had a fine voice, and many fine old English songs. The midshipmite, Reynell, had a beautifully trained voice, and all the latest popular London airs. But the bosun, the manipulator of Sambo, was the star performer, whether crooning a nigger minstrel air, which was apparently coming from Sambo, who was gesticulating or jigging to suit tune and time, or rolling out a song of the sea, and finally winding up in a strain carrying our thoughts back to bonnie Scotland, where

> " Shrined among their crystal seas
> Thus I saw the Orcades—
> Rifted crag and snowy beach,
> Where the seagulls swoop and screech;
> While around its lonely shore
> Wild waves rave and breakers roar,
> Gone the isle, and distant far
> All its loves and glories are."

THE BOSUN BOLD.

The boatswain was a big, powerful man, black haired, bearded and eyed, with a ruddy, bronzed complexion, and handsome countenance. He had been educated in George Heriot's Hospital in Edinburgh, and had roved the seas from his youth up. For several years he had been in the coasting trade in the West Indies, where he had acquired such experiences as are related in " The Cruise of the Midge " and innumerable diverting stories of the colored people there and their dialect, and the art of mimicking both. He was in every way a splendid specimen of the British sailor, and as he was then about fifty years of age, I feel sure that, like his friend of whom he often sang, " Old Tom Bowling," Aitchison has long ere this " gone aloft " for ever.

SPUN YARNS.

These amusements, under the boatswain's auspices, with the many well, fine-spun yarns of his life and experiences, and the long and interesting accounts given by Christie of the land of his birth, to which he was returning with fond anticipations, form my most pleasant memories of that long, monotonous and dreary voyage across the Atlantic. Of course we had our good young appetites sharpened by the sea, and a fine bill of fare to satisfy them; books and cards; sometimes little chats with Miss Mason; and occasionally the honor of listening to some of the captain's anecdotes; while the prophet Jeremiah—McPherson, chief mate—was ever ready to remind us of the blessings we were enjoying in the Paradise afloat, which he made out the *Prince Rupert* to be as compared with the Arctic inferno ashore to which we were journeying, impatient to enter on our career as voyagers and hunters of bear and buffalo.

EXERCISE BELOW AND ALOFT.

The cook's caboose on deck was the only place where a fire was allowed, except a miserable infrequent apology in the saloon—the danger of fire, with so much gunpowder aboard, being the risk always present in the captain's mind. So, perforce, we were obliged to tramp up and down the deck to keep warm, and always seized with alacrity every occasion to tail on to the end of a rope, which it was our privilege to do at the break of the poop in handling the main topgallant and royal sails. The skipper kept a fatherly eye on us, frowning on our going forward and mixing with those there, except during the frolics of the dog watch and in occasionally visiting his friend the bosun. When the captain was below I began to go aloft, a favorite amusement of all Lerwick boys from infancy, and the mate kindly cast his glance the other way. Christie joined me in these gymnastics, and soon could shin up a rope and the royal mast to touch the main-truck equally well. When the captain found out we had already " paid our footing " to the sailors, he never stopped us going up the rigging, except during very bad weather. So the setting and furling of the main royal, during the daytime, always were left for us to exercise ourselves upon.

Sail Ho!

Having now given an idea of the life we led aboard, I must continue the narrative of the voyage. We encountered light, baffling head winds on the 11th and 12th. On the evening of the latter we sighted a barque heading in our direction, S.W., homeward bound. We hoped she might be the Company's *Ocean Nymph,* which had wintered in the Bay on a whaling and trading trip with the Esquimaux. I immediately went below to write letters for home, but while so engaged the captain came down, saying it was not the *Ocean Nymph,* but probably a Danish craft from Greenland, which did not care to swerve a bit from her course to speak to us. Neither did she; but she gave us some pleasurable excitement for a while on that solitary sea.

Off Cape Farewell.

The 13th was a beautiful but calm day. Towards evening a freshening breeze favored us from the east, and increasing sent us along next day under full sail at the rate of eight knots till we rounded Cape Farewell, Greenland. We now began to maintain a bright lookout for icebergs. The next day was our second Sunday at sea. The wind had veered round dead against us during the night, and we stood in for the coast of Greenland till dinner time. The ship was then put about and the wind fell so that the sails no longer steadied her in the terrific cross swells, caused by the meeting of the three different currents, setting along the east and west coasts of Greenland and from the Atlantic respectively. These, crashing together, threw up pyramids of water composed of the opposing swells. The *Prince Rupert* wallowed, dipped her yardarms and pitched and tossed, helplessly becalmed, in this meeting of aqueous mountains, while every moment the straining threatened to dismast her.

GREENLAND'S ICY MOUNTAINS.

Next morning (the 16th) the ship was slipping along at one and a-half knots with a light air from the north, accompanied by mist and drizzly rain. We shot at a number of " whale birds," of which large flocks were to be seen during the last three days, and great numbers of " Mother Carey's Chickens " (the sign of coming storm) had been flying around us the previous evening. The monotony of the voyage was still further broken upon at one o'clock, when two big whales appeared playing within a hundred yards of us, affording a sight alone worth making the voyage to see. Then, just before dinner, at four o'clock, as we were taking our seats, the mate rushed down, reporting it had cleared and icebergs and land in sight to the nor'ard. The bergs were far off and the land still farther, but both were plainly visible, and were sights we had been longing to see as samples of the rest of the voyage. The land was supposed to be Cape Farewell, which is on an island lying north-westerly from Staten Hook, the most southerly point of the continent of Greenland. Seen through the glass the land showed, on the west, a comparatively low rounded outline, followed by a succession of four lofty, sharp peaks, the western sides rising perpendicularly from the water, and the eastern slopes running down at a sharp angle thereto, like the teeth of a saw. The color appeared black, flecked with snow, and a big berg, shaped like a corn stack floating in front, completed our view of Greenland's icy mountains. There was a beautiful rainbow and a lovely sunset this evening.

CROSSING DAVIS STRAITS.

During the next few days we made hardly any progress, being either becalmed or favored with very light airs; and nothing but one solitary seal and the whale birds, still numerous, were to be seen in crossing Davis Straits. On the 21st, however, we got a good fair wind at last, and with all sail set were making six knots an hour steering north-west for Resolution Island, which lies north of the eastern entrance of Hudson Straits. Next day (Sunday) was damp, but the wind had fallen, though still favorable. On the 23rd the weather was beautiful, the sea as smooth as a mill-pond, and we were doing four knots, the captain expecting to reach Resolution in two days more. In anticipation of getting some shooting when we reached the ice in the straits, the gunners among us began casting bullets.

During the passage across Davis Straits, the crew hoisted the crow's nest to the mainmast head, in which to accommodate the lookout when the ship got into the ice. The arrangement, always used by whalers, consisted of a large cask, with a trapdoor in the bottom, and open above. Then a temporary bridge was rigged up, athwart ship, near the mainmast, and projecting a few feet outside the bulwarks, to enable the officer of the watch to con the vessel through the ice. Fenders and long spiked poles to protect the vessel's sides and push aside the floes, were also got ready, as well as ice anchors to moor her to the ice, if necessary.

CHAPTER IV.

THROUGH STRAITS AND BAY—THE HUDSON BAY ROUTE.

OFF CAPE RESOLUTION.

ON Thursday, July 25th, with a heavy swell from the east and a strong breeze from the W.N.W., the ship, under top-gallant sails, was about seventy-eight miles off Resolution Island at noon. At six o'clock in the afternoon sighted Cape Resolution on starboard quarter, ship standing on to S.W.S. Sighted at the same time a large iceberg about five points off our weather bow, and were abreast of it two hours later. This was the first ice seen since that off Greenland.

July 26th.—At five o'clock in the morning an immense and ugly iceberg was seen about five miles off. It was flat-topped, stratified, and of a dirty bluish grey color. A fair wind sprang up after breakfast, accompanied by fog, compelling a bright lookout. About noon it cleared. Passed another berg on entering the straits, which appeared a mile long and its wavy pinnacles resembled a king's crown in shape. Next came a tall spire-like berg, which as we sailed by capsized, raising enormous rings of billows all round, into which our yardarms dipped. These and another smaller berg were all of beautiful variegated sheen to which neither artist's brush nor poet's pen could do justice. Open water ahead this evening.

27th.—In the morning the ship was surrounded by loose, brashy ice on every side. Stood out to the north-east, where it was least, and doubled round the northmost edge of the floes. Foggy most of the day, and cold, the braces being coated with ice. Towards evening it cleared up and I went aloft with a glass, seeing ice as far as the eye could reach, extending from south-west to north-east, with open water ahead.

28th.—A beautiful day. Ship slipping along through wide lanes of loose decaying ice, at three knots, over a smooth sea. Several icebergs in the distance. The ice gathered closer and stuck us up for about an hour in the afternoon until the tide turned. Saw several seals and a walrus, but being Sunday they were not molested by the gunners.

SAVAGE ISLANDS.

29th.—As there was more wind and the floes were more compact than yesterday, we were banging into big pieces every now and again, and finding plenty of exercise threading the lanes and dodging the heavier floes. This was quite an enjoyable change from the monotony of the open ocean. Lower Savage Islands, about fourteen miles abeam this morning.

30th.—Still slipping along in the right direction. About half way through the straits now. Anchors being shackled on to cables, ready for mooring at York. A long month at sea to-day.

31st.—Fine, strong breeze sending us at a great rate, banging into the floes, especially when the mates are on watch. The captain and bosun, being fine seamen, scarcely ever touch the ice when they are conning her. MacPherson seems to ram big floes for the fun of the thing, bringing us up " all standing "—on our aheads almost, occasionally. While we were at table, it being a fresh wind with frequent squalls he kept on sail till we were nearly on our beam ends several times and crashed into heavy ice that once brought the ship to a sudden dead stop, throwing Christie right over the dinner table with his plate of pea soup into Miss Mason's lap. Whereupon the skipper rushed on deck, shortened sail, backed the ship out of the ice, and gave the " false prophet " a dressing down. In the evening we reached altogether open water, with a slight swell on, which sent our seasickly passengers back to their sad state on the ocean. One poor young Orkneyman (an apprentice blacksmith) had been troubled that way from Stromness till we reached smooth water in the straits.

August 1st.—Sighted Upper Savage Islands.

2nd.—Between North Bluff and Prince of Wales Land. Fine weather, but the wind is light and contrary. Here we had hoped to be visited by the Esquimaux, but were disappointed, the more so as we wished ocular demonstration of some of the appearances and customs ascribed by the romantic-minded mate and other old voyageurs to these strange people. From North Bluff we crossed from the north side of the straits, which we had so far followed, to the southern shore and followed it thereafter, but always giving the land a wide berth, to avoid dangerous currents.

MEET A YANKEE WHALER.

3rd.—With a fair wind this morning the ship slipped along at four knots among loose ice, with land about twelve miles off on port beam. The weather was beautiful and warm. At about half-past eleven this morning we sighted a barque on the port bow close under the land. Thinking it might be the *Ocean Nymph* I again wrote letters for home. We stood in for the barque and fired two cannon to attract her attention, empty beer bottles being put next the wad to increase the noise. At two o'clock she hove to on our weather bow, and sent a whale boat, manned by a smart crew, with a very tall, thin and supple man at the steering oar. He came on board, leaving his crew strictly in their own boat alongside, and went down to the cabin with Captain Bishop, who gave him a glass of grog and sent him back to his vessel, bearing a nice present of beef, beer and wine for his captain. Our visitor was chief mate of the *St. Andrews* of New Bedford, returning from a short and unsuccessful whaling cruise in the Hudson Bay, and they were now bound out Hudson Straits up to Cumberland Straits in search of better luck.

So we were again disappointed about getting letters sent home.

While the Yankee mate was on board, the mirage of a vessel upside down appeared high in the western sky, which our captain thought might be our consort, the *Lady Head,* and perhaps several hundred miles away. When the mate returned, the *St. Andrews* bore down in the direction of the phantom ship for about half an hour, and then, changing his mind, her skipper hauled up to the wind again, and the ships exchanging courtesies by dipping their ensigns soon parted company.

Capes Wolstenholme and Digges.

August 4th (Sunday).—With a strong breeze from the south, coming off the land in heavy squalls occasionally, we ran for the first time pretty close along the land, which here, as on the north shore, rose steeply from deep water to high hills. But while every depression between barren black hills on the north side was filled with snow or ice, the brown, apparently heath-clad hills of Labrador presented a much warmer and more homelike aspect, much resembling the last land we had seen across the Atlantic—the Island of Hoy.

We doubled Cape Wolstenholme at two o'clock in the afternoon, and passed Cape Digges at four o'clock, having passed through the straits proper and reached the vestibule, between them and the main bay, extending from Cape Digges to Mansfield Island.

Storm and Fog.

Into this neutral zone, destitute of the protection afforded by the deep land-locked straits and of the free sea-room of the Bay, we shaped a course north of Mansfield Island, which was dreaded as the scene of the wreck of the *Prince Arthur* and the stranding of the *Prince of Wales* in 1864, through the inexperience of their commanders on a first voyage to the Bay. While on this precarious course making for the island towards dusk a dense fog enveloped us, and a storm with a heavy short sea arose from the south. The storm struck us suddenly, and it was fine to see the masterly manner in which Captain Bishop handled his crew and ship. He gave his commands in a clear trumpet-toned voice, which rang above the roar of the tempest, the rattle of rigging and clatter of canvas, and soon had her snugly under close reefed topsails and the foretopmast staysail.

August 5th.—The ship had been laid to during the night. In the morning it was still blowing hard, with a heavy sea, and the fog still continuing it was impossible to make Mansfield Island. So we kept sounding with the lead and pitched and tossed about all that day and the following night, during which the poor passengers who were liable to seasickness had a recurrence of its ghastly horrors, and were battened down below; while we all had an anxious time.

Round Mansfield Island.

Next day—the 6th—being now five weeks out from Stromness—the fog abated, and the wind fell and changed to the west, which was dead ahead, our course being north of Mansfield Island, to avoid the shoals which lie to the southward of it.

Got the anchors over the bows. Just before dinner a nice breeze from the north-east sprang up and carried us round the north of Mansfield, into the Bay proper. Still misty.

In Hudson Bay.

7th.—We are now fairly out of narrow waters into the open Hudson Bay itself, favored by wind and weather. As we are ahead of the usual time the captain intends to make for Churchill first and fire cannon to notify the schooner, which may be there, of her services as tender being required at York. We are 550 miles from the factory.

8th.—Got a splendid wind this morning at one o'clock, which kept on freshening and driving us along at nine knots.

CAPE CHIDLEY, SOUTH-EAST ENTRANCE OF HUDSON STRAITS.
Courtesy of Hudson Bay Railway.

SOUTHERN COAST OF HUDSON STRAITS.
Courtesy of Hudson Bay Railway.

NEARING CHURCHILL

"The fair breeze blew,
The white foam flew,
The furrow followed free."

We were now on the last lap of the voyage and were favored
by gentle breezes, a smooth summer sea, and bright balmy
weather to its end. The nights, too, were exquisitely lovely,
the full moon blending her radiance with the silvery crests
of the wavelets playing around, and blending her sheen with
the phosphorescent, whirling wake left by the ship as an
evanescent trace of her path across the deep.

OFF CHURCHILL.

On August 11th we were fifty miles east of Churchill and
one hundred and twenty north of York. A couple of cannon
were fired off Churchill on the faint chance of the reports
reaching the schooner and fort and intimating the safe
arrival of the *Prince Rupert* in the offing.

Next morning, by soundings, which had been taken regularly as we approached the coast, we were in twenty fathoms,
and by reckoning twenty miles from York Roads. The ship
was running at six knots, in smooth bright green water, with
the wind off the—still invisible—land. Though the low shore
was invisible, the wind wafted off a faint aroma of spruce, and
at the same time a few languid representatives of the most
numerous inhabitants of Rupert's Land—my bloody enemies,
the mosquitoes. These, after a little rest, proceeded to introduce themselves to us, and we submitted with curiosity to
these preliminaries to an acquaintance with the family of
ubiquitous and untiring tormentors, which became so intimate,
unendurable and infernal during all my summer journeyings
in the wilds.

ANCHOR IN YORK ROADS.

In the afternoon the anchor, last weighed in Cairstone
Roads, was cast in York Roads in the turbid estuary of the

Nelson River, twenty miles from the Factory, and out of sight of land, the high beacon, twelve miles off on the Point of Marsh, between the Nelson and Hayes rivers, only being visible from aloft. For the last time I ran aloft and stowed the main royal, and my voluntary services on the ocean wave were over.

To convey the glad tidings of our unusually early arrival to the people of the Factory, a cannon was fired at intervals during the day, and rockets and blue lights were set off after dusk, a lantern being also hoisted to the mizzen peak.

CRUISE IN THE GIG.

After the ship had been moored and tidied up that afternoon the captain lent the apprentice clerks his gig for a sail. With slack of the tide we tacked to windward towards shore, and upon the turn of the ebb to seaward, on a signal from the ship, we raced back before wind and current, and, catching a line thrown from the forechains, brought up smartly at the companion ladder. Armit, our most ardent gunner, then proudly passed up the sea fowl which had fallen to his aim; Christie, in exuberant spirits on nearing his native shore, had handled the foresheet; and I had been in my element steering. We had all enjoyed our little cruise so much that MacPherson must needs follow suit. So he set off, heading for the south, with a beam wind and free sheet, and an ebb tide carrying him to leeward and seaward. When dusk set in without his return the captain became quite anxious for the safety of the gig and its passengers. We were all relieved when they returned early next morning, after having run aground on shoals, and having passed a miserable night on the beach, somewhere between Hayes River and Cape Tatnam. The skipper gave MacPherson a dressing-down, and Christie, who was an expert at teasing, took occasion to contrast the lubberly conduct of the mate and his men, with the fine style in which the apprentice clerks had handled the gig.

Our Mentor the Mate.

Apart from the amusement afforded by the mate the object in mentioning the occasions on which he came to grief is to show the manner of man, who, when he obtained command of the *Ocean Nymph* a year or two after, made voyage after voyage to Hudson Bay without accident. The *Nymph*, too, was an abominable old flat-bottomed tub, which made about as much leeway as headway with the wind abeam. Her only redeeming qualities were that with a fair wind she made fine time, and her light draft also enabled her to ascend the Hayes River and anchor in front of the Factory, instead of, like vessels of deeper draft, discharging cargo into a tender at " Five Fathom Hole " out in the open roads.

The Hudson Bay Route.

Being eager and impatient to reach the new world, and begin our lives and adventures there, the non-eventful trip across the Atlantic appeared tedious. But from the time we got among the icebergs at the eastern entrance of the Straits till we reached the open Bay the voyage was full of interest and excitement, although we had missed two of the entertainments we had been led to expect. The first of these was football between the larboard and starboard watches on the icefields, the non-detention of the ship having afforded no opportunity for the annual match. The second was the graver disappointment in not having fallen in with the Esquimaux. For all that, every day we had passed some high cape or island marking our progress; and the tacking, backing and filling, the threading our way among the floes, and occasionally ramming into them, gave us plenty of joyous excitement and exercise. In the last lap over the summer seas of the Bay we were happy in the hope of soon reaching port.

Since then I have passed thrice through the Straits of Belle Isle, where the shores are as forbidding in appearance as those of Hudson Straits, and where, later in the season, I saw quite as many, in fact more, icebergs near its eastern entrance than we saw when entering Hudson Straits.

Most of the ice in Hudson Straits was rapidly decomposing, smashing in " candles " on contact with the ship. A steam-ship could have avoided the floes, or forced her way through any we saw with ease. There was a little fresh, clear, and heavy ice, also broken in floes, occasionally seen, which must have come from some other source than the main body of the floes.

We saw no ice in Hudson Bay, where ships have occa-sionally been beset for weeks by a stream of heavy ice flowing from Fox Channel towards the south-east end of the Bay. This ice sometimes draws so much water as to ground in six fathoms along the coast between Churchill and Chesterfield Inlet, my authority being a friend, Mr. John George Mowat, who made several boat voyages in as many years from Churchill to Marble Island. He also informed me that the ships manage to pass this heavy ice stream on the outward and homeward voyages by going round it or through it on a northerly, never a southerly, course.

I have selected the dates and calculated the averages here-under from the appendix to Dr. Robert Bell's " Geological Survey Report on Hudson Bay, 1879-80," giving the dates on which the ships arrived at and departed from York Fac-tory during the ninety-two years between 1789 and 1880 in-clusive :

Arrivals—Earliest, August 2nd, 1850, the *Prince Rupert;* latest, September 27th, 1811, the *Eddystone;* average, August 24th; exception, October 7th, 1836, the *Eagle,* wintered at York.

Departures—Earliest, August 27th, 1804, the *King George;* latest, October 7th, 1811, the *Eddystone;* average, September 18th.

Mr. Tuttle, in his book, " Our North Land," gives a list furnished by the Hudson's Bay Company, from their vessels' log books, for the years 1870 to 1883, of the dates on the outward voyage upon which their ships entered the Straits and upon which they passed out into the Bay, from which I derive the following averages:—

Entered July 31st; passed out August 13th; average passage through the Straits, fourteen days; exception, the *Ocean Nymph* once ran through in four days. Of the eighteen logs, six report "ice," eight report "no detention," and four report "no ice" in the Straits.

A comparison between the dates given by Dr. Bell and by Mr. Tuttle, of the time the ships passed through the Straits and of their arrival at York, shows an average passage of eleven days across the Bay, outward bound.

On the homeward passage to London, owing to the Straits being generally clear of ice, and the prevalence of the equinoctial gales from the north-west during that time of year, the ships make a much quicker run than when outward bound. A run of fourteen days from York to Land's End was not uncommon, and I have even heard of its being done in ten days. The vessels, of course, went straight for the English Channel, not calling at Orkney, and besides only carried a light cargo of furs, supplemented by ballast.

The immunity from frequent disaster on the voyage to and from Hudson Bay enjoyed by the Company's ships was very largely due to their being well built, well manned, and under able commanders of long experience. In former times not only the captains and mates but the seamen also were retained on pay all the year round, and the passengers always helped materially in handling the ships. The wreck on Mansfield Island in 1864 was due to a new captain, making his first voyage, paying no attention to the warning of his experienced chief mate, afterwards captain, Bishop. But it is remarkable that ever since the opening of the Hudson Bay route has been advocated in Western Canada an unusual number of wrecks have occurred on the Bay. While some of these must be merely accidental coincidences, others must be ascribed to the inexperience of the officers in uncharted waters.

I have read the arguments for and against the Hudson Bay route. I made the voyage related in these chapters. I was brought up among a seafaring people, many of whom made annual voyages to the Greenland and Davis Straits' sealing and whaling grounds, and others to Archangel and the Baltic; for twenty-five years in this country my companions were men who had come and gone by Hudson Bay, sometimes on several occasions; and having witnessed in my boyhood the revolutionary improvement effected in the sealing and whaling trade by the addition of steam power to the old sailing craft, I feel assured that properly equipped vessels, under competent officers may make, during at least four months of the year, the voyage through the deep waterways of Hudson Straits and Bay with even greater safety than they can that by the foggy banks of Newfoundland and through the dangerous Gulf of St. Lawrence.

Those who go down to the sea in ships and have business on mighty waters have ever taken the risk, and taking that risk the seamen of our race have carried our commerce and our conquests all round the globe. Are we, then, through fear of the dangers of the deep, so minimized by modern improvements, to leave unused the natural outlet for our products, explored " in tiny pinnace " four hundred years ago by Henry Hudson?

Of the heroic Hudson, to whom the united West should erect her first monument in bronze or sculptured stone, our western pioneer and poet, Charles Mair, in the oft-quoted lines of " Open the Bay," nobly says:

> " Open the Bay! What cared that seaman grim
>   For towering iceberg or for crashing floe?
> He sped at noonday or at midnight dim
> A man, and hence there was a way for him,
>   And where he went a thousand ships can go."

Of the influences antagonistic to its opening the poet proceeds to say:

"Open the Bay! Who are they that say ' No ?'
　Who locks the portals? Nature? She resigned
Her icy reign, her stubborn frost and snow,
Her sovereign sway and sceptre, long ago,
　To sturdy manhood and the master mind.

"Not these the foe! Not Nature who is fain
　When earnest hearts an earnest end pursue;
But man's old selfishness and greed of gain;
These ancient breeders of earth's sin and pain—
　These are the thieves that steal the Nation's due."

CHAPTER V.

YORK FACTORY.

York Roads and "Five Fathom Hole."

August 13th, 1867.—At nine o'clock the schooner *Marten* and the packet boat hove in sight, coming off from the Factory. The boat was of the model used on the coast, built to row and sail, rigged with two lugs and a jib, and with grip enough to tack against the wind, the last being the essential difference between the "coast" and the "inland" boats. She was manned by a crew of different races, the Scottish islesmen distinguished

> "By the tall form, blue eye, proportion fair,
> The limbs athletic, and the long light hair"

of their Norse ancestors, in striking contrast with the bronzed visages, brown eyes and long black hair of the North American Indians. The boat's crew of both races, all tanned by the fierce American sun, and arrayed with bright-colored sashes (L'Assomption belts) round their hips, beautifully silk worked yellow moccasins on their feet, and gaudy garters below the knee, showed a striking contrast to the fresh, rosy-cheeked recruits, who were generally well and plainly clothed in blue pilot cloth pea jackets and trousers, with well blackened boots.

Captain Bishop greeted at the gangway, as old friends, the chaplain of the Factory, the Rev. William Mason, who came to meet his daughter; and the chief accountant, Mr. Parson, and the surgeon, Dr. MacKay, who immediately had the crew and passengers mustered for inspection, with the most satisfactory result. We had had no illness on the voyage, but sea-sickness in three or four cases, and the recruits were a splendid lot of picked men from one of the hardiest races of Europe. The inspection over, Mr. Parson quickly took his departure with " the ship packet," that being the mail and documents from Britain. The doctor also returned in the packet boat, eager to get the letters from home when the seals of the packet were broken at the Factory.

Captain Tuckee, of the *Marten,* and a pilot had come aboard to take the ship from her anchorage in York Roads, in the channel of the Nelson to " Five Fathom Hole,"* in the channel of the Hayes River, over a course marked by buoys and bearings known only to those who take them each season. After lightening the ship of the dangerous cargo of sixty tons of gunpowder, by discharging it into the *Marten* and two sloop-rigged lighters, with a high tide and fair wind we set sail and hove anchor and were taken by Captain Tuckee and the pilot into " Five Fathom Hole " that afternoon. We were still seven miles from the Factory, but, after mooring and firing a salute, we could distinctly hear the thunder of the answering guns booming to leeward.

When the tide fell at low water we appeared to lie in a basin completely surrounded by mud flats and sand bars, and secure from every wind except a storm at high tide from the east.

August 14th.—The *Marten* returned from the Factory for more cargo, and to take the passengers ashore.

" OCEAN NYMPH " AND YANKEE WHALER.

During the day we sighted a sail in the offing, which, on nearer approach, was made out to be the *Ocean Nymph,* Captain Taylor, returning from a whaling and trading cruise and wintering at Marble Island, near Chesterfield Inlet. She anchored not far from us and lay rolling frightfully, while

---

* A recent visitor to York was informed by the Indians there that " Five Fathom Hole " no longer exists.

the *Prince Rupert's* motion was hardly noticeable. This I have learned from indignant passengers was one of the *Nymph's* specialties—she was wholly a roller.

Captain Taylor had had no luck whaling, and about five hundred white foxes were all the returns of his year's voyage. Some American whalers had wintered at the same place and not only spoilt his trade with the Esquimaux, but, after having helped themselves to all they needed of a cache of coal placed there by the British Admiralty, and before Captain Taylor, who had planned to help himself from time to time to the coal, knew, our American cousins had set fire to and destroyed the pile in wanton malice. After having suffered from want of fuel through this outrage, Captain Taylor's sentiments towards his Yankee rivals cannot well be reproduced in type, and they certainly were not calculated to cement the Anglo-American *entente*.

We Disembark.

We now were ready to leave our good home upon the deep and the fleshpots of the *Prince Rupert*. We bade a long farewell to our good friends the boatswain and others of the crew, and embarking on the *Marten,* slowly sailed up the Hayes estuary and river to the Factory, arriving there late in the evening.

The first thing that impressed me was the smell of the spruce, which seemed all-pervading and as characteristic of the country as peat-reek is in country places in Scotland. We were met with an enthusiastic welcome at the landing by Mr. James S. Ramsay, apprentice clerk of three years' service, who, at the request of Chief Factor Wilson, convoyed us to the " Summer House," the quarters provided for visitors of our grade. There were bedsteads but no bedding in the rooms given us, so Mr. Ramsay sent the steward for a bale of new blankets, which served as mattresses and covering till we got our own bedding.

BELLICOSE BACHELORS

OFFICERS' QUARTERS.

The rooms were bare and the furniture plain and scanty, for the quarters were only temporary " camping ground " for wayfarers. They may have seemed still more uninviting than they really were from the contrast afforded by the blaze of barbaric decorations on the walls of the rooms of the clerks in " Bachelors' Hall." These consisted of Indian silk and bead and wool work of every hue, which adorned the attire of these " veterans " from head to foot, also their gun-coats, shot pouches, firebags and snowshoes, all of which were hung up round the room, alongside of colored prints of prize fighters, race horses, hunting scenes, ships and yachts, and photographs of all kinds. Each of the bachelors seemed to be a performer on a different musical instrument—one had a violin, another a flute, a third an accordion, and a fourth a concertina, and I think they could all play the Jews' harp, a very cheap and easily portable instrument, and whether single or double or quadruple-tongued was much in vogue in those days in the wilderness.

BELLICOSE BACHELORS.

Perhaps because rival musical performers, or maybe afflicted by the malarial atmosphere of the marshes, there was not among the York bachelors the same cheerful comradeship and good feeling as prevailed throughout the interior among the officers and clerks. Some of the stern, strict discipline and formality of the old coast-dwelling Hudson Bay men, before the union with the more free and easy and affable Celts of the North-West Company, still lingered at York. Whatever the cause, York Factory was notorious for the clerks and others stationed there making themselves disagreeable to each other in a way we, who keenly appreciated the companionship of the few of our own tongue and kind with whom we met in the wilderness of the interior, could not understand.

But however much the old residents might " scrap " among

themselves, they vied with each other in showing us every attention and kindness, even as they did to every other visitor.

THE COMMERCIAL CAPITAL OF RUPERT'S LAND.

Although Fort Garry was the residence of the Governor-in-Chief of Rupert's Land (if an official whose duties demanded constant travel through the length and breadth of the vast Hudson Bay territories could be said to have any fixed abode), and also the headquarters of the government of the district of Assiniboia, commonly known as "The Red River Settlement," yet in the year 1867 and for four or five years afterwards the ancient York Factory still retained its pre-eminence as the seaport and storehouse for the imports and exports of the northern department of the territories, excepting only supplies brought from St. Paul, Minnesota, chiefly for the Red River Settlement, and the buffalo robes which were also sent *via* St. Paul to Montreal for the American market.

FAR-SIGHTED BUSINESS METHODS.

To guard against shipwreck and other accidents by flood, field and fire, two years' full supplies for the whole Northern Department (now Keewatin, Manitoba, Saskatchewan and Alberta and North-West and Yukon Territories) were stored in the ample warehouses of York. There also were received and repacked for shipment to London, the only exportable products of the country—furs and skins from the interior, and feathers, goose quills and whale oil from the coast.

The business accounts of every district in the Department were kept at York, and the personal accounts of every officer and man, excepting freemen and Indians therein. Copies of these accounts were sent each district and person by the winter packet annually.

But by far the most important duty devolving upon the officer in charge and the accountant of the depot at York was that of making out in advance the lists of supplies required and likely to be required by the various districts and posts for several years to come. To facilitate and make reference accurate these lists were all made out in alphabetical order under the general headings of "general goods," "provisions," "medicines," and "stationery," for imported articles; and "country produce" for the manufactures and products of the country. In the inventories taken at every post in the country on the 31st day of May, annually, being the close of the Company's business year, known by them as an "outfit" (for instance, "outfit 1867"), to the headings above given there were added "articles in use" and "live stock," and "area in cultivation." To the number of each article on the inventory were added the numbers received in invoices from York and transfers from other posts. These added together showed the receipts, from which the transfers to other posts and the inventory for the following spring were deducted to show the expenditure, upon which the indents or requisitions for the supplies for the coming year or years were based. Allowance for all kinds of contingencies had also to be made, such as good or bad years for furs, and possible competition, involving increased expense in procuring and purchasing the furs.

The work of preparing these requisitions, upon which depended the well-being of the trade and the lives of the employees and the Indians frequenting the posts, which could only be supplied once a year and afterwards had to be as self-sufficient as a ship at sea for a whole year, was one requiring great experience and good judgment, and it was generally performed with almost prophetic foresight.

The Manufactures of York.

The "country-made articles" consisted chiefly of articles made at the Factory, such as small and large "Indian axes," ice-chisels, fish and muskrat spears, ironwork for boats, and even nails and tacks, which when they reached the far interior were worth more than their weight in gold. Everything made of tin for service and trade was turned out by the tinsmith at York, such as half and one pint drinking pots (known as " porringers "), round and oval pans, open and covered kettles of various sizes, all so made that the smaller sizes "nested" within those larger, to economize space. The few earthenware cups and bowls taken into the interior were also without handles and "nested." There was also a cooper who made the kegs for the allowances of liquor, rice, raisins, currants, etc., and also firkins for butter. So York was really a factory in these senses of the term.

Packing Goods for Portage.

Only some of the merchandise was packed in London in packages of convenient size and weight to be carried on men's backs over the portages. These were called " whole pieces," and consisted principally of bales of blankets and cloth with tarred inside wrappers and tin-lined cases of small hardware; kegs of gunpowder (sixty-six and two-third pounds net) and sugar, chests of tea (of one hundredweight and half a hundredweight net); rolls and " serons " of tobacco, done up in red-painted canvas, and weighing one hundredweight; double canvas bags of ball and shot, each one hundredweight; cases of yellow soap and long cases of Indian flintlock guns.

Most other articles which came in larger packages from England were unpacked at the depot and made up in mixed and assorted bales and cases of the proper kind for inland transport. The chief danger being damage by water, wreck and weather, to provide against the whole supply of one article being so lost or damaged the articles would be divided among a number of packages, so that an outfit for a post, which might be fifty white blankets, fifty capotes and one hundred shirts, etc., would be made up into, say, five bales, each containing the fifth part of the total supply, and including other articles, similarly assorted, to make up the required bulk or weight. Hardware and breakable things were, of course, packed in cases or casks, and, no paper or other waste weight or bulk being allowable, these were wrapped up or separated by "dry" goods—a bottle of castor oil (one of the few medicines supplied) was generally enfolded in the coil of a woollen sash, and so on.

ALL EGGS NOT IN ONE BASKET.

The same precautions against having all the eggs in one basket were taken in packing the furs in the interior. If a post had, for example, ten silver foxes, one hundred red foxes, thirty common (unprime) bears, five hundred martens, etc., then in ten "packs" of ninety or one hundred pounds each, there would be in each pack, wrapped up in three bundles protected by the common bearskins, one silver fox, ten red foxes, and fifty martens, etc. Likewise in loading a "brigade" (a number) of boats the cargoes would be assorted, for it would have been fatal to have the whole supply of gunpowder sunk in one boat, nor would unassorted ladings be fair to the crews, for some "pieces" could be stowed and handled with far greater ease than others, and the trim and capacity of the craft had also to be considered.

Tinware was largely used about the stations, but the strong and less easily damaged copper kettles, open and covered, were preferred for travelling. These were of different sizes, the smaller fitting inside the larger, and, as cargo, were generally put up in casks.

The unpacking and repacking employed a large number of the people of the establishment, and the clerks had plenty employment making out packing accounts and invoices of the "outfits," the clerical work being done with the greatest neatness and accuracy and checked and rechecked to avoid error, which would be irremediable in the interior.

DESCRIPTION OF THE FACTORY.

The site is five miles from the mouth of Hayes River, and on its northern or left bank, and the pickets enclosed about five acres. On the open space between the river bank and the high wooden railing on the south side of the enclosure, stood two twelve-pounder and four smaller brass field pieces on wooden platforms on each side of the front gate. These guns and the tall flagstaff, with its topmast, were the only outward signs of anything military in the place, for the day had long passed since the French and English had captured and re-captured the old forts on the Hayes River. The bald facts have been told by many writers, but never by a pen which has taken full advantage of the abundant romantic material of the history of the stirring strife between our gallant and daring former enemies and present friends, the French—aye, " foemen worthy of our steel "—and the English on the Bay. They fought for furs, perhaps but dimly conscious that the battle was for the whole North-West, to which he who held the Bay held the master-key.

The site of the Factory was a mossy bog originally, and the " gardens " within its pickets were artificially formed by plac-ing thick layers of willows on the moss and covering them with a layer of soil brought from upstream. Frequent chilly winds off the Bay checked the growth of the few hardy plants tried in the gardens. But in a sheltered spot on Ten Shilling Creek, about three miles further up the river, and nearly a mile up the creek, there is good soil, where the Company formerly raised good potatoes, onions, carrots and turnips, small peas, and large rhubarb and cabbage. The wild fruits of the country near the factory consist of cranberries, moss and gooseberries, red and black currants.

The sides and rear of the enclosure were formed of high pointed pickets. Inside, running parallel with these, were rows of buildings, used as stores, dwellings, offices and work-shops. The whole enclosure was divided into a front and back quadrangle by the large depot—two hundred feet square —which faced the front gate. This warehouse was built with a hollow square or court in the middle, and was flanked by long low buildings on the right and left, used as the officers' mess and summer quarters for visitors respectively.

All the buildings were of logs, clapboarded, nicely painted, and plank walks led to and past them. The whole establishment was beautifully clean and neat; but since then, with the fallen importance of the place, many of the buildings have been demolished or have become out of repair.

A Valuable Library.

The library held many valuable old books of travel, with special reference to those on the Bay and North-West. It was kept up by subscription, ten shillings a year being contributed by each clerk, and a smaller sum by such of the men as patronized it.*

Outside the Pickets.

Outside the pickets, a few paces to the east and near the river bank, there was a large boat-building and repairing shed. About half a mile further down along the bank stands the Indian church of log and clapboard construction. And at the same distance past the church there was a large powder magazine—the only stone structure in the place.

The Graveyards.

Across "Schooner Creek," where the schooner was laid up for the winter, was the old Indian graveyard, upon which the Hayes River was encroaching and eating away the banks, while outside of that enclosure, within iron railings set on stone, arose the tombstone of an old governor of York Factory, before the union of the North-West and Hudson's Bay companies. The inscription reads:

* I am informed that although many books have been spoilt or lost, this library still contains many rare and valuable volumes. Could not the survivors of the old subscribers ask for its removal to the custody of the Provincial Library at Winnipeg?

Sacred

To the Memory of

WILLIAM SINCLAIR, ESQUIRE,

Chief Factor,

Honourable Hudson's Bay Company's Service,

Who Died 20th April, 1818,

Aged 52 Years.

" Behold Thou hast made mine years as an handbreadth, and my age is as nothing before Thee. Verily, every man at his best estate is altogether vanity."

Erected as a token of affection by his son.

GOVERNOR SINCLAIR'S DESCENDANTS.

This old Governor Sinclair is said to have descended from the old Earls of Orkney. He left a numerous family of sons and daughters, who married and intermarried with other Hudson's Bay Company's officers and others throughout the territories, Canada and Columbia, so that go where one may in all these regions the ubiquitous descendants of his family may be found, many occupying leading and influential positions. Generation after generation of his descendants have served the Company " with courage and fidelity " till the present day.

The son who raised the monument was another chief factor, William Sinclair, whose grandson, John George McTavish Christie (son of Inspecting Chief Factor William J. Christie, and grandson of Governor Alexander Christie, of Assiniboia) is assistant to the fur trade commissioner of the Hudson's Bay Company in Winnipeg to-day.

The ramifications of old Governor Sinclair's descendants are wide and varied, but the one who attained the greatest public eminence was his grandson, the late Sir Edward Clouston, Bart., of the Bank of Montreal.

OFFICIALS OF THE FACTORY.

Those stationed at York Factory in 1867 were, as I remember: Joseph W. Wilson, chief factor; Joseph Fortescue, chief trader; William M. MacKay (1), surgeon and clerk; George Mowat, clerk, " the second," in charge of the men; Samuel K. Parson (2), clerk, accountant; Thomas M. Anderson (3), clerk, in depot; James S. Ramsay, apprentice clerk; Captain Tuckee, of the schooner *Marten*. To these were added my fellow-passenger, Alexander Christie, apprentice clerk, and shortly afterwards Doctor Yarrow and James Hargrave (4), apprentice clerk, who came from Canada *via* Red River, to York.* Mr. Fortescue had been chief accountant for years, but had now been promoted to chief tradership, and appointed to the charge of Oxford House. Dr. MacKay had volunteered for special service in Mackenzie River and was about to start on his long journey.

PASSENGERS TO ENGLAND.

The missionary of the Church of England stationed at York, the Rev. William Mason, has been already mentioned. While I was there two of his brethren from the interior arrived to take passage with their families by the ship to London, the Rev. Messrs. Taylor and T. T. Smith. Mr. and Mrs. Alexander Dahl, of Red River, also arrived to go home on a visit to Mrs. Dahl's relations in England.

In charge of the missionaries on his way to be educated in Scotland, Christie's little brother, Duncan, had arrived, bringing the sad intelligence of the death of his mother, a lady whose virtues and high talents had endeared her to every one having the privilege of knowing her throughout the country. I grieved for my chum, whose fond anticipations of a happy

* Those surviving 1st May, 1913, are: (1) Dr. McKay, retired factor, Edmonton; (2) Mr. Parson, retired chief factor, Montreal; (3) Mr. Anderson, St. Laurent, Manitoba; and (4) Mr. Hargrave, Medicine Hat.

return home had been so direly disappointed, and for the little motherless boy going away from his native land. However, it was for his own good, and he would find a new home with his grandfather, old Governor Christie, in Edinburgh, and with his uncle, Dr. Isbister, and aunts in London.

THE OFFICERS' MESS.

Captain Bishop came and stayed ashore several times, and so did Mr. MacPherson once, looking quite sheepish when he beheld the fine fare of fish, ducks, geese and venison spread on the mess table, at which all the gentlemen mentioned assembled three times a day. The table was well supplied with milk from the dairy of the post, and rhubarb, lettuce and radish raised in the garden. At lunch we had beer or stout, and at dinner, port and sherry, partaking only of the latter in responding to a toast, or as sauce for the plum pudding, no other sauce being provided.

On the walls of the mess-room hung a life-sized oil painting of the famous Governor-in-Chief of Rupert's Land, Sir George Simpson, and a very large one of the battle of the Nile.

All were placed at the table in order of seniority, we apprentice clerks being, of course, near the foot, where the kindly " second " Mr. Mowat presided and saw we wanted for nothing eatable or drinkable, while we listened to the conversation of our seniors and the missionaries' yarns of the interior, at the head of the table.

GET BILLETS AND SET TO WORK.

All the way out we had been eagerly speculating upon the posts to which we might be allotted by the minutes of council. We were not long in hearing from Chief Factor Wilson that Christie was to remain—much to his disgust—at York; Armit was down for White Horse Plains in the Red River district, and esteemed himself lucky; while I was delighted to find that my main desire in entering the service would be gratified by my appointment to the buffalo hunting post at the Qu'-

Appelle Lakes, in Swan River district, among the wild tribes of the prairies.

Christie was at once permanently installed in Bachelors' Hall, and all three of us were set to work in the office the day after our arrival, for during ship-time no idlers were suffered at York. We did not at all relish thus being cooped up in an office instead of being allowed to get into birch bark canoes and go in pursuit of game in the marsh. I especially resented the rule prohibiting any " green hand " to get into a canoe, of which there were numbers belonging to the Swampy Cree Indians on the shore.

MINUTES OF COUNCIL.

I don't think our services in the office were of much help to the regular staff, who took great pains to initiate us into the style of work. When it was found that I then wrote a good hand and could copy accurately, as a great honor I was entrusted with engrossing the minutes of the council of the Northern Department, 1867, in an immensely strong leather and brass-bound book, with clasps and a padlock. The minutes of many years previous were therein engrossed in beautiful penmanship by various hands, and there was ample room for the transactions of many years to come. So it was not only with pride but also with awe that I commenced operations on this venerable and venerated volume. The matter, too, was most interesting and instructive, giving the names, rank, capacity, and stations of every chief factor and chief trader, clerk, apprentice clerk, and postmaster in the Department, and all the arrangements for the transportation, etc., of supplies to each district. The names of those officers " permitted to retire," and of those to be re-engaged, with their salaries, were also recorded in the minutes. Grants in aid of schools and churches, general orders and new regulations, in fact, everything of importance about the future conduct of the business had a place in the minutes.

A Wedding.

A few days after our arrival we were invited to the wedding of our cheery fellow-passenger, Miss Mason, to the chief accountant, Mr. Samuel K. Parson, to whom she had been engaged before her last visit to England. The ceremony was performed in the Indian church, and a warm reception followed in her father's parsonage in the fort. Mr. James S. Ramsay was best man, and the bridesmaids were Mr. Wilson's two beautiful girls, Mary and her younger sister.

Kindness and Hospitality.

We were invited to evening parties by Mr. and Mrs. Wilson and Mr. and Mrs. Mowat, who all did whatever kindness could suggest to render our stay at York pleasant. In fact, from the highest to the lowest hand everyone was good to us there, Chief Trader Fortescue, a very clever man, taking great pains to instruct us in the office, and Chief Factor Wilson giving us the benefit of his advice and experience on our conduct in the interior.

THE LATE MISS MARY WILSON.

EMMERLING'S HOTEL, WINNIPEG, 1866.

CHAPTER VI.

FROM INLAND SEA TO LAKE INLAND—YORK FACTORY TO NORWAY HOUSE.

OUR CHUMS AT YORK.

WE continued in the office and amused ourselves in the evenings at York for a fortnight, during which I fraternized with Anderson and Ramsay in Bachelors' Hall. Anderson was a son of Chief Trader William Anderson (who had preceded Mr. Wilson in the charge of the Factory), and had been educated in Orkney. He retired from the Company's service many years ago and took up farming at St. Laurent, Lake Manitoba, where he still resides. One of his brothers is a farmer at St. Andrews, and another is the Anglican Bishop of Moosonee—all worthy sons of a worthy sire.

James S. Ramsay was a son of a former minister of Stromness, and another victim of reading the tales of Fenimore Cooper and R. M. Ballantyne. With Dr. MacKay and my friend Duncan Matheson, of Swan River, he had been in the *Prince of Wales* when she was stranded in 1864 on Mansfield Island, and her consort, *Prince Arthur,* was wrecked. The flatbottomed *Ocean Nymph* was in the same squadron at the time, but escaped injury owing to her light draft, and assisted in salving.

Subsequently Mr. Ramsay was transferred to the Fort Garry office, and resigned to take the office of city chamberlain, in the newly formed city of Winnipeg, where he died, a few years later, leaving many friends. He had the distinction of being the only one who showed his head above the ramparts of Fort Garry when the 60th Rifles under Wolseley appeared before them. He was joyfully greeting his deliverers, but, being mistaken by the troops for an enemy, he immediately dropped under the shelter of the parapet.

Shortly before our departure a Red River boat brigade brought Dr. Yarrow to relieve Dr. MacKay and Mr. James Hargrave, apprentice clerk, to serve his time at the Factory. Yarrow was a Scotch M.B. and C.M.; Hargrave was from Ontario, and cousin of Joseph James Hargrave, the historian of Red River. Mr. Hargrave became a pioneer rancher at Medicine Hat, where he still lives.

PREPARE TO START.

After the arrival of this brigade, under old Guide Kennedy, Armit and I were told to get ready to take passage in it for inland. We had bought some heavy blankets during cold weather on the ship when the captain opened a bale, and we now bought green ones as counterpanes and pillows in highly-colored slips ("not to show the dirt"), and were provided with an oilskin to wrap the bedding in, and another to serve as a ground sheet in the tent, also provided by the Company. We had been advised at home not to bring great coats as the capotes universally worn were much better adapted to the country. It appeared the approved uniform for clerks on the boat journey was a greyish blue cloth "Illinois" capote with silverplated buttons, and a broad scarlet worsted sash, the regulation headgear being a fine navy blue cloth cap with leather peak. We had already been presented with several pairs of beautiful silk-worked yellow tanned moccasins, in which we took great pride; so when we had donned the sky-blue capotes and wrapped the red sashes round our waists we felt transformed into real voyageurs at last.

VOYAGING OUTFIT AND RATIONS.

Besides the oilcloths and tent, the Company supplied us with camp cooking and eating utensils, of tin, tinned iron, and iron. The smaller articles were stowed conveniently in a well-arranged box fitted with tin sugar

116

and tea cans, etc., called a "canteen" as it had square flagons for wine also. Besides the canteen there was a keg with a hinged and padlocked top, and a large water-proof canvas-covered basket, divided into several compart-ments, in which the provisions for the voyage were also under lock and key. These consisted of sixteen pounds corned beef, sixty pounds ship's biscuit, eight loaves of bread, ten pounds butter, two pounds tallow candles, six pounds cheese, two pork hams, half-pound mustard, quarter-pound pepper, fifteen pounds salt pork, twenty pounds loaf sugar, three pounds Hyson and two pounds Souchong tea, ten salted smoked buf-falo tongues, ten pounds buffalo dried meat, forty-five pounds fine buffalo pemmican, and two gallons port wine for each of us. One of us took sherry instead of port, and the doctor, as a senior, had brandy and shrub in addition. Out of this our cook was fed, and both guide and steersman expected a big share.

THE RED RIVER BRIGADE.

On September 4th, 1867, at two o'clock the brigade of four inland boats, manned mainly by Swampy Cree Indian trip-men from Red River Settlement, started for Lower Fort Garry from York. The guide, Baptiste Kennedy, a quiet and pious old man, who held worship with his men throughout the voyage, having for the steersman of his own boat a big powerful fellow, named Cameron, while the other boats were steered by William Prince (afterwards chief of St. Peters), and men named Spence and Cunningham. The boats were laden with some private property for the Company's people and missionaries, and an assorted cargo for the Company, partly gunpowder and rum. The passengers, obliged to work their way, were a number of the Highland recruits who had been our shipmates in the *Prince Rupert,* and were going to winter at Norway House, preparatory to being sent further into the interior next season. These were sent with the Crees rather than with the Metis voyageurs in other brigades, because those Indians were always kinder to the green hands.

Dr. MacKay had volunteered for particular service in the Mackenzie River district where a number of Indians were suffering from a constitutional disease. He was to winter at Norway House. He embarked in Prince's boat and had chosen for his fellow-passenger in the sternsheets James A. Lang, who, having served five years as tinsmith at the Factory, was now on his way to settle in Red River, where he was entitled to a free land grant of fifty acres, in lieu of his return passage to Scotland.

Mr. Armit (now a retired chief trader, farming at Elphinstone, Manitoba) and I were billeted in the guide's boat, in which Edward Scott, apprentice blacksmith from Orkney (now living at Fort Frances) and James Thomson, a fisherman from the Hebrides, were also passengers. Armit and I were fortunate in securing as cook for the voyage a fine active Swampy named Thomas Sandison, who pulled the stroke oar in our boat.

The Hayes River Route.

Although very much larger streams, neither the Churchill nor the Nelson afford such a comparatively easy boat and canoe route into the interior as the Hayes and its affluents. That pioneer pathfinder of genius, Radisson, therefore selected the mouth of the Hayes River for the original fur post, Fort Bourbon, which preceded York Factory. The distance from York to Norway House on Lake Winnipeg is about four hundred miles, the ascent seven hundred feet, in which there are thirty-four portages of from 16 to 1,760, averaging 175, yards, over which cargoes are carried on men's backs, and across many of which the boats themselves have to be dragged. The route lies up the Hayes to its forks, the Shamattawa and the Steel; up the Steel to its forks, the Fox and Hill Rivers, and up the Hill River through Knee and Oxford Lakes and Franklin River and Echemamis to the height of land at Painted Stone. A short passage over the Painted Stone is made into the western Echemamis and through Hairy Lake and Blackwater Creek into the Nelson River below Sea River Falls; thence up the Nelson to Little Playgreen Lake, upon which Norway House is situated.

TRACKING UP STREAM.

Unless they are favored by a fair wind the boats are towed up the Hayes by the crew scrambling along the shore through mud and brush and all kinds of obstacles, the oars being chiefly used to cross the stream to the side affording the best footing, which is seldom, if ever, good. Whilst thus " tracking " one-half of the crew remains aboard, while the other half tracks ashore, and they relieve each other every half hour. The men go at a quick pace, and even at a trot whenever the footing and the current favors them, attaching their portage straps to the towline and passing the browbands over their "inshore" shoulders. It takes a good ordinary walker going light to keep up with them, and the men require strong legs and lungs and good hearts to keep it up as they do, always seeming in good spirits and ready to laugh at every mishap of their comrades or themselves. In the long serpentine procession strung out ashore in advance of the boats the fresh-faced Highland laddies were harnessed with the brown boatmen, with whom they gamely kept up in speed and spirit. Whenever it was cold or rainy these recruits could always be distinguished by the white blanketing capotes, faced with blue and piped with scarlet, which was their regulation costume. Generally they were in high glee, attempting to teach Gaelic words to the Crees and learning scraps of Indian in exchange, with laughable results on both sides.

THE SPUR OF RIVALRY.

Of course, in this work, as in all other operations of the voyageur, there is keen competition between the men, and especially between the crews of different boats. This spirit of emulation leads them to perform wonders, and in the absence of another boat or boats, a single boat's crew will never make so smart a voyage as when in company and competition with others. An ordinary boat's crew are also unable to haul their boat over land across a portage by themselves, so as a rule, a single boat with a single crew is never sent on a voyage where these obstacles occur.

By Strength and Skill.

Whether tracking up against an ordinary current with a codline or slowly hauling, inch by inch, against the force of a rapid or fall with a whale or " main " line, the labor requires strength; and both strength and skill are required in rowing and poling up stream, and in running, at a trot, with two " pieces "—two hundred pounds—across a portage. Besides the activity, strength, spirit, and endurance required by these duties, the men had to be as hardy as a water-dog and as ready to plunge in, whether tracking, embarking, or disembarking, or to lift and push the barge over shallows and up rapids.

Fortitude in Distress.

Added to this strenuous toil, wet or dry, in heat or cold, and tormented most of the time by mosquitoes and black-flies, these hardy voyageurs endured, unflinchingly and with fortitude, agonies from hands blistered by the oar and feet lacerated by rough and sharp stones on land and in water. Despite these wounds and bruises the men made it a point of honor to keep on working when absolute rest and removal of the cause were the remedies imperatively indicated by the symptoms.

Their Food.

From dawn to dusk the toil continued, day after day, on a diet which ordinary laborers to-day might consider not fit for dogs. The dried and partially pulverized beef of the buffalo mixed with its melted tallow composed the highly nutritious

pemmican, which, plain or mixed with flour in " rouchou " or
" rubabou," appeased their splendid appetites and was converted by their vigorous stomachs into the energy required for
their mighty exertions. Flour bannocks, baked with water
and a little pemmican grease, without any rising, and, generally, only half " done," by exposing them on twigs and
frying pans before the camp fire, were a luxury attained by
the boatmen starting from Red River and York Factory
which was denied to their fellows in the interior, where the
flour of wheat was as scarce and more valuable than flour gold,
and animal food, generally dried, was the only sustenance
afforded by the country, and their sole reliance.

The Black Cup That Cheers.

But the thing which restored their strength and spirits
more rapidly than eatables was " the cup that cheers " in the
form of immense draughts of strong black tea. The first quaff
of this beverage, seldom with sugar, worked marvels, and
toil and fatigue seemed at once forgotten. They were consequently lavishly fond of the beverage, and so generally improvident of their allowance as to run short before reaching
the next available source of supply.

Muscle-Driven Transport.

The force supplied by steam to-day in transportation was
in those days furnished by the muscles of the men as just
described. Tribute has been paid to their almost superhuman
exertions and endurance by such famous travellers as Sir
John Franklin and Sir George Simpson, and lest we forget
these pioneers of railways and of nations—the grand old
voyageurs—the testimony of those two authorities is quoted:
On his voyage up from York Factory, in 1819, Franklin
writes: " It is not easy for any but an eye-witness to form
an adequate idea of the exertions of the Orkney boatmen in
the navigation of this river. The necessity they are under of

frequently jumping into the water, to lift the boats over the rocks, compels them to remain the whole day in wet clothes, at a season when the temperature is far below the freezing point. The immense loads, too, which they carry over the portages, is not more a matter of surprise than the alacrity with which they perform these laborious duties."

Sir George Simpson, who urged the French-Canadian voyageurs of his flying canoe from York Factory to the Pacific Ocean in thirty-eight days, says: " Such was the routine of our journey, the day, generally speaking, being divided into six hours' rest and eighteen hours' labor. This almost incredible toil the voyageurs bore without a murmur, and almost invariably with such hilarity of spirit as few men could sustain for a single afternoon. But the quality of the work even more decidedly than the quantity requires operatives of iron mould."

The Swampy Crees who manned our brigade were cast in like mould to the Orkneymen praised by Franklin and the French-Canadians extolled by Simpson. There were no better boatmen, none more amenable to orders, and their good nature was shown in their treatment of the young Scotsmen who were working their passage in the brigade and being initiated into the new labors and hardships of the life they were entering upon in the interior.

THE HIGHLAND LADDIES.

It was pleasing to see how soon the Scottish mountaineers and the American Muskagoes got on good terms with each other. Some of the former had not the two talks, while all the Swampies knew more or less English, generally the Orkney dialect. Their attempts to make themselves mutually understood were, therefore, very amusing. The finding of a few words in Gaelic and Cree, which sounded somewhat alike but had entirely different meanings, afforded great delight as exquisite jokes, which time could not wither nor custom stale by infinite repetition. Perhaps in a moment of fierce

TRACKING UPSTREAM.

Photo by C. W. Mathers, Edmonton.

"forcing" (a common tripper's term), such as when a heavy boat is being dragged uphill came to a standstill in spite of all efforts, one of the Crees would suddenly shout his rendering of the amusing Gaelic word, and instantly, in response, there would be a simultaneous yell from both races, and with it the boat would be dragged exultingly over the obstacle. The Highlanders were lively and active and seemed to adapt themselves to their new conditions and pick up both the Indian and French languages more readily than their staider brethren from the Orkneys.

Our First Camp.

We pushed off into the stream and set our square dipping lug sail to a fair breeze which carried us slowly along till evening, when we camped near Ten Shilling Creek, on the bare stones and boulders of the beach, in a downpour of rain, which lasted all night, and rendered our first night under canvas, unprepared as we were, very uncomfortable. The campfire was a miserable little one of driftwood, and we were glad to accept the invitation of the doctor to his tent to have supper. As a campaigner of three years' experience, the doctor had everything comfortably arranged in his tent, and had had a fine ham and some delicious cured buffalo tongues cooked before leaving the Factory. After disposing of these and fortifying ourselves with wine, Lang brought forth a concertina, upon which he was no mean performer, and we all joined in a sing-song till about ten o'clock, when we were surprised by Chief Trader Fortescue suddenly arriving in a canoe with papers to be placed in the packet box for Red River. We sat at the feet of Mr. Fortescue for hours thereafter listening to his clever and entertaining descriptions of life in the interior.

Yelling " 'Leve, 'Leve."

At an unearthly hour next morning, Sandison rattled the cold, wet tent down about our ears, and startled us from rosy sleep to the shivering realities of getting up and dressing in the open air of a chill, damp dawn. We scrambled aboard, where we found in the sternsheets a steaming kettle of tea and some biscuits which he had provided for our early breakfast. The boats started under oars, but the crews soon commenced the long and laborious job of tracking up the Hayes. The river was about half a mile wide, with a current too strong to make headway rowing against it. The banks were of clay and got steeper and higher as we advanced, with sometimes a wet, muddy beach and often none, when the poor fellows were obliged to scramble as best they could along the steep slopes in mud and through brush, driftwood, and landslips, while we on board took our ease as the boat slipped smoothly along.

THE SCENERY IMPROVES.

The tamarack, spruce, poplar and willows growing along the bank became of larger growth as we proceeded up stream. The scenery changed to beauty and variety. All vegetation had begun to put on the glorious hues of autumn. The weather, improving day by day and continuing delightful, with scarcely a break throughout the journey, rendered the travelling to us as mere passengers most enjoyable. The Steel River is three hundred yards wide where we left the Hayes, and its banks are, though higher, less steep than those of the latter, rendering the tracking ground easier, but the stream is more obstructed by rapids and shoals.

ABSENCE OF GAME.

The Steel winds its serpentine course through a lovely valley, then adorned with the varying shades of the season of the fall of the leaf in North America. The novel experience of this new country and mode of travel, and the ease and comfort we had now attained afloat and ashore in camp fulfilled all our fond anticipations of life in the wilderness. But to our intense disappointment there appeared to be a total absence of the game, the pursuit of which had been our chief lure into exile. The noise of the boatmen shouting and laughing as they went along tracking, and the rattling of our oars in the tholes and their splashing in the water, scared all game away. Ducks in the river ahead would take flight as the string of noisy boatmen marching in advance of the boats approached, and other game in the woods were equally alarmed by the unwonted noise of our intrusion; so it was only that mass of nothing but feathers and impudence, the ubiquitous "Whiskey Jack," which, presuming on its being no good and unworthy of powder and shot, ever gave us a chance to shoot, while under way.

Armit was a very ardent sportsman, however, and kept keen watch and ward for a shot in spite of continual disappointment. So he succeeded in bagging about four ducks and one mink between York and Norway House. We both missed a red fox, and were successful in trolling for pike, which furnished a welcome and much appreciated addition to our usual bill of fare. As we passed through the narrow grassy channels of the Echemamis, near the watershed at Painted Stone, the rabbits were numerous and in good condition too, and we had some satisfactory sport there.

Picturesque Hill River.

We made good progress, reaching the mouth of the Steel on the second day from York, and entering the Hill River two days afterwards. The Hill was shallow and rapid, the men often having to jump out and lift and push the boat over the shallows, and pole and warp up the rapids. The banks are higher than those of the Steel and more broken in outline, the clay cliffs some ninety feet high, surmounted by hills two hundred feet higher, but the woods were too thick to give any view further back. At Rock Portage the river is pent up by islands, between which it rushes down in many cascades of rare beauty. On the 8th we arrived at the site of the old depot for the Selkirk Settlement, Rock House, long since abandoned, which was in charge of Mr. Bunn, the ancestor of the well-known Red River family, in 1819, when Franklin passed it and stored some of his supplies there.

The "Tracking Grounds" being now passed, we entered into the fight with the rushing river by poling, warping and portaging up and over the many rapids and cascades formed by the rocky nature of the country. At Morgan's Portage the Hill River expands to three-quarters of a mile, and its low, flat, rocky banks permit of a wide and extensive view for the first time since leaving the sea coast. Among a multitude of conical hills scattered about, one of six hundred feet towers over the rest, and has given name to the river. From its summit over thirty lakes can be seen. The low-lying islands covered with spruce, birch, poplar and willow right to the water's edge, in their green, yellow and russet foliage, with babbling brooks and dancing cascades between, entranced the eye. We landed for dinner on one of these islet gems of the wilderness. Under an azure sky we lounged luxuriously on velvety couches of emerald moss, and I fain would have had the friends we had left behind in Scotland there to admire the perfect picture and partake of our picnic.

"WITH A LONG, STRONG PULL."

So day after day the crews rowed, poled, pushed, warped and carried upstream, in all which laborious operations we delighted to assist whenever a long, long pull and a strong, strong pull was required. Our best assistance was in rowing, when our oar, aft of that of the stroke in the stern, used to send our boat ahead of her competitors. At poling and warping up a rapid we were of some service, too, but at carrying, after almost wringing our necks in trying to imitate the voyageurs, we limited ourselves to shouldering the oars (which the tripmen considered the worst load) over the portages. In all these ways, too, " the recruits from Europe " assisted, and willingly worked their passage to the best of their skill, the mastery of the portage strap being the hardest to acquire.

MEET A PORTAGE BRIGADE

A Sailing Race on Knee Lake.

We had a fine, long stretch under sail on Knee Lake, where we enjoyed all the excitement of a regatta with the boats competing in a sailing race to the head of the lake. The crews, except the steersmen, all went to sleep, a well-merited repose, while the passengers tried every expedient in trimming the sails and the cargo of our rival crafts to outsail each other. After a while one of the Indians fished out a battered violin, which had seen much service and had evidently travelled considerably. This tuning up soon roused several of his companions from their slumbers, and they started to pound out the Red River jig on the bowsman's stand in the bow. The shaking spoilt the way of the boat, the wind being light, and we dropped astern of our rivals whilst the dance went on. I wished my friends, the bosun and the Frenchman of the *Prince Rupert,* had been there to get some fresh ideas in tripping the light fantastic toe.

The "Long" Portage Brigade Passes.

On the 17th of September we made a portage past Trout Falls, a sixteen-foot drop, and while at dinner above it we heard the regular rattling of oars at a distance, heralding the coming of a brigade down stream. Very soon the Portage la Loche brigade of four boats flashed past, and taking the cascade at full speed, disappeared one after the other over the brink, with a final flourish of the steering oar. The boats were under the veteran Red River guide, Baptiste Bruce, and manned by Metis, all gaily decorated in fancy shirts and feathers, just as they had embarked that morning at Oxford, after a ball, attended by the beauty and fashion of that vicinity, which had been kept up till daylight. As the crews swung to their oars in dashing style, they seemed as able to row all day as to dance all night. I subsequently found that dog-drivers were equally able to run all day and to dance all night, taking great pride in the double performance.

Oxford House.

We reached Oxford House on Holey (not Holy as it is often spelt) Lake* that evening, and spent the next day there, refitting. The post stands on high ground at some distance from the water's edge, and commands a lovely view of the lake and its varied islands. There were fields off which fine crops of barley and potatoes had been taken, and a garden which produced all common vegetables of first-rate quality.

We were most hospitably received by Mr. Cuthbert Sinclair —who was holding the fort till Mr. Fortescue's arrival from York—and Mr. William Isbister, of Island Lake post; and the table was laden with game and fruit from the forest, vegetables from the garden, and delicious trout from the lake, besides fresh butter, cream and milk from the dairy. Of course our boatmen took advantage of their stay there to invite the belles from the bush to an all-night dance, and the thumping of their jigging feet reached our camp on the lakeside all through the stilly night.

Through Hell Gates.

Bidding adieu to our kind entertainers, we left Oxford House on the 19th, under sail, and crossed the lake. Next day we entered the narrow chasm, bounded by sheer cliffs of eighty feet, for three-quarters of a mile, and called by the terrible name of Hell Gates. Whilst quietly pushing through this wild and gloomy defile, where it was too narrow for rowing, the sudden shriek of a Cree catchword, with a Gaelic twang, aroused its echoes, and being at once received with ringing and resounding laughter by the whole brigade, caused an aerial tumult fit for pandemonium proper. Crossing the Upper and Lower Hell Portages, we camped at the foot of the White Fall, or Robinson's Portage, on the 21st. The portage, over which all cargo is carried, is a mile long, over a level but slippery path, along which we noted the wrecks of several of

* Named because of a deep place in it, said to be bottomless!

the quaint Red River carts, with which I was soon to make long and intimate acquaintance. It was said these vehicles had been put on the portage in 1846 to help Colonel Crofton's troops, and those who succeeded them, over the carrying-place. Another tradition was that they were the relics of an attempt (which came to grief) made in the 1830's to improve the transportation between Norway House and York Factory by a road overland part of the way.

TOURNAMENTS OF THE TRIPMEN.

In those days the measure of a man was his courage, strength and skill as boatman on the river or hunter on the plain, and men were always ready to prove these qualities by vying with their fellows.

While the fierce conflict raged between the great rival companies, champion prize-fighters were kept in the train of the opposing officers, and when these met, a battle of giants was witnessed by the partisans of the opposite sides. Marvellous traditions of these encounters were handed down from generation to generation of voyageurs, but these had become so distorted by racial leanings by the time the legends reached my ears, that the French and English versions were entirely at variance as to victor and vanquished.

Even after the union of the Nor'-Westers and the Hudson's Bays the custom lingered, the rivalry between different districts succeeding that between the warring companies. Moreover, long after the plumed and pampered professional " bullyars " had disappeared from the lists the desire to emulate their performances would crop up, and the old ceremony would be revived by some aggrieved or perhaps merely vain voyageur defying all enemies and competitors.

At some encampment, portage or post, arrayed in all his finery with a plume of colored cocktail feathers on his head, the challenger would parade, " chanting the cock " (*chantant le coq*), in defiance of the best man (*le meilleur*) within hearing. But the challenge was generally addressed to " *le meil-*

leur " of the offending district, the men of which were known by such nicknames as " Les Blaireaux," or badgers of Saskatchewan; " Les Cygnes," or Swans of Swan River; " Les Rabisca," of Athabasca; or " Les Gens de la Grande Rivière," of Mackenzie River.

But in the year of grace, 1867, of which I am writing, the days of these ancient Homeric struggles were nearly over, and the race of the swift and the battle of the strong and many a quarrel during the year was left to be decided at the White. Fall on the annual voyage to York Factory. So the slippery trail, stretching for a mile over that portage, became the arena on which bets, challenges and quarrels were settled, by competing in carrying the biggest loads in the shortest time. It was also the track upon which a novice had to undergo the ordeal to qualify as a first-class tripping man, by running without a stop, with a load of two hundred pounds on his back, from one end of it to the other, and repeating the round till his share of the boat-load—twelve hundred pounds —had been carried across.

THE HEIGHT OF LAND.

The boats had to be dragged overland at this place, where we spent a whole day. Leaving the White Fall, passing through the river where Franklin was nearly drowned, and since named after him, through several lakes connected by narrow streams winding through a grassy marshland, being the eastern part of Echemamis ("a stream running two ways,") we reached the divide between the head waters of the Hayes and the Upper Nelson River at Painted Stone Portage during the 23rd. The portage here is short, over an even rock, and then we began to descend the Echemamis, which is a narrow and winding stream through a great grassy marsh, with tall reeds and rushes and willows on each side, the latter sometimes forming an arch over it. Here and there were rude dams, which we opened and closed as we passed through. Some of these were the works of beaver originally, but the

Indians could not be restrained from slaughtering these engineering animals, and the dams had to be kept in repair by the Company.

The Echemamis took us to Hairy (Bulrush) Lake, the outlet of which, Blackwater Creek, led us to the Sea River branch of the great Nelson River, here four hundred yards wide, with muddy white water. Sailing up the Nelson * with a good breeze, we portaged at Sea River Falls, and, continuing under sail up stream to Little Playgreen Lake, we arrived at Norway House on the 24th of September, three weeks' journey from York Factory.

* From Knee Lake to Nelson River we passed through a Huronian formation in which great mineral wealth may yet be discovered.

CHAPTER VII.

NORWAY HOUSE AND ACROSS LAKE WINNIPEG.

Norway House.

Norway House is beautifully situated upon one of the rocky islands of Little Playgreen Lake, near the mouth of the Jack River, so often resorted to in times of distress by the persecuted people of Lord Selkirk's colony at Red River. The first post of the Hudson's Bay Company in the vicinity had been opposite Mossy Point, where the great outlet of Lake Winnipeg, Nelson River, begins to send the mighty waters of the Saskatchewan, the Red and the Winnipeg Rivers into the North American Mediterranean—Hudson Bay.

The fishery of the old fort was at Jack River, and finding it more convenient for the fort to move to the fishery than for the fish—the staple food—to be moved to the fort, Norway House was established in its present site. The island is now overgrown with white clover, which, originating in the square of the fort from some hay in which crockery had been packed in England, was spread by the cows eating it to the native pastures, and has now very largely taken their place. There is a story, too, of a Norway rat having been transplanted in the same manner, but this pioneer perished, unwept, while the growth of clover persisted and gave to the milk and butter and beef of the establishment a fine flavor.

Norwegians.

The name of the post was first " Jack River " and is said to have received its present designation in honor of a large number of Norwegian recruits for the Company's service having been for some time stationed there. Many years after-

NORWAY HOUSE.

Photo by Chief Factor James McDougall.

Courtesy of Chief Factor William Clark.

ward—in the 1850's and early 1860's sometime—a mutiny,
which occurred among other Norwegians there, is one of the
historic events told round Hudson Bay men's campfires. Many
of the men engaged in Norway were splendid fellows and
well adapted for the service, but the agent employed to procure
the recruits there appeared to have thought more of the head
money allowed for his service by the Company than the moral
character of the men he engaged. Tradition avers that the
Norwegian authorities got rid of many of their able-bodied
convicts by permitting them to be deported as recruits for the
Hudson's Bay Company's service. On one occasion fifty or
sixty of them refused to disembark at York Factory, and
compelled the ship's company to take them back to Europe.
On another occasion others deserted from Moose Factory, and
of these the majority perished in the wilds in an effort to
reach civilization in Canada.

"DIVIDE AND RULE."

In a wild country, where the personality of the master of
a post, frequently entirely unsupported by any subordinate
officer, alone maintained discipline and order, it had become
a general rule, in view of possible mutiny, to man every post
by men of different nationalities and races, as affording less
liability to combined strikes or actions. Even a large number of the usually obedient Orkneymen at one post was unde-
sirable for this reason, and the more impulsive and clannish
Highlanders were more apt to " buck against the boss " when
more than two or three were gathered together. The Indians
engaged were generally chosen for exceptional docility, but the
French-Canadian and Metis voyageurs, who were nearly
always in the majority, were often difficult to manage successfully.

The same rule—" divide to govern "—was that adopted in
the management, by the Company, of the Indian tribes. By
diplomatic favors of various kinds full advantage was taken
of the mutual jealousies between different tribes, between

septs and families in these tribes, and by setting up Company's chiefs and headmen in opposition to the natural leaders amongst them, to prevent any united action which the few whites would have been utterly unable to successfully combat by force of arms.

IMPORTANT BASE.

From the place of an ordinary post on the Hudson's Bay Company's line of communication between York Factory and the inland districts, after the coalition of the companies had diverted the traffic of the North-West partners from the canoe route by Lake Superior to the boat route from Hudson Bay, the post at Jack River grew to be the great inland depot and assumed the official name of Norway House. In its warehouse was stored the outfit for Mackenzie River District, which, after being received from London in August and repacked during the winter at York Factory, was freighted to Norway House during the following season of navigation and stored there for the winter, in readiness to be forwarded during the succeeding summer to Portage la Loche by the Red River Brigade, which brought farm and other country produce from Fort Garry for use and distribution at Norway House.

At Portage la Loche the merchandise brought there, about the first of August, was exchanged for the returns of furs of the Mackenzie River District, which had been traded during the preceding winter at the posts east of the Rocky Mountains, and those of the posts beyond them, in the Yukon, which had been secured two years before, and had been hauled by dog trains over the divide to Fort McPherson during the winter. As the trading supplies, " the outfit " for the Yukon posts were sent over the mountains from Fort McPherson during the winter, and, if no delay occurred the furs reached York Factory by the Red River brigade, on its return, and were shipped to London in September, to be sold there in January and March, it will be seen that from four to seven years intervened between the purchase of the supplies in London and the conversion of the resulting furs into cash.

Until the Council of 1831 directed that Norway House should become the depot for Athabasca as well as Mackenzie River, men coming from and returning to posts on the Upper Peace River served in the Athabasca Brigade, going to York Factory with the furs and returning with "the outfit." At first their boats were drawn back and forth across the twelve miles of muskeg and sand and the eight hundred feet hill of Portage la Loche; but subsequently two sets of boats, one on each side of this really "Long" portage, were provided, and the voyageurs who had dragged the boats across the divide and made the longer journey to York Factory, considered carrying cargo only over it and going merely to Norway House child's play compared with their former labors.

THE FIRST HUDSON'S BAY ROAD.

Freighting between Norway House and York Factory for the benefit of these districts was carried on by brigades equipped at both depots, and manned principally by Swampy Indian tripmen; while the transport of supplies to and from Red River was largely performed by two-decked sailing crafts, of light draft and twelve tons burden, manned by crews who wintered at Norway House. These were employed for some years in cutting out a winter road, between Oxford House and the head of the tracking ground on the Hayes River, to avoid the multitude of rapids and portages intervening in summer. After a number of winters' work on this overland road, superintended by Chief Factor Lewis at Oxford, and assisted by men and material from York and Norway House, this project, which at first appeared to promise a great reduction in freight charges and a general benefit to the country, was abandoned; but the straight clearing made through the thick bush is still visible in many places to this time. It will be unusual if this old trail be not yet followed by some railway en route for the Bay, just as the old Red River cart trails have been so often succeeded by the railways on the prairies, in following the line of least resistance.

Besides being a receiving and distributing depot, the establishment built boats for other districts; and other boats built at Rocky Mountain House at the head waters of the Saskatchewan and coming down laden with leather and with pemmican and dried meat, to be given at Norway House to districts where the buffalo were not, and to the boats' crews as rations, were turned over for general service at Norway House. These Saskatchewan boats were floated down with half crews, which on their return upstream, assisted by the European recruits for the Columbia department, provided full crews for the other boats, retained by the Saskatchewan district.

Where East and West Meet.

Norway House continued to grow in importance as the inland centre from which the whole boat transportation system of the Northern Department was controlled and at which it focussed. It advanced a big stride when it, instead of the distant York Factory, became the regular annual meeting-place of the officers coming from and returning to such immense distances as Fort Vancouver at the mouth of the Columbia River, New Caledonia, and Mackenzie River.

To the inland depot on Playgreen Lake there came in state by flying express canoes manned by mighty French-Canadian and Iroquois voyageurs, bearing the great Governor Simpson from Montreal. Other great voyageurs coming from Columbia, New Caledonia, Mackenzie River, Athabasca, Saskatchewan, Swan River, Red River, and Lac la Pluie, brought their *bourgeois* to Norway House, and were welcomed with *regales* of rum on arrival.

While the grandees were holding solemn conclave in the council hall, and sealing the fates and fortunes of the fur trade and its *engagés* for the year, the voyageurs in the encampments outside the stockades held high festival, frater-

A YORK BOAT—SAILING.

A YORK BOAT—ROWING.

nized with old long-separated comrades, related and discussed
the news of the uttermost parts of the wilderness from which
they had here converged, engaged in friendly trials of strength
and skill, boat and canoe races, and the great annual fair
nearly always ended in a battle between the rival prize-fighters
of the different brigades.

The Old Transportation Problem.

The officer in charge of Norway House as chief of inland
transport occupied an arduous position. The movements of
the brigades had to be so regulated that those starting from
points as far apart as Norway House on Lake Winnipeg, and
Fort McPherson on the Mackenzie, should meet within a day
or two of each other at Portage la Loche. People who have
never been without the convenience of regular mails and telegraphs in the civilized world can form little conception of
the skill and care required to conduct such transport operations in a wild country where communication between the
officers at each end of the long line of travel only took place
twice a year. The operations were very similar to those
planned by a great military commander in the days before
electric messages.

Manning the Boats.

Besides these complications there was always the difficulty
of finding men willing to man the boats. The expense of
keeping men with big families all the year round for the
purpose of freighting in the open season only, was ruinous,
except at such places as buffalo and whitefish abounded. The
chief supply of voyageurs for general service during the summer was derived from the Metis of the Red River colony,
whose ambition was to be counted as good a boatman on the
river as he had proved hunter on the plain. Unless one had
made the trip creditably to " the Long Portage " he was not
counted and could not without challenge have the right and
title to proclaim himself on festive occasions to be a man—

"*Je suis un homme.*" To earn this *éclat* he was willing, after the proceeds of the fall buffalo hunt had been wasted away in more or less riotous living, to engage during the winter for the trip to Long Portage and thence to York Factory to catch the ship. Besides the desire for glory as a voyageur, the temptation of procuring a large advance on his wages, in the shape of decorative raiment and rum from Fort Garry, was not to be resisted. When the time to start had come such a man would have managed, by continual coming to the store, to draw nearly all the wages which he was yet to earn.

THE BUCKING BRIGADES.

Then the trouble began. The Red River officials had the time of their lives every June to coax, persuade and threaten those who wished to back out of their engagement and betake themselves to the buffalo plains. The people of Fort Garry would heave a deep sigh of relief as the last boat of the brigade disappeared round Point Douglas, but trouble travelled with the brigade to torment the master at the Lower Fort, and so on at every post along the line, where supplies which these improvident men desired could be had. The climax, however, was always reached at Norway House, both on the outward and the downward voyage, and never a season passed—in later years they got worse and worse—without a rebellion of the "Long Portage brigade" at Norway House. The officer in charge had then to use his best wits and diplomacy to prevent a general collapse of the transport system through these strikes. Sometimes they were persuaded or bribed to complete their voyage. On more than one occasion they refused to wait for the Mackenzie River boats at the Long Portage and returned light, or else refused to take the furs down to York Factory from Norway House.

When the strike was general, of course the officials were powerless to resist. But when only a few malcontents started and tried to incite the others to join, it was sometimes quickly settled by giving the ringleaders a good licking, and such fellows were less likely to start trouble when they knew that they had a fearless officer, handy with his fists, like Chief Factor Stewart, to face.

THE OLD YORK BOAT FREIGHT RATES.

It will be of interest to compare these with the much-complained-of railway rates of the present day.

The freight rates authorized by the minutes of the Council of 1831, chargeable by the district performing the service against another, and subsequently adopted for the payment of the Red River settlers who engaged as contractors in the business were:

For "piece" of ninety pounds, from York Factory to Red River, 18s., or $4.50; from York Factory to Norway House, 14s., or $3.50; from York Factory to Oxford House, 10s., or $2.50; from Oxford House to Norway House, 4s., or $1; from Norway House to Red River, 4s., or $1; from Red River to Norway House, 1s., or 25 cents; from Norway House to Oxford House, 2s., or 50 cents; from Oxford House to York Factory, 3s., or 75 cents.

By the standing regulations the lading of a boat was not less than seventy "pieces" cargo, exclusive of the allowance for passengers and their effects. The allowance for chief factors and chief traders was ten pieces, for chief clerks five pieces, for junior clerks and postmasters three pieces.

The annual equipments of clothing, etc., supplied from the depot to the officers and employees in the interior, at cost or a little over, were limited in weight to one-half the above number of pieces, that of the employees under the rank of postmaster being one piece. Anything over these limits was charged to their private accounts as follows:

Per "piece" of ninety pounds, from York Factory to Mackenzie River, 50s., or $12.50; to Athabasca, 40s., or $10; to Saskatchewan (Edmonton House), English River (Ile à la Crosse), Lac la Pluie (Fort Frances), Upper Red River (Brandon House), 30s., or $7.50; to Swan River (Lakes

Manitoba, Winnipegosis and Fort Pelly), and to Red River Settlement, 18s., or $4.50; to Lake Winnipeg posts, 18s., or $4.50; to Norway House, 14s., or $3.50; to Oxford House, 10s., or $2.50; to Nelson River, 10s., or $2.50; to Churchill and Severn, 2s., or 50 cents.

The rates of pay given to the boatmen for the whole season were: £16 ($80) for steersmen, £14 ($70) for bowsmen, and £12 ($60) for middlemen. For the trip from Red River to York Factory and return the rates were, respectively, $40, $35 and $30 for these classes. These were the wages of men hired for these limited periods only, and they were paid partly in cash, but chiefly in goods priced much higher than those sold once a year to the regular yearly servants as " private orders for equipments." As the rates of annual pay to the regular servants employed as boatmen were at about the same rate for the time, and they largely occupied themselves during the rest of the year in providing food and fuel for themselves, and their large families, maintained all the year round at the Company's expense, their position was much better than that of the temporary servants, or tripmen.

WINTERING AND TRAINING RECRUITS.*

Most of the green hands, or, in the language of the minutes of Council, " the recruits from Europe," intended for service in the remoter interior were sent inland to pass their first winter. A few of these were sent to Swan River district, but the majority wintered at Norway House, where they were initiated into the work for which they individually might appear best fitted. A number went to the sawyers' shanty to

* Before 1840, instead of those required for service on the Columbia and New Caledonia being sent by the Pacific, they were selected on landing at York and worked their way up to the Saskatchewan, in a boat with two experienced men left annually for the purpose. After wintering in the Saskatchewan, next summer they accompanied the party taking the leather supplied yearly to New Caledonia, and the otter skins to pay the rent of the strip of Russian America leased by the Hudson's Bay Company.

provide plank for boat building, etc. Others assisted the fishermen, and so on. After passing through this course of setting-up drill they were drafted into the brigades as voyageurs and expected to perform full duty as such, portaging or otherwise. The majority of those who wintered at Norway House were drafted into Athabasca and Mackenzie River, where they were preferred to the French-Canadians because these only enlisted for three years instead of five, and when leaving seldom got out to Norway House in time to obtain a return passage in the canoes going by Lake Superior to Montreal.

The drill sergeant of these recruits was the " second " at Norway House, and during the time of trial of both drilled and driller while Mr. Cuthbert Sinclair (a native of Red River, whom we passed at Oxford, where he was then in temporary charge till Mr. Fortescue's arrival) was the " second " everyone of the Scottish lads who served under him had a good word to say of his impartial kindness and good treatment of them, which was received the more gratefully because so many others were wont to make fun of the green hands and their ignorance of new work and conditions, some of their own countrymen being often the worst in that way.

PLACE WELL-KEPT, WITH FINE GARDEN.

The place was in apple-pie order in 1867, and I believe it is still decently preserved, unlike York Factory, which is now the mere wreck of its former self. The photograph herewith is a good one, and beyond the buildings shown there was a very fine vegetable garden, which Chief Factor James Green Stewart took pride in showing us. There were many berry bushes in it, too, and a sundial, erected by one of the Arctic explorers, in passing.

The large summer-house for visiting officers and the Council chamber of the Northern Department were under one roof but at opposite ends of the building. After York Factory had ceased to be the regular meeting-place, the Council came to be held usually at this place and only occasionally in Red River Settlement at Lower Fort Garry. We were lodged for the time in the summer-house, and were invited to the chief factor's own bungalow that evening for music and bagatelle and refreshments. He was the soul of hospitality, looking every inch of his tall stature the officer and the gentleman. Mr. Stewart came of one of the best old families of Quebec. He had served in the rebellion there in 1837 and was full of military spirit. He was a splendid snowshoe walker and traveller, and as such had been accepted as second on the Arctic expedition in search of Franklin under Chief Factor James Anderson, of Mackenzie River, for which he bore Queen Victoria's (octagonal) medal " For Arctic Exploration, 1818-1852."

To anticipate in my narrative: During the Red River trouble of 1860-70, furious at the surrender of Fort Garry and determined that no such thing should occur at Norway House, Mr. Stewart felt in his element in putting it into a state of defence under military law, and in drilling his men, of whom he had a goodly number of Scotsmen to arm. Every precaution was taken to guard the fort, and the large quantity of supplies for the northern districts stored therein. He soon had the whole garrison as full of warlike ardor as himself, and when he got tired of waiting to be attacked in his stronghold he sallied forth with several barges, manned by his well drilled levies, Highland Scots and Swampy Crees, to join in the recapture of Fort Garry. Reaching Red River in time to accompany Colonel Wolseley's Rifles on the march from Point Douglas, mounted on a steed as fiery as himself, and eluding the restraints of discipline, he raced full speed ahead of the troops into the square of Fort Garry in time to utter shouts of wild defiance at Riel and O'Donoghue as they were making their hasty retreat.

Mr. Stewart was rewarded for his warlike ardor and loyal spirit by being—in the euphemistic formula of the Hudson's

Bay Company in such cases—" permitted to retire from the service." Upon his retirement he took up residence down the Red River at Marchmont, where for years he kept open house and dispensed unbounded hospitality to his numerous friends, of whom the officers of the Canadian garrisons at the forts were not the least welcome. In return he was always a welcome guest at the forts, the soldiers competing with each other in their eagerness to attend to his horseflesh, for with lavish hand Colonel Stewart always dispensed something *pour boire.*

Later, having become financially embarrassed, he received the appointment of Indian agent at Edmonton, where shortly afterwards he died, leaving behind him that good name which is better than riches.

The Swan River Boats.

Chief Factor Stewart told me that he had held, awaiting my arrival for a week, the brigade of boats which came every fall from Swan River district to meet the private freight and passengers which came out in the ship; but he had sent them away without me a day or two before, for which I was very glad, because had I gone by the Little Saskatchewan and through lakes Manitoba and Winnipegosis, and then up the Swan River to the landing near Fort Pelly, it might have been years ere I should have had a glimpse of the far-famed paradise of the fur-traders on the Red River.

Mr. Stewart had been for a time in charge of the post at Touchwood Hills, quite near to Fort Qu'Appelle, for which I was booked, and he spoke of the country and the people I should meet there. He asked if we had everything we required for the rest of our journey, across Lake Winnipeg, and gave us much more than we asked or expected.

Other Good Fellows.

Besides being so well received by Mr. Stewart, we found other good folks at Norway House, in the persons of the clerks, Messrs. Anderson, Alexander Sinclair, and Donald C. McTavish.*

I had a long talk with Mr. Anderson, who was a native of the Island of Bressay, opposite the town of Lerwick, where I was born. His people had all died of consumption since he left home, twenty years before, and it spoke well of the climate that he enjoyed splendid health.

ON LAKE WINNIPEG.

Norway House was altogether a nice place to live in, and seemed to combine the advantages of a good outpost with many of those of York, and we were glad that our fellow passengers, Doctor MacKay and the jolly Hielan' laddies, were to pass the winter in such pleasant quarters. Armit and I set out again on the 25th of September, on the voyage over Lake Winnipeg. The next day, after a fine run under sail, we put ashore to boil the kettle where we espied the Swan River boats lying windbound, as they had to cross to the west side of the lake at that point. The guide, who I think was a son of our old guide, good old Kennedy, urged me very earnestly to embark with him, as he had waited so long for me at Norway House. I excused myself by saying that I had been shipped as a passenger to Red River by Chief Factors Wilson at York and Stewart at Norway House, and that it would be as much as my high position as apprentice clerk were worth were I, in defiance of these officers and the bill of lading, to take it upon myself to embrace the opportunity of joining the brigade of the district to which I had had the privilege of being appointed by minutes of Council. Apart from these considerations which I stated to the now indignant guide, I was determined to see Red River, and I also feared that Chief Factor Campbell might keep me at Fort Pelly,

* Mr. Anderson died suddenly, in 1869; Mr. Sinclair met his end, like so many Hudson's Bay men, by drowning, twenty years after, near La Cloche, Lake Huron. Mr. McTavish, as a retired Chief Factor, is now living in well-earned leisure at Colborne, Ontario.

where the prospects of adventure amid buffalo and wild Indians were more remote than away out on the plains at Qu'Appelle.

So after having a good meal ashore, we again embarked with a splendid wind on our quarter, leaving the wind-bound brigade of Swan River to kick their heels in the sands of the lake shore for a few days longer. I forget when they reached Fort Pelly, but I had been at Qu'Appelle some days, after a leisurely journey, and taking in the Red River Settlement, the Republic of Portage la Prairie, and Fort Ellice, before the fall carts with the green hands and freight, coming by Fort Pelly, reached Fort Qu'Appelle, with the intimation from Chief Factor Campbell that Apprentice Clerk Cowie had offended by going in to Red River, where he might be kept for good by Governor McTavish, and Mr. McDonald would have to do without an assistant.

The wind did not continue to favor us, and we lay wind-bound on an exposed beach, where we had been obliged to unload and haul up the boats, for twenty-four hours. On Sunday, the 30th, we passed a Hudson's Bay trader, named Chatelaine, from whom the crew obtained rum in some quantity in exchange for furs, which they had got hold of from Indians along the route, and we had our first opportunity of witnessing what was described in a report of a literary clerk at Touchwood Hills, as " the variegated and diversified effect of alcohol upon the natives."

We were now sailing along with a light fair wind for the mouth of the Red River. With the exception of the guide who was steering, and some decent fellows who were sleeping, all the rest of the crew had imbibed for better or worse. The merry boys chanted and kept time on the tom-tom—a battered tin pan—the fiddler got out his severely sprung instrument, and some tried a jig on the thwarts. The Swampies were all good-naturedly full, but in the crew there were two Bungies, partly of French extraction, as may be inferred from their names—Sergent and Richelieu. The former was a tall, snaky-looking fellow, who cast malignant eyes at me, because in Hill River I had hit him under the chin and landed him on the small of his back on a sharp stump for stealing ducks and then calling out insulting names to us when remonstrated with. The other was the bowsman of the boat, and on imagining himself in his cups to be entitled as an officer to come on that one occasion and sit in the stern-sheets, he made himself ridiculous by shouting at intervals in admiration of the sound of his name and all the glory it appeared to imply "Richelieu! Richelieu!" Then he would hug himself in self-satisfaction and glorification. At first we were amused and took sufficient notice to satisfy him, but the thing became tiresome. He deserved to have been heaved overboard and ducked to sober him. But very soon the rum overcame him, and he went forward and slept.

We slept that night, as we had done on many previous occasions, very comfortably in the stern-sheets. When we awoke next morning the boats were lying along the rushes in the mouth of the Red River. The crews were ashore, boiling the kettle in high glee and dressing up for their arrival, with *éclat,* in the St. Peter's Settlement.

CHAPTER VIII.

IN THE RED RIVER SETTLEMENT.

St. Peter's.

WE landed in the marsh at the mouth of the Red River on the 1st of October. It was a glorious morning, in fact after we left the Hayes River till my arrival at Qu'Appelle, and long after, the weather was without a flaw, and I do not remember to have since enjoyed a more prolonged and beautiful autumn. Ducks were flying about, and the pot hunters were busy at their harvest, but we had no time for sport, everyone being eager to reach the end of the journey at Lower Fort Garry.

We started under oars, boat racing against boat. When we got out of the marshland and reached the dry banks of the river, the men strung out on the line ahead, and went lightly as if the St. Peter's girls had got hold of the towline too. Joyful cries of greeting were exchanged as we sighted and passed the comfortable cabins of the Indian settlers along the river, and we could see that a procession was following us to the fort by the road further back.

The men were not long unloading the boats and carrying the cargo uphill to the warehouse in the fort. And then, being now united with their families and friends, they eagerly entered the shop to be paid off. We gladdened Sandison with a suitable reward for his kind attention to us on the voyage, and I am sorry that I never saw him again. In fact, the only one of the crew I have since seen has been William Prince, the late chief of St. Peter's.

147

THE COMPANY OF ADVENTURERS

AT LOWER FORT GARRY.

The Company's officers stationed there were Mr. George Davis, in charge, Mr. Alexander S. Watt,* accountant, and Mr. E. R. Abell, engineer of the steamboat *International,* and of a mill outside the fort. Staying there, preparing to start for Montreal, were two gentlemen who had lately arrived by the Portage la Loche brigade from Mackenzie River, Messrs. C. P. Gaudet† and Thomas Hardisty. Mr. Gaudet was on leave for a year, after sixteen years' service in the north, and was taking his family to see his friends in Quebec. Mr. Hardisty was being transferred to the Company's office in Montreal.

Besides these we saw at the lower fort retired Chief Trader A. H. Murray, ‡ a fine, genial and accomplished Scot, Mr. Thomas Sinclair, a very popular native magistrate and counsellor of the colony; and the Rev. J. P. Gardiner,§ of the English Church at St. Andrew's. My friend Hardisty got a buggy and we went up to the rapids to call on Chief Trader Alexander Christie, father of my shipmate. On the way we met two young ladies going to the fort, the daughter and the niece of Mr. Christie, then attending Miss Davis' admirable seminary at St. Andrew's, and qualifying for the positions they afterwards so well filled as wives of chief factors.

The clerks stationed at the fort were assisted by several shopmen and storekeepers, there being a considerable trade with the settlers, of whom at that time some of the best farmers resided in the parish of St. Andrew's. There were shops dependent on the fort at St. Andrew's and St. Peter's, and of course there was the general Indian and fur trade.

* Now living in Stromness, Orkney.

† Living as a retired Chief Trader at his station for a life-time—Fort Good Hope.

‡ Builder of Fort Yukon. Designed that relic of Fort Garry—the Gate—still standing.

§ Resided for many years as a beneficed clergyman in England, and died 1913.

A few years before the large farm attached to the establishment had been under a very able agriculturist from Scotland, Mr. A. R. Lillie, but he had forsaken the plough to follow the fur trade and become a chief trader. The farm was still carried on in a way to provide employment to a number of temporary servants, but the intensive methods of Mr. Lillie had been largely abandoned.

The place was also important as the residence of high officials when visiting the settlement, and until 1910 was used in that way by those seeking rural seclusion. The general store and grog-shop in it were closed at about the same time.

FROM LOWER TO UPPER FORT GARRY.

We remained next day about the lower fort, and on the forenoon of the 3rd of October Mr. Davis, as a great favor, provided us with one of the rather few American buggies thereabouts to take us to the upper fort, supplying also a native driver who was to bring the precious vehicle back at once, lest it should be annexed at Fort Garry. This was a precaution quite generally taken throughout the service to prevent useful horses, dogs and other things used in travel, from being retained or exchanged for inferior animals or articles by the post from which they were supposed to be returned " in good order and condition as per bill of lading."

I was as yet not aware of the prevalence of these tricks of the trade, so when Mr. Davis told me to leave all travelling kit, which had been provided for Armit and myself, at York Factory, as I would get a fresh outfit at Fort Garry, I thought it was all right, and did not discover that it was all wrong until leaving Fort Garry.

I do not remember the driver's name, but he was one of the hangers-on about the place, and evidently a favored one, for he smelt strongly of rum when we took our places on the one seat at his side. He looked and spoke as if he regarded us with disdain as green

149

hands, and spoke of himself as our "guide"—not a mere driver —on the perfectly plain beaten road between the two forts. Armit, being a crack whip, asked for the reins, but was refused with contempt at such presumption. Then the "guide" began to brag of feats by flood and field, of his mastery of all useful arts of the country, and the general inferiority of all other races to that to which he belonged. The Hudson's Bay Company's rum had evidently been given in a horn of plenty, for he kept up steam in this way till we got what, he said, was about half-way, where there was a house of entertainment kept by a gentleman with the suggestive name of "Whiskey Jack." And there he decided to tarry "to give the poor horse a drink." We found that Jack lived up to his name, and not only consumed but made and sold whiskey on the premises, in defiance of the Governor and Company of Adventurers of England. On hospitable thoughts intent Jack asked us to sample his barley bree. The smell was about all that Armit and I could stand, but "the guide" had no hesitation in mixing the Red River with the Demerara brand of firewater which had preceded it. Fearing dire results, we told him to get into the buggy and start, which he regarded as an impertinence and took another swig. Then we started again, but very shortly he began to show that Demerara and Red River had gone to war in his interior. So Armit took the helm, while the "guide" alternately bragged incoherently, swore at the pony, and gave the warwhoop as the spirits moved him. Next he began to sway about in the seat and required to be held to prevent his upsetting himself and the rig. We soon decided that we might manage to find our way on the well-marked road without his valuable services and pleasant company; also I was getting tired of holding on to him; so, seeing a fine large and invitingly soft mud hole in the wheel rut ahead, I prepared to let him go full swing as we passed through it. Just at the spot the rig and the "guide" gave a simultaneous lurch, I let go, and away he went right into a fine sanitary mixture of mud and water. The pony took fright at the sudden splash and let out as if he were after buffalo. Just as we were rounding a woody bend in the road I looked back and saw the guide in his shirt, waving his capote frantically and yelling for us to stop. I made him a polite bow as we flew round the bend, and we set out as full-fledged explorers to find Fort Garry for ourselves.

We had no difficulty in keeping to " the King's road," as that on which the electric line between Winnipeg and Selkirk now runs was then called. There were very few, and far between, houses along the road at that time, but along the river these were closer together, so that when we were told that we would first come to " the town " and then to Fort Garry, we, expecting to see the buildings in " town " much nearer together than those on the river bank, were surprised to find ourselves at Fort Garry without having recognized in the straggling buildings scattered about the prairie on each side of the track the germs of the future metropolis of the great West.

At Fort Garry.

Upon reporting ourselves to Dr. William Cowan, the chief trader in charge, he handed us over to the attention of Mr. A. R. McKenzie, the accountant in the shop, and Mr. Joseph James Hargrave, the Governor's private secretary, the only member of the general office staff on duty at the time. Mr. John H. McTavish, chief accountant, and Mr. John Balsillie, cashier, were both off on their fall shooting holidays at Lake Manitoba, along with Mr. Alexander Matheson, the clerk in charge of Pembina.

Governor McTavish and Chief Trader Magnus Linklater, who was in charge of the shop and all outside work, and Chief Trader William Anderson, in charge of the Red River depot, were the other officials at the time in fort, besides Mr. James Anderson, foreman, and Color-Sergeant James Rickards, pensioner of the Royal Marines, who guarded the fort as night watchman.

McKenzie and Hargrave installed us in the clerk's quarters over the general office, and made us feel at home. Mr. Linklater introduced us to his wife (a Kildonan lady) and their two pretty little daughters. Governor McTavish came to see us, and enquired about his old friends, whom Armit and I knew in Scotland, and examined the shot guns we had brought with us.

The day after the arrival we were summoned into the presence of Doctor Cowan to answer the complaint laid against us by the " guide " for non-support in the buggy and desertion, also for running away with the buggy and pony entrusted to his special care by the officer in charge of Lower Fort Garry, without his consent having been first asked and obtained. Our accuser looked seedy in countenance and muddy in costume from the effects of the late mix-up between Demerara and Red River, and the mud and water along the King's highway. He desired a solatium in the shape of an order on the Fort Garry shop " for some things "—probably imported from Demerara—which he required very urgently. The doctor heard the charge and our defence with well-assumed judicial gravity, and said that while withholding judgment on us, he could not presume to interfere with the unknown financial arrangements entered into between the " guide " and the authorities at the lower fort, by giving him any supplies other than food for his return.

I had a letter from the Rev. Mr. Brand to his brother-in-law, the Bishop of Rupert's Land, and Hargrave kindly undertook to be my " guide " to Bishop's Court. The Bishop spoke of experiments he was making with crab apples in his garden, and of parasites which had been observed on, and which were hoped would be the destroyers of the locusts, which had already done much damage to the crops of Red River and threatened more—a threat which was most direly fulfilled. On the way back Hargrave pointed out the famous hotel of

" Dutch George," and the buildings of other leading inhabitants of the town, but the only place we entered was that of Doctor Schultz, with whom we had some conversation.

Hargrave had been educated at St. Andrew's and Edinburgh in Scotland, where we knew many people in common, so we had plenty to talk of as we walked along. He was known to be one of the wealthiest men, by inheritance, in the service, but he was a man of method and had confined his annual expenditure within the limit of his first year's salary as apprentice clerk, which was twenty pounds, and had not exceeded that amount ever since, although his pay had advanced yearly thereafter. During Balsillie's absence he had been taking his place as cashier, and in three weeks had lost unaccountably the sum of two shillings and sixpence. " I wish," said Hargrave, earnestly, " Balsillie were back, for if such loss continues, the consequences will be perfectly ruinous to me." Curiously the loss Hargrave deplored was not due to love of money itself, for he was most generous and liberal in spending it on his friends afterwards, but from his love of methodically following a rule once adopted. Even at table this characteristic exhibited itself in the precise and orderly manner in which he arranged the fish bones on the edge of his plate.

Joseph James Hargrave was a man remarkable as the most painstakingly accurate historian of Red River. The book, brought out at his own expense, was never pushed on the public, and he lost £600, it is said, in the venture. Copies of it are now rare. But everyone writing on the history of the country, since its publication in 1869, has made use of it, often without the slightest acknowledgment to its mine of officially acquired information. He was the son of Chief Factor James Hargrave, who served principally in command of York Factory. His mother, the daughter of the Sheriff of Argyleshire, and a laird there, was sister of Governor McTavish, to whom he became private secretary. As such he had access to all fur-trade and colonial records, and came into personal contact, at Fort Garry, and in attending the Council of the Northern Department, with all the notables and veteran officers in the country. Consequently he had unique facilities for acquiring information, which he had the natural ability and education to make use of, and the moral courage and love of truth to state without fear or favor. He had the absent-minded simplicity of a student non-observant of common affairs, which made him the butt of lesser wits in the service, who failed to understand that he had written a *magnum opus* to outlive them all.

Few people ever passed through Red River at that time without experiencing the kindness and hospitality of Mr. Andrew G. B. Bannatyne, the leading merchant of the " town." We were no exception, and were most pleasantly entertained at his comfortable abode, which was furnished in a manner surprising to see after the plain furnishings provided by the Hudson's Bay Company for the quarters of their officers. Mr. Bannatyne's and my father's people had been old friends in Orkney, and I had met several of his relatives in Stromness, so from that time on, whenever I got leave to visit the settlement, I always went to see Mr. Bannatyne. Under Mr. Bannatyne's roof I had the privilege of meeting Mrs. Kennedy, the accomplished wife of Captain William Kennedy, commander of the Arctic expedition in search of Franklin in the *Prince Albert*. The captain and my father had been schoolmates at St. Margaret's Hope in Orkney, and great friends, and my cousin, Robert Cowie (afterwards of the United States navy), had been surgeon of the *Prince Albert*.

Besides the Hudson's Bay people of the fort the only others whom I recollect having seen around it were the Rev. Cyprian Pinkham, of St. James, now Bishop of Calgary, and Mr. James Murray (son of the highly respected pioneer of Kildonan, Donald Murray) and the lady he was about to marry, Miss Christy McBeth, daughter of Mr. Adam McBeth, then in charge of the Shoal River post in the Swan River district.

The Company had a store * in the town also, of which an American, Mr. Burbank, assisted by Mr. Henry Moncrieff, had charge. I spent much of my time visiting Mr. Moncrieff on that occasion, and on every subsequent visit to Red River, while he remained there, as he came from Scalloway, the ancient capital of the Shetlands, where our people were well acquainted. During a visit to Moncrieff a young man, with a jaunty and genial air, came into the store and introduced himself as Dan Devlin, clerk for Mr. Bannatyne, and son of Bryan Devlin, an army pensioner, who had taken his discharge from the Royal Canadian Regiment when they left Fort Garry in 1861. Dan was very communicative and said he had been born on the Rock of Gibraltar. He talked about the " town " as if it were already a city of renown. He agreed with an English halfbreed pedlar, who had forced himself on our notice at the mouth of the Red River, and with the newspaper, *The Nor'-Wester,* that the Hudson's Bay Company's days were numbered, that in their opinion the Company had been weighed in the balance and found wanting. Knight, Dan and the editors of *The Nor'-Wester* have long ago gone the way of all flesh, but the venerable Hudson's Bay Company still exists and amasses riches from the people who were going to overwhelm it, according to the seers of the sixties of the last century.

Dan was cheerful and obliging, and told me where I might buy an unrestricted supply of American-made matches, of which the supply was very limited in the interior, flint and steel and touchwood being universally in use, and burning glasses much in vogue. In sunshine the burning glass quickly sets fire to touchwood or tinder, but for general service the flint and steel was the main reliance, and the natives were wonderfully expert in their use, making the sparks fly like a blacksmith's forge. But till the art is

---

* The building, about the best in town in 1867, is now dilapidated, and used as a blacksmith's forge on Fort Street.

acquired the novice often uses up a lot of skin and fiery language before getting a light.

McTavish, Balsillie, and Matheson returned from their outing laden with ducks and wavies, of which the officers' mess got a share, and on the occasion of the first dinner after their holiday Judge Black had come to mess from his place down the river. There were several clever and well-informed men at table, and their conversation was brilliant and interesting. The rule that an apprentice clerk should not speak at mess unless spoken to, which was observed at York Factory, was not so much in evidence at Fort Garry, and I ventured to tell of certain negotiations going on for the transfer of the government of Rupert's Land to the new Dominion of Canada, reported in the newspapers at home in June. Neither Judge Black nor Doctor Cowan had seen these reports and they were quite interested; but they did not seem surprised that the London board of the Company were making arrangements, which though leaking out in the old country, were being officially withheld from their " wintering partners " in North America, whose lives were much more vitally affected by the reports than were the merely financially interested English stockholders.

PREDISPOSING CAUSES OF THE RED RIVER TROUBLES.

In the secrecy of these negotiations and the withholding of confidence from their own officers and men and the people of the North-West at large lay the root of the Red River troubles of 1869 and 1870. On two historically and legally most important occasions previously had the London board acted in the same stealthy fashion, and the people in and of the country only discovered these transactions of great magnitude from outside sources, while they were still officially concealed from them by the London committee. The first occasion was that of the transfer of the whole estate of the heirs of Thomas, Earl of Selkirk, in the district of Assiniboia, an area of 116,000 square miles (which included the smaller municipal

"District of Assiniboia," better known as the Red River Settlement), from these heirs back to the original grantors, the Hudson's Bay Company, in the year 1834 (which may have been ratified by "the wintering partners" when a new deed poll between them and the London shareholders was also made in 1835), but without the knowledge and consent of the colonists generally. In the original grant from the Hudson's Bay Company to Lord Selkirk one-tenth of the 116,000 square miles, had been granted in trust to him for such employees of the Company as, after three years' service, should retire therefrom and settle in the country. This transaction was concealed from the colonists until the year 1845, when the secretary in London, in reply to the Kildonan settlers' request for the fulfilment of Lord Selkirk's promise to them of a Presbyterian Gaelic-speaking minister, wrote inadvertently that such was not one of the obligations mentioned when the Selkirk property was relinquished to the Company.

As soon as "the wintering partners" had become party to this, which Judge Martin calls "a transaction of great magnitude," in 1835, the Northern Department Council of that year passed a resolution for the purpose of depriving their servants, who had not yet reached Red River, which they could not do without the Company providing passages, of their right to claim and obtain their free grants under the Trust created as above mentioned in their favor, which resolution reads as follows: "Resolved, (84) that no servants be permitted to settle at Red River Colony unless they become purchasers from the proprietors of the soil of at least fifty acres of land at 7s. 6d. ($1.87) per acre, payment thereof to be deposited with the gentlemen in charge of the depots to which they have been attached previous to their departure for the settlement." Note the words, "*proprietors of the soil.*" Who were they supposed to be?

Hargrave, in his book, "Red River," page 81, says "the repurchase by the Company from Selkirk's heirs was without prejudice to the rights of all the colonists." Perhaps because the deed of reconveyance safeguarded these " rights of all the colonists " (and colonists all Company's servants of three years' service certainly were) its terms have never been made public, and even its existence had been denied. If it be non-existent then the right of the retiring employees to share in the one-tenth put in trust for them by the original grant remains unquestionably. And if it exist, concealed in the law archives of the Company or of Canada, for the benefit of the non-resident absentee stockholders of the Company, but to the injury of the Company's retired servants who were colonists of the country, it should be produced and the public made acquainted with its terms. That the deed or a copy of it existed and was accessible to Hargrave, when he wrote as above, is a fair inference. If there be nothing to conceal, why this silence?

The second " transaction of great magnitude," completed without proper consultation with and the consent of the people of the country, was when the old proprietors of the Company in London sold out in 1863 to " The International Financial Association," under circumstances related by Hargrave, pages 298, 299, and on the other hand by Sir E. W. Watkin, in his " Canada and the States, Recollections, 1851 to 1886."

The " wintering partners " were first stupefied and then filled with indignation, when the news of this deal reached them. *The Nor'-Wester* gleefully jeered at them, saying, " the hardy, active and intelligent factors," which the new Company called them in their prospectus, " had been sold like dumb, driven cattle." But the deed poll gave these gentlemen certain legal rights which could not be disposed of without their consent, and these were not quite adjusted when the coming of confederation began to cast its shadow before.

A Contented Community.

But, however important these transactions might be to the Company's employees and the wintering partners—the chief

factors and chief traders—by the majority of the people of the
colony and the vast country outside of the Settlement the
changes were either unknown or unnoted. To read *The
Nor'-Wester,* and the declarations of some gentlemen of repute
and lovers of their native country, one at a distance would be
apt to think that the country was seething with discontent
and groaning under the iron despotism of the fur-trading
monopolist government.

The very opposite was the case. I do not think there could
be a more contented community anywhere than that of the
old Red River Settlement. By comparison with the poor
cottars and crofters in the old country, with the poor in the
slums of the big cities, the lot of the Red River people was
cast in very pleasant places. Each lived, so to speak, " under
his own vine and fig tree " on his own land, rent free. He
could hunt, fish, and shoot without restriction; he had building material and firewood for the cutting and hauling; his
animals roamed on free pastures, and there was hay in abundance. Even their churches and schools were largely supported
by contributions raised in the old country, from many classes
of people, some of whom were in much less prosperous circumstances than themselves.

The good substantial clothing they wore never got out of
fashion, for they did not follow those of the outer world. In
a community where exchanges were made by barter more than
in money, and where a man was measured more by his physical,
mental and moral qualities than by the mere possession of
money, people did not sacrifice their time and health and
character to its pursuit. Everyone could get clothing, shelter
and plenty of good substantial food, and a rich man could buy
little that his poorer neighbor might envy. There was very
little class distinction outside the Hudson's Bay semi-military
service.

As to the want of a market for all the farmers could have
raised, they had deprived themselves of that advantage by
planting themselves away from all facilities for freighting

anything heavier and less valuable than furs. The same handicap was on the merchandise imported for their use, and those of the settlers who became importers and opened stores as merchants did not undersell the Company, rather the reverse.

GOVERNED BY CONSENT OF THE GOVERNED.

The opponent of the Hudson's Bay Company, *The Nor'-Wester* newspaper, would one day represent them as a grinding and merciless and mighty monopoly, and next describe them as a contemptible lot of impotent and cowardly old wives to be laughed at and defied with impunity. The truth was that without military force in the Settlement the Company had to govern it just as they did the Indian country, by the consent of the governed. While there were no such things as elections, of the approved pattern, which are now so pure and expressive of the sovereign will of the political bosses of the people, the counsellors were selected for well-known and respected qualities, from among the natural leaders and elders of the different classes composing the population. Among them were the bishops of St. Boniface and of Rupert's Land; such men as Sutherland and Fraser representing Kildonan; McDermot, Bannatyne, Inkster and Sinclair for other British; and Pascal Breland, Solomon Amlin, and other good men and true for the French element. Every one of these would have been elected by popular vote, had that machinery existed. The enterprise of the petitioners, who asked this Council to appoint Doctor Schultz to a vacancy in it, might be paralleled nowadays by a similar effort to induce the Hon. Sir Rodmond Roblin to give the leader of the Opposition a seat in his Cabinet.

A BENEVOLENT DESPOTISM TEMPERED BY RIOT.

But even the rule of these benevolent despots, appointed by the governor and committee in London, was tempered by riot, whenever anything done by the Council or the legal authorities was sufficiently displeasing to any considerable section of the population. Without an imperial military force which might be considered impartial, it was impossible, in cases of trouble when the British and French as a whole took opposite sides, to call upon one side to support the government without plunging the Settlement into all the horrors of a civil and religious war, which, like a prairie fire, would have spread throughout the length and breadth of Rupert's Land, and involved the Indian tribes as well. Possibly the British element in the Red River Settlement might have held their own against the skilled hunter-warriors of the Metis, but every post and Christian mission station from Red River to the Rocky Mountains and from the boundary line to the Arctic Ocean might have been swept out of existence. And it was that consideration, I believe, which dictated the " peace at any price " policy for which the good Governor McTavish was so severely criticized in the troubles of 1869-70.

The Stone Forts and Their Builder.

To the forty men of the 39th Regiment, who accompanied Commissioner Coltman to Red River, in 1817, to enforce the Prince Regent's orders for the restoration of peace and property between the great rival fur companies, belongs the honor of being the very first expedition of British regular troops to the Red River.

When peace was restored, and subsequently, in 1821, the union of the companies effected, the memory of old feuds did not die out immediately, so instead of retaining the old North-West Company's name of Fort Gibraltar for the new union fort on its site, the name of the deputy-governor, Garry, who came to Red River to complete the arrangements of the coalition, was given to the new establishment. It was damaged by the flood of 1826 and rebuilt as before of wood.

In 1830 the Northern Department Council, held at York Factory, passed this resolution:

" The establishment of Fort Garry being in a very dilapidated
state, its situation not sufficiently central, much exposed to the
spring floods, and very inconvenient in regard to the navigation
of the river and in other points of view, it is resolved (51) that
a new establishment to bear the same name be formed on a site
to be selected near the lower end of the rapids; for which purpose tradesmen be employed or the work done by contract, as may
be found most expedient; and as stones and lime are on the
spot, these materials be used, being cheaper and more durable
than wood."

The reference to the site being inconvenient to navigation
is accounted for by decked vessels being used between Norway
House and Red River, which could not ascend the St. Andrew's
Rapids.   Another reason is said to have been to remove the
chief fort to a site less exposed to hostile attack from the
plains.

The work at the lower fort seems to have gone on slowly so
that it was not completely surrounded by a wall till 1837 or
1838   But while the lower fort was slowly being added to
from year to year, there came a master builder from the
charge of York Factory to take command of Red River district as chief factor, and of the colony of Assiniboia as its
governor, in the person of Alexander Christie, in 1834.   During 1835 and 1836, instead of abandoning the commanding
site at the forks of the Red River, he erected thereon a fort
of stone with a frontage of two hundred and eighty feet on
the Assiniboine River and a depth of two hundred and forty
feet, with high bastions at each corner, loopholed for mus-
ketry and pierced for cannon, with neat and substantial
stores, dwellings, offices and barracks therein.   Afterwards, to
this stone fort, he added, during his second term as governor,
a square of about equal size in the rear of the stone part, the
walls being of big squared oak logs laid horizontally, and
pinned together.   The only remaining part of old Fort Garry
now in existence is the old stone back gate of this otherwise
wooden addition to the stone part built in 1835-6.

ARCHIBALD McDONALD,
Clerk in charge of Fort Qu'Appelle,
1867.

CHIEF FACTOR ARCHIBALD
McDONALD,
At Fort Qu'Appelle, 1911.
Courtesy of Grand Trunk Pacific R'y.

INSPECTING CHIEF FACTOR THE
HON. WILLIAM J. CHRISTIE.
Courtesy of Mr. J. G. M. Christie.

CHIEF COMMISSIONER JAMES ALLAN
GRAHAME.
Courtesy of Mrs. Cowan.

MONUMENTS TO GOVERNOR CHRISTIE

GOVERNOR CHRISTIE.

In the old Fort Garry gate in Winnipeg and Lower Fort Garry, Mr. Christie has left two monuments to his skill and ability as a builder as well as to the memory of the old fur-trading rulers of Rupert's Land. To the courtesy of retired Chief Factor MacFarlane, whose good wife is a granddaughter of the old governor, I am indebted for the following notes, and to his grandson, Mr. John G. M. Christie, assistant to the Hudson's Bay Company's fur trade commissioner, Winnipeg, for the use of the governor's photograph, from which the picture herewith has been copied.

Chief Factor MacFarlane writes:—

"At the coalition of the North-West Company, of Montreal, with the Hudson's Bay Company, of England, in 1821, Mr. Alexander Christie (a native of Aberdeenshire) was one of the twenty-five senior officers of both fur-trading concerns to receive a chief factor's commission under the deed poll of the united companies.

"Mr. Christie had much to do with the rebuilding of Moose and York Factories on Hudson Bay, and also with the erection of both Upper and Lower Fort Garry on the Red River, while he was chief factor in charge of the fur trade in Red River district, from June, 1833, to June, 1839, and from June, 1844, to June, 1849.

"During these periods in which he superintended the fur trade of Red River he held the commission of governor of the colony of Assiniboia—that is the Red River Settlement. Mr. Alexander Ross, in his history of Red River Settlement, erroneously stated that Colonel Crofton was governor of the colony from June, 1846, to 1847, and Major Griffith from June, 1847, to 1848, and this error has been repeated by writers copying him. But according to these officers' own evidence they merely had seats in the council of the colony, *ex-officio*, as commanders of the British troops then in garrison there. The Minutes of the Council of Assiniboia also show these military officers attending as members at meetings presided over by Governor Christie. Mr. Christie was succeeded, as governor, however, by Colonel Caldwell, commander of the enrolled pensioners, who relieved the Imperial troops under Major Griffiths, in 1848."

Mr. MacFarlane continues:—

"In 1849 Mr. Christie retired from the Hudson's Bay Company's service and settled in Minto Street, Edinburgh, Scotland, where he died in 1874, at the age of eighty-two years. He was probably the most influential and respected chief factor of his time, and in proof of this it may be stated that, in addition to the seven years' retiring interest in the profits of the fur trade to which he was entitled, Mr. Christie was accorded by the Company, with the approbation of his brother officers and Sir George Simpson, governor-in-chief, two years' additional shares in the profits.

"In 1833, Mr. Thomas Simpson, afterwards celebrated as an Arctic explorer, wrote to his brother, Alexander, of Mr. Christie, to this effect: 'Chief Factor Christie, you will have heard, is now governor of Red River, and has, besides, the summer management of York Factory; so that he is now, in fact, the second man in Rupert's Land. And well does he merit such a situation, for a worthier or a more honorable man I believe never existed. I feel particularly happy in acting under him. . . . His sound judgment, his integrity, his liberal and enlarged views, entitle him to my respect, while his genuine kindness of heart and manner ensure my esteem.' "*

There was an old saying of the great Governor Simpson that with three good officers stationed each respectively at York Factory, to make out the requisitions; at Norway House, to superintend the transport; and at Red River, to manage the Settlement, it did not much matter if the rest of the officers in the Northern Department were of mediocre calibre. Mr. Christie was for years in charge of York Factory before being appointed to Red River, and certainly filled every position he occupied with credit to himself and advantage to the Company.

Of his family, his daughter married the highly respected Chief Trader, John Black, afterwards Judge. His elder son, Chief Trader Alexander, a man of gigantic physique, has been already noticed. His second son, William Joseph, was edu-

* Strong votes of thanks passed by meetings of the Council of Assiniboia, in 1839 and 1849, presided over by his successors, also show the high esteem in which he was held by that body.—*I. C.*

cated splendidly in Aberdeen, and after many years as the leading chief factor in charge of Saskatchewan district, became, under the reorganization, inspecting chief factor, and retired in 1873. Upon the formation of the North-West Council, by Canada, he, with Donald A. Smith and other gentlemen of high standing in the country, was appointed a member, and as such became entitled to the courtesy prefix of " honorable " to the already honored name of Christie.

CHAPTER IX.

THE RISE OF FORT GARRY AND THE DECLINE OF YORK FACTORY.

INCREASING TRAFFIC WITH UNITED STATES.

THE gradual advance of settlement in Minnesota and of the railway system of the United States nearer to the Red River Settlement; the placing of a steamboat on the river; and the generally increased business relations consequent thereon, had already, in 1867, raised Fort Garry into a port of entry which was rapidly overtaking York Factory in importance. The increasing "luxury of the age," as compared with the bare necessities of existence originally imported for the fur trade and the fur traders; the forsaking of the simple life of the original settlers by their descendants, who plied with the carts to St. Paul, Minnesota, and set American fashions on their return; the larger supplies of trading goods required by the Company to meet increasing competition in the trade of which they no longer retained the monopoly; and the ever-increasing difficulty of manning the boats for the voyage to York Factory, all gave evidence of a time when, by the nearer approach of American railroads to the boundary, the old Hudson Bay route, handicapped by the absence of a railway from the bay to the interior, would cease to become the main inlet and outlet of the commerce of the Company.

So in the log stockaded enclosure, which had been added to the back of the stone walls of Fort Garry, there was a large warehouse known as the Fort Garry depot, under the management of Chief Trader William Anderson, who had behind him long experience of similar duty at York Factory. In this depot were stored the " Canadian and American goods " which

166

always appeared separately in the alphabetically arranged requisitions, invoices, and inventories of the Company's account books. At that time the principal articles under the heading were axes, L'Assomption belts, American matches, Perry Davis' Painkiller, steel traps and tobacco.

YORK FACTORY SIDE-TRACKED.

But the warehouse also contained large supplies of the regular English goods required, not only for the settlers but to outfit the " commercants," generally Metis, owning a large number of ponies and carts, who traded all over the plains west of the Red River, between the Missouri and the Saskatchewan, following the buffalo and buffalo hunters in their migrations. Besides such supplies, increasing portions of the regular English outfit for the Settlement, the Saskatchewan and part of that for the Swan River district had begun to find their way by St. Paul, Minnesota, to Fort Garry, instead of by York Factory; and these supplies were freighted by carts over the plains as far as Edmonton.

While this traffic grew in successive years that by way of York Factory diminished proportionately. Year after year district after district in the interior ceased to send boat brigades to the Factory on the Bay, and began to receive all their supplies, with the exception of gunpowder, through Fort Garry. When at last the iron horse reached the waters of the Red River which were navigable by steamboats, shortly after the transfer of the North-West to Canada, the old historic seaport on the Bay became merely the depot for posts on the coast or much nearer the coast than to Lake Winnipeg.

THE STEAMBOAT AGE.

With the advent of the American railway to and of lines of steamboats and strings of flatboats on the Red River, the York boat as well as York itself ceased to be the foremost factors in the traffic of the country at large. The steamboat age succeeded, the Hudson's Bay Company placing steamers on Lake Winnipeg, and several stern wheelers on the Saskatchewan, running from the head of Grand Rapids to Edmonton, whereby the old reliable Red River cart, which had taken the place of the York boat in Saskatchewan freighting, was also rendered, on the Saskatchewan trail, relatively a thing of the past.

Next, as we all know, the age of steamboats was succeeded by the present railway age, and it again will probably be succeeded by a time when waterways, improved by modern science, will resume much of their ancient importance for the carriage of bulky produce to market.

JOURNEY RESUMED.

After a few days spent pleasantly and profitably at Fort Garry, I was ordered to put my baggage on a cart driven by a French-Canadian voyageur, named Dufresne, who was returning to Carlton on the Saskatchewan. Dufresne had for fellow travellers two Saskatchewan Crees, who had been hired for the trip with a boat taking the remains of Chief Trader Arthur Pruden, from Carlton, for burial in Red River Settlement. I was to travel in their company as far as Fort Ellice, and Dufresne, who had been for many years a "master's man," stationary and travelling, was to act in that capacity for me on the way.

Armit and I had left, at Lower Fort Garry, the complete camp outfit and tent with which we had been supplied at York, on my being assured that "everything" would be furnished me again at Upper Fort. Dufresne, who knew "everything" about travelling, assured me that he had it on the cart, and Chief Trader Magnus Linklater gave the following order on the provision store for my trip from Fort Garry to Fort Ellice: Twelve pounds "biscuits," four cured buffalo tongues, eight pounds salt pork, ten pounds dried buffalo meat, six pounds fresh beef, one pound Congou tea, four pounds loaf sugar, half pint country salt, half gallon port wine. Besides this, Dufresne and the two Indians received full rations for themselves.

An Attractive Start.

Dufresne drove out of the fort, with as much style as he could forcibly persuade the cayuse to put in his paces. What the pony lacked in energy the driver made up for in gesticulation and profanity, and the pace kept up when they hit the prairie trail showed that Dufresne was determined to make a record journey, and that I should have to lose no time in starting for our rendezvous at White Horse Plain.

Deserters, Mormons and "Rouge."

On the 7th of October, 1867, Armit and I started in a buggy driven by him, for the last lap of our long voyage together, on his way to the post to which he had been appointed at White Horse Plain. On the way we met a large party of American cavalrymen, who had deserted from Devil's Lake with horses and accoutrements, and, shortly afterwards, a party, said to be Mormons from Salt Lake, who were distinguished by the men wearing immensely wide-brimmed felt hats and having a number of mules in train. Mr. W. D. Lane, who was in charge of the post, was ordered from Fort Garry to supply me with a saddle horse, and picked out of the band one which he alleged to be a "buffalo runner" for the purpose, and as a special mark of favor, for which upon further acquaintance with "Rouge," the beast's name, I did not fail to express my full appreciation. "Rouge," said Lane, being a buffalo runner *par excellence,* was too proud a pony to put up with the degradation of hauling a cart, but would make a fine saddle horse.

Cuthbert Grant.

At White Horse Plain post the Company raised cattle and did some farming, besides supplying the northern band of Metis buffalo hunters, who made it their winter quarters.

Formerly for many years it had been the station of the " Warden of the Plains," Mr. Cuthbert Grant, whose name is so well known as the clerk of the North-West Company, who was in charge of the provision brigade of Metis when attacked by the greenhorn, Governor Semple, with a force of Hudson's Bay servants, greatly inferior in number, untrained, almost unarmed, but animated by " courage and fidelity." That Grant was able to restrain his wild warriors from massacring the defenceless Kildonan settlers, after the slaughter of the poor Hudson's Bay employees who followed the fatuous Semple, showed the future warden of the plains to be a born leader, a humane and merciful man, and well worthy of the position of authority he gained as chief of the Metis hunters of Red River, and as their recognized leader and representative in the Council of the colony of Assiniboia.

Metis' Warlike Virtues.

Under Grant, the Metis of the buffalo hunting brigades were organized as a disciplined force which repelled every hostile Indian attack so successfully as to win renown as the most skilful and bravest warriors of the prairies. Recognizing no boundary to their hunting grounds, save the range of the buffalo they pursued, they roamed at will, protecting themselves from overwhelming numbers of Sioux by barricades of carts round their camp, and by the fame of their prowess guarding the agricultural settlers of the Red River colony from molestation by the bloodthirsty " Tigers of the Plains " and other warlike tribes.

The warlike qualities of the Metis often were most favorably commented upon by military men who hunted and travelled with them in the old days. All alike expressed surprise at the excellent discipline they maintained among themselves when on the grand annual buffalo hunt, and British officers mention them in their reports as magnificent horsemen, and splendid marksmen, whose services would be invaluable in war on the frontier. At the time when Lord Selkirk's agents

FORT SMITH. H.B.Co's POST, SHOWING THE OX CARTS LOADED WITH FUR. MAKING THE 16 MILE PORTAGE TO AVOID THE RAPIDS ON SLAVE RIVER, 200 MILES NORTH OF EDMONTON.

A HUDSON'S BAY COMPANY'S TRAIN OF OX CARTS.

Photo by C. W. Mathers, Edmonton.

were proclaiming such game laws in the Wild West as were enforced in Europe, even decreeing that the natives of the country should not hunt buffalo on horseback, it seems wonderful that these bold and freeborn plainsmen were not provoked to attack the feudal lord's colony, without any incitement by the North-West Company.

A Burden of a Beast.

Dufresne and the Twin Wolves—so the Cree brothers were named—arrived in the afternoon of the 8th, and we set out for Fort Ellice. I at once found that " Rouge " was absolutely no good for anything. At a walk he constantly stumbled and fell behind the cart, and to compel him into a trot to catch it up was violent exercise. Neither would he lead light nor follow. Instead of being useful as a beast of burden he became a burden of a beast, for we could not leave a pony, which had been charged at full tariff price by Red River district against Swan River district, loose on the prairie, and I had to take him to be exchanged at the next post for an animal which could be used.

My French Chef.

That night I made my bed for the first time under the body of a cart, a canopy with which I became accustomed during many a following year. With a tent or paulin thrown over its shafts, wheels and body, and opening on a camp fire in front, one has good lodging in wind and rain; but I had only the bare cart and an oil cloth under my blankets, and the night was keen and windy. While I fixed up my bedding my new French chef was busy and noisy about the fire, and I expected some fine French cooking for supper; but when Dufresne came to set the meal before me and, spreading a piece of dirty bale cover for a cloth on the ground, put down on it a flake of uncooked dried meat and lumps that looked like the limestone of which Fort Garry was built, and said they were "biscuits," I was quite disgusted. The meat was of the look and texture of rawhide, not a speck of fat, and the hardness of the biscuits was in exact keeping with their appearance. I had asked for bread and the Company had given me a stone. Moreover, on asking Dufresne what had become of "everything" in the way of cooking and eating utensils, he said that these consisted of a frying pan, a tea kettle, and a cooking kettle, with three tin drinking pots all belonging to him and the Indians, and each of them had a scalping knife in his scabbard. Dufresne lent me his drinking pot, in which we soaked the "biscuits" after crumbling them with the axe, and cutting up the dried meat with my pocket knife as one shaves a plug of tobacco, I managed to make a kind of a meal.

However, Dufresne was a lively and interesting talker, and had lots to tell of his travels and his general prowess and adventures and hairbreadth escapes on flood and field. His conversation was voluble, but, of course, Frenchy English and full of strange oaths as well as incidents. And he, too, was pious, crossing himself before eating and kneeling down to pray before lying down to sleep. He was a thin, wiry, little man, as active as a cat, and so hardy that all he wore, without underclothing or hose, was a pair of moleskin trousers, a coarse cotton shirt, and moccasins, adding a cloth cap and a capote occasionally.

POPLAR POINT.

The Indians were constantly visiting any place they saw people camping or dwelling along the way, but they did not appear to see anyone who appreciated their company till we reached Poplar Point, where they found the father and brother of a halfbreed they knew on the Saskatchewan, by whom they were well received, and I was made welcome. The old man had been sent from a post on Hudson Bay, by his Orkney father, to be educated in Stromness, and he was delighted to talk about that place with me. I let Dufresne and the Indians depart, towing "Rouge" with them, and remained with the

Taits for some time, and then the son lent me a nice saddle
horse and came on another with me to catch up the cart. I
enjoyed on that occasion the first fine gallop I had yet had
on the prairies, and more than ever disgusted with " Rouge,"
I did the rest of the trip to Portage la Prairie on foot, to my
great relief and pleasure, for there is nothing more trying to
a man's patience, and even his body, than sitting on a lazy,
stumbling pony following a slow-going cart on the plains.

PORTAGE LA PRAIRIE.

On the 10th of October we reached the Hudson's Bay post
at Portage la Prairie. The place derived its name as the
portage over which the early French traders, coming up the
Assiniboine, carried their cargoes to Lake Manitoba, a distance of nine miles, and forwarded them up the lake to Fort
Dauphin and their other posts beyond. In seasons of high
water the floods of the Assiniboine find their way by the
course of Rat Creek (River Champignons) into Lake Manitoba.

In 1737 the intrepid Verandrye established a post here
named Fort la Reine, which he made his base for exploration
to the Missouri. The British Canadians who followed his
footsteps towards the end of that century had three rival posts
here, which were attacked by the Assiniboines, and only the
men of one post succeeded in defending themselves and making their escape. The route by Portage la Prairie seems to
have been preferred over that by Lake Winnipeg by the early
traders to reach the Saskatchewan, and of course it was more
convenient to their posts on Lakes Manitoba and Winnipegosis,
as well as those on the Swan River. For some time before
1832 there does not appear to have been any post between
White Horse Plain and Brandon House; but the Northern
Department Council of that year appointed John Richards
McKay, P.M., to the charge of the " new Post of Portage la
Prairie," and the Company has had a store here ever since.

THE HONORED FOUNDERS.

Shortly before 1857 the venerated and Venerable Archdeacon William Cochran established an Indian mission at the Portage to endeavor to repeat in the case of the savage Indians surrounding it the success which his untiring and zealous labors had attained in the Indian settlement of St. Peters, with the further object of pioneering the way for agriculturists from other parts of the Red River Settlement who might wish to take advantage of the splendid soil of the Portage plains. A number of native families, numbering in 1858 some one hundred and twenty people, took advantage of the opportunity, among whom may be named with honor the Garriochs, Birds, Cummings and Gaddies. To these later on were added the first Canadian farmers, the McLeans, and others from Ontario, who were the vanguard of the mighty host who have brought the whole western prairies beyond under the plow —the conquerors of the wilderness.

The Hudson's Bay Company and the Council of Assiniboia tried to discourage this western advance of settlement into a district beyond the municipal limits of the latter body, which only extended fifty miles in a circle of which Fort Garry was the centre. But none of the dire consequences apprehended by the Council of Assiniboia followed the settlement, which persisted and increased under the wise direction of the patriarchal Archdeacon until the time of his death in 1865.

"GOVERNOR" SPENCE—HIS REIGN.

After the death of the great and good missionary, Hargrave, in his history of "Red River" (page 109), relates:

"With regard to the political aspect of affairs at Portage la Prairie, I regret to have to record that the evil forebodings of the secular authorities have been fully justified by the event. . . . The petty colony has been a source of much disquietude to the magistracy in the Red River Settlement of late years;* that two instances of murder have already occurred in its his-

* Written in March, 1869.

tory, and that, after an abortive attempt to organize a private government of their own and to force an oath of allegiance and a customs duty on the general public the Imperial government was memorialized on the subject by the so-called 'Governor.'* The result was an intimation from the colonial secretary advising him (Governor Spence) that the course he was pursuing was illegal, and that he and his abettors were incurring what might become a grave responsibility, seeing the British Government could not recognize their authority which might be legally resisted by any person so minded."

BILL WATT, O'DONOGHUE'S CAPTOR.

At the Portage post I was heartily welcomed and well entertained by Mr. William H. Watt, an Orkney gentleman, who was in charge. Mr. Watt was an ardent sportsman and had lost an arm in pursuit of game some years previously, but its loss did not prevent his seizing the Fenian O'Donoghue when he made the raid on Pembina in 1871, and holding him till arrested by the American troops who intervened so opportunely on that occasion. The Twin Wolves had succeeded in making away with all their own rations for the voyage from Fort Garry to Fort Ellice, and besides had devoured all my share also by the time we reached Portage. They declared that they also required to be supplied with other " things from the store " on account of their wages for the trip. In Watt they thought they had found a " Moonias " (the Indian contemptuous term for a white newcomer), but they soon discovered they had met a Tartar whom they could neither fool nor bully. He gave them, of course, some pemmican and ammunition to find them on their way to Fort Ellice, but nothing more than a dressing down for their waste of food on the way from Fort Garry.

In Mr. Watt I found a friend whose people at home had been well acquainted with my father's family there. So I passed a very pleasant time in his hospitable quarters and we sat up long into the night exchanging information, in

* Thomas Spence.

12

which I was greatly the gainer, for he was a chief clerk shortly expecting promotion, and had seen service all over the southern and Montreal departments of the Company. With him I exchanged Mr. Lane's alleged "buffalo runner," the aggravating "Rouge," for a pony of a different kind and color— *noir* this time, and he supplied me with plenty of flour and other food for the trip to replace that devoured by the Twin Wolves of Saskatchewan.

Next day—the 11th—I bade my kind host farewell, and we never chanced, in our roving over the plains which followed for years after, to meet again; but I rejoice to know that Mr. Watt is still hale and hearty in the enjoyment of a liberal pension as a retired factor and resides in his native and beloved Isles.

Join Swan River Men.

I only travelled with Dufresne and his tripmates till noon, when I joined two men belonging to Swan River district who were returning after obtaining medical aid at Fort Garry. They were two fine young Metis named Antoine Genaille and Henri Hibert, and had a horse and cart with their baggage. I was sorry to leave Dufresne, who was lively and amusing, with his laggard fellow-travellers, but both Antoine and Henri spoke good English and were smart and obliging. Next day we caught up a brigade of Company's carts belonging to Fort Pelly, under a guide named William Johnstone, taking flour and American goods to the district. Two of Johnstone's cart drivers had deserted him on the way, so he kept Genaille, and Hibert and I pushed on ahead, after we had remained long enough with the brigade to use their frying pans in cooking enough bannock to serve us to Fort Ellice.

The magnificent monotony of the level plain was now relieved and varied by wooded vale and hill, over which we moved at a pace which was exhilarating after the dull lagging behind the Saskatchewan men's cart. We had good shooting, too, and the tough dried meat disappeared from the bill of fare and was replaced by fine prairie chicken and ducks, which Henri cooked in woodland style to perfection.

At first Henri was very polite, but also very silent; but when he saw that I was glad to fall into the ways of the voyageurs and to be fond of fun, he completely unbent, and before we reached Fort Ellice he and I had formed a friend-ship which lasted till his death many years afterwards. It was from him that I first learnt the many good qualities, generally unsuspected by strangers, of this kindhearted, hos-pitable people, so ignorant of books other than the great book of nature, and such splendid travellers and hunters.

CHAPTER X.

SWAN RIVER DISTRICT.

BRANDON.

WE crossed to the south side of the Assiniboine River by fording it above the " Grand Rapids," below what is now the city of Brandon, which has perpetuated the name of the old fur trade post, " Brandon House." This famous post was, according to Doctor Bryce (who gives an interesting description of its site, seventeen miles below the city), established by the Hudson's Bay Company in 1794, and remained their chief business centre for twenty years, when it was burnt.

Probably the Hudson's Bay Company reached Brandon by crossing from Lake Manitoba to the Assiniboine at Portage la Prairie, in which vicinity another post was begun two years later, and—to quote Doctor Bryce again—" the Red River proper was taken possession of by the Hudson's Bay Company in 1799."

As an illustration of the immense distances travelled over by the early fur traders in the ordinary pursuit of their business, I may cite the fact that Governor Vincent, of Albany, was wont to visit Brandon to obtain buffalo products for his district, and married a wife born there, from whom the highly respected Truthwaite family of St. Andrews is descended.

The Brandon House was resorted to by a number of different tribes, but principally depended upon the Assiniboines and Crees for its fur trade. To it also came the Mandans of the Missouri, bringing, besides the skins and meat of the buffalo, their Indian corn for sale. These interesting Indians were painted and described by the famous artist, Catlin, and believed by him to be descended from the Welsh, who hun-

178

dreds of years before sailed out into the western ocean and never more were heard of.

Brandon continued to be a post of importance and the only one of the Hudson's Bay Company's "Upper Red River District" till 1831, when the Northern Department Council held at York Factory directed, "in order to protect the trade of the Assiniboines and Crees from American opposition on the Missouri, a new post be established at or in the neighborhood of Beaver Creek, to be called Fort Ellice." At the same time Doctor Todd was transferred from Brandon to the new post, and old Brandon was left under the charge of a veteran North-West partner, Mr. James Hughes. This old gentleman had been well known in the struggle between the rival companies at Edmonton, and, having retired with a competency, had lost all his money, so that in his old age he was obliged to ask re-employment in the fur trade, which had been granted in the capacity of clerk, on the understanding that he should have no expectation of regaining his old status as a "wintering partner" in the united company.

The names of "Upper Red River District" and Brandon disappeared off the minutes in 1832, when Mr. Hughes succeeded Doctor Todd at Fort Ellice, and that establishment was added to Swan River district, in command of which Doctor Todd succeeded Chief Factor Colin Robertson, with headquarters at Fort Pelly.

Chief Factor Colin Robertson.

This gentleman at the time of his taking furlough in 1832, in anticipation of his retirement from the service, was the senior officer who sat next Governor Simpson in Council, Northern Department, and signed its minutes immediately after the governor. His name appears sixth on the seniority list of chief factors created in 1821 in the United Hudson's Bay and North-West Companies. Originally he had been a Nor'-Wester, but he was won over by Lord Selkirk and became his guide and counsellor, at the same time joining the Hudson's Bay service. By the North-West partisans he was hated accordingly, and feared too, for he was a man of great physical and mental power and experience. Under Robertson the Hudson's Bay Company adopted the Nor'-West Company system of employing French-Canadian voyageurs to carry the war into the northern preserves discovered by his former associates. The best account given of his deeds and his captivity in the hands of the Nor'-Westers is that of Miss Laut, who has made splendid use of his hitherto unpublished writings in her "Conquest of the Great North-West." There also will be found how the able and experienced Robertson, who (by the stupidity which has too often characterized the Hudson's Bay home authorities in such appointments) was merely adviser and "wet nurse" for the ill-chosen greenhorn, Governor Semple, had unavailingly warned him of the preparations being made by the Nor'-Westers to prevent any further pillage of their posts and property. Like that of many another of these old-time worthies, the life of Colin Robertson and the prominent part he took in the strife would make a large and interesting book of itself.

JOHN RICHARDS McKAY, P.M.

In 1833 Mr. Hughes yielded the charge of Fort Ellice to Mr. John Richards McKay, postmaster, under whom the trade was extended greatly, and among so many tribes as to require the service of interpreters speaking seven different languages. The remnant of the Mandans came to it at peril of their lives, and it was resorted to by natives from a wide tract of country quite regardless of the international boundary, with no posts nearer than Portage la Prairie on the east, Fort Pelly on the north, and Carlton House on the northwest, and none on British territory to the west.

Over this wide domain Mr. McKay held sway as chief for a generation. The admiration of the many tribes who resorted to Fort Ellice was aroused by feats in which he displayed his skill and dexterity as a horseman, a swordsman, and a sure shot, and by other sprightly and spectacular accomplishments. His friendliness and fair-dealing, his courage and cordiality, combined with his knowledge of Indian character (he was, I think, born at Moose Factory), and his tact in managing the natives established an influence over the tribes which descended with the name of " Little Bear Skin " to his sons and grandsons, who were, and still are, worthy scions of this worthy sire. One of these is Mr. Thomas McKay, who took so brave and loyal a leading part during the Saskatchewan rebellion of 1885, and who ably represented Prince Albert in the North-West Assembly for many years. Another is the talented James McKay, K.C., M.P. for that constituency in the Dominion House.

FORT ELLICE.

Henri and I journeyed on pleasantly, following the well-marked wheel ruts of the cart track which branched off the broader road which led the buffalo hunters to the Turtle and Moose Mountains. We met and saw no other people on the way, and no notable sight was seen until the 16th, when big prairie fires arose ahead, in which we were soon enveloped. That sight alone was worth making the long voyage to see, and one of my boyish objects in persisting, against the wishes of my people, in coming to Rupert's Land, was accomplished. That night the grandeur and magnificence of the display of fireworks extending on every side over the rolling prairies far exceeded the conception formed from the printed descriptions which I had so often devoured.

Next morning early we put on a spurt and dashed to the front gate of Fort Ellice, in the style which Henri informed me was the fashion of the country. No one coming out of the master's house to meet us, as was also the fashion of the country, I was looking round for a hitching post before dismounting, when in there galloped in hot haste a dashing horseman, clad in buckskin shirt and leggings, carrying a gun crossways in front in the bend of his left arm, and a quirt dangling from the wrist of his right. His blackened face proclaimed that he had passed through the fires raging around the fort. Approaching me he jumped off his restive steed, and I followed suit, each advanced with outstretched right hand while we led our steeds with the left. "Mr. Cowie, I presume," said the horseman, and just as our hands came within grasping reach his horse reared backward and dragged him back. So did mine with me. We made some other attempts, indulging at the same time in some far from complimentary language to our respective steeds for their lack of manners, ere completing the greeting. We then had a laugh at the not unusual interruption of a ceremony strictly enjoined by "the fashion of the country," and intended to be observed with dignity proper to the occasion. I often afterwards enjoyed the ludicrous sight of two polite Metis, with their respective steeds attached to their left hands, eagerly advancing with "*Bon jour, mon ami*," checked back and pouring out a succession of "*Sacrés*" and "*Diables*" the moment thereafter.

In this manner I made the acquaintance of my good friend Walter J. Strickland Traill, apprentice clerk of one year's seniority to me in that grade. He had been out since the day before with Chief Trader William McKay and men fighting the prairie fire, and saving the haystacks, not yet hauled in to the yard at the fort, where a large herd of cattle was kept. In former times, ere the buffalo had been gradually driven further west, they were frequently so numerous right at Fort Ellice, as to require watchmen round the hay-yard to keep and drive them out of it, in winter when the snow was deep.

Fort Ellice was beautifully situated at a point on the level of the prairie where the deep and picturesque valley of the Beaver Creek joined the broad valley of the Assiniboine River, which could be seen wending its winding way for miles to and fro in the parklike bottom lands to join the Red River at "The Forks," by which name, or its equivalent in French and Indian, Fort Garry was known throughout the great plains. Pointed pickets of round spruce, about fifteen feet high and eight inches to nine inches in diameter, surrounded a square in the rear of which, facing the front gate, stood a large and commodious two-storey house, occupied as officers' quarters, and containing a large Indian reception hall, and an office off which the clerk had his bedroom. On the west side of the square there was a row of one-storey houses occupied by the men and their families, with a workshop next the front pickets. Facing these on the opposite side of the square was a similar row of stores, for provisions, harness, furs, and trading goods. In the middle was a fur-press and a tall flagstaff, on which the British red ensign, with "H.B.C." on the fly, was hoisted on Sundays, holidays and in honor of visitors. On this occasion I was the recipient of that honor for the first time.

WALTER TRAILL.

Traill ushered me into his quarters, where I met a warm welcome and enjoyed a long talk, the precursor of many more I had in that same room with his successors in after years. And here again there was evidence of the breed of the Orkney Isles in Rupert's Land, for the name Traill had been for ages an honored one there and borne by leading lairds, one of whom as the Magnus Troil of "The Pirate" had been immortalized by Sir Walter Scott. But Traill could not claim the complete distinction of coming from Orkney, for his father, with other army officers who had fought the French at Waterloo, had settled near Lakefield, Ontario, with his English lady, whose sister, Mrs. Moody, also the wife of a member of a very old Orcadian family, and herself were the talented authoresses of well known books on settling in the backwoods of Canada. Literary talent ran in his mother's family, for their maiden name was Strickland, and their sister, Agnes, the celebrated authoress of "The Lives of the Queens of England." Traill

183

was a tall, restlessly active fellow, who inherited the maternal talent, as our later correspondence amply showed. He had preceded me as clerk at Qu'Appelle—"Cape Hell," he said, was the English halfbreed pronunciation. His elder brother, William Edward, had joined the service two years before him, had preceded him at Fort Ellice, and was that fall placed in charge of the wintering post of Egg Lake, north of Touchwood Hill post, but subject to Fort Pelly.

Traill's talk was of swift hunting horses, on which he had chased the red deer, assisted by train dogs, for hours, till they were brought to bay. This was splendid sport. Lynxes were also hunted in the same way in the fall, and were fine eating—like mutton, he said. I thought that a cat, wild or tame, could not possibly be good to eat, but he assured me that only greenhorns thought so. But Traill's talk was not all of sport. He was a clever, energetic young fellow, full of progressive ideas for the reformation of the Hudson's Bay antiquated methods of doing many things, which he had seen better ways of doing in Canada, or thought theoretically might be done in a new way. But the whole force of public opinion in that day and generation was extremely conservative, and one venting such radical ideas was regarded as a presumptuous greenhorn to be quizzed out of them by the older officials. Moreover, such innovations were regarded with utter contempt and abhorrence by the men and natives especially, who, when he tried to get them to do something in some style they had never seen, opposed either the most provoking passive resistance, or inertia or stupidity—real or assumed—thereto. So his own everlasting activity and impatience of sloth and slowness in others, while they gained the esteem of his superiors, led to his having lots of trouble with those under his orders. I never met a Company's man who was so tirelessly and zealously devoted to their business.

Of course I did not discover all about Traill during the first few hours after the beginning of our friendship, which, although we have wandered many a weary foot since those days of auld lang syne, has continued to this day.*

"Billy" McKay, Chief Trader.

Before dinner time at noon, the Chief Trader, accompanied by his good wife, who loved life in the open, returned with his fire-fighters, and successful. William McKay, if not born at Fort Ellice, had been brought up there in the great days when half of the whole business of trading in the famous Swan River district was done under his father, the Mr. John Richards McKay before mentioned. "Billy," as the Indians, who had known him from boyhood, fondly called him, had inherited the popularity of his father, with his tact and talent as a trader, but the fiery blood of his dashing father had been tempered by that of a gentle mother of the old Hudson's Bay family of Ballenden. Struck by his character and conduct, a British nobleman, who had penetrated into these distant wilds for buffalo hunting, described him as one of nature's gentlemen, in which opinion all who knew him concurred. In his family he was a good husband and a fond father. Ever, with devotion to his duty to the Company, he was just and kind to the Indians, into whose affairs he brought the sympathy of knowledge, while his well-known courage prevented their attempting to impose upon him. He was the model of what a really good Indian trader should be. The only guile I ever heard him accused of by anyone was in his horse-trading operations, which were most extensive, for these were not only in the way of everyday business with the Indians, but also, as the Fort was a half-way house between Fort Garry and Carlton on the main route, with passing traders, freighters and other travellers who resorted to him to buy or exchange horses to enable them to pursue their journey.

* After leaving Fort Ellice in the summer of 1870, Traill was placed in charge of the Company's business in the American portion of the Red River, with headquarters at Grand Forks. He has since, for many years, resided in the Kalispel Valley.

Horses, too, like furs, formed the currency of the country. The tricks of the horse trade are universally practised throughout the equine world; and men in it look on it and enjoy it as a game of skill, a contest of wits in which the wittiest wins, without much regard to the quality of the animal he may succeed in palming off on his opponent. In this game " Billy " had the wonderful advantage of always being able to recognize any horse he had ever seen, no matter how altered by change in condition, season, or age. So he was always ready for and keenly enjoyed a horse trade. Of course he only exercised his art in this line when engaged with a foeman worthy of his steel, and there were many who were great experts, or considered themselves so, amongst the traders and hunters passing and frequenting Fort Ellice. He was fond of a joke, too, and of quizzing those who had come to shear and had got shorn, when he met them again.

REV. THOMAS COOK.

Outside the fort, but near at hand, there was a Church of England mission, under the Rev. Thomas Cook, who was Mrs. McKay's brother. The wandering habits of the Indians, who had to follow the roaming buffalo for their living, must have been a great hindrance to this good old missionary at Fort Ellice, and he was moved to Whitemud River, not far from Portage la Prairie, within a year or so after, to minister to a settled congregation. At Fort Ellice he certainly was favored by the assistance of Mr. and Mrs. McKay, and had it been possible to keep the Indians for any time around the fort, another instance of the power of the trader, when so minded, to influence the Indians to accept Christianity might have occurred. Many of the successful missions throughout the Indian country seemed to owe quite as much to the assistance of a Hudson's Bay trader of the same persuasion as to the devotion of the missionary himself.

Buffalo " Go West."

Just as old Brandon House in 1830 had become too far from the general habitat of the buffalo for the convenience of the hunters, so had Fort Ellice become to a large extent already in 1867. The first step in diminishing its supremacy was taken when the post at Big Touchwood Hills, on the Saskatchewan trail, was established about fifteen years before. This was followed by an outpost from Fort Ellice, on the prairie, south of the site at the fishing lakes upon which Fort Qu'-Appelle was built by Mr. Peter Hourie, postmaster, about 1863. Fort Ellice, too, had its regular fur-trading outpost in the wooded Riding Mountains, from which it derived large quantities of fine furs trapped by the splendid hunters of the Saulteaux tribe, of whom the family of the Little Bones (Ouk-an-nay-sic) was the most expert. The buffalo hunters were provided for by trading parties sent out after them in the summer, and wintering at Turtle or Moose Mountain, near the herds. But the many tribes, which had resorted to the fort when its trade was at its zenith under Mr. McKay's father, had become customers to Fort Union on the Missouri, and to the posts at Touchwood Hills and Qu'Appelle, leaving appertaining to it only the Wood Indians before mentioned and other Saulteaux who followed the buffalo on the plains. The Mandans, who first occasionally frequented Fort Ellice after Brandon House ceased to exist, had long since become a tradition, and tales were told of the attacks made on them by the other tribes when visiting the place.

The Sioux.

To make up for these lost tribes, a band of Sioux-Yanktons, who declared that they, while trying to farm in peace, had been forced by the hostiles to rise against the Americans during the massacre of the whites in Minnesota, had taken refuge from the vengeance of the Americans by coming to

Fort Ellice when others of their tribe came to Portage la Prairie.

These Sioux were very different from the other Indians about the place, in their active and thrifty habits. Instead of taking contracts to make hay and cut cordwood and expending all their art in trying to secure advances in full before the work was even begun, far less done, the Sioux went to work first and saved their earnings for a time of need. My own experience with them subsequently was that they secured in time of abundance of buffalo provision for the winter and for other times of scarcity, while our own Crees, Assiniboines and Saulteaux were eager to sell every bit of provisions to us or other traders with no thought for the morrow. One of the most industrious among these Sioux at Fort Ellice was one named Enoch, who spoke good English and sang the hymns he had learnt from the Methodist missionaries in Minnesota, and practised the Christian religion too. He was the leader of several such among them and was a really good and respectable man.

PAZ-ZY-O-TAH—BUFFOON OR FIEND?

Another was a most amusing fellow, named " Paz-zy-o-tah," who made the Indian hall of the fort his lounging place. He seemed to be simply a lounger and fond of doing and saying things to make people laugh, regardless of the personal dignity assumed by most Indians. Of course he could not read English, but whenever he saw a newspaper lying on the table he would take it up, and, solemnly holding it upside down, would sit for long pretending to be deeply engrossed in its contents. If he thought he had, by these means, imposed upon or impressed any envious and jealous Saulteaux with his erudition, he would look round behind the paper and give one of us a wink with a merry eye. He always acted, as far as we ever saw or heard at Fort Ellice, the lazy, though innocent, good-natured and amusing fellow; but it was whispered in secret subsequently that he had distinguished himself by the active part he had taken in roasting the Minnesota settlers' babies in cookstoves, and in tying pairs of babies together by the legs and leaving them hanging by these on a washline to die. I sincerely hope that this accusation was untrue, for he was apparently one of the merriest and most good-natured Indians I ever had the rather unusual pleasure of knowing.

A GOOD TIME.

My good fellow-traveller, Henri Hibert, belonged to Fort Pelly, to which he had to proceed direct. Mr. McKay's men were all required for the regular duties of the place and busy preparing for the winter, the parties to winter at Riding and Turtle Mountains having been already despatched. So he had to detain me till some Indian suitable to guide me to Qu'-Appelle should chance to visit the place. The weather still continued perfect, and the Indians' meteorological predictions by observations of the flora and fauna, all indicated its long continuance. Mr. and Mrs. McKay were hospitality itself. The mess table was laden with all kinds of wild flesh and fowl, and gold-eyes from the river. There was also a variety of preserved wild fruit put up by the skilful hands of the good housewife, and the vegetable garden had supplied everything in that line excellently. A large number of cows furnished delicious cream, milk and butter. Traill's company was good, and the chief trader was old and deep in the lore and legend of the fur trade, and everything connected with it. So I had a really good time at Fort Ellice, and I do not remember feeling very anxious to continue my voyage to the station to which I was appointed by the minutes of the Council of that year, which I had copied into the ponderous tome at York Factory, from which I may now give the appointments and those of the interpreters whose names do not appear in the minutes.

APPOINTMENTS FOR SWAN RIVER DISTRICT OUTFIT, 1867:

(NOTE.—Those marked (*) are still living.)

COMMISSIONED OFFICERS.

Chief Factor Robert Campbell, Fort Pelly, in charge of district.
Chief Trader William McKay (c), Fort Ellice.

FORT PELLY.

Robert Campbell, chief factor.
*William Thomson Smith, clerk, accountant of district, (now London, Ontario).
*Thomas McKay, postmaster (now of Prince Albert).
William Daniel, district guide and interpreter.

FORT ELLICE.

William McKay (c), chief trader.
*Walter J. S. Traill, apprentice clerk (now Kalispel, Montana).

FORT QU'APPELLE.

*Archibald McDonald, clerk (now retired chief factor near Vancouver).
*Isaac Cowie, apprentice clerk (Winnipeg).
John McNab Ballenden McKay, interpreter.
*William Kennedy, apprentice interpreter (Prince Albert).

TOUCHWOOD HILLS.

Joseph Finlayson, clerk.
Peter La Pierre, interpreter.

EGG LAKE.

*William Edward Traill, apprentice clerk (now a retired chief trader, Meskanaw, Sask.).

SHOAL RIVER.

Adam McBeath, clerk.
*Angus McBeath, postmaster (now a pensioned clerk), Kildonan.

WATERHEN RIVER.

*Alexander Munro, interpreter (now a pensioned clerk, Minitonas).

FAIRFORD.

*Donald McDonald, interpreter (now clerk in charge there).

SWAN RIVER DISTRICT, 1867

Manitobah Post.

Ewan MacDonald, clerk.

*Duncan Matheson, apprentice clerk (now a retired "real" factor, Inverness, Scotland).

Angus Murray, interpreter.

Of the above some were only wintering posts, abandoned for the summer. For instance, Egg Lake was an outpost of Fort Pelly, and Waterhen of Manitobah Post. There was an outpost of Shoal River at Duck Bay, on Lake Winnipegosis; while under Manitobah Post salt was manufactured for Swan River and other districts at Salt Springs, Lake Winnipegosis. Fort Ellice had a regular winter outpost at Riding Mountain, besides flying posts wherever the buffalo were numerous, at such places as Turtle and Moose Mountains. The district in which the city of Brandon stands to-day was also in a fur-trade sense tributary to Fort Ellice. Similarly, buffalo hunting and trading parties were sent out from Qu'Appelle and Touchwood Hills, following the migrations of the herds in summer, and wintering at the nearest points to the herds, provided with wood.

The missionaries in Swan River district in the winter of 1867-8, were: Church of England—Rev. Thomas Cook, Fort Ellice; Rev. George Bruce, Fairford; Mr. Charles Pratt, catechist, Touchwod Hills; Rev. Luke Caldwell, Fort Pelly, and, I think, possibly, Rev. James Settee, at Manitobah Post. The Roman Catholic Church had missionaries on Lakes Manitoba and Winnipegosis; but the Rev. Father Decorby did not re-establish the mission at Qu'Appelle till 1868. Both he and the Rev. George Bruce are still on active service.

Gaelic Predominates.

Of the twenty Company's servants above named, all were of Scottish descent except Daniel and La Pierre, the one being an Irish and the other a French Metis. Other natives of the country of partly mixed origin were the chief trader,

13

McKay, his son Thomas, and his brother John (alias "Jerry"), also Mr. Finlayson and young Kennedy. The two Traills were born in Canada, and, like myself, proud of the old Norse strain in their blood. Smith was a Lowlander from St. Andrews, Fifeshire; about all the rest were pure Highlanders, whose mother tongue was Gaelic, and all born in the land of the mist and the mountains, except Mr. McBeth and his nephew, Angus, who hailed from that transplanted parish of Sutherlandshire—Kildonan, on the Red River. The two McDonalds were brothers of the Glencoe branch, while the chief of the district was a descendant of that Campbell of Glenlyon who almost extirpated their clan in the infamous Massacre of Glencoe. Of course all of these Highlanders "talked the two talks," and the interpreters, McDonald, Munro and Murray, with the facility in acquiring a language in which the Celt so excels the Saxon, all spoke the Indian language fluently as their employment indicates. The McKays and Mr. Finlayson had a smattering of Gaelic, too, in addition to the Indian dialects, and French, which they all spoke fluently, and in which the latter wrote as well.

It had been my lot to have never heard Gaelic in the North Isles nor even in Aberdeen and Edinburgh, except a chance expression. My mother, whose people had lived for two centuries in Shetland, and who loved me to read Sir Walter Scott's novels and to explain every word I did not understand to me would sometimes talk of her people, the Greigs, who came originally from Perthshire, and belonged to the clan McGregor. Occasionally my father talked of his grandfather—my namesake—as a gigantic Highlander of Huntly, who wielded his claymore for Bonnie Prince Charlie at Culloden; but as a boy I had been imbued with the idea prevalent in the old Norse archipelago that the Scots of the mainland were not our kin, although we all belonged to Britain, for which the Islesmen had fought as fiercely on the sea as ever did Highlander or Lowlander on land. In Shetland, the Scots, too, as a rule, were not nearly so well liked as were the

English, in whose ships the Shetlanders always preferred to sail, for the Islesmen had about the same reason as the Irish to dislike " foreigners " from the mainland, who came to convert their commons into enclosed sheepfarms, and to collect tithes and taxes. Besides, Scots officials tried to interfere with the right to smuggle, inherited from the freebooting rovers of the seas by the Shetlanders, and considered a profitable and meritorious means of spoiling the Egyptians who oppressed them.

OLD HIGHLAND FEUDS.

So when these Gaelic-speaking gentry got together and began bragging about the Highlanders and saying that a Shetlander was not even to be classed with the common Lowlanders whom the Gael despised, I felt all the humiliation of an oppressed minority, and that too in a strange land. But I soon had my revenge, and it was sweet, for in their excitement and boastings the member of one clan would say something to revive the slumbering memories of hereditary feuds, and then each clan gave the other its far from complimentary character to me in English as referee. In such exciting moments the hereditary hatred of the McDonalds of Glencoe against the Campbells of Glenlyon was only tempered by the consideration that the representative of Glenlyon was the Company's chief factor in command of Swan River district, whom all good and true Company's men were dutifully bound to honor and obey. For the moment the cause of the Company called, every ancestral and personal feud and ill-feeling was forgotten, the war of words ceased, and every clansman was ready to unite with his comrades in the Company with as much loyalty and devotion as ever his forebears had shown in following their chiefs to the field in their own and every other country where Highlanders had won renown.

CHAPTER XI.

QU'APPELLE.

LEAVE FORT ELLICE.

AFTER six pleasant days spent at Fort Ellice, on October 23rd, 1867, I set out for Fort Qu'Appelle, on horseback, with my baggage, consisting of two *cassettes* of the regulation pattern, made in Lerwick though, and containing a good outfit of clothes, and a few first-class books, several being on medicine and surgery, also a few surgical instruments. As the weight allowed an apprentice clerk was only two hundred pounds baggage, nothing but the most useful articles was in my outfit. Mr. McKay had kindly added to my bedding the buffalo robe which the Company supplied to everyone in the district. With provisions for three days besides, the cart was light and its driver, Old Lamack, rode in it.

Lamack was counted among the Saulteaux Indians frequenting the post. On the Bay he would have been called one of the "Homeguards," for he never went far from it, and was available for odd trips or work which haughtier, or lazier, hunters would not condescend to perform. I rather think from his appearance and genial character that he had some European blood in him, probably French, as his name would indicate. Mr. McKay informed me that although Lamack understood enough English to catch the meaning of anything I might require of him on the trip, he could not be induced to speak it except when, after he had been treated to a dram, he wanted another so much as to ask for it in English.

INDIANS AGAINST BI-LINGUALISM.

In this respect Lamack followed the custom of his countrymen, who considered it bad form to appear to comprehend

194

DR. WILLIAM COWAN.

WALTER J. S. TRAILL.

A German Noble Apprentice Clerk,
COUNT WILLIAM BERNSTORFF,
Lieutenant 16th Hussars, Schleswig-
Holstein.

CAPTAIN HENRY BISHOP, OF THE
Prince Rupert,
A splendid British Sailor.

any language but their own, and—being exceedingly sensitive
to ridicule themselves and prone to ridicule others—they considered it undignified to speak in a strange tongue, even when
they were quite competent to make themselves understood in
it. Besides, an Indian who had the gift of speech in French
and English and used it freely was very frequently a worthless fellow upon whom neither the Indians nor the whites
placed confidence. But of course this did not apply to the
halfbreeds, who generally took pride in the number of different languages and dialects in which they could make themselves more or less understood.

Tom Lamack.

My guide and guardian on the trip was accompanied by his
little son, Tom, a lad of ten, who, proudly carrying the pater-
nal flintlock in the fore front of our procession, showed
wonderful skill in laying low rabbits and prairie chickens
along the way. He was a smart, active boy, of the true hunting breed. But, instead of later on taking to the bush or the
prairie and following the paths of his ancestors, Tom came
to be employed by the Company as a cart-driver in summer
and a dog-driver in winter. In this capacity he made voyages
to the seats of civilization in the Red River and Minnesota,
and casting away the breech-clout as the sign of his emancipa-
tion from Indian customs and pursuits, and easily acquiring
and using English, he became a wild voyageur instead of a
respectable trapper and hunter. The coming of the white
settlers was bad for such men as poor Tom, and in a drinking
bout with a fellow Saulteau, Josiah Matoney, near Fort
Qu'Appelle, in the fall of 1894, Tom shot and killed Matoney.
Making a daring and successful escape from the Mounted
Police, Tom took refuge amongst his kind, who harbored him
until finally, after many hairbreadth escapes, he sought concealment in Montana. Eight years after shooting Matoney—
very probably in self-defence—he was arrested at Butte and

brought to Regina. After a trial before Judge Richardson, in which the Crown provided Mr. James Balfour as counsel for the defence, Tom was found guilty of murder and sentenced to be hanged in six weeks. But before the date (June 27, 1902), arrived, the Governor-General commuted the sentence to imprisonment for life, which Tom Lamack began to undergo at Stony Mountain Penitentiary, and conducted himself as a model prisoner. For so wild a bird to be cooped up in such a cage must have been worse than the bitterness of death. After suffering imprisonment for seven years and being reduced thereby to a decrepit old man, the authorities mercifully released him. But the confinement had been too long, and after lingering for about a year on Pasqua's Reserve, near Qu'Appelle, poor Tom departed on his last long voyage.

WOODED COUNTRY.

The cart trail from the fort led first through what might be called—comparatively speaking—a wooded country, in which among the prevailing poplar a stray oak and a chance spruce might be seen. Soon the woods were gathered into groves, like islands in an undulating sea of grass. All these wore the glorious hues of autumn, under a bright sun and azure sky flecked with fleecy clouds. The bracing breeze by day and the comfort of the blazing fire of our bivouac, night and morning, and the shortening day alone betokened the lateness of the season. Lamack wished to make a quick trip to get out to his trapping grounds, and I was anxious to see the end of my long and slow journey, although I was thoroughly enjoying it. So we did not waste time in shooting, merely firing at anything that came in our way, of which we got an abundance which might soon have laden the cart had not the splendid appetites of the party disposed of it otherwise. In these feasting feats, mine, though grand, fell far short of those of my companions.

THE INDIAN GUN

An Ancient Firearm.

I was also outclassed as far in the getting of game as in
the " getting away with it." The Lamacks led the way, sitting in the cart, and keeping the pony at a steady jog-trot,
while I followed behind, falling back at a walk and then coming up at a canter. Nothing in the way of fur or feather
ahead and along the trail escaped the keen eyes of the
Lamacks. I think they scented as well as saw the game, for
Tom would leap out of the cart (their pony would not stand
fire) and bang away at objects quite invisible to me and then
rush into the brush or long grass to retrieve the rabbit or bird
he had shot. When we unhitched and unsaddled, while the
old man made fire and cooked, Tom and I would set out to
shoot, but, even on ponds where the ducks were quite visible,
the little lad with the flintlock, longer than himself, always
did better than I with my double barrel percussion gun,
loaded with four times the quantity of shot. I had won a
marksman's badge, and had been officially gazetted as one of
the best shots in the rifle corps, and, besides, had shot lots
of wildfowl at home, so I wondered if my own gun were not
to blame, and if Tom's long gun were the better. Anyhow
I wanted to see how the flintlock went, and so I tried the
family weapon at a mark. The sight was coarse, the stock
straight, and the trigger very hard. At last when the flint
struck the steel, sparks as from an anvil flew in every
direction, followed at what appeared a long interval by a flash
in the pan, and then by a kick like a horse, for while the
native did spare shot he did not spare powder, and wadded it
hard, too. Of course the strong pull, and the startling flare-
up quite spoilt my aim, and I never did get up to the
use of the " Indian gun," nor get over my surprise at the fine
shooting the natives did with it.

Long Barrels.

These guns came in three lengths, three and one-half feet
barrel being the longest I ever saw or heard of, although

there still lingers a legend, which has descended from old detractors of the fur traders, that beaver skins were exchanged by the Indians for guns lengthened enormously so that the pile of beaver skins to reach from the ground to the muzzle—which was the measure—would be so much higher. The shorter ones, two and one-half feet, were those most in use on the prairies, and these were usually still further shortened by the Indians, for lightness as well as concealment under the robes or blankets they wore, and because in running buffalo with a good horse the hunter got so close as to singe the buffalo when he fired.

The wooden stock of these guns ran out under the barrel to within an inch or so of the muzzle. The groove for the ramrod had brass clasps at intervals and two brazen serpents decorated the grip of the stock. To these " Brummagem " decorations the Indians added others of their own device, in brass-headed tacks, without which the weapon seemed unconsecrated in their eyes.

ELK ANTLER HILL.

As we went on the poplar groves became more sparsely scattered over " the parklands," the ponds shrank in size and were less frequent and of these many had been dried up during the long lasting fine weather. So for our second night's camp we had to reach Elk Antler hill, alongside of which a pond generally yielded in such times a certain water supply, just as the trail passed on to the bare, dry prairie through which Ay-cap-pow's Creek runs into the Qu'Appelle. Expecting to find water as usual we unhitched on the knoll, and prepared for the night, while Tom went down to the old pond to fill the kettles. Suddenly he hailed his father and they exchanged some mournful and complaining sounds. Tom came back with the kettles, driving the ponies, which had been hobbled, back from the watering-place. The old man began loading the cart again and turned to me, saying, " Cawin gaycou nepe," which, of course, I did not understand, so, impatiently bursting the barrier of his dignity, he said, "None water, boy," and signed that we would have to go on till we found it.

CALLING RIVER.

We had made a good day's journey for the time of year already, but we had to travel far into the night before reaching the banks of the Qu'Appelle valley, into which, by a steep trail in a coulee, we descended, and were soon camped on the Calling River.

Next morning—October 26th—we forded the river a little above our camp, at a place where a cart had evidently been hauled up the short steep bank before. Lamack's pony found the place too steep, and both he and his boy waxed wroth at the poor animal's inability to haul up the cart with its load. They began to unmercifully belabor the pony, when I intervened and made them take the little trouble of unloading and carrying the stuff up the bank. Then the little "plug" eagerly and easily hauled up the cart. The old chap looked sulky, and some not very complimentary remarks about me appeared to pass between him and his son, but they were not translated into English, so neither my bones nor those of the faithful pony were broken.

We followed up the wide and beautiful valley on a good, well-beaten trail, till afternoon, when Lamack, now all smiles, managed to make me understand that if I pushed on ahead on horseback I might reach the fort before bedtime. He drew on the ground a line representing the river, which expanded into a lake, followed by another line to another lake, at the end of which, he said, "McDonald," meaning my future boss. As I could not very easily get lost with such a clear course in the deep valley before me, I was only too glad to set off ahead at a gallop to reach my station at last. At that time, however, I did not know the marvellous power of endurance of the Indian pony, and as the one I bestrode was very willing, and I did not like to impose on him, it was dark before we had passed the first lake. Riding on a little beyond I saw a light across the valley for which I made, the pony following a path which took us to a ford, through which we splashed and shortly after stopped before a little shanty from which the light of a blazing fire shone through the open door, before which stood the occupant, Thomas Favel, *dit* Mango.

FAVEL A FISHERMAN.

Favel was making his fall fishery and preserving the fine whitefish he was catching in the usual way, by spitting them with willow wands above the tail in tens, and hanging them up, heads down, on a stage to drain and dry. Although it was his busy season he at once offered to show me " a short cut " to the fort. The night was dark as he led me up the steep south side of the valley on to the prairie above. He was surprised that I should get off and lead my good pony up the hill, saying it was no use having a horse if you did not ride him, and I afterwards discovered that dismounting to spare the horse in a steep place, going up or down, was generally considered undignified and even cowardly by the bold, hard riders of the plains. I also found by later experience that at the end of a long, quick journey my mount, by being eased at hard places, would remain comparatively fresh, while those who stuck to their saddles everywhere often had to get off and run behind, driving their ponies, which could no longer bear them. Another despised custom, imported from home, was that of rising in the stirrups at a trot whenever I found my pony beginning to fag. This immediately eased and put fresh life into the animal. And I was abundantly rewarded for my care and consideration, too, for the relief from using a tired steed enabled me to come off a long journey " fresh as paint " and in good humor, whilst my companions were often in the opposite state of body and mind.

ABOUT THE PONIES.

Although I had the advantage from childhood of being used to the pet ponies for which my native isles are famous, of course, I had much to learn about the ponies of the prairies and the wonderful things they and their masters could perform. Such a brute as Mr. Lane had given me at White Horse Plain, in " Rouge," would have tried the patience of the most saintly member of the Society for the Prevention of Cruelty to Animals; but he had probably been the victim of a course of brutal treatment and so trained as to do nothing except under the most violent compulsion. A great many Indians were horribly cruel to their ponies, but the Metis were much more humane, especially caring for their splendidly trained buffalo runners. Owing to their style of riding most of the Indians' ponies had sore backs, and too many of those of the Metis and the Company likewise suffered in that way, but not to the same extent. Collar galls on the carters were also strongly in evidence, and their prevention and alleviation was a chief duty of those in charge of a train.

But to return to my journey, after this lapse into talking horse, which was a perennial subject with the people who lived and moved and had their being among horses and buffalo, with whom I was about to sojourn for seven long years. After ascending the wooded slope from the valley to the upland prairie, Mango led me over it for a mile or two and then plunged down into a deep and steep ravine, by a path through the bush, to the borders of the lake, then across low ridges and shallow intervening valleys, till we emerged upon the flat bottom land between the second and third lake, on which the Qu'Appelle Post is situated—I use the present tense, for the lineal successor of the old post, in the shape of a modern shop, stands on the same old site in this instance.

At the Fort.

It was a beautiful, calm, starlit night. The occasional neighing of a pony to his fellows, and the frequent barking and howling of dogs echoed from afar in the stilly night of the valley. Jets of sparks flying straight upwards, from fires being replenished for the night in the big open chimneys of the men's quarters, showed how near the fort lay before us. The night was clear, but in the shadow of the vale I could see no other indication of its existence. Not so the ever-watchful train dog, and while we were about a mile off one of these videttes, ever skirmishing round and seeking what he might devour, gave a warning bark, which he kept up at quickly increasing intervals as we advanced. By the time we got near, the whole pack in and about the place had taken the alarm and was in full cry, blending bark and yelp in a canine chorus which resounded and awoke all the echoes of the well-named " Echoing Valley." The next customary sign of the coming of strangers to a fort was the banging of doors as the inmates rushed out to see the cause of the loud clamor of the dogs. As some of these doors were made of parchment stretched tightly on a light wood frame, their banging resembled that of drums, and each person following at intervals— until the whole male, female and child population emerged— banged the doors behind them, so that we approached the front gate and entered it amid a chorus of the canine band now escorting us (punctuated by some snapping and snarling at myself, in whom they scented a stranger, while at Mango they barked not), and the intermittent banging of these door drums.

" Where is the master?" asked Mango of George Sandison, the watchman who had entrusted his function to the dogs.

" He is off spearing fish with Harper; but the mistress is in the big house."

So Mango led me to the door of the " big house," which faced the gate from the back of the square. In the Indian reception hall and office, on which the front door opened, the lady of the Qu'Appelle lakes gave me kindly welcome, and sent a messenger to Mr. McDonald to tell of my arrival. He soon came, accompanied by Harper, his man, bearing carefully the first coal oil lamp which had found its way into those regions, where candles made of buffalo tallow had been, and were, with

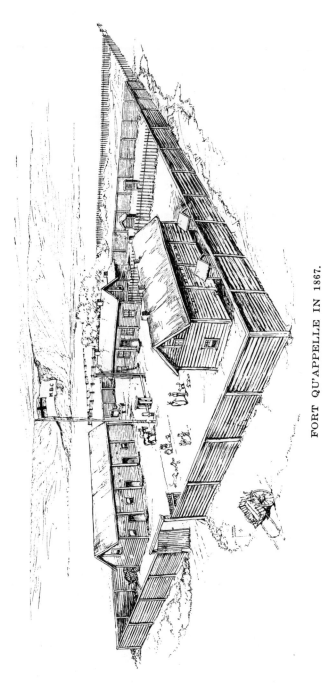

FORT QU'APPELLE IN 1867.

Specially drawn by Mr. Lawson, artist of the *Manitoba Free Press*, from rough sketches and diagrams of the Author.

this one brilliant exception, the illuminating medium. The lamp was Mrs. McDonald's own property, as well as the oil, for the Company had not yet come to supply such modern luxuries to its frontier establishments. So Harper had been very particular not to damage the lamp of his good mistress, which her husband had taken, as he had no birch bark or pine knots to lure the fish within reach of his trident, in the use of which he was an expert from the time he was a boy spearing salmon in the streams of his old home in the Highlands.

The McDonalds.

I was not only well welcomed as the new clerk, but also as the bearer of a packet of letters and other mail from Red River and the great world beyond. It was pretty late, but Harper soon had a good supper for me, and after a chat the master ushered me into my future quarters—a bedroom off the office, which the good Mrs. McDonald had beforehand made comfortable for the newcomer who had been expected for some time. Next morning I was introduced to the family of my new-found friends—John Archibald, who trotted about on his own little legs, and Donald Hogarth, who was still a baby in arms. I had always been fond of children, and soon made friends with these two, and passed in pleasure in their company many an hour which would have been weary otherwise in the time that followed. I am glad to say that both these little chaps are now big men, the elder still living at Qu'Appelle, and a member of the Saskatchewan Legislature, and the other a capitalist and president and director of several large financial companies in Winnipeg.

Mrs. McDonald came of the best of old Hudson's Bay people, her grandfather being the Governor Sinclair of York Factory, whose monument there was noticed in a previous chapter, and her father, another Orkneyman, widely respected as John Inkster, of Seven Oaks, and a councillor of the colony of Assiniboia. She had been well educated at Miss Mills' academy for young ladies in Red River, and as a devout member and active worker of the Church of England, at St. John's, and afterwards as the mistress at Manitobah Post, had been highly spoken of by the Bishop of Rupert's Land, when I told him that I was on my way to Qu'Appelle. To the wisdom and good counsel of such ladies of old Rupert's Land many a gentleman of the Hudson's Bay Company, besides Mr. McDonald, owed much of their success in overcoming difficulties, and in maintaining the Company's influence over the natives.

Mr. Archibald McDonald, chief clerk—as he then was—was already a man of mark on the plains of Swan River district, in which he served the Company " with courage and fidelity " from the time he came to the country on the ship *Prince of Wales,* in 1854, up to that of his retirement as their oldest chief factor on 31st May, 1911; and for the most of that long period with Qu'Appelle as his headquarters. It has been already said that he was of the clan McDonald, of Glencoe, and of course he was proud of it. He was also naturally proud of having been mentioned by the Right Hon. Edward Ellice, in replying to a question of the Select Committee on the Hudson's Bay Company, at London, in 1857, as one of the carefully selected young men sent out to be trained to the important position of Company's officers in Rupert's Land.

From the time that Mr. McGillivray and he arranged the union of their North-West Company with that of Hudson's Bay, Mr. Ellice had been the leading director. His reply to the question was: " I took great care to send out the best men we could find, principally from the north of Scotland, sons of country gentlemen, clergymen and of farmers, who had been educated at the schools and colleges of Scotland." He stated that the appointments were not made by individual directors, but by the Board on recommendation of one of them, and went on to say: " My son recommended a boy, the son of our forester in Scotland, brought up at our own school where he turned out a quick, clever boy; that boy has never seen a town, nor known anything of the vice and habits of towns; he has gone out as an apprentice, and will rise, if his merits justify the council in promoting him, to be one of our chief men." The steps by which this boy, Archibald McDonald, rose in fulfilment of the promise of his youth and of the prediction of the right honorable director are too many and too interesting for me to attempt to do justice to in these cursory memoirs. The details should come from the fountain-head himself, but, like the majority of makers of history, he may never be prevailed upon to write it.

THE ASSINIBOINES OR "STONIES."

Already in 1867 Mr. McDonald's absolute fearlessness and vehement energy had conferred upon him the post of honor on the frontier, back from which the Crees and Saulteaux were pushing the Blackfeet as they followed the buffalo into the country of the latter further west, while the Assiniboines of Wood Mountain and along the Missouri to the south, although nominally friendly, were a greater source of anxious uncertainty than the Blackfeet, who were open and certain enemies. These Stonies were of the hereditary caste of professional horse thieves from friend or foe, dexterous sneak thieves and pilferers from strong parties and open plunderers of weak ones, on the members of which they were wont to inflict the most beastly and degrading ill-usage, only letting them escape with their lives. The Assiniboines were also false friends of the Americans at the posts on the Missouri, and made it a practice to murder the haycutters and woodchoppers employed to provide for those establishments; and then they would take the mutilated bodies of their victims to the Americans and claim the reward (fifteen dollars I think was the amount) offered for such as had been killed by the Sioux, who were generally more or less at open war with the whites on the Missouri. The Stonies considered this a very smart thing to do, and boasted to our Indians of the base performance.

THE BLACKFEET.

Although the Blackfeet and their allies were friendly to the whites at Edmonton and Rocky Mountain House, they considered Fort Pitt, Carlton House, and the Touchwood Hills and Qu'Appelle posts and the trading and hunting parties belonging to all of them as allies of their enemies, the Crees, and objects of attack as such, because supplying with arms and ammunition these aggressive invaders of the hunting-grounds of the Blackfeet, the daring lifters, too, of their scalps and live stock.

RELIGION AND RUM.

Liquor from the American side of the line could be and was brought in amongst our Indians by "free" traders without hindrance, for when the Company passed their self-denying ordinances against its use in their business in Swan River and Saskatchewan districts, the Indians besought other traders to bring it to them. To quote Professor Youle Hind, of the Canadian exploring expedition of 1858, on this subject:—"When the Rev. James Settee arrived at the (Qu'Appelle) mission last autumn, the Crees of the Sandy Hills having received intelligence that the bishop had sent 'a praying man' to teach them the truths of Christianity, directed messengers to enquire whether 'the great praying father had sent plenty of rum; if so, they would soon become followers of the Whiteman's Manitou.' The messengers returned with the intelligence that the great praying father had not only omitted to send rum, but he hoped that the Plain Crees would soon abandon the practice of demanding rum in exchange for their pemmican and robes. The messengers were directed to return to the missionary with the announcement that 'if the great praying father did not intend to send any rum, the sooner he took his praying man away from the Qu'Appelle Lakes the better for him.'"

All the old hands who had been in the Company's service on

the plains when liquor was still given, chiefly as a treat on state occasions or as a present, in parts where the Indians might get it from across the line, united in saying that while the liquor trade was in their own hands it was regulated so that comparatively little damage was done. For when a band came in to receive their semi-annual regale of rum, all their weapons were first delivered up for safe-keeping in the fort. Then the bravest and ablest men were selected to keep order among their fellows while the latter were drinking; and these keepers of the peace only had their turn after the general spree was ended. Then, too, if one became too annoying and clamorous for more rum, and could not be kept quiet by any other means, a good big knock-out drink was given him to put him to sleep. So, said my informants, they never had the same trouble as with the Indians, who, getting all the drink they could buy with their furs or horses from the "free" traders, immediately came over to torment the Company's people and rake up all their past grievances, while the teetotal Company's men had none of the former medicine wherewith to soothe the savage breast.

A Post of Danger and of Honor.

Even among the friendly tribes themselves there were many dangerous characters thirsting for glory in battle, tribal or personal, and their thirst for blood became acute when that for rum had been first indulged.

But wild man was not the only danger. The trading and hunting parties sent out over these treeless prairies had many a battle with the blizzard in crossing them in winter by "traverses" occupying days between the infrequent patches where wood was to be found. In summer, too, there was the great dearth of water, and when it was to be had at all it was often horribly alkali, or, if the buffalo were numerous, tainted with the foul excretions of the wallowing herd. In every other part of the prairies, save those tributary to Qu'Appelle, over which the Company's men travelled in winter, there were clumps of wood to be reached within comparatively short distances. True, dry buffalo dung lay almost everywhere beneath the snow, but it only made, even when heaped up like a haycock, a smouldering "smudge," on which the kettle boiled and the frying pan served its purpose; but without shelter from the cold blast sweeping the bare plain the "buffalo chips" were a very poor apology for a wood camp fire. Anything in the shape of a tent or lodge was considered too great an impediment on a trip performed with already heavy laden dog trains, carrying, besides the regular load, a few sticks of dry wood to make the shavings necessary to start the buffalo dung to burn.

"LA BELLE QU'APPELLE," LOOKING TO SOUTH-EAST ACROSS
VALLEY. THE SITE OF OLD FORT, SURROUNDED
BY LOW TREES, TO RIGHT.

Courtesy of Grand Trunk Pacific Railway.

"LA BELLE QU'APPELLE." LAKE ABOVE FORT QU'APPELLE,
LOOKING NORTH-WEST. BUILDINGS TO RIGHT ON
SITE OF OLD FORT. ENGINEER'S GRAVE
IN FOREGROUND.

Courtesy of Grand Trunk Pacific Railway.

CHAPTER XII.

A BUFFALO "PROVISION POST."

LA BELLE QU'APPELLE.

THE valley of the Qu'Appelle is of ideal beauty throughout. When the earth was ages of years younger a mighty river, the continuation then of the South Saskatchewan, swept down through it to join the Assiniboine. A great geologic dislocation at the elbow of the South Saskatchewan diverted its waters at a right angle to its old course and sent it to unite with the North Saskatchewan at the Forks. The drift of the great sand dunes in the vicinity also partially filled up at its head the old river valley of the Qu'Appelle, which then became the beautiful stream which winds about and in and out in the broad flat bottom land of its mile wide and magnificent valley, which the ancient river had scooped out for its course and deepened from two hundred to three hundred feet below the level of the great plains on its borders.

Rills and brooks, bearing the drainage of the upland prairies, have fretted the banks of the valley into gentle dales and deep ravines, which, fringed with flower and shrub and aspen, hurry down to the verdant lowlands, through which they bend their still fringed courses to mingle with the willow-bordered river. The bold spurs and ridges of the southern slopes of the valley are also adorned by the white stems and trembling leaves of the aspen, with here and there the beautiful bark and lovely foliage of the birch, mingled lower down with scattered maple, ash and elm. But across the valley the ridges, though covered with short grass, are bald of brush or bush, and only in the intervening hollows and coulees, sheltered from the scorching sun and succeeding frosts of spring, is tree or shrub to be seen.

The Lovely Lakes.

Framed between the graceful, curving slopes of the long reaches of the deep and wide valley, the Qu'Appelle River sweeps through its prairie lowlands in endless bends from slope to slope, glinting in silvern sheen through the greenery of its borders.   Lovely as is this shining river in the valley while alone in its beauty, it is when the stream expands into its rosary of lakes and links them together that the full glory of the scenery is revealed.   Each lake, a limpid gem of azure, fills the valley from bank to bank, which, embowered in verdure, sweep in the stately curves whereby they and the lakes in their embrace are finally concealed in the distance.

Upon the prairies between the second and third lakes stood Fort Qu'Appelle, in the middle of the valley, and within a hundred feet of the right bank of the river, some few hundred yards east of the upper lake.   There were no fixed habitations of man, on British territory, between the fort and the Rocky Mountains to the west, while on the east the cabins of Favel, Parisien and Denomie, between the next two lakes, and those of Alick and John Fisher on the lower lake, were the only buildings between Fort Qu'Appelle and Fort Ellice.

Fort Qu'Appelle.

The fort was an enclosure of about one hundred and fifty feet square, the stockades were framed of squared poplar logs, serving as foundations and plating, supported by posts every fifteen feet.   These posts were grooved on each side, and into these grooves were inserted thick slabs and planks, with the sawn surface outside.   The height of the stockade was about twelve feet.   The fort faced north; and in the middle was a gate amply wide for laden carts to enter between its double doors.   The stockade was well whitewashed, as were all the buildings within it.

At the rear of the square, facing the front gate, was the master's house, forty by thirty feet, one story, with light high loft above, built like the stockade, but with squared logs instead of slabs, and thickly thatched with beautiful yellow straw—the best roof to keep in heat as well as to keep it out that I have ever lived under. This and the interpreter's house were the only buildings in the place which had glass windows, which consisted each of an upper and lower sash, with six panes of eight and one-half by seven and one-half inch glass, all the other windows in the establishment being of buffalo parchment.

The west end of this building was used as the office and hall for the reception of Indians transacting business and making speeches. My bedroom opened off this. The east end contained the messroom and the master's apartments. Behind and connected by a short passage with "the big house" was another building, divided by log partitions into a kitchen and cook's bedroom, and into a nursery for Mr. McDonald's children and their nurse.

The rooms were all floored, lined and ceiled with white poplar, tongued and grooved and planed plank and boards— all hand-work. The furniture was also all made on the spot out of white poplar, which is a fine wood for inside work, and makes beautifully white flooring. The Company only supplied a few one-pound tins of paint to adorn the head of a dogsled or carriole, or perhaps to cover the folding board used by grandees in camp in place of a dining table, or maybe the wooden frame for the beaded mossbag, which so beneficially served the purpose of the rocking cradle of civilization. So, Mr. McDonald had painted his own quarters at his own expense, and the rest of the house, which represented in the eyes of nearly all the Indians who visited it the last word in European architectural art, was left in the unadorned beauty of the native wood.

On the west side of the square there was a long and connected row of dwelling houses of the same construction as the master's, divided into five houses by log walls carried up to the ridge pole, and each with an open chimney of its own for cooking and heating. In the officers' quarters only were there any iron stoves. The Company had provided a large sheet-iron one, made at Fort Pelly, for the office, and Mr. McDonald had bought a small Carron stove for his apartments, while Mrs. McDonald owned the American cook stove, imported from St. Paul, Minnesota, in the kitchen. The immense open fireplaces and chimneys were all made of mud. They provided a splendid system of ventilation and made a cheerful blaze. In fact, the blaze was required for lighting purposes, for tallow was too much in demand in the making of pemmican to permit of its being used luxuriously in making candles merely to light " the men's houses."

Each of these five houses in the row was about thirty by thirty feet. The floors were of planed tongued and grooved plank; the walls were smoothly plastered with clay and whitewashed, and except in the interpreter's house, which was ceiled and had two bedrooms partitioned off with boards, the beams were open or covered by poles, on which rested buffalo parchments or dry rawhides to form a ceiling. The doors were sometimes of parchment, stretched on a wooden frame, but those of the interpreter's house and the workshop, at each end of the row, were of wood, and had big iron latches and locks, the others having only long, heavy wooden latches which opened by a thong through a hole in the door. The door was in the middle of the wall with a window on each side of it facing the square; there was none in the rear of the buildings. Although the parchment, if a good one, afforded a fair enough light, it hid from the inquisitive eyes of the women of the establishment what was going on in the middle of the fort, so that the peepholes in the parchment, left by the bullets which brought down the buffalo, were the coigns of vantage where, unseen themselves, the gossips of the post could observe everything going on in the square.

Directly opposite the row of men's houses, on the other side of the square, was a row of similar construction and size, used as trading, fur and provision stores, with, at the south end, a room for the dairy, and at the north end a large one for dog, horse and ox harness and the equipments—called *agrets*—required for sleds and carts on the voyage. All these buildings had, of course, strong doors and locks, but none had a chimney, for the fear of fire in a fort where gunpowder was the chief article kept for trade was too great to permit of even the trading shop being heated in the coldest day in winter. This was the rule all over the country, and the men who defied the intense cold when travelling in the open used to dread the more intense cold which seemed to accumulate in the trading store, where one had to spend hours at a stretch writing down each item as the band of Indians brought in their credit slips from the master's office.

To the right of the front gate stood the flagstaff, on which the British red ensign, with the white letters H.B.C. on its fly, was hoisted on Sundays and holidays, and in honor of the arrival and departure of visitors of importance and the brigades; and in the middle of the square was the fur-packing press with its long beam lever and huge slotted post into which it was inserted.

The duty of scrubbing their own and the big house and keeping the square clean, making a certain number of tracking shoes for the voyageurs, and of planting and harvesting potatoes, was all that was required of the women of the fort in exchange for the board and lodging furnished by the Company. At least once a week they turned out with brooms and raked the stuff or snow up in heaps, which were hauled outside by an ox hitched to a rawhide instead of a cart or sled, and which served the purpose better. The place was the abode of the numerous train-dogs, which wandered about loose; the square served as a corral in which to round up the horses and oxen required for a brigade; in it the sleds and carts were laden and unloaded, and big snowdrifts were often formed during the winter, so the women of the place were sometimes kept quite busy and furnished with plenty of good exercise. After a snowfall it was a pleasant sight to see them all, arrayed in bright colors, with cheerful faces and active limbs, enjoying themselves, assisted by their children, large and small, sweeping up the snow in piles for half-witted Geordie Gills to draw out, if some one did not, while his back was turned to another teasing him, tip Geordie's load over to have the fun of hearing him denounce the perpetrator in phrases peculiar to himself.

Behind the stockades was a kitchen garden of the same size as the fort, protected by pointed pickets set in the ground and about ten feet high. Again, behind the garden was a field, fenced with rails, about ten acres in area, one-half of which was used for potatoes and the other half for barley.

To the west of the garden there was the hay-yard, and, facing the yard, a row of old log buildings on a ridge of a few feet elevation, which had first been used as store and dwellings, but had been converted into a stable and cattle byres.

Outside, within a few feet of the north-east corner of the stockade, stood a log ice-house, with a deep cellar, in which were preserved fresh meat and fish in summer, and where frozen fish was stored in winter.

THE PEOPLE OF THE FORT.

The regular complement of engaged servants of the Company in the winter of 1867-68 were:

Archibald McDonald, clerk (of thirteen years' service).
Isaac Cowie, apprentice clerk.
John McNab Ballanden McKay, interpreter.
William Kennedy, apprentice interpreter.
Nepapeness (Night Bird) Steersman, a Saulteau.
Jacob Bear, bowsman. (A Swampy Cree.)
George Sandison, watchman.
George Sandison, jun., middleman.
William Sandison, carpenter, at Wood Mountain.
George Thorne, cattlekeeper and woodcutter.
Olivier Flemmand, voyageur.
  (All these, except Mr. McDonald and myself were natives.)
Gowdie Harper, laborer, from Shetland, in 1864.

EMPLOYEES OF FORT QU'APPELLE

John Dyer, laborer, from Orkney, in 1866.
Alexander McAuley, laborer, from Lews Island, in 1867.
Alaister McLean, laborer, from Lews Island, in 1867.

The monthly employees were:

Alexander Fisher, horse guard, at the east end of the lakes.
Joseph Robillard, cartwright and carpenter.
Charles Bird, Cree, voyageur.
Henry Jordan, laborer.
Charles Davis, laborer.

The two latter were deserters from the American troops at Fort Buford, Missouri River.

Besides these there were a number of natives hired as " temporary servants " and others occasionally by the trip or by the day, as the occasion required.

The families of those having rations and quarters from the Company were, as far as I can remember:

Mrs. Archibald McDonald, and sons, John A. and Donald H., with their nursemaid, Mary Adams.
Mrs. McKay, with children Sarah, George and Archie.
Nepapeness' wife, Necanapeek (the leading woman), with son, Kenowas, and a baby daughter.
Jacob Bear's wife, Nancy (an English-speaking Swampy like himself), and two children.
G. Sandison's wife, Mary Whitford, with daughter, Mary Jane, and son, William.
W. Sandison's wife, Nancy Finlayson (no children).
G. Thorne's three children—Julie and two boys.
O. Flemmand's wife, Helen Brule, and two sons.
J. Robillard's wife, LaLouise (no children).
C. Bird's wife, Caroline Sandison, and child.
Cree widow, " Curly Head," with three children.
Alexander Fisher's allowance, two rations.
   Thirty train dogs, each two-thirds of a man's rations.

At the fort the daily allowance for each child was one-quarter and for a woman one-half that for a man, which was twelve pounds fresh buffalo meat, or six pounds dried buffalo meat, or three pounds pemmican, or six rabbits, or six prairie chickens, or three large white fish, or three large or six small ducks, besides potatoes and some milk for the children, and occasionally dried berries, with a weekly allowance of tallow or fat. Rough barley was also given to those who cared to prepare it for themselves.

Daily to feed the establishment required, in the form of fresh buffalo meat, the tongues, bosses, ribs and fore and hind quarters of three animals, for the head, neck, shanks and inside were not considered worth freighting from the plains to the fort. The product of three buffalo in the concentrated form of pemmican was equivalent to the daily issue of fresh meat.

JERRY McKAY, INTERPRETER.

In a previous chapter the commander of the fort, Mr. McDonald, and his family have been introduced, and I cannot tell my tale without introducing myself perhaps too often in its course. So the other people of this place, of importance in the days when the fur traders were the forerunners of the police and the pioneers with the plough who followed them, may be described here.

Interpreter John McNab Ballanden McKay was a younger son of the famous trader, John Richards McKay, of Fort Ellice. His mother was a fine and fair daughter of Chief Factor John Ballanden, whose father and grandfather had been masters of Forts Severn and York, on Hudson Bay during the previous century. The name McNab, I think, descended on his father's side from John McNab, chief of Albany Fort in 1789-90. Except in formal contracts the Christian and hereditary names of our interpreter were never used, for he was known by all, including his very wide circle of Indian acquaintances, affectionately by the name he had given himself as an infant—" Jerry." He wore his hair long, according to the prevailing fashion of the place and time, and it, like his beard and moustache and complexion, was fair, which, with his clear blue eyes, showed that, if a Celt in name, he was also of the Orkney blood of the Norsemen.

He was under the middle stature, because his well-built body was on relatively short legs, which, however, more than made up for that by their marvellous activity. He could run foot and snowshoe races and with dog-trains for days and nights in succession with the best in that land of runners. From his father he had acquired all the athletic feats which had astonished the natives frequenting Fort Ellice of old; the art of dancing the sailor's hornpipe, the Highland fling and the sword dance; also the equestrian skill to suddenly spring from the stirrup to his feet on the saddle of any horse he happened to be riding and balance himself on one foot whether the animal were going at trot or gallop. Then, resuming the saddle, he could pick up any small object on the ground as he passed it at a gallop, or imitate the Indian warriors of the southern plains by throwing himself on one side of the pony and shooting at an imaginary foe under the animal's neck as he circled round at full speed.

I don't know if there were any better buffalo hunter on the plains, for, mounted on an ordinary runner, and armed with a common Indian single barrel flint-lock (such as that used by Lamack), he would commence firing as soon as he came within range, often killing two selected buffalo before his companions considered it worth while to waste ammunition at such a distance, and continue the race till his mount was blown and he had slain thirteen choice animals in all. As the Indian average in such a run was only two, and that of the better mounted and armed Metis about five, Jerry's repeated record of thirteen under these circumstances was hard to beat. With a double-barrel cap gun he did better, and when he and his brother Joe procured Henry repeating carbines a few years after, I was told they each killed twenty-eight buffalo in a run.

Besides being good with the gun, Jerry had been from infancy familiar with the bow and arrow, which from time immemorial had been the chief plaything of every man-child in the country. Arrows used for such play and practice were called "bluffies," because the business end was bluff—the full size of the willow instead of being pared down to that of the shaft—not pointed. There was great competition in daily contests with these bluffies between all the boys in the fort or camp, in which everyone else were interested spectators; and Jerry's father used to get the boys at Fort Ellice to shower bluffies at him while he warded them off with his sword twirling around in the moulinette, so as to keep himself in practice to astonish the Indians when he challenged them to a similar friendly contest. Another child's play was that of throwing the lasso, at which many natives became very expert.

Even in Red River Settlement itself in those days nearly every man was a jack-of-all-trades, while in the wilds a man who could not do everything and make anything required by the mode of life with his own hands was considered no good. So, of course, Jerry could chop cordwood or square logs, repair carts, make horse and dog sleds with an axe and a crooked knife only. With a tree, these tools and rawhide, such plainsmen worked marvels in travelling gear of all sorts; and, when the Metis hunters were overtaken by winter, making for the first convenient woods, they would with equal dexterity and rapidity knock up a shanty, plaster it and provide it with a chimney of clay, and be warmly housed for the winter in a few days. And here may I say that very few of these wintering cabins were ever occupied again, for the Indians made it an invariable practice to burn all such buildings after they had been left by the traders and hunters in the spring, to prevent any permanent possession being secured by those invading their hunting grounds.

But to return to Jerry. That fine type of the old native frontiersmen, while highly learned in the book of nature and skilled in all the arts and crafts of the voyageur and hunter, also knew enough of "the three R's" to do all the clerical work pertaining to his business as a trader, but lacked the inclination and practice to become able to keep the general accounts of a regular post. His business there was to interpret between the tribes speaking Cree, Saulteaux or Assiniboine, or the Metis speaking Indian or French, and the master or clerk of the fort. Not only was he required on important occasions simply as interpreter, for his sympathetic knowledge of the diverse ideas and interests between natives and the European officers of the Company enabled him to act the delicate and diplomatic part of the mediator, in the not uncommon event of the Indians making unreasonable demands and the master refusing reasonable concessions. Too little credit entirely has been given to such really good interpreters in so preventing trouble between the Indians and the whites; while many an Indian war has been occasioned by incompetent or wilfully malicious ones. Under the head of the incompetent I include a large number who, while speaking both languages well, were afraid to give offence to either side by translating what was said. These fellows are entirely too polite to be of use in time of trouble, unless the principals or either of them happened to understand the general meaning of what was said, although unable or unwilling to speak the language themselves.

Qu'Appelle was frequented by different tribes of warlike Indians, and amongst them many professional "bad men," so that my being able to write this to-day is owing to the kind and skilful mediation of Jerry McKay, peacemaker, on more than one occasion. The ability and desire to use it beneficially resided in numerous members of the McKay family with whom it was my good fortune to come in contact, and I must say that the great West owes such men a big debt of gratitude for good service alike under the old regime of the Company and the new rule of Canada.

As Jerry was at the head of all the hunting, trading and wintering parties which went to the plains, and the trading done at the fort itself was of minor volume, it is due to the memory of this worthy man to take up space in telling of him, more especially as he was of that fine type of Hudson's Bay employees, with just enough Indian blood to give the sympathetic insight into the native mind and inspire reciprocal good understanding in them, who enabled the isolated European servants of the Company to hold without regular military forces and garrisons the Great Lone Land, until the advance of American settlement and modern means of transportation rendered it available for the pioneers with the ploughshare, who have converted the once happy buffalo hunting grounds of the red man into the great granaries and cities of the white man which we see to-day.

ALICK FISHER, HORSE GUARD AND COUNSELLOR.

Another person of great influence, in what might be termed the political relations between the Company and the natives, was Alexander Fisher. He was son of Chief Trader Henry Fisher, who had succeeded Mr. John Richards McKay in the charge of Fort Ellice, and who had been a North-West Company's man originally. Alick's mother was a Metis, and French was his mother tongue, although he talked good English. "Alick," as he was so popularly called, had the tall form and fine figure so characteristic of the English-French blend, and most gentlemanly manners and instincts, while his uprightness, intelligence and geniality commanded the respect and liking of his fellow Metis; and his "loyalty to the Company," in whose posts he had been brought up, was always in evidence whenever occasion demanded.

Although Alick was paid for his services in guarding the band of several hundred horses belonging to the fort, which found safer range in the valley below his place at the end of the lakes, his remuneration was for that special service only, and did not put him under the orders and discipline to which regular and temporary servants were subject. So Alick was important to the business as a frank, outspoken friend and counsellor of experience, and in touch with the Metis community, and knowing the character and reputation of each of

FORTS PEMBINA AND DAER IN 1822.

From a reproduction in black and white, by Mr. Lawson, artist of the *Manitoba Free Press*, of a water-color by a Swiss Colonist, in the Dominion Archives, Ottawa.

these who came as strangers to the place. In fact his assistance in these ways with his own people was on a par with the services of Jerry among the Indians.

Besides seeing that the horses were properly herded on well-watered pasture and protecting them from prowling Indian horsethieves, who infested the plains, Alick was a good horse-doctor and judge of horseflesh, who knew every animal he had seen once whenever he saw him again. In those times, next to the scarcity or plenty, the nearness or remoteness of the buffalo, the greatest subject of conversation and argument was the horse, especially as a buffalo runner. Mr. McDonald and Alick would talk for hours on this absorbing topic of universal and never-ending interest. Wherever two or three were gathered together it was always the same, and nearly all the quarrels I ever saw among the Metis originated in disputes about the relative merits of their favorite ponies. Besides, the wealth and influence of a person depended on the number and quality of his horses; and as they were always in demand they served in exchange and barter the same purpose as furs and preserved provisions, in a land where money was of no use except in the form of orders on Fort Garry.

The Rest of the Garrison.

Next in the roll of the fort comes William Kennedy, apprentice interpreter, a boy of about twelve years old at that time, now an elderly settler of many years and good standing, near Prince Albert, Saskatchewan. He also came of good old Hudson's Bay officers' stock, his grandfathers being Chief Factors Alexander Kennedy and Roderick McKenzie, and his name father and uncle, Captain William Kennedy, the well-known Arctic explorer.

Space cannot be given to all I would like to say about my other friends and comrades at Fort Qu'Appelle, and as their names will come up in course of the narrative I shall only mention them briefly here. The three Sandisons and Thorne were English halfbreeds and so were their wives, and Mrs. McKay; Flemmand and Robillard and their wives were French halfbreeds, although the latter looked a very fair Frenchman and the former a pure Indian. Of the Europeans, besides Mr. McDonald and myself, Gowdie Harper was the only one permanently attached to the fort, the others being only sent there to pass the winter where provisions were plentiful, and to be drilled to their duty by Mr. McDonald (who had a reputation for breaking in green hands as well as bronchos) preparatory to being sent elsewhere—Dyer to Lake Manitoba and the other two to Athabasca, next summer. Of the two Americans, Jordan, who remained in the country, will be mentioned again, and Davis returned to the States after a year or so. Nepapeness was a tall, splendid-looking fellow. Neither he nor his wife was a Christian. On the other hand, Jacob Bear and his wife were well instructed Christians from St. Peter's, both speaking, reading and writing English, also syllabic.

CHAPTER XIII.

MY INITIATION.

ORAL INSTRUCTION.

THE day following my arrival was Sunday, on which Mr. McDonald took me for a walk around the premises and introduced me to the people about. He wanted to hear all about my voyage and the people I had seen and the news I had picked up on it; and then he began giving me his own experiences on coming to the country and afterwards. This was only the beginning of many a long talk in the evenings, in which he took pains and pleasure in initiating me into the customs of the country and the rules and policies of the Company, exemplifying the same from the stores of his own experience and those of the older officers under whom he had served. In this respect he had been most fortunate in having been a pupil of such able and educated men as Chief Trader Alexander Hunter Murray and Chief Factor William Joseph Christie, and they had had an apt pupil, for he was gifted with a marvellous memory.

GOOD READING.

Then, turning from matters of business and his own long and often exciting experiences in the country, he would show that his heart was still in the Highlands, by the pleasure he took in telling of his doings among the deer and the salmon in his native land of the mountain and the flood, during the happy days of his boyhood. Letters from his relatives and from his patron, Mr. Edward Ellice, M.P., still kept him in touch with his native glen, and subscriptions to those fine old, newspapers, the Inverness *Courier* and the *Scottish American Journal,* afforded him full intelligence of public affairs. Nor did the periodicals, to which he freely gave me the benefit, end with these newspapers, for he subscribed also to the Leonard Scott American re-publications of *Blackwood's Magazine* and " the three Reviews." Besides all this good reading he had the, also familiar, red leather-bound thick volume of Oliver and Boyd's Edinburgh Almanac sent out to him yearly, and, as he either knew personally or through friends of a number of the celebrities and others mentioned in it, he searched that almanac as one devout might search the Scriptures, and with such effect that he could quote the pedigrees of all those given in it as quickly from memory as he could do that of any horse in the band of hundreds attached to the fort.

He had, too, the history of every Highland clan and regiment at the tip of his tongue, and similarly knew that of every Hudson's Bay officer and family of importance in the Northern Department.

Lynx and Whitefish.

On Monday Mr. McDonald ordered ponies to be brought round and we set out to visit the fishery up the lake. Of course several of the train dogs followed us, and among them his steering dog, " Beaver," who, running ahead of us, started a lynx from his lair along the trail. We at once dashed after him, but after taking first one long leap, next a shorter, and then one quite short, as is the nature of the beast, the lynx took refuge from the dogs in pursuit by scrambling up a tree, from which Mr. McDonald brought him down dead with a shot from his double barrel. Now at last, I thought, I had reached the happy hunting grounds of my dreams, for he treated the matter as one quite common in a sally from the post.

We found Jacob Bear with a big stage laden with whitefish, hung, in tens by the tail, to freeze for winter's use, and although those caught up to that time were a little gamey, on account of the fine warm weather still continuing during the day, that would only make them more palatable than quite fresh fish as an article of frequent diet. Jacob had also split, slightly salted and smoked some of the finest of his catch, like finnan haddies, for the mess. He gave us a few ducks, caught while diving in the net, to take back with the smoked fish and the lynx, to the fort, all being equally good to eat; for roast lynx was thought to be a great delicacy.

THE ACCOUNT BOOKS.

I was soon set to work to open a new set of books. These were a day book, copied in ink from the pencilled blotter which was carried round in the stores, an Indian debt book, a fur receipt book, and one for the receipts and expenditures of provisions. In all these the money and other columns had to be ruled, for the books were all plain horizontally ruled only. At the head of each column in the fur book the names of each kind of skin and whether large or small, prime or common, were written alphabetically across the double page, beginning with badgers and ending with wolves; and at the end of the year the totals of these columns had to tally with the totals of the " returns of trade " packed for shipment, and if they did not correspond there was a strict investigation. Similarly the receipts and expenditures of provisions were supposed to balance, after allowing a large margin for waste and weighing, but I seldom saw any such accuracy in this book as was so strictly required in the fur receipts. The expenditures of provisions were under the headings of " Officers' Mess," " Servants," " Temporary Servants," " Labor," " Voyaging," " Visitors," " Charity," " Dogs," and " Transfers to Other Posts." The columns also showed separately the rations issued to the families of each class of people under the headings; and under these general heads there were the descriptions of provisions, each with a column for itself headed: " Meat—fresh and dried," " Pemmican—common and fine," etc.

In the Indian debt book every article had to be strictly itemized, whether debtor or creditor; and even in what was called "prompt trade," in which the customer simply exchanged his hunt for its exact value in goods, it was better to make a balancing entry in his current account, for reference in case of dispute, as well as to show the total amount of his yearly earnings and ability as a hunter. But although the Company had to have a written record, the Indians were endowed with such extraordinary memories as to recall each item they had given and received during the year, and in many cases for many years, if not for life. Both Mr. McDonald and Jerry had a good deal of the same faculty, and relied very largely, as did most of the free traders, on their good memories and did not often require to look at a book to tell exactly how an Indian's account stood.

Of course everyone knew the prices of each kind of goods which never varied in the trade, although those for furs fluctuated from year to year according as competition compelled; and the price of provisions rose and fell according to the distance from the fort at which they were bought and their abundance or scarcity. But I had been used to putting things in writing and depended on that almost entirely for prices and everything else, while new to such work. So I wrote out the tariff for goods and furs in the alphabetical order used in the " Post Accounts."

Post Accounts.

These " Post Accounts " were those between the Post and the Company to exhibit the profit and loss, as far as that could be ascertained by returns of trade in furs and provisions, valued at an arbitrary rate which had been established in 1834 and had never been altered to suit the times. For instance, the post only received credit for ten shillings for each prime buffalo robe, when they were being purchased for as many dollars in cash by the Company at Fort Garry from the traders who competed with us at Qu'Appelle. Pemmican also rose and fell with the plentifulness or scarcity of the buffalo, and yet the post only got credit for it at an old, out-of-date valuation. Again, at some posts in the woods the valuation price was much higher than that to which unfashionable furs had fallen in many cases, so that such places exhibited gains which were only apparent. Of course it was impossible to tell exactly how a post paid until its furs were auctioned off a year or so after in London; and I don't think the management there was ever anxious to let the men on the spot know when their individual charges were making a big profit, although when a loss obviously occurred the gentleman in charge was sure to hear all about it.

The Journal of Daily Occurrences.

This was, like the log of a ship, supposed to contain a complete record of everything taking place at the post. The weather occupied the first place, as upon it depended the general business which was all done out in the open by the hunters and travellers of the establishment. Notable weather often had an important bearing in fixing dates on which particular events had occurred at places far apart and at a period when the natives generally reckoned time vaguely by moons. Arrivals and departures of all " comers and goers," the employments of the servants, the state of the crops, the receipts of furs and provisions, and births, deaths and marriages were all fully noted, with occasional grave or gay comments thereon.

To a new man coming to take charge of a post the old journals provided a mine of most useful information for his guidance in the management of the routine work as well as the insight it, along with the Indian debt book, gave him of the character and capabilities of the people. To a young apprentice clerk whose penmanship and spelling were not up to the proper standard old journals were given to copy for his improvement in the arts he should have learned at school, as well as to enlighten him about the business in which he might qualify to take a part. Those who received their education in this way at the Company's expense were never more than a favored few, foisted into the service by family influence, for the greater number of the apprentice clerks were young men of sufficient education and ability to require to serve no apprenticeship in anything but the mysteries of the fur trade, the customs of the country and the lone miseries of the life into which their longing for adventure had plunged them.

Many of these journals were kept by " a summer master," who was quite often a very illiterate laborer, who could barely scrawl phonetics in the book during the real master's absence on the annual voyage to and from headquarters with the furs and for the outfit. And some of these made most funny reading, not because of the writing and spelling being unconventional, for the efforts were most praiseworthy under the circumstances and served the purpose, but because of the quaint remarks and reflections at odd times committed to paper, and occasionally by the man's boastful record of his own skill and good works and the disparaging references he made to those of his companions " summering inland." I remember seeing a record at Touchwood Hills where the writer, in recording the only employment of himself and one companion "summerer" was shooting ducks for food daily and making hay, says: " Myself killed six large and ten small ducks, but Thomas only killed three very small ones." And " Myself cut eight big loads of good hay, and Thomas only four small ones of poor grass." And so on through the summer about everything else. As no mention was made of there being any other human beings about the place to consume the enormous number of ducks which "Myself," in the huge bag he records daily, must have slaughtered, it is to be presumed that his capacity to devour was equal to that to kill, and he seemed to have neither sympathy nor compassion for " Thomas " and to have allowed that poor fellow the meagre returns of his own shooting only.

Occasionally a journal afforded the only outlet its keeper could find for feelings which it might not have been to his advantage to give vent to in any other manner. For instance, his private opinion of some influential and unbearable Indian on whom it would be bad policy for the Company to use the rod; or maybe of the master of another post who had encroached on his rights to furs and hunters. The comment might even throw out hints against that high potentate, the chief factor of the district himself, yea even cast doubts upon the supreme wisdom of the infallible Council and the august governor and committee at home.

Even the unspoken enmity between officers living at the same board and under the same roof burst out now and again in the form of derogatory and belligerent remarks written in turn by each party to the quarrel in the other's absence, both having access to the book.

PERISHED HISTORICAL RECORDS.

As these complaints were more plain than pleasant, revealing opinions and a state of affairs which it was impolitic as well as impolite to leave lying around, I am sure that many an old journal which contained other most valuable records, having been disfigured by such spiteful entries, was purposely destroyed by individuals from motives of concealment apart from the gross carelessness shown by the Company in no effort being made to preserve records whose historical value would now be so great. Through the destruction of these ancient and interesting records by such carelessness or of set purpose, much of the material which gives life to history has been lost forever, unless what may be contained in those deemed worthy of preservation in the archives of the venerable Company in London.

The interesting and valuable data furnished in the chronicles of Severn Fort on Hudson Bay for the years 1788 to 1790, which were recently, with such commendable enterprise, given space in the magazine section of the Manitoba *Free Press,* are mere vestiges of a history that seemingly has been allowed to perish in a connected form. Though day after day the one may be but a repetition of the other, embedded in this monotony every now and again some important item is to be found and extracted for historical purposes, by eyes that see and minds that understand its value. Evidently the journal of Severn House at that time was written to be sent home for the information of " Their Honours " in London, where it is to be hoped many such records are still preserved and which may yet be presented by the Company to the archives of Canada.

THE INDIAN DEBT BOOK.

In this record, too, uninviting as its name would appear, occasionally between the lines might be found elements of history and romance. For apart from the number of buffalo and grizzly bear which had fallen to the bow and spear of the hunter, his wanderings in pursuit of game all over the wide plains might be traced by entries of supplies charged and furs and provisions credited him in the course of a year at places as far apart as Qu'Appelle, Wood Mountain, Milk River, Elbow of South Saskatchewan, and Last Mountain. The man might so be shown to have been a mighty hunter by the furs he had given, or a man of many wives by the amount of pemmican and dried meat, buffalo robes and dressed leather, which were the result of their labors, for their lord and master stooped not to such laborious industries. Among the items, if he were credited with the value of a good buffalo runner, the probability was that the animal was the result of a successful raid on the Blackfeet herds and incidentally on their scalps, or possibly one won in a gambling game from an original owner, who, especially if he were an Assiniboine, might be expected to lift it on the first favorable opportunity, and so it was well to sell it to the traders to be lost sight of in that way. Finally, the account might be and very often was closed thus: " By balance to profit and loss, £23 10s.," followed by the explanation ("Killed in battle with Blackfeet at Belly River, August, 1871 ").

Besides getting a glimpse of his life in the way just described, at the head of the page opposite his name the officer previously in charge of a post, upon being transferred, was in duty bound to leave his experience and opinion of the Indian, for the guidance of his successor in office. The idea of those unacquainted with Indians, that all of them are alike, would be confounded by the various characters given in these debt books. And another thing I not infrequently found was, that a man with the character of an utterly unreliable rascal from my predecessor, or another with a first-class certificate from him, turned out in my experience to be each the reverse. So I came to the conclusion that many Indians in their conduct towards the traders were very much what the conduct of the traders made them. There is a great deal of real human nature in an Indian, and they vary individually nearly as much as every other race and nation.

MY FIRST TEMPORARY CHARGE.

Mr. McDonald continued to initiate me into my duties, taking me on his regular rounds to see the men at work, to which he roused them at dim dawn in the morning—a hateful job to me, for once I had settled down off a voyage, I fell at once into my old habit at home of reading, or working to all hours of the night. He was anxious to make a trip to the plains to see how Jerry had succeeded with the fall hunt for fresh meat, and the best sites at which to post the winter trading parties. So, as soon as the fall fishery was over, and he had everything arranged, so that (if I had the sense to act well my part as figurehead over the experienced hands, who each knew his work) all would go well during his absence, he took Jacob and Harper with him and left for the plains about a fortnight after my arrival. Instead of Harper he put into the kitchen Alaister McLean, who, with John Dyer and Alexander McAuley, had arrived from Fort Pelly a few days after me, with a letter from Chief Factor Campbell, saying that he had sent Dyer in charge of the two others who had come out in the ship, but that the clerk expected had not come with them by the Swan River fall boats from Norway House.

The men thus left under my nominal charge were George Sandison, a very decent, quiet fellow; Thorne, another of the same and a splendid worker, and Robillard, a competent cartwright, but rather consequential. Besides these were the newcomers, Dyer, McAulay and Alaister, and, of course, my assistant, Kennedy. I had to do the abominable duty of going round to rouse up the men in early morn, and to make the regular rounds several times a day, although none of them except Alaister required the supervision, which none resented except Robillard.

A REAL GREENHAND.

Alaister had been a general favorite on board the *Prince Rupert* for his abounding good nature and desire to take an active part in every work going on on deck. Unfortunately he "had no English" and very little intelligence to direct his ever active and willing bodily power. He was a short, well-built man, with fine, rosy complexion and an ever-cheerful countenance, most willing and obedient to do anything he could be made to understand and to keep doing it till further orders. As a man for the kitchen—I can't call him a cook— he was entirely out of place, for he had no previous experience except in the herds of the Hebrides and the herring fishery, and neither Mrs. McDonald nor I "talked the two talks." So we had to employ his friend and compatriot, McAulay, to interpret whenever we wanted him to do anything—for he would never budge without orders—and then again to tell him to stop. As it was very inconvenient to get McAulay every time a fresh order to give him a fresh start had to be given, I took lessons from McAulay in how to say in Gaelic, " Get up out of bed," " Go to bed," " Go and milk the cows," " Get in wood," " Go for water," " Eat this," and so on, for he would sit up all night if he were not told to go to bed, and so on with everything else. One day we had a big buffalo boss on the table which Mrs. McDonald and her maid had seen roasted, and in the evening as he was taking it—we had hardly eaten any of it—out of the mess room, the mistress told him in some way that he understood to eat it. It was a very big boss, and next morning McAulay came to see me before breakfast to say that Alaistar had gone to him in great trouble, fearing Mrs. McDonald would be annoyed at his not having obeyed her orders by eating the whole of the boss, although he had sat up all night trying to do so, and had sickened himself in the attempt. When I told Mrs. McDonald of this gross act of disobedience, we joined in one of the many hearty laughs everyone had at Alaister, who, when he found out his mistake, was just as ready to enjoy the laugh as anyone else. He was the most good-humored and willing fellow, and a favorite on that account with all, and when he got routine work outside which he understood, he was none of the Company's bad bargains.

A Native Dandy.

Shortly after Mr. McDonald had left for the plains, one afternoon Kennedy came in to report that a free trader's man, named Donald Sinclair, with liquor, was visiting the men's quarters, which was strictly prohibited by the rules. I met the man just as he was going from one house to another, and he at once greeted me in good English and by name, although an utter stranger to me. He was a smart, good-looking, medium-sized fellow, and evidently self-satisfied as a dude of that day. He wore his black hair in long oily ringlets reaching his shoulders, under a low crowned, broad brimmed, soft black felt hat, adorned with a " black foxtail feather," which was an article of trade at the time and resembled a small ostrich plume. He wore a new navy blue cloth capote, with double rows of flat gilt buttons in front; trousers of the same material, over which, of the same cloth, were leggings reaching half-way up the thigh, heavily decorated by broad stripes of beadwork on the outer sides and fastened below the knee by broad garters completely covered with beaded patterns of flowers and leaves. Beautifully made, yellowish brown moose moccasins, topped with fine silkwork, embellished his finely formed feet. To support his trousers was a broad, vari-colored L'Assomption belt, under which was tucked a profusely ornamented firebag, in which flint and steel and tinder were always carried with the ubiquitous pipe and tobacco. Waistcoats were not usually worn, and he was strictly in the mode by exhibiting a fancy colored flannel shirt—of the " Crimean " variety of the time—with a big black silk handkerchief tied in a sailor's knot round his neck. On his left hand was a finely silkworked buckskin glove, and in it he held its mate while greeting me with the right.

Attempt to " Play Over a Moonyass."

As mentioned before, the self-denying ordinance of the Company prohibiting the importation of liquor into Swan River and some other districts, while affording the Company none of the profits, had subjected their people to great annoyance by Indians made drunk by free traders. Another trouble was the habit the traders had of upsetting the Company's business by treating the employees to too much. This was generally done on the sly, but occasionally in open defiance of the Company's rule against bringing it into their premises. A case of the kind a few months before had involved Mr. McDonald in a fight with a trader. Donald would have taken particular care to avoid the fort had the master been at home, but when he heard of his departure leaving a young new clerk in charge, he thought he would have a fine chance of strutting about in gorgeous attire, proudly bearing, in a big tin flask slung by a strap over his shoulder, enough over-proof spirits to intoxicate all the Company's people who would accept his " treat."

I asked him what he was doing in the fort and he answered saucily that he was visiting his friends and treating them with liquor from Sousie Thomas, a big trader by whom he was employed. The people had all come out to see what would happen. I ordered him to get out immediately, which he did promptly, amid the jeers of the people before whom he had been bragging how he could " play over a Moonyass " a minute before. The next time I had the fun of seeing him his actions, which will be related, were as good as a play.

A Real Indian Missionary.

Our next visitor was both very different and very welcome, in the person of Mr. Charles Pratt, Catechist of the Church of England Missionary Society, stationed at Touchwood Hills. Mr. Pratt told me that he was a pure Indian of the mixed Assiniboine and Cree blood of the sept known as " Young Dogs " or " Puppies," in the Cree equivalent. He had been born at the fish-barrier, about a quarter of a mile below the fort, about fifty years before, when that part of the country was considered well within the recognized hunting grounds of the Blackfeet. He was a man of pleasing appearance, strong and hardy, a good hunter and tireless traveller, and a modest, sincere and unworldly Christian. In searching the Scriptures of the Old Testament he had recognized so many traits and customs of the Israelites to be so entirely like those of the Indians of the prairie, as to have become convinced that these Indians were the Lost Tribes. This was his favorite subject of conversation, and very interesting it was, as well as plausible. Such was the faith of this single-minded missionary, and upon it he founded original ideas for the conversion of his countrymen, which met with little encouragement from his clerical superiors. As far as I can recollect it was his idea to begin by ingrafting the religion of the old dispensation as more suitable to the understanding and conditions of the Indian than the higher truths of Christianity, which, I understood, would be taught in due time after they, like the Jews, had been prepared to receive and comprehend them.

Mr. Pratt held services on Sunday, which were attended by all the Protestants in, and a few Indians around, the establishment. He returned after a day or two to his station at Touchwood Hills whence it had been shifted from the site of Fort Qu'Appelle, on which the first mission had been founded by the Rev. Mr. Hillier, of the same society, in 1853.

A Traveller From New Caledonia.

During Mr. McDonald's absence, an American, who stated that he was an engineer employed by the Western Union Telegraph Company, then connecting Alaska with the States by a wire through British Columbia, arrived bearing a letter from Chief Trader Peter S. Ogden, of Fort St. James, Stuart's Lake, directing " Officers in charge of posts on the route to Fort Garry to provide the bearer, Mr. Schovil, with transportation and requisite supplies, to be endorsed on the letter " Mr. Schovil also had a like letter from Chief Factor Christie, at Edmonton, saying that, as Mr. Schovil had been forwarded so far, it would be expedient to continue to speed him on his way to Fort Garry. I entered copies of both these letters of credit in the Journal and, after a day or two to allow Mr. Schovil a welcome rest and to procure the means of sending him to Fort Ellice, sped him on his way. During his stay he was a most entertaining guest, full of news about New Caledonia and Saskatchewan districts, so I was sorry when he left. But afterwards there was an indignant enquiry from Governor McTavish as to the authority upon which the adventurous gentleman had secured passage, for he had neither reported at Fort Garry, where the account was to have been settled by draft on the Western Union Telegraph Company, nor had he paid his board bill to " Dutch George," the Winnipeg village hotelkeeper, before slipping away secretly to the States. It was fortunate that I had taken copies of his credentials, by means of which the governor was able to fix the responsibility for them on the proper authorities, and he was so good as to write to Mr. McDonald in acknowledging the receipt of the extracts from the Journal, that " it speaks well of that young fellow to have been the only one along the route who thought it worth while to take a copy of the letters."

An Imperialist Free Trader.

The Assiniboine Indians had a pre-eminence, of which they were proud, in the way of horse-stealing and plundering weak parties of traders, also for their beastly treatment of those they pillaged. On one of the first dark, blustering days (which ended the exceptionally long and beautiful Indian summer of 1867) there stopped near the fort two men, who came over to buy provisions. One was a Metis, surnamed Racette, who went by the name of Pa-pe-nay, and the other a white man, who introduced himself as Mr. Farquharson, father-in-law of Doctor Schultz. He said they had gone out trading on the plains and had been plundered by the Assiniboines, who only left them with the clothes on their backs, and they had found their way back to Qu'Appelle in a starving condition. Mr. Farquharson was boiling over with rage at the loss of the property and the indignities to which he had been subjected, and had been compelled by overwhelming force to submit to escape with his life.

His wintering shanty was about six miles from the fort on the upland prairie north of the valley, alongside of the place of old George Racette, the trader, who was Papenay's father. I was glad to get Mr. Farquharson to stay till next day with me, and to hear him discourse, from his point of view, on the state and problems of the country, and on things in general also; for he was a clever, well-informed man, who had travelled extensively since leaving Aberdeen. He spoke of Demerara, where the inferior brand of Hudson's Bay rum came from, also of Jamaica, from which came the best, and then went on to his favorite subject—the development of the great West by a British transcontinental railway, which he predicted would be built in a few years by the Imperial Government itself, in spite of the opposition of the Hudson's Bay

Company. I was quite interested in hearing the other side of the question, for, of course, I had had little opportunity of hearing anything adverse to the Company, for the *Nor'-Wester* newspaper, being tabooed, was not among the periodicals which reached Mr. McDonald.

Mr. Farquharson, before leaving, gave me a pressing invitation to visit him and to partake of a feast of curried chicken and plum-pudding, the anticipation of which had cheered him on his famishing trip in from the plains. I was only too glad to accept, and a few days after enjoyed the feast and his most interesting conversation accompanying it.

FOOLED ON A SILVER FOX.

The only other occurrence, during my first charge of a post, which may be of interest to relate, was how Kan-o-cees fooled me about a silver fox. He was a very " cute and interesting ne'er-do-well " by reputation, which neither Kennedy nor I had as yet heard of, and I did not become acquainted with his redeeming qualities till making his intimate acquaintance some years after. He came in at this time and told us that he had found the burrow of a fine silver fox, which was very rare on the plains, and so I was eager to make my brief " reign " remarkable by securing one. He required, he said, provisions and some other supplies to enable him to keep watch and ward over the burrow with certainty of capturing the valuable prize, which was worth £10 according to the fur tariff of the post.

He wanted these supplies in advance on account of the fox, which could not possibly escape him, if so provided. I at once referred to the Indian debt book, where I found he was already in debt, but there was nothing otherwise to show his character and standing. Thinking that he must be good for a little more, I let him have what he asked, and waited expectantly till he came back to say he had run out of provisions and now intended to smoke the fox out of his hole, if he could get some more supplies. After luring me into giving these also, he departed, and I did not see him again till he turned up drunk the following summer, again in the absence of both Mr. McDonald and Jerry, demanding tribute for the use of the site on which the fort stood. But I had been chaffed so much about his fooling me on the imaginary fox that I met his demand for tribute in forcible English only, for, like other "bad" Indians, he understood that kind of language, and could use it, too, on occasion.

KA-NO-CEES.

Ka-no-cees was a brother of "Poor Man," the Cree chief of Touchwood Hills post. He was of a roving nature and travelled about far outside the confines of his band—down to Red River, up to Edmonton, and south to the Missouri. Being an inveterate gambler he never kept horses or wives any time, and consequently was of no account as a hunter for the Company. To retrieve his losses and to satisfy his inordinate craving for adventure his chief occupation was horse-stealing from the Blackfeet and the Indians along the Missouri. On such errands he generally went alone, and never came back empty-handed. With the proceeds he would then purchase a wife or two, although occasionally he stole these from friend or foe, and set up in style till he lost all in gambling again. Such I found to be his record, and, although his brother, the chief, who was a much-respected man of known bravery, often said Ka-no-cees was a braver and more intelligent man than he himself, none of us thought of him as other than a worthless, wandering ne'er-do-well, till at the big battle on Belly River, in 1871, Ka-no-cees, by his skill and courage, saved the defeated Crees, flying before the victorious Blackfeet, from the fate of the one hundred and thirty-five of their fellows who fell in the fight.

It was after that that I became well acquainted with him, and discovered that he was full of fun and fond of a joke, besides being quite a diplomat in influencing the Indians, apart from his reputation for courage. So, during the latter years of my stay at Qu'Appelle, I found him often a useful ally, who became a respectable and loyal customer.

CHAPTER XIV.

A WINTER TRIP TO THE PLAINS.

ENTER JACK FROST.

By the time Mr. McDonald returned from his tour of observation winter had set in, and I had begun to experience the effect of a degree of frost I had never before witnessed; for although the Shetlands are as far north as the south end of Greenland, they lie in the track of the warm Gulf Stream, so that we thought ourselves lucky when the ice on the lakes allowed us skating for a whole week in a whole winter. In the Northern Isles the short winter day is gloomy with dripping clouds, frequently borne on storm, with few glimpses of sunshine to lighten the peaks of the heather-clad hills and the crests of the rolling waves, which roar without ceasing on the rock-bound shore. North-easterly winds then changed the rain into snow and sleet, and these the children were told were the feathers of the Christmas geese they were plucking in Norway. There we did not need a glass to tell us it was cold, for we felt it in good earnest, while on the sunlit, snowy prairies, Jack Frost had to bite nose-tips to make us feel his presence, although the glittering snowfields and glistening gems bedecking each blade of grass and crystallizing every twig bore eyewitness to his transforming presence.

"TENDER FEET" AND NATIVE-BORN.

Like every vigorous person fresh from the old country, none of us green hands felt the cold during the first year as did the natives. While the native-born were going about wrapped in big capotes, with huge mittens on their hands, the new-comer Scots went about in their blue serge shirts and bare-handed at work round the fort. As the cold increased they also had to put on coats and mittens, also moccasins—especially moccasins. Even after longer residence had made the Europeans more susceptible to cold, my experience showed that they were able to stand it with the hardiest of their native fellow-servants; but how almost naked Indians endured it was marvellous.

The weakness of the European was in his tender feet, which, stunted and cramped in boots, had become partially atrophied, so that the circulation was too poor to keep them warm in contrast with the free circulation and free play afforded by the yielding moccasin. Until continual use of moccasins had revived the dormant circulation and spring of the feet, and practice had also developed the legs, the green hand was inferior to the native-born as a traveller. The latter came of a race of walkers, while the Islesmen came of a race of oarsmen, so by inheritance one was strong in the legs and the other strong in the arms and back, also notably in the hands. As a rule the picked natives engaged by the Company were taller and bigger men than the Europeans, but not generally so healthy.

Chief " Growing Thunder."

The first Indian of distinction to come in for an outfit on credit was the Assiniboine chief, Growing Thunder, who looked as if he had stepped out of Fenimore Cooper, with every frill and feature of the nobility of the red men. He was tall, finely formed, with aquiline features, of stately gait and dignified manners, looking every inch the daring leader of warriors. Besides gun, tomahawk, and scalping knife, he carried a long bow and quiver of arrows on his back ever ready to let loose on the instant.

He belonged to the Assiniboines frequenting Wood Mountain and the Missouri River, where he as often traded with the Americans as he did with the Company on our side. Very few of his tribe were worthy of trust with an outfit, and he himself was doubtful in that way. After several unsuccessful attempts to intimidate the Company's traders, he had become friendly and had shown both his friendship to them and the respectful awe he exacted from his brethren by falling upon a mob who were about to pillage Big William Daniel, when on a trading trip to the plains, and driving them off, helter-skelter, using his long bow as a rod of correction. This affair occurred before liquor had ceased to be given by the Company to the Indians. Daniel was renowned for giant strength as well as daredevil courage, and guarded the keg with double-barrel at the ready, but he would have had no chance of escape had not the Indians so closely surrounded him that they were afraid to shoot lest the missile passing through or by him might kill one of their own people. Before a clear chance to shoot him occurred Growing Thunder appeared in wrath and saved Daniel and the firewater.

As a matter of course, every man who gained influence and respect by such feats as this and by having killed more than one of his rivals in single combat, had to maintain the prestige by being ever ready to fight all who dared question it. Within a year after I first saw him Growing Thunder was slain in such an affair of honor.

The chief had come in unattended except by two of his ten wives, and there was no one who could talk Assiniboine well enough to interpret speechifying. So he and Mr. McDonald managed to do the necessary business in broken Cree, which the chief ably supplemented by the sign language, in which the Stonies were the most proficient. He exchanged his "fall robes" and leather for the strong cloth called "Hudson's Bay strouds"—taking dark blue for gowns and red cloth for leggings for his wives. Also he "took debt," to be paid to Jerry during the winter, consisting of guns and ammunition, tea and tobacco principally; and then he received his gratuities as a leading man in his tribe. He was not regarded as a regular chief, duly appointed by the Company and recognized by the Assiniboines, such as "Loud Voice" was for the Crees and "Oukima" was for the Saulteaux of Qu'Appelle. Each of these had a scarlet, gold-laced and epauletted frock coat sent for him in the outfit yearly, besides a tall black silk hat with colored cocktail feathers. Growing Thunder wanted the red coat very much, but it could not be given him. He also desired the high hat, and the Company had none. However, I had one, which in its case had been an object of derision on the voyage. Christie had said that I had better keep it and give it to a chief rather than throw it overboard; and now it just suited the Assiniboine chief, who gave me a fall buffalo robe for it. Having decorated it with broad gold-lace and a couple of colored plumes from the store he seemed to be quite proud of these marks of distinction, topping the blue cloth capote and trousers, shirt, belt and handkerchief with which Mr. McDonald had transformed a magnificent, robed and leggined savage into a most uncomfortable looking voyageur. However he only endured this penalty of greatness until he got out of the fort, and took his ease in his lodge with nought about him but his painted robe, his leather breechclout, leggings and moccasins, and perhaps the shirt. The European raiment was too uncomfortably stylish.

THE MIS-NY-GAN AMULET.

Besides these " gratuities," the chief was insistent on obtaining a little bit of writing ("mis-ny-gan" in Cree) from Mr. McDonald, certifying that " The bearer, Growing Thunder, is an influential warrior among the Assiniboines of Wood Mountain, who has always been friendly to the whites, and deserves a piece of tobacco from any of the Company's people when they meet him," or something to that effect. Such a scrap of the written word was considered very precious and of occult value apart from the material benefit in tobacco and the good introduction it gave the bearer to strange white people. " These presents " were highly prized, not only for the distinction and privilege they conferred on the bearers above their fellows, but also as amulets to ward off the terrors of the unknown. They were placed between two thin sheets of wood, hinged at one corner so that they slid over each other. On one of these sheets a three-inch round mirror was neatly embedded, and the whole outfit was placed in a beaded or quilled buckskin bag, which was suspended in front from the necklace, often of bear's claws, always worn by a warrior. In the little bag might also be some other " big medicine " and also vermilion to decorate the face.

HELIOGRAPHED SIGNALS.

The little mirror was used for signalling purposes as well as for the toilet, for the Indians had long anticipated the art of heliography in that respect. Besides being useful for signals to friends engaged in hunting or in war, the mirror was used as a "joker" very often by hostiles who did not intend to attack, but merely to annoy their foes by playing the flash on them to keep them on the alert and guessing what might be the next move. The Blackfeet often would let us know of their invisible presence by flashing at us as we passed over the plains on our trading or hunting expeditions, in mockery as much as for wanton annoyance, for by so revealing their being in the vicinity we were put doubly on guard against a raid on our camp or cattle.

TAY-PUT-AH-UM PERISHED IN A BLIZZARD.

This was a Cree who came with his son to get " debt " at the fort, for it was against the usual policy to give any supplies on credit to Indians away from it. He had left his two wives and children at " The Turn," a bend of one of the branches of the Souris River where the last woods occurred on the route between the Pile of Bones Creek and the Old Wives' Lakes. There was nothing particularly striking about Tay-put-ah-um, and I only recollect that he got £10 worth of supplies; but on his way back, in making the traverse from the last point of woods which fringed the valley of the Qu'-Appelle to those on the Pile of Bones Creek, he was overtaken by one of those frightful blizzards so frequent in that country, and he and his poor boy perished within a short distance of the woods in the valley.

ON THE FIRST ICE.

It did not take much time to exhaust the interest derived from the novelty of life at the fort, and I was eager to experience that of winter travel. Meanwhile, shortly after the lakes froze fast, old George Sandison made me a pair of skates out of two six inch flat files let into wood. It was too cold to use boots and the tight strapping over moccasins was torture. However, one Sunday forenoon I set off for the end of the lake, about five miles below the fort, to see a very sick man, Joseph Parisian, who had asked for my services.

My next outing was on Company's business to John Fisher on the lower lake, and I went on horseback half way down that lake on the north side, where I discovered that his place was on the other side, and so I set off across the smooth, newly frozen lake. The ice was not yet very strong, it cracked all around, in the calm air making a great noise.

On fore feet only the pony had flat shoes, without calks, made of the copper hoop off powder kegs, and with difficulty he managed to keep his feet, as I led him across the cracking and undulating surface of the lake. Fisher had seen me taking the ice, and had tried to signal by firing his gun that he did not consider it safe. I did not understand the intended warning, and went on, while he anxiously watched, expecting the pony and myself to break through every moment. " Well," he said, " you are a greenhorn to do such a thing," when I landed safely. He had never seen the thin ice on which skaters in the old country venture, on the infrequent occasions for such sport occurring during the generally rainy winters there. I returned to the fort by land.

CHRISTMAS AND NEW YEAR.

On Christmas Day Mr. McDonald read the Church of England service in the morning, and we had roast buffalo boss and plum-pudding for dinner. There was no midnight mass for the Roman Catholics at the lake that winter, for no successor had come to take the place of the Reverend Father Richot, who had been there the previous year, and of whom Mr. McDonald spoke very highly, although he had objected to have the mission planted alongside of the fort, and advised its being placed between the third and fourth lakes.

"Christmas Regales" in the shape of some flour, rice, raisins, sugar, chocolate and extra rations had been issued to all the people of the fort, and I don't recollect anything special, except that they were all in holiday attire and temper.

New Year's Day was ushered in at daylight by a volley, and the men all came crowding into the hall to shake hands and wish the master and all "A Happy New Year." They were immediately served with clay pipes and tobacco, and after a little conversation, sat down to a feast of buffalo tongue and boss, cakes and plum-pudding, accompanied by chocolate and tea. After they had trooped out, their places were taken by the women and children of the fort, and each lady greeted us with a smacking kiss, according to the custom of that day and generation. Some of the elderly ones expected pipes and tobacco, but the others were happy with cakes and chocolate and tea, with some suitable sweets for the children.

Next came the Indians, who had flocked to the fort for the occasion from far and near, bringing in their furs to trade at the same time. The number of these was not large and was composed of the few who trapped in the wooded country thereabout, for the rest of the Indians were far out on the buffalo plains for the winter.

The proceedings on both days terminated with dances in the men's quarters, and these went off merrily despite the absence of anything stronger than tea.

MY FIRST TRIP WITH DOG TRAIN.

During all that long lasting fall of fine weather I had been anticipating the joys of snowshoeing and dog driving as soon

DOG TRAINS CROSSING A LAKE.
Courtesy of Hudson Bay Railway.

CAPE DIGGES AND ISLAND.
Courtesy of Hudson Bay Railway.

as the snow fell; and the moment it did fall, with Kennedy as my instructor, I commenced to practice these arts of travel. After amusing himself by watching my efforts with a scratch team, Mr. McDonald began to allow me to use his splendid train occasionally. They were four big yellow dogs with some collie in them. The beautiful and benevolent Beaver was the steering dog (next the sled); the leader or foregoer was Seresto; next the proud Tiger, always with high-cocked tail; and then Saquilla, who hauled too hard if in front. They were a most powerful, willing, and splendidly trained team. Beaver alone could race along the smooth tracks about the fort with Mrs. McDonald and the boys in the cariole and her husband standing on behind; and the other dogs were little less powerful.

After New Year, Jerry came in with four men and their dog trains to fetch supplies for his winter post at Wood Mountain, and I was delighted when Mr. McDonald told me I could go with him and take a load out on this fine team. I slept little, with excitement, the night before, starting early on the morning of January 10.

A BLIZZARD ON THE PRAIRIE.

The first day's journey was through the parklike country which bordered the valley, following the big cart track to the plains. At the last point of woods we took on a few billets of wood on each sled, to kindle and augment the dried buffalo dung, which was to be dug up everywhere from under the snow, when stopping to eat or camp on the bare prairie. While making the traverse across the treeless plains between the last woods and a place in the valley of the Pile of Bones where there was some bush, we were overtaken by one of the terrific blizzards for which the winter travelling grounds of the Qu'-Appelle traders were notorious. Fortunately, on this occasion we did not have to resort to the usual plan of safety, which consisted in scooping a hole in the snow and spreading robes and blankets under and over one, and lying down to let the snow drift over and protect one from freezing to death from exposure. We had six sleds with large lodge leather wrappers, and these the clever hands of Jerry and his men soon converted to serve the purpose of tent poles and their covering. Arranging the loads of the sleds as a barrier outside of the lodge so formed and taking inside all eatables and the harness to protect them from the dogs, we got inside, and made ourselves secure against the piercing blast, covering the ground with buffalo robes and ourselves with blankets and robes. Then a smoky smudge was started to boil the kettle for tea and to melt snow to drink.

We spent the next twenty-four hours huddled together in this rough refuge from the cold blast of the blizzard, passing the time mostly in sleep, with intervals of eating and smoking, and considered ourselves fortunate in such shelter near where Tay-put-ah-um and his son had perished a short time before.

At Pile of Bones.

On the evening following we were to camp in the woods of the valley of the Pile of Bones, and I was coming behind the long train of sleds, following the brow of the bank, when my leader, Seresto, catching sight of Nepapeness, who had gone ahead to start a fire in the bottom of the valley, swerved, in spite of my yelling " Choo," to the right, off the trail he had been following, and heading straight for the fire led his team and sled to the brink of a big snowbank overhanging the slope, and the snowbank breaking off crashed down, an avalanche of snow, dogs and sled to the bottom of the valley. The dogs were all twisted and twined up in the harness and the load lashings were loosened in the spectacular descent, but nothing worse came of it; so it was witnessed and commented on, in Indian, with much laughter at my expense.

At The Turn.

On our fourth day out from Qu'Appelle we reached The Turn, and got lodgings in little wintering cabins of Paul and

Xavier Denomie in its wooded valley. A Saulteaux Indian rejoicing in the name of Tep-is-couch-kees-cou-win-in, which being interpreted, means approximately " Man in the Zenith," had arrived the evening before with loads of freshly killed buffalo meat, and we and our dogs procured from him a very welcome change of diet. Jerry had some trading to do, and he also required to buy some more dogs to take the place of several useless brutes in his men's trains, so we did not leave our warm and comfortable shelter in the Hotel Denomie (16x12) till the 16th.

During all our stay there there arose, night and day, the monotonous wail of woe of the wives of poor Tay-put-ah-um, for him and his son. In token of grief they went about with dishevelled hair, in garments rent, and seemingly willing martyrs to the custom by which all the property of their dead husband had been parted among relatives of his own blood, leaving them destitute.

BUFFALO BULLS.

Jerry had a smart, swift train of grade deerhounds, and they were always on the lookout, whether loose or in harness, for any game along the way. The day after we left The Turn we sighted a few buffalo bulls ahead, and Jerry at once threw off his load and set after them on the light sled, with Nepapeness running on snowshoes after him. The younger bulls took the alarm and to their heels before Jerry came near enough for a shot, but one old veteran faced about and stood his ground. Jerry fired twice, but the bull, already maddened by the dogs let loose upon him, although mortally wounded, still kept his feet and showed fight, till Nepapeness ran up, and while his attention was held by the hounds, plunged a long hunting knife into the old hero's heart, and pushed him over, as he died fighting.

His meat was too poor for anything but dog feed, and we camped on the spot to give them the full benefit, after the carcase had been cut up with the marvellous speed of these skilled hunters. The dogs held high carnival that night, and held off the wolves, which had soon gathered about, till we broke camp in the morning, when there was little left for the wolves, which soon began to lope after us on the trail. As we went on that day we started a band of buffalo again, and wolves became more numerous, sitting on every knoll, but always out of range of our guns. Then as we passed them, they, too, would follow on and take advantage of our beaten track in the snow, till one could see a long string of them behind, always keeping at a respectful distance.

PRAIRIE WOLVES.

There were two kinds of wolves, the smaller being those known to-day by the familiar name of coyote, and then called " togony," an abbreviation of the longer Cree word. The others were the real big prairie wolf, " Me-hin-gen " in Cree, which, fattening on the bison and as scavengers on the field of slaughter, often attained an immense size. These were of various shades, from white to grey, with occasional patches of black, and were esteemed good eating by the Indians. They were generally fat, and yielded a large proportion of the grease eaten by the Indians and made into the finer kind of pemmican by them. These big brutes took the lions' share of the prey, while the coyotes acted the part of the jackals.

I had, of course, read many a terrible tale of travellers in the snow being pursued by packs of ferocious wolves, and when I saw them abounding along our route I was surprised to see the perfect indifference of my companions. Instead of men being afraid of wolves, the wolves were afraid of men. I was told of their wonderful intelligence in keeping out of the range of gunshot, and afterwards when repeating long range rifles came into use they soon learnt to keep out of range of them, too. During after years several different Indians at different times and places assured me that wolves could count up to seven, and the way it was proven was this: They have a habit of following in a trail beaten by travellers, and on a rolling prairie or mounting a rise over which the party they were following had disappeared, the wolves would halt till they got a clear sight of them again. Then, if one of a party of seven men had forked off to watch the trail to get a shot at the wolves following it, as they passed the place he had concealed himself, the animals would stop and follow no further on that trail. But if the number exceeded seven men, then one might detach himself from the party and not be missed by the wolves.

I am sure that my informants believed this story of the wolf's ability to count, and I know that a band following us would stand for a while on the top of a knoll before coming on again after us. As to both wolves and other wild animals and birds wonderfully soon discovering the longer range of newly introduced guns there is no doubt whatever.

The only time the wolves were ever considered dangerous on the plains was in the month of March, when an occasional old male went mad, so mad in fact, as to come within range or striking distance of hunting people, who courted the opportunity to get the hide. It may be said the wolves on the prairie of which I am speaking were not the same animals as those found in the woods. But they were exactly the same, and I have seen thousands of them alive, and handled thousands of their skins, and in the very much smaller number of timber wolves I have seen, " on the hoof " or in the hide, I have noticed no difference except that those reared in the woods were darker in color and on an average not so large as those who feasted on the buffalo. The difference between them in any desire to attack mankind or to leave him severely alone was occasioned by the one in the woods being famished and the other on the buffalo plains being well fed as a class; while the latter's greater familiarity with the power of hunting men inspired him and his with a wholesome dread not experienced by his kind beyond the seas in Europe and Asia, and even in the forests of North America.

Even when the buffalo had migrated afar and food could not have been plentiful, the wolves never plucked up courage to attack people in the way described in tales of other countries. On the contrary, they then became more the prey than ever of man, who found his chief resource for food, in the absence of the buffalo, in the wolves he poisoned with baits of strychnine. The only part not eaten in such cases, was the stomach containing the bait, and our own men often were compelled to live on poisoned wolves, and glad to get them.

CHAPTER XV.

WOOD MOUNTAIN, OLD WIVES' CREEK, AND RETURN TRIP TO QU'APPELLE.

CROSSING THE COUTEAU.

So we travelled on, as described in the last chapter, day by day, seeing a few scattered buffalo, which went off at a seemingly slow and ungainly gallop at our near approach. Sometimes one was either stalked on foot or Jerry threw off his sled load and let loose his hounds after them; but this was only done about "camping" time (if our hole in the snow around a buffalo-dung smudge be worthy of that word of comfort), so that no time might be lost on the journey nor the meat of the animal wasted by merely taking the tit-bits on the march and leaving the rest for a feast of following wolves. Our route crossed ridge after ridge and valley after valley of the Couteau Missouri, frequently requiring us to pull uphill with the dogs, and break the rush down the slopes. That was hard work, but the worst was along the slope of the ridges, where the utmost exertions of the steering dog and the driver with his tail line were required to keep the sled on the beaten course and prevent an upset.

We were making that night for a spot where there were a few small willows, a sort of oasis in that treeless desert, where something resembling a camp fire instead of a smudge could be made in those wind-swept hills. So we travelled after dark, guided by the instinct of Jerry's foregoer on an old track which had been travelled that winter but was now obliterated by drift so as to be imperceptible to the most experienced voyageur except by feeling it with his feet, divested of snowshoes. The leading dog lost the trace often and the men had to beat about in moccasined feet repeatedly to find it; while Jerry lamented the death of a very wise old dog named Fox, which was never known to have lost a trail, however old and obliterated. The crossing of the Couteau was the most dreaded part of winter journeys, for the region was peculiarly subject to sudden storms and blizzards, which neither man nor dog could face. So that part of the route was always got over as quickly as possible and advantage was taken of fine weather to cross it during the night.

There was the double danger of losing the trail in a storm as well as of the travellers losing each other, and perishing as had a Canadian named D'Amour, a year or two before, when out for a trip from Touchwood Hills Post.

Safety Beneath the Snow.

In such a storm of snow and drift one could not see the foremost dog in his train, and shouts could not be heard above the roar of the tempest. The expedient of connecting each train with the next by life-lines to keep them together was then resorted to, if the party expected to find some kind of fuel and shelter ahead. But if there were no prospect of reaching these before man and dog became exhausted, the party immediately shovelled out a hole in the snow down to the grass, and with robes and blankets under and over them found shelter and warmth by being soon deeply buried under the snow-drift. Under this snowy shelter one could eat pemmican and perhaps quench his thirst by taking a covered copper teakettle into his bosom to melt the snow it contained. But, however thankful a traveller might be for this safeguard from the fury of the storm, it was distinctly uncomfortable, unsanitary, and malodorous, and I know what I am talking about, for I spent two days and two nights in such a shelter on the Couteau in the following winter. Jerry and Harper had had three days and three nights of it on a previous occasion about the same place.

A LICK AND A PROMISE

ARRIVE AT WOOD MOUNTAIN.

We reached the clump of wolf willows, and had a fire that night, which, after finishing cooking, we raked to one side, and spreading our bedding on its site, previously covered with willow twigs, we lay down and enjoyed a good warm bed, for it is from the ground more than from the air in ordinary winter weather, that the cold comes to the couch of the winter traveller in the open.

On our last day we made good time and then travelled long into the night over the foot hills and a lake at the base of Wood Mountain, where our arrival was hailed with joy by Harper, who had been left in charge, and his companions in the big log hut, the common abode of Jerry and his men for the winter. We were all eager to hear the news of that world of magnificent distances in which our lots were then cast. So amid a torrent of tongues, Cree, Saulteau, French and English, we sat down to a comfortable " square " meal, accompanied by that rare and costly dainty of the time and place— bannocks, made with lots of buffalo fat and baked before an open fire in a frying pan. To say a man is hungry as a hunter is comparatively mild, for the appetite of a driver of dogs, after a winter trip when the term " camp " did not signify warmth nor any cookery save a lick and a promise and the boiling tea in the drinking pot was often frozen before one could drink it, would put any hunter but an Indian to shame.

HENRY JORDAN.

Besides Harper there were at the wintering house two American army deserters, Henry Jordan and Charles Davis. Another American of the same kind was at Fort Ellice, named Miron. These poor fellows must have had powerful reasons to take the risk of deserting from posts surrounded by hostile Sioux, ever ready to slay and scalp any stray Americans. Miron and Davis were able-bodied men, and willing and

17   255

obedient. But my friend Henry Jordan at that time was almost a skeleton. He appeared to have been brought up from infancy in such perfect terror of all Indians that during the seven years subsequently in which I had the happiness of knowing him, and in which he became thoroughly familiar with our Indians and their language, he never lost this dread when trouble was brewing or brewed. He had started as a drummer boy, had been some years with a circus, and had acquired a number of the " catches," songs and dances used in such shows. So Jordan was the great entertainer and quite an acquisition in that line to Jerry's brigade. Besides he was always in good humor and obliging and willing to do anything he was at that time physically fit for. In another year he had developed into a strong and athletic man, and a first-rate traveller and dog driver.

He was always well liked by everyone, and deservedly so, and latterly when I succeeded Mr. McDonald in the charge of Fort Qu'Appelle, he became most useful in the trading store there. After I left Qu'Appelle, in June, 1874, Jordan drifted away from the Company and found employment with the firm of I. G. Baker & Co., who had established themselves near my old wintering post at Cypress Hills, where he received in a month as much as the Hudson's Bay Company had been paying him for eight months' wages. He did not live very long afterwards, and his bones lie somewhere about Medicine Hat.

THE AMERICANS ON THE MISSOURI.

I record this bit of the biography of Jordan, in whose cheery company I passed many a happy hour, for it is his due, also to show what manner of man it was from whom I derived information concerning the Americans on the Upper Missouri in those days. From Jordan, and Dick Niven, a wolf hunter, both highly American in sentiment, and from Edward McKay, the elder brother of Jerry, and other reliable Metis, who had been employed at the trading posts on the

Missouri, it appeared that the life and conduct of the Hudson's Bay men in the wilds were saintly in comparison with those of their fellows on the Missouri.

Jordan said that the colonel in command of the post from which he deserted, crimped his men and sold the liberal supplies of food provided by the government to the traders; also, the reason for the stationing of the military under him being to check the hostile Sioux and prevent arms and ammunition being supplied to them, that he actually sold these arms and ammunition to them himself or through traders in collusion with him. This story was corroborated by his fellow deserters, as well as by other parties.

The men who had been employed by the Missouri fur traders said they all got big wages, especially if they were much addicted to gambling, in which their master took a part and kept the bank. Consequently they never could save a cent, while the Hudson's Bay servants at smaller wages always did so in the interior. Assiniboine women were openly bought, sold and exchanged as an everyday occurrence; and liquor was illegally but freely used in the trade. The Americans were continually being killed and scalped by the Sioux, and many fatal fights occurred among themselves, for which no one was punished, although there were military posts planted at intervals all the way up to Benton.

These were our next door—civilized (?)—neighbors, immediately across the international line, which no man knew, for it was not surveyed for years afterwards. And to them was due the trouble we were always having with drunken savages, who obtained their supply from French halfbreed and Indian traders fitted out at the posts along the Missouri.

At Wood Mountain.

My instructions having been to take a list of the furs, robes and provisions purchased, and the goods on hand, besides those we had just brought out, at Wood Mountain, I found the following on hand, and detail it as shedding light on the trade of ancient days.

List of furs, etc., at Wood Mountain, 23rd January, 1868— 485 prime buffalo robes, 22 buffalo bosses, 79 buffalo tongues, 21 prime badgers, 1 grizzly bear, 21 red foxes, 132 kitt foxes, 16 hares (Jackrabbits), 3 skunks, 1 wolverine, 59 wolves.

List of Goods—Blankets, 1 red, 12 green, 13 white, 3 points; cloth (" H.B. Strouds "), 34 yards red, 13 yards white, and 20 yards blue; cloth, green, 4 yards; Capotes, 30 Indian white from 1 to 4 Ell size; 53 yards printed cotton; 40 yards red woollen Tartan; 2 Tartan shawls; 2 pairs moleskin trousers; Belts, 1 narrow L'Assomption, 8 colored worsted, 2 to 4 inches; 1 roll striped gartering; 16 yards half-inch colored ribbon; 1 gross gilt ball buttons; 2 pounds white and 1 pound blue beads; 23 scalping knives; 14 fire steels; 5 small tooth combs; 2 large combs; 26 gun flints; 1 gunworm; 1 keg Tower-proof gunpowder, 66 pounds net; 122 pounds ball, 28s; 110 pounds plug tobacco; 2 carrots tobacco; 9 Indian awls; 1 pound linen thread.

To supplement this outfit we had brought out more gun-powder and ball, two rolls Canada twist tobacco, each about one hundred pounds, and last but not least in the Indians' estimation, several half chests Congou tea, each half a hun-dredweight, and two cases of Indian trading flintlock guns. Besides these were blankets and clothing, also hardware, such as files, copper kettles and needles, axes, and a few traps. I have no memorandum of these, but certainly vermilion for painting their faces, and brass wire to twist around the ends of their hair, and hawk bells to jingle as they walked, would be part of the outfit, and Jerry may have secured, to sell to specially favored Indians, in not greater quantity than one pint each, a keg of crushed loaf sugar—sixty-six pounds. The bag of that precious commodity—flour—which he brought out was for his own use only, but he was too open-handed and good-hearted to keep it for himself.

EPIDEMICS OF SMALLPOX

THE ASSINIBOINES.

The Indians wintering in the wooded valleys of the mountains were principally Assiniboines, and amongst them the Chieftain, Growing Thunder. They were living in abundance, making occasional raids out to the open plains after buffalo. Their leaders vied with each other in proffering breakfasts, dinners and suppers, and other intervening meals, to Jerry, to a number of which I had to accompany him. Fine " back fats " of the rump, and bosses and tongues were the chief items in these feasts, with frequently a calf, unborn and cooked in its own juice, as a special delicacy, for declining to partake of which I should have given offence, had not my hosts kindly excused me on account of my " greenness."

These Assiniboines, as a body, when unadorned with vermilion, had the palest faces of all the Indians I ever remember seeing. Although they often traded with the Americans on the Missouri, they spoke of them bitterly as supplying an inferior quality of goods at higher prices than ours, although they had the advantages of steamboat freight up the Missouri, and we had to carry everything on men's backs from the Hudson Bay. These steamboats also conveyed epidemics of smallpox to the Assiniboines, and through them the infection spread to the north. The Missouri was also the source from which came among our Indians occasional cases of unclean complaints.

The notoriety of the men as horse-thieves incarnate has been mentioned before; and the women were equally adept at pilfering any stray article they could squat down on. Harper, the zealous and honest, was particularly furious against these women, and gave as an instance that of one who had walked off slowly, and to all appearances innocently, but with the helve of the axe, which had been thrown down for a moment, protruding an inch or two below her short skirt. He declared the squaws had some concealed device which enabled them to carry away anything that they could squat down on.

The women of this tribe of Assiniboines were an exception to the modesty of demeanor which distinguishes those of all other tribes on the east of the Rockies, including, I believe, those down the Mackenzie and the Loucheaux, on the Yukon. A Stony squaw appeared to have as little self-consciousness, while standing around trading, as a cow.

It was amusing to see the entirely naked little boys, stuffed full with such plenty that their stomachs would have done credit to an alderman, running about barefooted on the hard-beaten snow around the lodge, whipping up their tops, which, like everything else of native make, were of some part of their universal provider, the buffalo. In this case the tip of the horn was the boy's top. After perhaps ten or twenty minutes playing barefooted in a temperature several degrees below zero the little chaps would come in and thrust their calloused soles against the fire, which seemed to have as little effect on them as had the frost outside.

My Friend Flemmand.

I spent a few pleasant days under Jerry's hospitable roof, and with Jordan's aid we had several sing-songs, Jerry's contribution being, " The North Counteree " and mine " The Jolly Dogs," which latter charmed the ear or fancy of Olivier Flemmand, who was a jolly dog himself. The chorus was " Slap, bang, here we are again," in which Flemmand turned the " slap " into " frappe " in his rendering. Flemmand was a tall, lithe, active fellow, who justly prided himself on his prowess as a runner, for on one occasion he had run the distance of one hundred and thirty-five miles from Fort Qu'-Appelle to Fort Ellice within twenty-four hours in the heat of summer, carrying an urgent letter. He was polite, good-natured, full of fun, and talkative. He was a good-looking fellow, although as dark skinned as most Indians, but inside he seemed to be all French with one exception, for he was an arrant coward. This he sought to conceal by brag and bluster, and bullying young fellows under him with most savage threats. He talked French, Saulteau and Cree, and spoke English amusingly.

Flemmand wanted to get a trip in to the fort to see his family, so Mr. McKay sent him with me, *via* Old Wives' Creek, where Jacob Bear was wintering in the lodge of Ookemah, the recognized chief of the Qu'Appelle Saulteaux. The American, Charles Davis, and William Sandison, with a train of dogs each, came with us on the homeward journey.

OLD WIVES' CREEK.

On the 27th of January I note that Jacob Bear had on hand ninety buffalo robes, seventy buffalo tongues, five badgers, five red foxes, twenty kitt foxes, one lynx and twenty wolves as the result of his trade up to that time. My visit afforded old Ookemah the unusual opportunity of putting his grievances in writing. The old fellow was in a sulky mood, probably arising from disturbance of his liver from overeating, for he was living on the fat of the land, and he was far too fat himself anyhow to be healthy. Obesity is not common among male Indians, but it is, I think, more frequently found among the Saulteaux than the other tribes. He and his son, White Bear, appeared to be conjoint chiefs in some way, which Flemmand failed to make me understand. Neither could I understand and get any comprehensible explanation of the chief's bitter complaint that he had not been paid in full for the " present " to the Company with which he had celebrated, according to custom, his arrival in state at the fort in the fall. The alleged present consisted of two horses and some furs and provisions, and all those who contributed towards it had been paid in full but he himself, said he. He also grumbled that his gratuities as a chief had been forced upon him against his will, and for these he might be called upon to pay when he was unable. Bewildered between what he regarded as my childish questions for an explanation, and the inadequacy of Flemmand's interpretation in such a case of delicate diplomacy, I finally simply wrote down what Flemmand said the chief had said, leaving Mr. McDonald to solve the problem himself.

Start for the Fort.

We passed a day with Jacob, and on the 30th of January, 1868, set out for the fort, the trail to which, after reaching the Hotel Denomie, at the River that Turns, would be that followed on the outward voyage. Although Jacob had plenty of carts to carry in to the fort all he was likely to trade by spring, we loaded up our sleds with robes, or rather Jacob and Flemmand loaded mine, saying that my dogs were strong and well able to draw forty large prime robes. While the stuff I had taken to Wood Mountain on my sled probably weighed as much, yet in bulk it was not half as high as the load of loose, unpacked robes they piled on it. Flemmand, having no dog-train to drive, set off ahead, on an old trail hard enough to hold up a man without snowshoes. He seemed to be in a great hurry and kept us busy attempting to keep up with him. But the roadway was over rolling ground and side slopes where my sled was continually swinging off the narrow track and upsetting in the soft, deep snow alongside. The ground seemed to be honeycombed with badger holes, and nearly every time I got off the track to right my sled down one of my legs would go full length in one of the holes. Sandison and Davis, having lighter and well-snugged loads, did not have so much difficulty and were more experienced in the work; but they, too, had had enough of Flemmand's furious rush at the start and were glad when he halted at my signal. I came up to him hot in body and in temper, for I suspected he had done as he did " to play over a greenhand." I said:

" We will stop and make tea, and then you and I, Flemmand, will go back to Jacob's while the others go on. We will catch them up in the morning."

" What for, m'sieu, you want to go back ?" asked Flemmand, with feigned surprise.

"Because I did not come out here to do the work of a cart-horse, with a sled that you have loaded as high as a haystack," I answered, hotly. "We will make a cariole at Jacob's and you will drive me in, in style, to the fort."

TERROR OF THE OLD WIVES.

Next morning we caught up to the men within a mile of where we had left them the day before, going slowly along at a walk. Flemmand was delighted and proud of the splendid train he was driving, and we passed on ahead to give them a lead and encouragement. Before us lay the Old Wives' Lake, with the high rolling ridges of the western slopes of the Couteau on its farther side. Flemmand pointed out the direction we had to go, which towards evening I saw lay almost directly over the willow-clad island in the middle of the lake, which was supposed to be frequented by the spirits of the old wives from which the lake derives its legendary name.* There was no wood anywhere on the way, except the willows on the isle of the spirits, which we could have reached just about the right time to stop for the night. I told him to make for the island, and he at once declared that no living man had ever dared to go there, and it would be a terrible thing to rouse the wrath of the ghosts of the old wives.

"Nonsense," I said, "there is no such thing as a ghost."

"Ah, m'sieu, maybe dare be none in de old country, but dare is plenty en ce pays sauvage. Day not baptime and le diable help dem."

We had now got on the lake, and the track had disappeared, so I told him to go ahead and give a lead for the dogs to follow. But the swift and joyous runner of yesterday now went forward with slow and saddened step, wavering in his line of march and always edging away from the isle he

---

* There are two Old Wives' Lakes, connected by a creek. These were named on maps, respectively, after the Rt. Hon. Henry Chaplin and Sir Frederick Johnstone, who hunted buffalo near them in 1861.

dreaded. I tried over and over again to keep him on the course, but he always edged off, and I suppose I must have fallen asleep for a while, for when I awoke we were far from the island and in the middle of the lake, where we were obliged to stop for the night, after a cup of tea boiled over a little kindling wood which we each carried at the tail of our sleds.

I slept in the cariole quite comfortably, but was aroused every now and again by the cracking, rumbling and thunderous resounding of the ice as the cold took a firmer grip on it and upheaved it into pressure ridges. I daresay Flemmand, who belonged to a family of fishermen, and had heard other lakes make an equally noisy disturbance, fully imagined that those that night were caused by some devilish cantrip slight of the Old Wives, aroused to wrath at our approach to their abode of terror.

Again Cross the Grande Couteau.

We got off the lake bright and early, Flemmand requiring no urging to keep a straight course, and we found the trail again, which took us to the foot of the main slope that forenoon. After stopping to boil the tea kettle, the track getting better, Flemmand proposed that we should go ahead of Sandison and Davis and try to reach Denomie's, at the River that Turns, for the night. The hills were often steep and the dogs required Flemmand to assist them in parts, so he proposed that I should get out and walk up hill, if we were to reach Denomie's that night.

"I only weigh one hundred and sixty-four pounds," I answered, "and yet you expected me to take four hundred pounds of loose robes, piled up high, over these hills. I won't walk."

When we came to the next hill he said:

"M'sieu, take pity to de poor dogs. Day force, an' me, too, I force very hard."

"All right," said I, "but if I get out once I will stay out and run all the way to the Turn."

"No, no, jump on going down hill."

"No, I shan't," and I did not either till we had crossed all the hills and had come quite a way on the plain. There we found the two lodges of Cowesess, one of the very best hunters of the Qu'Appelle Saulteaux, whose brawny wives insisted on our stopping for something to eat with them before making the few more miles to Denomie's. The two wives were sisters, and good, steady housekeepers and workers.

THE FURY OF FLEMMAND.

So, after a well-served meal of buffalo tongue and tea, I was glad to get into the cariole to enjoy a smoke, while Flemmand, delighted at the chance of showing off, started the dogs with a furious, but quite unnecessary, flourish, for they now knew where they were going to camp. He was soon glad to jump on the tail of the sled, for it took a mighty good runner, when that train "took the bit in their teeth," to keep up with them. Standing on the tail end of the cariole, he began wrathfully to tell that the Cowesess women had reported the arrival of Donald Sinclair (the native dude mentioned in a previous chapter) with alcohol for trading purposes at The Turn. Between Flemmand and Donald, the dude, there was personal animosity and rivalry, and now Flemmand was aroused to fury at Donald's intrusion among the people whose furs, by reason of the outfits given them by the Company, belonged to Fort Qu'Appelle. Moreover, the attempt of Donald to introduce the seductive beverage amongst the women of the fort, which has already been related, filled Flemmand with virtuous and warlike wrath.

"Let me catch dat leetle trash, and you'll see what a proper pounding I been give him," exclaimed Flemmand. "I been waiting de chance for long time now."

He continued to rant and rave as we sped along the well-beaten path, and urged on the dogs to still greater speed in his eagerness to give Donald the thrashing, to wipe off old scores and to show me that although he was afraid of the ghosts of old women he dreaded nothing in the shape of mortal man.

We were, with the customary kindness and hospitality of the Metis, warmly welcomed by Paul Denomie and his wife, and invited to remain over the night in their snug little cabin. The door was of clear parchment and gave a good light, so that only one little window "glazed" with a piece of cotton, was cut in the log wall. Under this was a cassette—a wooden trunk—which was used as a seat by visitors, and there were two bedsteads made of poles and covered with several soft and downy robes, one of which was kindly given to me to sit and recline on.

THE FURY ABATED.

We had a good supper, during which Flemmand anxiously enquired where he could find Donald, the transgressor, and in French and Indian proceeded to repeat much more fluently than he had in English the terrific consequences to Donald, which would result when he got within arm's length. After a little in came Paul's brother, Xavier, evidently laboring under a big dose of Donald's fire-water, although he remained perfectly mute, squatted down in a corner. In the midst of one of Flemmand's most blood-curdling threats against him, the door quietly opened and in stepped Donald, looking as cool as a cucumber and impudent as a "Whiskey Jack." Flemmand's tirade at once was cut short, and to my astonishment he sprang up and grasping the hand of Donald, warmly greeted him as "Mon cer ami, mon associe," and expressed his delight at meeting him. Probably Donald had been eavesdropping before he quietly slipped in, but the only sign he gave was to immediately begin:

"Flemmand, you are a liar and a boaster and a coward. I can beat you travelling in the boats and with dogs; I can outrun you on foot, and beat you running buffalo, and I can wrestle you down and pound you with fists."

"Oh," replied Flemmand, "my friend and comrade, you are joking; we always been friends."

"You are a liar," coolly answered Donald. "We never were friends. I never would make friends with such a bragging liar and coward as you."

"Ah," said poor Flemmand, soothingly, and looking round to us for sympathy, "my friend and comrade, you joke too hard."

"If it is too hard," tauntingly replied Donald, "take up my challenge like a man and come outside."

"Oh, my friend, my comrade, don't carry your fun so far," besought Flemmand.

The reply was voluble and abusive, in Indian this time, which being understood by Xavier, who had remained during the English portion of the debate still and silent, aroused him to instant action on behalf of his fellow Metis, just as I, at first thoroughly amused at the instantaneous collapse of Flemmand's fury, was about to take the part of my amiable and amusing travelling companion. With a "*Sacré diable!*" Xavier sprang to his feet, and Donald, who was sitting on the casette under the cotton window, seeing him coming, with amazing nimbleness sprang up, turned round, and took a header right through the window, his heels just disappearing as Xavier reached the cassette. Xavier instantly made for the door to pursue, his pent-up feelings and the firewater bursting out in French and Indian execrations. But his brother Paul was too quick for him, and blocked the doorway, whereupon Xavier became more enraged than ever; so that, with the assistance of his wife and Xavier's, who had rushed in from her cabin next door, Paul was obliged to tie his brother hand and foot with buffalo cords, and lay him in bed.

ANOTHER FLARE-UP EXTINGUISHED.

No sooner had Xavier been subdued than up sprang Flemmand, full of renewed fury against Donald.

" First I tink he been joking, and I not want to make troube in nodder man's house, but now, me properly mad at dat Donal," he declared. " Just let me see him again !"

Just as he was uttering the words the door again opened quietly, and Donald reappeared, unabashed, and with as much effrontery as ever.

" Here I am again, you bragging coward," he said.

Poor Flemmand at once wilted, tried to assume an ingratiating smile, and was beginning, " Oh, mon ami," when Paul sprang up, opened the door and kicked the presumptuous Donald out without resistance; for in boasting and cowardice Donald and his " camarade, Flemmand," were equal and well met.

Pile of Bones and Their Ghosts.

We departed in peace next morning to make the little clump of wood in the valley of the Pile of Bones Creek. Every now and again Flemmand would jump on behind and make excuses and explanations and express his regret at not having smashed Donald. Still he was hopeful of getting another chance, when the indignities which he had borne with Christian patience would be wiped out in gore and glory. The decisive action of Paul in kicking the fellow out had evidently aroused again in Flemmand the hope which springs eternal in the human breast. So the delinquencies of Donald and the frightful vengeance which he, Flemmand, had every intention of taking upon him " next time " were uppermost in his talk as we went along. At first when we started and had gone a mile or so that morning, I said that as he felt so bad about it we might turn back and have the affair of honor over and done with. But Flemmand would not hear of such a sacrifice of the Company's time. Yet as we put mile after mile between us and his " friend " and enemy, his fury against him increased instead of abated.

We arrived that evening at the Pile of Bones Creek in time to make a good camp. We started a fire and Flemmand was busy getting wood for the night, when I began to talk about the poor Cree who had perished with his son, in the attempt to reach these woods that winter—Tay-put-ah-um. Flemmand had talked of merely making fire and having something to eat at the Pile of Bones, and then going on through the night across the traverse over the bare plain to the last wooded point out from Qu'Appelle. But I was not in such a hurry as to pass a rare wooded oasis in that treeless snowy plain, from which we could easily make the next woods in a day's run with four fine dogs.

"Don't say dat name," cried Flemmand in alarm.

"Why should I not?" I exclaimed in surprise.

Pausing in his wood chopping and coming to the fire he warned me:

"You not know how bad dese Indians are. Dey partners of le diable, and if you speak about him his ghost will come and bodder us."

I was amused at the poor fellow's superstitious dread, and after he resumed his chopping, suddenly called out:

"Hello, Flemmand, what's that?" pointing to a rabbit that was just disappearing in a thicket.

With a yell of terror the poor chap rushed to the fire, and throwing himself down on the brush by it, enveloped himself from heel to head in his green blanket. There he lay till next morning without stirring, for neither reasoning nor persuasion could elicit a word out of him; and I was but too slightly punished for my folly and cruelty in playing on his terrors by having to pack the wood into camp and cook my own supper, to which he treated the invitation to join in silence. Presumably after dawn the spirits of the departed took a rest, in Flemmand's opinion, so at broad daylight he got up briskly, but in haste to make breakfast and resume our journey. He was in a desperate hurry to get away from that haunted ground, and we were soon bowling away on a good hard trail for the woods bordering the valley of the Qu'Appelle.

The Driver Driven.

His spirits rose as we left the place behind and he began to think that if the track kept good we might make the fort that night. Every stride took us farther away from Donald and the cold shade of Tay-put-ah-um, and before long he desired me to add to his various accomplishments by teaching him " properly " that fascinating ditty " The Jolly Dogs." As " by special request " I trolled out the air, the dogs, who knew quite well they were nearing home, increased their speed and gave him hard work to keep up, holding on to the tail line. Every once and a while he jumped on behind, but finally he asked me to make no more noise as the dogs might over-exert themselves early in the day and become too tired to reach the fort that night.

We made the first woods early and had tea and something to eat, and went on till, towards evening, we came to Duck Lake, where we stopped again for a meal. It had become warmer, and on starting again I noticed the dogs were getting a bit fagged, as Flemmand more frequently and for longer spells got on and rode behind. We went on for a few miles, and as it was getting dark he jumped on and the dogs slowed down, when he said:

" Bien m'sieu, I not tired, mais I sick."

" Oh, then, get in the cariole and I will drive you to the fort," I replied.

The poor chap gladly got in and lay there contented while I drove the remaining ten miles to the fort; but when we got near he asked me to stop and change places with him, so that he might enter the gate with *éclat* instead of ignominy. But I had him " properly " secured in the cariole so that he could not get out, and I had the pleasure of driving into the square the man who had set out with a rush from Old Wives' Creek with the object of showing his superiority and my inferiority as a winter voyageur.

CHAPTER XVI.

THE CLOSE OF THE FUR TRADE YEAR.

The Winter Packets.

The winter packets from York Factory and Fort Garry, which had met at Norway House, and went on from there to Carlton House, where the packet from Mackenzie River and other northern districts met them, returned south-easterly by Touchwood Hills and Qu'Appelle en route to Fort Garry by way of Fort Pelly and Lakes Winnipegosis and Manitoba. With this packet Mr. McDonald went in March to Fort Pelly, to attend the annual council of the officers in charge of posts in Swan River district, presided over by Chief Factor Campbell.

Spring the Busy Season.

Spring did not linger in the lap of the winter of 1867-8, coming on with a rush and quickly merging into summer. As soon as the snow had uncovered the southern plains around Wood Mountain and Old Wives' Creek, Jerry and Jacob loaded up their carts with the buffalo robes, furs, provisions and leather which they had traded during the winter, and followed the thaw into Fort Qu'Appelle. The rate at which the thaw advanced northward was generally about the same rate as that which the carts travelled in a day—some twenty miles. Indians and the few Metis hunters, who then regularly resorted to the fort, also made their way to it to pay their debts and trade the balance of their hunts.

Day after day these arrivals took place and the fort presented a busy scene. Each arrival first reported to the officer in charge, who sat, in clouds of tobacco smoke, in the com-

18   271

bined office and Indian hall, to receive them and hear an account of their doings during the winter, and the news of different places of the plains from which they had come or heard. In return he would, with the assistance of an interpreter in particular cases, give them the news of the world, at large and of the country in particular, for the first question a visiting Indian would ask was: " What is the news? . Tell it truthfully, my friend."

INDIAN DEBTS.

Then the Indian's fur packs would be opened and sorted out according to value, in the office, and his robes, leather and pemmican similarly dealt with in the fur and provision store. When these were reckoned up and placed to his credit, any credit balance he might have was settled by an order on the trading store, which would specify if any amount of such limited supplies as tea and sugar should be given the Indian over the regulation limit. In case the hunt did not come up to or exceed the amount of the hunter's debts, the master arranged with him how much should be paid on account and how much he would be allowed to exchange for his present needs.

Any officer who neglected to personally meet and talk with the Indians, and arrange for their requirements in accordance with their needs and abilities, and consider the prospects of the grounds upon which they hunted or planned to hunt, in fact, to acquire a sympathetic knowledge of the Indian, his character and capabilities, was no good as an Indian trader. For to be a successful one he had to judiciously furnish in advance the outfit required by the Indian if he were to be successful in his winter and summer hunting. The trader having arranged how much of the vital essentials—such as ammunition, guns, axes, and traps, and such luxuries as blankets, tea and tobacco—without which he would be miserable,—the Indian should get on credit, he was allowed to take a few other things for his personal adornment. All these were marked down in the order on the trading store, otherwise the Indian would most likely take all the unnecessaries and, the amount of the advance agreed upon having been made up in these, try to have it increased by the addition of the absolute necessities which he pretended that he had forgotten. The Indian generally was as void of any care for the future as is the field of a farmer, and even as a skilful farmer had to cultivate and take the risk of seeding his land in anticipation of remunerative returns, so had a well trained fur trader to cultivate a knowledge of each Indian and take the risk, after duly weighing his capabilities and prospects, of advancing to the hunter an outfit adequate to his needs and ability. In this way alone could the trade be conducted with Indians whose hunting grounds lay hundreds of miles from the trading post, and whose visits thereto were limited to once or twice a year.

From the time the fort gates opened at sunrise till they closed at sunset the Indians thronged the hall, singly and in family groups, and Mr. McDonald listened and talked to them with admirable patience, and managed them with tact and firmness. The natives were no fools, and quick to notice any flaw or inconsistency in an argument against them. Moreover they were all intensely jealous of each other, and strove to have similar favors, in the shape of debt and gratuities, bestowed upon each as had been given to those more deserving in the opinion of the master. No such favors could be given without being publicly proclaimed and boasted about by the recipients and their families; so it taxed all the diplomatic ability of the trader to smooth over and explain such matters.

ARRIVAL OF CREE CHIEF.

The chief of the Qu'Appelle Crees was Kaw-keesh-e-way, which was rendered in English as Loud Voice, and his voice was used always in the cause of peace and good-will between the different people and the tribes frequenting the post. There were a number of his band who had won greater names in war, but Loud Voice added to his reputation in the arts of Medicine Man, in which the more straightforward and simpler-minded Crees were much behind the more cunning and intelligent Saulteaux.

When the chief and his followers had reached a camp about a day's journey from the fort he sent in two runners to announce his intended visit, and to receive the usual present of tea, sugar and tobacco. On the day appointed, his band of mounted warriors, all painted and plumed in battle array, suddenly appeared careering on the plain to the east of the fort, performing various evolutions as they gradually approached. These became more exciting on nearing it, as they delivered charge after charge, accompanied with wild whoops, volleys from their guns and frantic brandishing of bow and spear. Each charge just before being driven home on the line formed by Mr. McDonald and all hands, who had turned out with arms to salute and receive them outside the pickets, was suddenly diverted from the centre into a right and left half wheel of the wings, which then swept at a furious gallop in a semicircle to the rear, where they again united and forming line again charged furiously towards us.

After a number of these feints, in their last charge they came to an abrupt halt within a few yards of us, and dismounted. Loud Voice at once advanced, leading a fine pony, by a line which he held in his right hand, and on Mr. McDonald advancing to meet him and shake hands in that process he slipped the leading line into the hand of the latter, thereby making him a present of the pony. Immediately following the chief came two warriors, each leading a pack-horse laden with presents of robes, furs, pemmican and buffalo marrow. Jerry and I shook hands with the chief and his immediate followers and, the ponies with their presents being handed over to four men, we followed the chief and Mr. McDonald as they marched together into the fort. At its gate the rest of our men and a number of visitors, who had previously arrived, opened up a narrow lane for us to pass through, as they delivered volley after volley in salute, and they took special pains to let our ear-drums get the full shock by letting off close to them. They followed us to the door of the " reception " hall, and let off several *feux de joie* after we had entered.

Amongst the things sent out to meet Loud Voice was his great ceremonial calumet and decorated stem, which, wrapped up with much mysterious medicine, in coil after coil of different colored cloth, and trappings of leather, decorated with quill and bead, had been hung conspicuously in the hall, as a token of friendship between the Crees and the Company, ever since his last visit to the post. And while all his followers came armed to the teeth, with bow and quiver on back, flintlock in hand, and knife and tomahawk in belt, Loud Voice met the master and entered the fort bearing only his long, and highly decorated, stem and pipe of peace.

He was given a chair of honor, and his band disposed themselves on the forms around three sides of the room, or squatted in front of these in a manner more comfortable to them on the floor. At the inner end of the room Mr. McDonald sat, with Jerry and myself on each side. The ceremonies opened by Loud Voice taking the pipe from the functionary, who filled and lit it according to the Cree rules of etiquette, and offering the mouthpiece to deities presiding over the four quarters of the compass and zenith on high and depths below. Then he took a whiff or two, exhaling the smoke through his nose, and handed the pipe to Mr. McDonald, who took a whiff and passed it on, with the sun, to the next man, and so on till all had taken a draw. Then followed the speeches of the chief and other headmen, which were duly responded to by Mr. McDonald. Next a feast was spread on the floor before them, consisting of bannocks, tea, chocolate, sugar, and a sort of hasty pudding containing raisins and currants. At the conclusion of the feast Loud Voice was taken into another room and clothed in a shirt, trousers, a chief's scarlet, gold-laced surtout, and a black silk high—very high—hat, adorned with three big plumes of coloured cockstail feathers. Upon returning, so arrayed, to the hall, he was presented with the semi-annual gratuities—tea, tobacco, ammunition, etc.—which his written and carefully wrapped up certificate as a Company's chief specified.

Meanwhile the "presents," except the pony, made by the chief and his followers, having been piled in the hall in front of Mr. McDonald, were removed to the store and appraised at market value, to which was added about twenty-five per cent. Quantities of tea, tobacco, sugar, and perhaps some other rare and expensive luxuries, such as flour, rice and raisins, were then brought in and presented to the band for a general feast, preliminary to the individual payment in full to each of those who had contributed to the "presents" strictly according to his proportion.

Loud Voice only wore his uniform for a few days, and immediately after his departure from the fort he parted these garments amongst his followers; for he would have been considered unworthy of being considered a chief and too stingy for the office had he kept anything he obtained in virtue thereof for himself. How different a disposition is made of "the spoils of office" amongst civilized Christians; but Loud Voice was only a simple heathen Cree chief, who retained as the only insignia of his office the long-stemmed pipe of peace before mentioned and a very big lowland Scotch blue bonnet, which deserves to be described. It was similar to those worn by curlers, with a red knob on the top, and red and white checks round the band. All around the broad rim were little brass hawk bells and round gilt ball buttons alternately, with bows of vari-colored narrow ribbon at intervals. Attached to the top knob there were either colored plumes from the store or three eagle quills, decorated with heraldic devices of his own.

PACKING THE FURS.

While Mr. McDonald was busy in the hall, outside we were all equally busy. When the trading parties from Wood Mountain and Old Wives' Creek arrived I had to take account of the goods returned and the robes and furs for which the rest of the outfits had been expended, also the Indian debts paid and the supplies given to servants there. And then commenced the lively scene of packing the robes and furs in the big lever fur press in the middle of the square. Before being pressed into packs, each containing ten, folded hair side in, the robes had to be beaten of the dust and mud clinging to them, in the same way as carpets are beaten with sticks. The men worked in pairs, one catching the head and the other the tail end of the robe, which was folded in the middle with the hair out. Day after day the resounding whacks of the beaters kept up from morn till eve, accompanied by the merry shouts of laughter of the men at some catchword which served its purpose as a provoker of mirth whenever uttered and which never seemed to lose by repetition. Original and new mirth-making phrases and antics were, however, frequently put on the stage by that gifted burlesque actor and farceur, my friend Flemmand, who was as active in keeping up the spirits of his camarades as he was in the work of beating and packing the robes.

Each pack had attached to it a wooden stave on which were branded its consecutive number, weight and " '67—H.B. F.Q." meaning Outfit 1867, Hudson Bay, (F) Swan River district, (Q) Fort Qu'Appelle. The furs were also hung up on lines like a wash to get rid of the dust in the wind, and the larger and stronger hides beaten like the robes. The finer and weaker-skinned furs were parcelled up in strong-hided summer bearskins, and several bundles of these made up the pack to about ninety pounds weight. Each of these fur-packs was of assorted skins, and as many packs as possible made up of a uniform number of assorted skins. This was done for the same reason as assorted bales of "dry-goods" were made up at York Factory and assorted cargoes shipped into the interior from there by boats—to avoid the risk of all the articles or furs of one kind being lost in case of accident. Into each of these packs was put a slip of paper with an unpriced list of its contents and the marks and numbers before mentioned. This slip served to identify the pack or bale if the branded stave became detached, and also it enabled the person in charge of a shipment, which had got wet on the voyage and required to be opened and dried, to replace the furs belonging to different packs in rebaling them after being dried. The priced packing account of the furs, at the valuation allowed the post in general accounts, was not for the eyes of the men on the voyage with them.

OUTDOOR ATHLETICS.

The fur-packing season was one of mirth and jocundity, for the men were all glad, after a winter of many hardships, to be enjoying all the good things provided by the fort, which seemed by comparison with their life on the plains to be the acme of luxurious civilization. For the first time since fall they had all met together, and could, in the admiring presence of the women and children of the fort and groups of Indians, exhibit their favorite feats of strength and agility, in which, to encourage them, Jerry took part, and as I passed from office to the stores, back and forth, he always invited me to join. In the evening, too, these games would be continued outside, while I was busy posting up the long entries, made in pencil in the stores, into the regular pen and ink books of the post. In these labors he was always coming in and interrupting me by urging me to have another trial of a short footrace, in which I always beat him. But Jerry was a man who never gave in in any sport or feat at which he had been worsted—he went on to try and try again, and nearly always succeeded in the end in besting all competitors.

The best wrestler and about the best long distance runner was Gowdie Harper, who entered into the sports with impetuous alacrity. Others were of gigantic strength, but these, by practice and perseverance and agility, Jerry nearly always contrived to beat.

TRADING IN STERLING AND SKINS.

I was kept continually on the move attending to the packing account, telling the men whose provisions were weighed how much they came to at so many pence per pound, and then marking down each article they got in exchange, with frequent pauses to tell the Indian how much in pounds, shillings and pence he had left. The same with furs, merely exchanged for their value in goods; for our traders and interpreters found it difficult to calculate in the complicated pounds, shillings and pence standard which had recently been introduced, instead of the well and easily understood Made Beaver standard. Whoever was the Hudson's Bay official who superseded the simple " skin way " for the " money way " of trading with Indians, he certainly gave us no end of torment and trouble. It was alleged that the object of the change was to meet competition by paying the Indians full value for their products and do away with the old established system of giving them gratuities in the way of ammunition and other articles, including, I think, " regales " of rum before Swan River was put on the Hudson's Bay Company's list of teetotal districts. Now an Indian was never satisfied with a trade which was a fair and exact exchange at the fixed prices of the time, until he had received " something for nothing " on the top of the transaction. It did not matter if a trader raised the prices of furs and lowered the price of goods to him on the distinct understanding that no present was to be expected or given, the Indian always insisted on that " something for nothing," so dear to all man and womankind, at the end of the barter. So what between the elaborate lecture on the mysteries of British sterling currency, without the aid of the never visible actual coin for demonstration purposes, which I had to deliver on nearly every important trade in which I took part, and the absolute failure of the exposition to enlighten the Indian on it, I had many a vexing hour, and in explaining too that it was beyond my power to alter the new and odious system. All our other accounts were kept, of course, in sterling, and I often wonder why they cling to it in the old country, when the decimal system is so entirely simple and easy.

The standard of exchange throughout the Hudson's Bay territories generally was the well known Beaver Skin, but in some localities and circumstances other mediums of exchange were used. For instance, among the Blackfeet a buffalo robe took the place of the beaver skin, and a common pony and a buffalo runner were mediums most frequently used to obtain wives, and to pay gambling stakes or bets on races. And what is known in commercial language as the financial standing of a man was measured in those days on the plains by the number of his horses, also in the case of Indians, by the abundance of his wives.

CLOSING THE OUTFIT.

The end of each business year—called "Outfit"—was May 31, upon which date the inventory of everything belonging to the Company at the fort was taken. At this Jerry, Kennedy, Jacob, Harper, and I worked from dawn to dark till everything was weighed, measured and counted, both outside and inside the establishment. The live stock, cattle and horses were each enumerated and described, the list of horses comprising several hundred, known by their colors, and the names of those who had sold them to the Company or the post at which they had been reared. The colors were all named in French, and a large proportion had also French surnames, such as Nez Blanc Paranteau, Rouge LaRoque, Noir Denomie, and Blanc Peltier. Also Brun Fort Ellice and Pinto Fort Pelly, and Nez Blanc Lord March, the latter being an expert buffalo runner, which had been used by the present Duke of Richmond, in 1866. Each of these was branded H.B.F.Q.; and as horse-trading and exchanging was a very frequent occurrence, many were stamped with many other brands. We only put the number of horses, mares and colts on the inventory, but had a great list on several huge sheets of cartridge paper posted up on the office wall, with the name of each animal, and space for pencilled remarks, such as, " Sent to such and such a place," with date, so as to keep track of them. But Alick Fisher, the horseguard, Jerry and Mr. McDonald required no such artificial aid to memory.

Once the list of merchandise, etc., and articles in use had been made in pencil it became my task, day and night, to recapitulate them in alphabetical order under the various headings, and enter the result duly priced in the post account book for Outfit 1867. To get that book complete so as to find out the apparent gain or loss on the year's trade before the time came for the boatmen to start for the annual voyage to York Factory took up all my time.

Lastly came the private orders of the regular yearly servants for their year's supply of clothing, etc., from York Factory, which were sold them there at very low prices, brought up freight free and supposed to last them for the whole of the coming year; for the goods brought back for the Company were intended for trade alone and the payment of temporary laborers and voyageurs. The enlisted men got a half-holiday to make up these lists, and derived much pleasure and some excitement in doing so. The articles supplied from York Factory were all strong and suitable to the country, and a man, careful in making out his order, seldom required to ask the favor of being permitted to buy, at a price fifty per cent. higher than at York, anything out of the trading supplies in the interior, unless his order had suffered "waste, spoil or injury" on the boat voyage, and those were frequent; while the damage to outgoing furs and incoming supplies for the Company itself was of yearly occurrence. The annual loss in tea, sugar, tobacco and gunpowder, damaged by water, to Fort Qu'Appelle was always considerable, and occasionally three-quarters of the outfit, for these articles came as whole pieces not specially packed and marked for any particular post in the district, and Qu'Appelle being the last post got the rejections of those on the line of route.

CHAPTER XVII.

OUTFIT 1868 BEGINS—WITH CARTS TO INDIAN CAMP.

The Brigade to York Factory.

THE post accounts had to be made out in duplicate for the purpose of sending one copy to district headquarters and retaining one at the post. The copy for headquarters from each post was handed there to the officer in charge of the Swan River brigade of boats yearly going with the furs to York Factory. The boats also took out to Norway House the pemmican, dried meat, salted and smoked buffalo tongues, tallow and marrow fat, also the dressed leather, parchments, specially prepared pack cords, common rawhide lines—known as shaganappi, the sinews—used in sewing leather articles, and the moccasins for the boatmen's tracking shoes, also well-smoked leather lodges for covering the boats' cargoes. After landing the quantity of these, called for by the requisition, at Norway House, the rest and the furs for shipment to London were taken on to York Factory, where the brigade was laden with the return cargo of " Sundry Merchandise for the Trade of Swan River District, Outfit 1868," and the private orders of the servants.

The chief factor in command of the district accompanied the brigade to Norway House, where he remained to attend the annual council of the Northern Department of Rupert's Land, while the officer in charge of the brigade went on to York Factory. Besides the gentleman in charge, a good junior clerk travelled in the boats to assist him in making up the General Accounts of the District, which were made up from the post accounts before mentioned, and handed in at York Factory to be embodied in the General Accounts of the Northern Department. These two clerks had certainly no sinecure, for the work could only be done while the boats were stopping for the night, and amidst the clouds of pestiferous mosquitoes which infested the route from end to end.

Although the brigade was under a guide, and Big William Daniel was a good one, still Joseph Finlayson, as officer in charge, had many other duties, besides his nightly labors with the district accounts, to perform. But Mr. Finlayson was an able and accomplished all-round officer, and he was fortunate in having as his assistant Duncan Matheson, **apprentice clerk,** who was to join the brigade at Fairford—the outlet of Lake Manitoba—and could wield beautifully a rapid pen.

JOSEPH FINLAYSON.

Mr. Finlayson was descended from old North-West and Hudson's Bay officers on both sides. His uncle had been one of the best of the chief factors governing the Red River Settlement, and his father was Chief Factor Nichol Finlayson. He had passed through an apprenticeship in all grades and risen by his talents to that of chief clerk, justly expecting a chief tradership as his reward. He was a man who could do everything himself that any Company's servant, interpreter or accountant, could be expected to do; he did everything excellently, and took pains and pleasure in training others to their duties. His geniality and kindness endeared him to everyone with whom he came in contact, and he was universally known, not as Mr. Finlayson, but by the popular name of " Joe."

Mr. Finlayson was in charge of the neighboring post at Touchwood Hills, only forty-five miles north of Qu'Appelle by a beautiful cart trail. When he had finished the business of Outfit 1867 at Touchwood Hills, where the trade was not so large as at Qu'Appelle, he came with his good wife and family on a visit to Mr. and Mrs. McDonald, and with his usual kindness at once gave his efficient aid to Mr. McDonald and me in winding up accounts and requisitions for Qu'-Appelle.

My father, on one of his three voyages as surgeon on the Hudson's Bay ships, had acquired the friendship of Mr. Finlayson's father at York Factory, and the retired chief factor had come in 1866 from Nairn to visit him during his last illness. The old gentleman on that occasion took much interest in me as I eagerly listened to his reminiscences of the wilds of Rupert's Land and Ungava. So the Finlaysons and I became great friends at once, and forever. And they were both interesting and instructive in conversation, for they had been in the great Mackenzie River District, and were still in touch through correspondence with friends there.

Mrs. (Flora Bell) Finlayson was a beautiful daughter of Chief Trader John Bell, well known as the able Hudson's Bay officer who rendered so material aid to the British Government's Arctic exploring expeditions. Mr. Bell was also a notable explorer himself. In 1839, he explored the Peel River; in 1840, leaving the " Fort McPherson " which he had built thereon, he crossed the Rocky Mountains and descended the " Bell " to the Porcupine River. Yearly extending his excursions down stream, he reached the mouth of the Porcupine in 1844, at its junction with the Yukon whose head waters had been named the Pelly-Lewes by their discoverer, Robert Campbell, whose name often occurs in this narrative as chief factor in command of Swan River District. Rather curiously, in that charge, one of Mr. Campbell's predecessors, Chief Trader Alexander Hunter Murray, was the officer sent in 1847 to utilize Mr. Bell's discoveries by establishing the old Fort Yukon at the great forks of that grand river. Mrs. Finlayson's mother was a daughter of Chief Factor Peter Warren Dease, who, with Chief Trader Thomas Simpson, commanded the highly successful expedition of the Hudson's Bay Company, to connect the discoveries of previous explorers, from Point Barrow to Cape Britannia on the Arctic coast.

Shipping Out the "Returns of Trade."

Mr. Finlayson had already sent to Fort Pelly his servants
and the voyageurs engaged for the trip to York Factory with
the furs and other supplies from Touchwood Hills. But he
had brought the buffalo robes to Qu'Appelle, to go with ours
and other products of the buffalo by cart to Fort Ellice,
whence they were annually taken by batteaux down the Assiniboine River to Fort Garry. Thence the robes were sent
to St. Paul, Minnesota, for transhipment to Montreal for
sale. Mr. McDonald was usually in charge of the batteaux
to Fort Garry, and returned overland with a supply of new
Red River carts and flour, also American goods for the district; a band of ponies from the plain posts being driven
light to Fort Garry to meet him there.

The expiring contracts of servants, considered worthy,
were renewed; voyageurs for the voyages to York Factory
and Fort Garry were engaged and advanced necessary clothing
and other supplies; and the carts destined for Port Pelly and
Fort Ellice respectively were laden and started, thus completing the yearly round of the trade.

Early Summer.

The new year or outfit now began. Messrs. Finlayson
and McDonald each followed the carts after giving them a
few days' start, leaving the ladies to pass the summer at
Qu'Appelle in company. Jerry and I equipped the remaining Indians and a few Metis for the summer campaign
against the wild cattle of the plains. The women of the fort
and some of the bigger children were employed from time
to time in weeding the garden and hoeing the potatoes. The
fisherman attended the nets, and the fort hunter went gun-
ning after ducks, geese and chickens and an occasional cabri
or antelope. We had many mouths to feed, for we had to
provide for the families of most of the voyageurs, as well as
those of the regular servants.

As soon as Jerry thought the hunters had had sufficient start to have provisions on hand by the time he reached their camps, he took all the remaining ponies, carts and men and set out for the summer provision trade on the plains.   He also took with him two or three good buffalo hunters, who, with himself, well mounted on the best ponies belonging to the fort, would largely add to the provisions to be purchased from the Indians and " free-men."

NEWSMONGERS.

After Jerry's departure, there remained in the fort, besides the women and children, only the watchman, George Sandison, Robillard, the cartwright, Kennedy, and myself, for Geo. Thorne had, on Alick Fisher's going for a hunt on his own account on the plains, been appointed horse and cattle guard. Amongst the women folk at the post, there were always all kinds of gossip and stories in circulation, mostly originating in the idle imagination of people having nothing else to exercise their minds upon.   Amongst those at Qu'Appelle, the leading spirit and circulating medium of evil omens and malicious scandal was a middle-aged woman descended from one of the old Hudson's Bay English governors of York Factory.   Her activities in these lines could not find full scope in the fort, so she marched from one end of the lakes to the other in search of news and in the dissemination of gossip.   It being impossible to answer the ever-recurrent question, " What is truth ? " in the case of these old wives' tales, we came to act on the principle of believing nothing we heard, of hearing as little as possible, and letting it go at that.

And the women were not the only sensational newsmongers by any means, for Indians would come in with rumors of bloody battles and successful horse-stealing raids, which they alleged had occurred so short a time before and at such a great distance away that it seemed impossible for the news to have travelled so quickly to Qu'Appelle. And the unaccountable thing about these rumors was, not that the majority were the baseless fabrics of a dream, but that they, in not a few cases, turned out to be more or less distorted accounts of events that had actually occurred, the intelligence of which, in the absence of telegraphs, had been conveyed in some mysterious way known only to the Indians.

PROWLING SIOUX SPIES.

George Sandison closed the gates and patrolled the fort all night, and the train dogs kept up keen watch and ward, ever ready to give the alarm on the approach of strangers. The women began to complain that strangers were prowling about and even inside the pickets at night, but I only laughed at their fears, for neither did Sandison report anything unusual nor did the dogs make any noticeable outcry. At last, Mrs. Finlayson, who was no coward, told me that an Indian had peered into her window during the night, and that she had heard the dogs barking at someone. I often sat up late writing by a window in the office, but never heard anything alarming myself, although occasionally there would be a little outcry among the dogs, which I attributed to one of their frequent quarrels over a stray bone and thought nothing more about it. Sandison was sure there were no prowlers, although we were not too far off for Blackfeet spies to reach us by getting in behind our hunters on the plains, and the Assiniboines, of Wood Mountain, were quite near enough. Having no apprehension myself, I tried to laugh the women-folk out of their alarm, but it continued until Mr. McDonald returned with his men from Fort Garry.

It was only in 1873 that I discovered that these alarms had not been baseless, for that summer there came to me a delegation of the Sitting Bull band of Teton Sioux warriors to try to make arrangments to become customers at the fort and occupy part of our Indians' hunting grounds. One of their spokesmen, in an effort to persuade me that their intentions were peaceful and friendly, pointed to the window and desk at which I used to sit at night in the summer of 1868, and said, " If we had any bad intentions, I could have killed you many a time when five years ago you used to sit at night writing there." I was never afraid of Indians, but when this ferocious eagle-faced warrior said the words a thrill ran through me, and I would have rejoiced had it been permissible to shoot him on the spot. He went on to say that, night after night, they used to get into the fort while they were on a scouting expedition to find a country where they would be safe from the pursuit of the American troops. I saw this same most savage-looking warrior in the fall of 1884 at Carlton just before· the Saskatchewan rebellion of 1885, in which he and others of his tribe joined, and he himself was killed.

My First Summer Trip to the Plains.

Mr. McDonald having returned from Fort Garry on horseback ahead of the carts, and the supply of provisions for rations having run low, there being no word of Jerry nor of any of the hunters from the plains, I was ordered to go out to meet him with a fresh supply of trading goods, and, after exchanging them with him for loads of provisions, return to the fort. Six ox carts and an English half-breed, named William Francis Whitford, and a Bungie Indian, named Metas-we-" Ten," were given me, with a brute of a cart pony to ride; while as rations we were provided with lots of ammunition for shooting game and a few layers of dried meat, which was covered with a growth of half an inch of white mould. Mrs. McDonald, with her usual kindness, augmented this supply by a donation of a dozen buns from her own private store of flour.

We started on the forenoon of the 17th of June, 1868, on the cart trail which I had followed from Old Wives' Creek in January. While going through the park-like country bordering the Qu'Appelle valley, we shot plenty of ducks and prairie chicken to keep the pot boiling, and at the last point of the woods I killed an antelope—better known by the local name of "cabri." We saw no sign of our own or any other hunters returning, nor of buffalo, but after crossing the Grande Couteau de Missouri, we fell in with free-traders, who, like ourselves, were in search of the camps of the Qu'-Appelle Indians.

There were three traders—Augustin Brabant, St. Pierre Poitras, and the Saulteau Indian dandy, Tip-is-couch-kes-cou-win-in, or "The Man in the Zenith." Brabant and Poitras were from Red River with ordinary trading outfits, but the Saulteau, who was a splendid hunter, had attained the zenith of his ambition by having bought at St. Joe, on the American side, a puncheon of over-proof alcohol to trade. Each of these traders had a couple of men, the two Metis each ten or twelve carts, and the proud proprietor of the puncheon three. As we were then in the country of which the Blackfeet had not yet been dispossessed by the Qu'Appelle Indians, it was fortunate for us all to join forces.

SURPRISED BY INDIANS.

We struck an old trail of the Qu'Appelle Indians, going westerly and not far from the South Saskatchewan. In the forenoon, as the long line of carts was following a long valley, in which there was no sign of either buffalo or man, suddenly there sprang from concealment in the grass a number of Indians, scattered at long intervals in skirmishing order to our left. St. Pierre at once yelled out in alarm, "Les Assiniboines, make a ring with the carts." But before this could be done, the Indians began running swiftly towards us, converging at the same time together and soon forming a "thin red line," which advanced with whoops and yells, apparently of the most threatening kind, and brandishing their arms. None of us had rifles, but, just as the Indians were coming within range of our shot guns and we were about to give them a volley, they yelled that they were Crees and friends, and, ceasing to run and to yell, they walked up quietly to the carts.

They were a war party of North Saskatchewan Crees and they were delighted to fall in with us in the nick of time, for they were being pursued by Blackfeet, who had just defeated them, and had killed five of their number. Moreover, they were starving, and the howl they had set up when they sprang out of the grass was one of joy at being delivered from the fear of their enemies by the sudden arrival of our brigade of carts on the scene. They said the Blackfeet were near at hand and were evidently very much scared of an immediate attack. But we went on till we found a good watering place along a little lake before unhitching for mid-day. Meanwhile, seeing that I was only a young " greenhead," that the Company's carts were not overloaded, and the drivers offered no objections, the braves of the North Saskatchewan began to jump into my carts to ride. I asked Whitford if they had asked leave to do so, and he said they had not, so I told him to order them to get out. This he did not care to do, so I made signs to them to dismount, to which they responded with smiles of disdain, thereby raising my temper and my voice in good strong English, of which they understood the general meaning, and its being further enforced by poking the foremost one in the ribs with the muzzle of my gun had the desired effect.

DEFEATED WARRIORS.

We were quite out of decent food, except what we shot on the way and had been living from hand to mouth, but had never got so low as to tackle the mouldy dried meat we got at the fort. We had gathered some saskatoons (service berries) on our way and Brabant sold me a few pounds out of the single sack

of flour in his outfit. With these berries and flour and the
dried meat, with the mould washed off and cut up small,
Whitford made a big kettle of soup, which the defeated
warriors ate with great gusto and wound up the meal with
the tea and tobacco presented according to custom on first
meeting the Indians. So scared were these fellows of the
Blackfeet that they at first protested against our party
making a fire lest the smoke should attract their enemies.
Next, while Louis Racette and I were shooting black gulls,
which hovered about the lake shore, they came to him and
implored us to quit firing, as the sound might be heard by
their dreaded pursuers. As Louis and I were more afraid of
going without something to eat than of the enemies of the
Crees, we continued our profitable sport. No sooner had
they finished the "feast" prepared by Whitford, and what
the other traders had fed to the rest of them, than everyone
of these valiant warriors disappeared from what they considered the dangerous vicinity of our camp-fire and firing.

SCOUTING AHEAD

From Gull Lake onward, the trail of the hunters ahead
became fresher and more easily followed. I was
eager to catch them up or to meet Jerry returning, but the abominable brute of a saddle horse
was too lazy and slow to go on ahead. Brabant, however, was a very obliging fellow and lent me his fine buffalo
runner, cautioning me at the same time to peep over every
ridge before crossing it, and, if I saw sign of Indians or
buffalo, to ride back and forth across the trail on a spot
where I could be seen from the carts, till he and other
men galloped up to me. Being now well mounted and
armed with a shot gun and a heavy revolver, I set off in glad
anticipation of long-sought adventure, either in running
buffalo for the first time, in scouting against Blackfeet, or
in meeting my friend, Jerry. It was a beautiful afternoon,

and I went at a swinging lope over the rolling ridges and across intervening valleys till the decaying remnants of buffalo carcasses scattered profusely on every side showed that an old encampment could not be far off. On reaching a stream, the poles of a Sun Dance lodge and hundreds of old lodge fires and other discarded evidences showed the site of a very large camp, with cart tracks running away from it in every direction. Being too inexperienced to circle round at a distance to find the main trail on which the people had pitched off, I wasted some time following different tracks which led out to the open and branched off here and there to each side till I was following the track of a single cart only. While I was still hunting in this labyrinth for the main trail, I caught sight of three buffalo, which disappeared behind one of the sandy knolls. I at once rode up to the nearest knoll, and, dismounting, crawled up to the top and peered over, when I saw one of the objects I had taken for a buffalo transforming itself into an Indian, covered with a huge buffalo robe, raising himself erect on the back of the pony, over which he had been stooping. He was looking in another direction from which he was apparently expecting me to come. Fortunately, the knoll up which I had ridden was high enough to be seen from the carts, several miles away, so I made the signals as instructed, and soon saw by the dust flying up ahead of the carts that Brabant and others were galloping up to my assistance.

I was always suffering the disadvantage of the want of that long sight whereby the natives could see things at a distance without field glasses far better than I could with them. Very likely, a keen-eyed Indian would have at once seen that the animals which I had taken for buffalo bulls were mounted Indians in disguise. But the smooth slopes of the sharp-peaked knoll on which I took my stand were covered with short buffalo grass only and no one could get within gunshot of me without being plainly seen; so when I saw

Brabant was coming, I went to the top and looked around continually for a possible attack. By the time Brabant and Racette came galloping up, the Blackfeet-Buffalo had slunk entirely away; and, after making a sweep about the old camping ground, Brabant hit the trail and set me out again on it.

FRESH BUFFALO MEAT.

The route which the Indians had followed was now marked by four tracks running, with little spaces between, parallel to one another, for in the enemy's country the long line of such a big party travelling in single file would have extended for miles from front to rear and been exposed to attack in detail. The route was marked here and there by the remains of buffalo, but not a live one was to be seen. Towards sunset, as I was riding up the long slope of a high ridge, two wolves, one after—but at a considerable distance behind—the other, passed me at a quick lope, and every now and again looking back, as if something were coming after them. Before getting on the skyline, I jumped off horseback, and with the end of the long line always attached to the pony's neck in my hand, I peered over the crest. The sun was setting, and the great valley which I beheld in front was darkened in shadow, but at its bottom I could make out a dark moving mass of animals flowing like a black stream. My sight could not show me whether this stream were buffalo or mounted men, but anyway it was time to signal the party again.

It was dusk before Brabant, Louis Racette and The Zenith dashed up with panting ponies. They peeped over into the valley and at once exclaimed: " Les animaux." Brabant then quickly said to me: " Let Louis have my horse, his is blown, and let him run to make sure of fresh buffalo for supper." Racette was by this time on the pony, and off he went, followed by Zenith. In a short time, we heard the rattle of firing, as Racette, with the last glimmer of light, killed a fine, fat young bull, alongside of which the carts on coming up were unhitched. Racette, Brabant and Zenith took no time to skin and cut up the animal ready for the kettle, the frying pan and the roast. By the time the camp had been made and the animals attended to, a splendid and long-looked-for supper was ready, and we had all sat down to enjoy it, when, out of the darkness, like thieves in the night, into the circle of the firelight, noiselessly slunk the warriors who had vanished after being fed at mid-day. They were, of course, made welcome to share in the feast, but no sooner had they eaten than they again quitted our dangerously attractive company, and disappeared in the night, during which, I afterwards found, several of them reached the big camp of the party whose trail we were following.

Indian Legends.

Regarding these panic-stricken horse-thieves, who had gone out for wool and had got themselves shorn, in 1892 I was employed by the celebrated ethnologist, Dr. Franz Boas, of the American Museum of Natural History, to make an ethnological collection from and take physical measurements of the Indians of the North Saskatchewan. I was also asked to write down some of their unprintable folk-lore and legends. At Bear's Hills, near Wetaskiwin, I had met with some obstruction in the attempt and was only able by the liberal dispensation of flour, bacon, tea and tobacco to make any progress, when I made the acquaintance of a big, fine-looking Cree, named, he said, " Head Man," and christened Edmund. He was one of the obstructionists, and, in the expressive old phrase of the fur-country, " was making himself awkward," in order to show his importance as a warrior of former renown and gain thereby an extra allowance in consequence. Upon my asking him to tell some of the ancient legends of his people, he instead began to boast of the mighty deeds of valor which he had performed in war and in horse-stealing, both being equally honorable in his eyes. I listened, in the hope that, after blowing his own horn, he might be in good humor to relate the traditions handed down by the ancients. At last he began to tell of one of the most brilliant victories in which he had taken the leading part away beyond the South Branch, near Swift Current Creek. I asked him how long ago that was, and he answered twenty-four years ago in July. Then I knew I had him and encouraged him to go on lying to his heart's content. When he had exhausted the stores of his imagination and was expecting to be highly complimented and admired for his heroism, I said: "Do you remember meeting a party of traders after that fight with the Blackfeet?" He looked rather surprised and said: "Yes, we did." "There was," I said, "a young clerk of the Company in that party." "Yes," he replied, "quite a young fellow, with no hair on his face yet." "Well," said I, "I am that fellow, and I remember how you fellows came running away from the Blackfeet, scared to death. I am glad to see you did not die after all."

From that time on, "Head Man" was foremost in all good work to assist me, in fact, my own headman, ever willing to divulge his secrets as an alleged medicine man, and yielding up unto me as samples thereof some common pepper, salt, bluestone, cinnamon buds, cloves, and brimstone, to which he ascribed all kinds of wonderful properties as yet unknown to the scientific world. He also gave me some bits of bark, roots, and leaves possessed of magic virtue. As I had as little faith in his virtue in the profession of medicine as I did in that in the profession of arms, I did not send his materia medica to Dr. Boaz; but I did not tell any of his fellows at Bear's Hill how I had witnessed his retreat, in bad order, from Blackfeet who did not know they had been licked.

CHAPTER XVIII.

THE CAMP OF THE ALLIED TRIBES.

A FIELD OF SLAUGHTER.

NEXT morning, the four lines of cart and travois tracks were fresher, and on every side the bones of the buffalo, off which the hides and flesh had been stripped by the hunters, were scattered over the undulating plain. Mixed with these were the bloated and blown-out carcasses of hundreds of the noble animals wantonly slain in the sheer love of slaughter, and left untouched by the young bucks to provide a festering feast for the flocks of villainous vultures, which, slimy with filthy gore, hovered over the field and disputed with the ravening wolves for the disgusting prey. For miles, the air stank with the foul odors of this wilful waste, so soon to be followed by woeful want involving the innocent with the guilty. Neither warning nor entreaty of their elders could restrain the young men from the senseless massacre of the innocent herds of the universal purveyor of the prairie Indian.

ESCORT INTO CAMP.

Passing at intervals through such sickening scenes, in the afternoon we approached the big camp for which we had been so long in search. When within a mile of it a hundred horsemen sallied out to meet us and escort us into their be-leaguered encampment, for it was surrounded by hovering bands of Blackfeet, and the escort came forth to protect the needful supplies, which we were bringing, from being cut off before reaching them. The valiant refugees, whom we had fed on the previous day, had heralded our approach when they had sneaked into camp during the night.

Under the tumultuous escort of these bronze-bodied warriors, stripped to the breech-clout and prepared for fight, surrounding us on front, flank and rear, we reached and entered the camp, where an excited crowd of men, women and children greeted us. ' But the whole camp was in mourning for the loss of sixty of the finest young men, who had been slain by the Blackfeet, two days previously, and its population were living in the midst of alarms. The supply of arms and ammunition, sorely wanted for defence, and that of tea and tobacco, craved for solace in their grief, which we brought, were gladly welcomed; while the puncheon of firewater, imported by Zenith, was hailed with joyful anticipation of a grand spree to come.

Unfortunately for me, Jerry had been permitted to depart with his carts, all heavily laden, about a week before, and had taken a different route to the wavering one we had followed. However, after we had passed through the outer lines, amidst the seething mob of black-haired, brown-bodied men, women and children, some in gorgeously colored raiment and many divested and dishevelled, I descried the dignified and dandified figure of a gentleman arrayed in the height of the mode prevalent amongst Les Metis Francaise.

The crowd cleared the way for him, and he came up to my horse's side and introduced himself politely as the Company's interpreter from Touchwood Hills. I was well acquainted with him by reputation, especially for that of putting on style, which was an amusing trait of an otherwise sterling character disguised by it. La Pierre laid me under the first of the many friendly obligations which I owe to him and his memory by telling me that Loud Voice wished me to put all my outfit for safe keeping in the Qu'Appelle Crees' " warriors' lodge," and, after that had been done, by inviting me to his own comfortable lodge to have a wash (which I sadly needed) and something to eat with him.

Accordingly, my carts were unloaded and the goods put into the tent of the Qu'Appelle Cree warriors to be guarded by them; and, after making them a suitable present in tea and tobacco, I accepted La Pierre's kind invitation.

PETER LA PIERRE.

His father was the French-Canadian postmaster after whom La Pierre's House, on the Porcupine branch of the Yukon River, was named, and who had died before giving his son any schooling. But the lad had ambition to become something above a mere voyageur, and, despite every difficulty and the sneers and ridicule of his fellows, he took every chance to learn, or rather to teach himself, reading and writing in English and arithmetic. Mastering these in a very creditable manner, considering the want of willing helpers, he had risen to the grade of interpreter, and could write an intelligible letter and keep the accounts of his trading business quite well. Of these accomplishments, so unusual at that time amongst his countrymen, in which he had so perseveringly educated himself, he was naturally proud, and this, combined with his love of display, made him the envy of many detractors. He was a brave, well set-up, medium-sized man, who loved the glorious sport of charging after buffalo, in which he informed me that he took even greater delight than "in reading and writing and keeping accounts." In this, he took me much by surprise, for I had never dreamed that "keeping accounts" could be a fascinating delight to any normal being.

He led to a large lodge, highly decorated outside with Indian totems and devices, supposed to represent, in colors, hunting, horse-stealing, and battle scenes. Inside, all around the sides were, similarly decorated in native art, curtains of dressed buffalo skins, and spread on the grass and rushes covering the floor were couches of many folds of robes, over which, in his own place, were a number of bright, various-colored and striped blankets, besides many downy pillows covered with brilliant chintz, or turkey red cotton.

Divesting himself of his fine blue cloth, brass-buttoned capote, he ordered a wash basin, scented soap and towel to be set before him. After using these and dressing his long curly hair carefully, he put on a light linen jacket, and ordered the table to be laid. The table was without legs, being merely a board, about four by four feet, hinged in the middle so as to fold up, and nicely painted in different colors, with rays from the centre representing the sun. The handsome wife of Baptiste Bourassa, his second in command, managed the *ménage,* and set before us dainty dishes of luscious buffalo meat and friend doughnuts, to which I did full justice, and we washed all down with tea and the luxury of sugar. I felt, in my travel-stained flannel shirt and trousers, quite out of place amid such elegant surroundings, but none the less did I enjoy the change from the unpretentious cookery of Whitford and The Ten, and the contrast between the soft couches of the mosquito-free lodge and my lay-out on the journey on mother earth under the tail-end of a cart, with venomous mosquitoes rushing in the moment the smoke of the smudge was wafted to one side. The number of fires and smudges freed that camp from the pestilential mosquitoes, ubiquitous outside.

PEE-WA-KAY-WIN-IN, PEMMICAN PURVEYOR TO THE QUEEN.

We were exchanging information and enjoying a smoke after the repast, when an Indian, who had evidently already visited The Man in the Zenith, and whose hair and paint showed that he was in mourning, came in and began haranguing La Pierre in tones of irritation. La Pierre evidently tried to soothe the savage breast, but did not succeed until he had given Pee-wa-kay-win-in a striped cotton shirt and some tea and tobacco "as a present." This satisfied the beggar for a very short time only, and he came back and made a speech to me, which La Pierre interpreted, that, in order to feed the few white people in the world, whom the Indians vastly exceeded in numbers, the allied tribes in camp had been compelled to follow the buffalo here far inside the hunting grounds of the Blackfeet and their allies. In consequence, two of the sons of Pee-wa-kay-win-in had been slain, with the other fifty-eight young men, in the recent battle, therefore he demanded of me a large present in ammunition, tea and tobacco. I told him that I was very sorry for the poor young men who had been killed and for their relatives, but I thought the supplies I had brought to sell to them, not to give away, were fair exchange for the provisions we might buy and for which they required to follow the buffalo to feed themselves, anyhow. At this he became angry and said: "What would become of the Great White Queen and her people if we did not send them our pemmican? Of course, they would all starve to death," he conclusively replied to himself. I told him he was quite mistaken, that Queen Victoria had probably never seen pemmican, no more than most of her numberless people. "That is a lie," he said. "We Indians are the most numerous people on earth. Why, in all this big camp of three hundred and fifty tents, you are the only European, and we never see, even at the forts, more than five or six of you." Then he was told that, as he did not belong to the Qu'Appelle, but to Touchwood Hills post, I could only exchange goods for anything he sold me, and he must make his complaints to the master at Touchwood Hills. He went away in bad humor, and La Pierre said he expected more trouble as soon as Zenith's grog began to circulate generally; for Pee-wa-kay-win-in had a spite at him for giving him a thrashing when trying, with some others, who had got drunk on " free-traders' " liquor, to break in the gate of the post at Touchwood Hills.

BIG CAMP OF THE ALLIES.

The annual northern migration of the buffalo herds from across the Missouri River had been deflected from the old hunting grounds of the Qu'Appelle and Touchwood Hills Indians, and the country from which they had pushed the Blackfeet back, lying to the east of a north and south line running approximately along the west side of the Old Wives Lake. I forget whether the alteration of the course of the herds was at that time ascribed to prairie fires or the combined action of the Indians along the Missouri. But whatever the cause, our Indians had been compelled to seek their prey farther west, well within the lands of the Blackfeet and their allies.

To collect all their friends and allies together in one camp, a big Sun Dance had been proclaimed by runners, and, as they gathered together in strength for the purpose, they extended the programme by deciding to keep together, so as to allow the buffalo to return to the east without being scared and driven back to hostile territory by small parties of hunters scattered all over the plains, and only caring for the success of their own individual hunts without thought of the general weal. Parties of braves—"soldiers" they were called in the language of our interpreters—were, therefore, sent out to search for and to compel all such stragglers to come into the big camp, and at the same time strengthen it sufficiently to penetrate farther into the enemies' country to hunt, while their own fields were being replenished.

So it had come about that the allied Crees and Saulteaux, the semi-Stony and Cree "Young Dogs," of Qu'Appelle and Touchwood Hills, a few English and French Metis belonging to these places and Fort Pelly, also some Assiniboines from Wood Mountain and a few from the North Sasatchewan, were all gathered together in a camp consisting of three hundred and fifty large leather lodges, containing a mixed population

302

of probably two thousand five hundred or three thousand people, of whom about five hundred were men and lads capable of waging war. Unfortunately, the inhabitants of the camp, while united in the common purpose of attack or defence on or from the Blackfeet and their allies, were very far from agreeing on other matters among themselves. The Crees and Saulteaux were all very friendly and took common cause against their ill-behaved allies of Assiniboine or semi-Assiniboine origin, and every one of the Indians resented the intrusion of the half-breed whites on the plains for hunting purposes. To prevent the latter from uniting for mutual help, which might end in their deserting the camp in a small, but formidable, body, the Metis were compelled to pitch their tents at wide intervals apart, separated from their fellows by many an Indian lodge, whose occupants kept them under continual supervision and espionage, besides subjecting them to many other annoyances.

Cypress Hills.

The camp was pitched in the Big Sandy Hills, which lie about twenty miles north-east of the north-east end of Cypress Hills. These hills from the level of the plain to the east rise four hundred feet, and the treeless plateau at their top is rent by numerous ravines, fringed with trees, running down to the surrounding prairie. Owing to the prevalence in these woods of the jack pine, the range—for it is a long hill—received the French name Montaigne de Cypre, which has been erroneously translated into English as " Cypress."

As far back as the memory and traditions of the Crees then living extended, these Cypress Hills—" Me-nach-tah-kak " in Cree—had been neutral ground between many different warring tribes, south of the now marked international boundary, as well as the Crees and the Blackfeet and their friends. No Indian for hunting purposes ever set foot on the hills, whose wooded coulees and ravines became the undisturbed haunt of all kinds of game, and especially abounded in grizzly bears and the beautifully antlered and magnificent was-cay-sou, known variously by the English as red deer and elk. Only wary and watchful war parties of any tribe ever visited the hills, and so dangerous was it to camp in them that it was customary for such parties to put up barricades about the spots on which they stayed over night.

BLACKFEET MASSACRE SIXTY YOUNG WARRIORS.

A few days before we arrived at the camp, sixty of the most esteemed young men of it had sallied forth on an excursion to the dreaded hills to procure chewing gum for their lady loves and for general use as dentifrice. The act was one of bravado, for ever since the camp had crossed the frontiers that summer the Blackfeet in large numbers had hovered around it as an army of observation, prepared to take advantage of any opportunity of successful attack. The young Cree braves and their companions of other tribes were coming back rejoicing in the success of their dangerous venture, when, they, being on foot (the Crees did not go on horseback to war, although they always hoped to return thereon), were surrounded by overwhelming numbers of Blackfeet horsemen on an open level plain, which afforded no protection. Mounted on swift, well-trained ponies, the Blackfeet circled round the fated band, out of range generally, but with occasional swoops near enough to shoot under their ponies' necks, while they lay on the far side of their mounts, protected and concealed from the Crees. What feats of valor these performed have never been told, for not one of the sixty escaped to tell the tale. They were found by a party, sent out next day to get tidings to account for their non-arrival at the expected time, lying all dead on the plain, scalped and " with their bodies as full of Blackfeet arrows as a porcupine is full of quills."

When we came into the camp Rachel was weeping for her children and would not be comforted, and the fathers were full of plans of revenge on the Blackfeet, and also ripe and ready to demand atonement from the people whom they alleged were responsible for the calamity by coming from afar to live on buffalo and by encouraging the Indians to risk their lives in the enemies' country to procure the pemmican upon which, they believed, the whole British nation relied for subsistence.

CAUSES OF CONFLICT.

Amongst these Indians there were no all-powerful nor any hereditary chiefs. The Sioux and Blackfeet called them the people without chiefs. This state of affairs was very largely the result of the Company's policy of " dividing to govern." The chiefs recognized and subsidized by the Company were influential men as peacemakers rather than as warriors, whose operations against other tribes who were customers of the Company at other posts, such as the Blackfeet, trading at Rocky Mountain House and Edmonton, were always discouraged by the traders. But the Indians belonging to the plain posts of Swan River district were comparatively poor in horses, while the Blackfeet were rich; and, moreover, the buffalo were ever receding from the eastern to the western plains, and for self-preservation the Crees and Saulteaux of the east were obliged to encroach every year farther into the realms of the Blackfeet. And these regarded the traders, whose posts supplied their enemies, as enemies also, so that while the Blackfeet confederacy was at peace with the Company at " the mountain fort " and Edmonton, they were hostile to the employees of the same Company at Carlton and in Swan River. The same rule applied to the freemen hailing from these vicinities.

Under these circumstances the Indians of Swan River district, from the time they were first supplied with firearms by the traders, had been the aggressors and the invaders of the

Blackfeet country, and the diminution of the buffalo in general intensified the strife.

WARRIORS' COUNCIL LODGE.

Even when there were mighty chiefs amongst the Indians, all important legislative and executive functions were vested in Councils of Warriors, who, as the defenders of the tribe, alone had the right to take part in its councils, to the exclusion of those who had not performed and did not perform military duties. (This reasonable rule might well be "taken into consideration" by our politicians in limiting the franchise to those citizens only who have been trained to arms.)

The matters of pressing moment coming before the council on this occasion were the maintenance of a united camp of all the allies for protection against the common foe, and to prevent straggling parties from leaving the camp and frightening the buffalo herds from moving from hostile ground to their own hunting territory in the east. Generally the men most gifted in speech or in spirit as warriors carried the council with them; but their motions could be upset by anyone opposing them making presents of sufficient magnitude to buy over the councillors, in the most frankly open manner, to his views.

REVENUE TARIFF.

Apart from such objects of tribal importance as are above outlined, the personal objects of the councillors were largely what is known to civilized communities as "private graft." True the Warriors' Lodge had to be supported by contributions, voluntary and otherwise, from the camp at large, but that the warriors should have unlimited tea to drink in sufficient quantities (mixed with a little tobacco to inebriate as well as to cheer) and an equally unstinted measure of tobacco to smoke, a system of import and export duties was devised to compel all traders to render tribute on entering and leaving camp. This impost was intended also as a special punishment to the Company for ceasing to give them the old and highly appreciated presents of rum as "regales" on state occasions, and also for changing the old, well-understood system of trading on the "Made Beaver," or skin standard, with the presents, called "gratuities," of ammunition and other necessaries which went with that way of barter, and for adopting instead the "money way" with its complicated and incomprehensible pounds, shillings and pence and avoirdupois weight in valuing pemmican and other provisions, instead of so many skins for a bag or bale of provisions of ordinary size.

TRADERS RESIST THE IMPOST.

To this impost the traders, especially those under the sway of Archibald McDonald, invariably offered resistance, complaining that it was an imposition and a breach of the bargain whereby prices of goods had been lowered and that of Indian produce raised upon the adoption of the "money way" of trading, under which the old gratuities were abrogated in exchange for better values. Mr. McDonald was particularly indignant whenever he heard that the rules against gratuities had been transgressed by traders belonging to other Company's posts. And as for the "blackmail," as he considered the import and export tribute which the Indians imposed whenever they were strong enough and the traders weak enough, he ordered us all never to submit to it unless compelled by a force which it was hopeless to resist. In such a case Mr. McDonald admonished me never to allow the Indians to go that length, but always seek to anticipate their demands by granting them as an apparent favor what they could otherwise exact by force, and by so doing preserve the prestige of the whites. In the general absence of reliable interpreters and spies on such occasions, a trader had to rely on his own ability to read the signs of the times and the countenances of the Indians in coming to a decision.

THE COMPANY OF ADVENTURERS

SMOULDERING ENMITIES.

In this camp of the allies each tribe had set up a Warriors' Lodge of its own. Only one common bond, the dread of their common enemies, united these in action. Apart from that the jealousies and enmities between the Assiniboines and the semi-Assiniboine Young Dogs on the one side, and the Crees and Saulteaux, who freely intermarried, on the other, smouldered as fires ready to burst into flames of war on any inciting occasion. In previous chapters the evil repute of the Wood Mountain Stonies (the traders' common name for Assiniboines) has been referred to. That of their offspring of partly Cree or Saulteaux blood, " The Young Dogs," might be most fittingly expressed by calling them the sons of the female canine, in the vernacular meaning thereof.

DESTRUCTION OF A PRAIRIE SODOM AND GOMMORAH.

In the fall of 1873 I was at the Sandy Hills near the Elbow of the South Saskatchewan and took the occasion to visit the site of a camp which had been destroyed by fire from heaven some time in the middle 1860's, which I had often heard about from different Cree Indians, who witnessed the tragedy. My old good friend and brother officer, Mr. William Edward Traill, now a retired chief trader living at Mackinaw, Saskatchewan, first told the tragic tale to me, and I am sure he could amplify the brief account of what I recollect of it.

The Crees, among whom white slavery did not exist, extended their hospitality to strangers to a height at which prudes would be shocked, but which the Cree children of nature regarded as a virtue instead of a vice, and a bond of peace and good-will. But liberal-minded as they were, the Crees witnessed with disgust and abhorrence the crimes of incest and bestiality, of robbery and murder, practised by the Young Dogs. So dreadful were these in their eyes that, on the occasion now referred to, although on the dangerous frontier of the Blackfeet, they would not allow fifty or sixty Young Dog lodges to be pitched in their camp.

A VITRIOLIC DOWNPOUR

So it happened that the Young Dog camp was pitched about a mile from that of the Crees in the Sandy Hills that summer day. In the afternoon a cloud no bigger than a man's hand arose in the north-west, came on swiftly and enlarging till it burst in roaring thunder and forked lightning, with a torrential downpour over the site of the doomed camp of the Young Dogs. That downpour was not of water, but of a liquid acid, which quickly reduced to ashes everything on which it fell. A few, near the shores of a small lake on which the camp stood, sought refuge from the burning rain in its waters, but while their bodies were protected by the water their heads above it were reduced to ashes.

When the storm ceased, the Crees, who then ventured to the scene, found the forms of men lying under covers of robes and skins, and the moment these were touched they crumbled into dust and ashes. Carts, lodges and poles left standing also crumbled away at a touch or breath of wind. The grass, turf and soil, down to the clay subsoil beneath, were also consumed, and when I visited the site in 1873, the circle in which the camp had stood could still be distinguished by the barren clay supporting scattered growths of weeds in a depression which was surrounded by an open and grass-grown prairie.

The miraculous nature of the occurrence is heightened by the statement that every living creature in that camp miserably perished, except a young and beautiful Cree maiden, who had a day or two before been kidnapped and taken into his harem by one of the Dogs. She is said to have escaped by diving till she crossed the lake.

Such, then, were the people and the state of affairs when I, young and inexperienced, and without any idea of the combustible elements in it, came to that big camp near Cypress Hills where I was to undergo the ordeal of initiation as a fur trader.

CHAPTER XIX.

A CAMP IN TURMOIL.

The Dogs Demand Tribute.

Up to our arrival there had been a famine in tea, tobacco, and ammunition, so next morning there was a general rush to trade, which kept Whitford, The Ten and myself busy, with no sign of slackening till the middle of the afternoon. We were then attending to the wants of importunate customers when an interruption occurred and these suddenly cleared out of the lodge without finishing their business.

The stampede was caused by the intrusion of two "braves" who, under the inspiration of the firewater of The Zenith, and at the instigation of the Warrior's Lodge of the Young Dogs, had come to demand tribute of me, as an attribute to their lodge, which they deemed to have been slighted by my taking up quarters in that of the Qu'Appelle Crees, to whom they were well aware presents had been made for the accommodation. A party of forty-two Young Dogs had therefore been sent to exact the tribute, headed by one of their chief men, named Yellow Head, with Big Beak, one of their loudest speechmakers, as his second, while the rest surrounded the lodge outside. But all this I did not learn until the trouble, which is about to be told, was over.

The Ten disappeared with the other stampeders. Loud Voice's men squatted stolidly in a circle within the eaves of the lodge and made no sign of disapproval of the interruption. Usually an Indian shook hands with a trader on meeting him for the first time, but these fellows did not, and squatted down near the middle of the lodge, which was large and made up of several lodges put together. Whitford told me they had not come to trade but wanted tea and tobacco "for nothing." Seeing that they were evidently under the influence of liquor and knowing the number of people who were waiting to trade, I thought it better to let the pair have a little tea and tobacco. Accordingly Whitford placed on the dressed buffalo skin which they had placed on the ground before them, two pint measures of tea and a yard of thick Canadian roll tobacco.

At first when these gifts were placed at his feet Yellow Head said nothing, but upon being incited by the reptilian Big Beak, who sat in his usual place—behind—he scattered the tea off the skin on to the ground and into the fire; and then, standing up, he threw the tobacco back to us with a gesture of contempt, growling out something in an angry tone at the same time. I was astonished and looked towards Whitford for an explanation, but only to see his heels as he dived under the eaves out of the lodge, leaving me without any means of knowing what Yellow Head continued to say, although I could see that its purport was far from friendly. The hasty retreat of my sole interpreter and the continued impassiveness of mine hosts, the Crees, and the intoxication of his own eloquence, emboldened Yellow Head to advance up to me, and before I realized that the gesture was not merely a waving of the orator's hands, he slapped me on the cheek. He made a second attempt to do so which I fended off, and said, in the only English he was likely to understand, " Damn you, don't try that again." He did, and the next moment, virtuous wrath adding might to the blow, I sent him sprawling across the fireplace to the feet of the reptile, with his two front teeth knocked out and a bloody nose. " Get up, you brute, if you want more," I cried, striding up. But in an instant he was dragged out of the lodge and it was just as quickly cut up in ribbons by his band outside. Down came the leather covering, leaving the bare lodge poles, between which forty Young Dogs with guns and arrows were pointing ready to shoot. I quickly caught the butt of my revolver and was drawing it, determined to die fighting, when up sprang all the Crees, who had remained so long passive spectators, and three of them seized me, and bore me, struggling desperately, to the earth. There they struggled with and held me down till I was utterly exhausted.

LED TO JUDGMENT.

Then they suffered me to sit up, but closely guarded, and the Crees were again seated, under bare lodge poles, round their council fire, but all the raiders outside had disappeared. In a little while a big procession of warriors marched up and surrounded the lodge and I was taken out and marched, surrounded by them, to another big Warrior's Lodge, in which I was received in solemn silence by the occupants, amongst whom, with a gleam of satisfaction, I saw La Pierre. One warrior got up and in an angry voice made a short speech, the only part of which La Pierre interpreted being, " White man, what have you got to say for yourself?" Thinking the whole Indians in the camp, including my late hosts of the Cree lodge, were all against me, I told them white men always defended themselves when attacked, that I would do the same again if I got the chance even if it were against Indian ideas. Whereupon, this being interpreted by La Pierre, up sprang " The Broken Sword " and coming to me, he shook me heartily by the hand and warmly uttered a few words. Then going back to his place in the circle of the council he made quite a speech, the purport of which La Pierre informed me was: " White man, the Young Dogs are very bad people, they have tried to rob and murder you to-day. The Whites are our friends and the Young Dogs are people whom we detest. We have seen to-day that your arm is strong and your heart is strong—and if you will say the word we—the Crees and Saulteaux of Qu'Appelle and Touchwood Hills—will fall upon them and kill the whole odious and villainous tribe of them. We have held and surrounded you to prevent your being killed by these rascals. Now you are free to do as you like, and we will do as you say."

FROM PRISONER TO DICTATOR.

So to spring at once from the position of what had appeared to have been a prisoner into that of a dictator of war or peace, was certainly a most agreeable surprise and relief to me, for I had made up my mind to die like a man, fighting, if I got a chance. La Pierre now for the first time spoke his own mind instead of interpreting only, and advised.

He said that Yellow Head was a warrior of high standing, chief of a harem of eight or ten wives, by whose industry and that of his sons-in-law, who by Indian custom were bound to hunt for him, he was able to sell to the Company at Touch-wood Hills many bags of pemmican and bales of dried meat, and several hundred buffalo skins and robes yearly. He was an important customer, and, for a Young Dog, was considered a good Indian. Consequently La Pierre was sorry that he had been incited by others and by firewater to lead the raid upon me. La Pierre reminded me that the Company's policy was always to try to keep the peace among the Indians, and that it would be against that policy to start a fight between the Crees and Saulteaux on the one side and the Young Dogs and their relatives, the Assiniboines, on the other, which would endanger the property of the Company and the lives of its people for years to come. Moreover, the two friendly tribes would be continually demanding compensation for the lives of warriors who might fall fighting, as they would claim, for the Company. The Company's determination never to show fear of the Indians and to defend themselves had been carried out, said La Pierre, in giving Yellow Head the smashing blow he deserved; so, he pleaded, "Don't set them to fight. They will play hell, and we will never be able to stop them once they begin."

GREAT SLAUGHTER OF BLACKFEET.

La Pierre was a man of experience, and he had taken part in the big battle between our Indians and the Blackfeet in

March, 1866, at Red Ochre Hills, on the South Saskatchewan, when no less than six hundred Blackfeet were slain. He had been in the Cree camp at the time it was attacked, and had supplied them with fresh arms and ammunition, besides taking a leading part in the fight. On that occasion a very large war party of Blackfeet had set forth to repel the invasion of their hunting-grounds by an inferior force of the Cree and other Swan River Indians. The Blackfeet, who generally fought on horseback, came down the South Saskatchewan valley on foot on this occasion. The snow had already melted, except in the shelter of the ravines, and they had no snowshoes. From the valley they descried two Cree lodges on the skyline of the hills, and they heard the chopping of axes in a ravine which led down from the hills to the valley. They at once knew the Cree women were getting firewood in the ravine, and had no idea that the two solitary lodges on the top of the bank were outliers of a big camp beyond and out of sight. Accordingly they proceeded up the snow-filled ravine and shot the two old Cree women who were chopping wood there. Then, following up the woodchoppers' trail, they proceeded up the ravine to attack the two lodges seen from the valley. All were eager to get there, and they crowded into the deep and melting snow on each side of the track in their eagerness. Stumbling and falling in the wet snow the powder in the pans of their flintlocks got wet also.

Meanwhile the Crees in camp behind the brow of the Red Ochre hills, hearing the volley echoing through the ravine, had taken alarm, and the warriors rushed to the brink commanding a full view of the ravine, now filled with a helpless crowd of enemies who had failed to keep their powder dry and were expecting an easy victory over the people in the two lodges to be attacked. That was a black morning for the Blackfeet, as, floundering in the deep, rapidly thawing snowdrifts of the ravine, and unable to use their guns, the well-armed Crees lined its brink on each side, and, firing in front, on left and right of them, slaughtered them as they were wont to slay unarmed herds of impounded buffalo.

In the fall of 1871 I camped for some time, when on a trading trip, alongside this ravine. It was still full of the grim skeletons of those who fell in March, 1866; and I followed, from the mouth of that death trap of the Blackfeet, for miles up the flat bottom lands of the South Saskatchewan valley a trail of bleached bones of the Blackfeet who had fallen, in the panic-stricken retreat, to the fury of the pursuing Crees. The ravine was a perfect Golgotha, and that trail of dead bones could be plainly seen, from a height, stretching for miles along the burnt surface of the bottom lands of the valley.

Most Indian accounts of their victories are, like the prematurely reported death of Mark Twain, apt to be highly exaggerated; but this defeat and massacre of the Blackfeet, I had the evidence of my own eyes, was not and did not require to be exaggerated—" it was a glorious victory." Curiously, for very seldom did such reports reach British newspapers from Rupert's Land in those days, an account of this defeat of the Blackfeet appeared in the Edinburgh *Scotsman* in the summer of 1866, and was read with great interest by myself.

THE COMPANY'S PEACEFUL POLICY.

But to return to the problem of peace or war set before me, as the representative of the Company of Adventurers of England, who then had the chartered right of making war upon any non-Christian prince or nation. After listening to the good counsel of my friend, Interpreter La Pierre, I decided that it would not be in the interest of the Company to precipitate by any further action of mine a war between the different sets of Kilkenny cats of which that camp was composed. Moreover, as far as I was personally concerned, the smashing blow I had given Yellow Head was ample satisfaction for the slap in the face he had given me.

So I got up and thanked my new found friends for their compliments and the tempting offer to clean out the " Young Dogs " they had made; but they all knew that the Company, which I had the honor to represent, had always tried to preserve peace and prevent war—except in self-defence—amongst them. Therefore I begged them accept, in token of appreciation of their friendship and the protection they had afforded me and the Company's property, also, some tobacco to smoke in the pipe of peace, along with tea to cheer them in their councils. They appeared to be very much disappointed at my not giving them the word for war, but the proffer of the present met with warm approval and applause.

So, under their voluntary escort, La Pierre and I went over to the lodge of Loud Voice, and the tea was measured out by the pint pot and the tobacco by fathoms, and with these the escort returned rejoicing to their fellows. While this was taking place Loud Voice and his braves were looking on in solemn silence, but as soon as the bearers of presents to the other Warriors' Lodge had gone, Loud Voice got up and made a speech explaining that they, while feeling grossly insulted by the conduct of the Young Dogs in invading their lodge and surrounding it in so hostile a manner, had abstained from resenting the affront put upon them as hosts and to me as their guest lest a fight should start, which, involving internecine war in that combined camp, would lay it open to its common and powerful enemies of the Blackfeet Confederacy. So they had put up with the bad conduct of Yellow Head and his band till the latter added injury to insult and, ripping up the lodge, were about to shoot me to avenge my blow, when he, Loud Voice, and his men, to save my life, had thrown me down on the ground and jumped up to their feet to surround me, so that the Young Dogs could not shoot at me without shooting them also. Then they had turned on the Dogs and ordered them off with their bleeding leader. So the said Loud Voice, together with his fellow tribesmen of the Touchwood Hills Lodge, had rendered the Company good service in protecting their merchandise and in defending me, and they equally deserved such presents as they had seen given to the others.

Although I had thought they had looked on with undue apathy, if not with approval, when the *fracas* occurred, I was not in a position to refuse this explanation and the accompanying request. But for all that I still think that, if I had shown any fear of Yellow Head, they might not have prevented the outfit of which I had charge from being pillaged by his band. However, making a virtue of necessity, I thanked them for their assurance of continued friendship to the Company, and for continuing to guard my outfit in their lodge. The tea and tobacco which La Pierre and I measured out to them was received with many a " How How " of thanks.

A GRAND WHOOP-UP.

Some years later, Kan-o-cees, who had by that time become quite a chum of mine, in relating the battle between the Crees and Blackfeet at Belly River in the summer of 1871, complained that the defeat and pursuit of the Crees and their allies by the Blackfeet had been quite unfair to the former, because the Blackfeet had been inspired by the firewater of which each swigged off a whole " min-ne-quag-i-kun," just before the battle, while the poor Crees had had none. It was perhaps to prevent the Young Dogs, who had already begun to tipple, from gaining any advantage in this way of Dutch courage that my friends in the camp started in on a grand spree also. They had all been preparing to take advantage of the " skoot-e-wah-bo," which Zenith had been mixing with swamp water into the state of dilution most profitable to him since his arrival. The Yellow Head incident brought this general desire seemingly to a head, and the warriors and chiefs who were the only constituted guardians and constables of the peace, divesting themselves of the robes of office, and everything else but the breech clout, joined in the common throng of boozers and "whooped it up" in every sense of the expression. As the spree grew fast and furious, the camp became a very pandemonium of red raging demons.

"Hell broke loose" alone conveys the impression it made on me at the time, and the end would have been that of the Kilkenny cats for every full-grown buck in that camp had it not been for the restraining influence of the brave and brawny women. These, denied the privilege, the glorious privilege, of partaking the highly-priced and rare vintage of Zenith, took up the neglected duty of their lords and masters in preserving life and property. Every one of the obstreperous bucks carried weapons and each was ready and anxious to use them at a moment's notice. They danced, they sang, they shouted, and they yelled shouts of joy and of anger as the spirit moved them. They embraced and wept over each other; they marched proudly boasting of their feats, and they challenged the best to meet in single fight or mixed affray.

FEMALE POLICE.

But whenever combatants proceeded to actual blows, out rushed the women of the harem from the surging throng, and, their muscles hardened by continual exercise in all the hard work and drudgery of their lives, they would seize their spindle-armed sultans, bear them to their lodges, where, trussed up in many plies of shaganappi (rawhide lines) they were placed on their couches of robes to sleep off their fury. Even man to man, or rather woman to man, these mighty strong females often mastered their males. Ministering angels of peace they were, not such as are depicted in art galleries, but brawny squaws whose services to-day might be welcomed to the ranks of militant suffragettes. To these latter these simple Indian women might have appeared mere down-trodden slaves of man, but the able-bodied squaw despised any woman who allowed her men to do any work of the order ordained for women, and if the work so ordained for the Indian woman might be considered by the new women of civilization as shameful, the redskinned wife gloried in the shame.

Nevertheless the Indian's wife or wives (the irreducible minimum at that time and place was two, for any respected family) were far from being mute mates. They always had their say in men's affairs, private and public, too, as is the wont of women the whole world o'er. And they had a right to do so, for although the man killed the buffalo, it was the woman who prepared its meat and skin for use and trade. So that, with the buffalo hunting Indians, the more wives a hunter had, the wealthier was he, and, I was often told by the men, the less trouble he had in keeping them in order, for they vied with each other for his favor. Anyhow, in that day, owing to their frequent loss in war and by other causes (seven hundred braves were killed in battle, by murder and by sudden death, in the circle of our acquaintance at Fort Qu'Appelle between 1867 and 1874), the number of females largely exceeded that of males, and had polygamy not been the custom these surplus women would have had no one to hunt for them, and would have perished from starvation.

ALL TRADERS RETIRE.

As soon as the general " whoop up " began all the traders, excepting, of course, The Zenith, packed up their outfits snugly and retired from business, seeking such little seclusion as their tents afforded. All the Metis hunters did likewise, for it was unsafe to be seen outside during the grand drunk. Alick Fisher, whose tent was pitched next that of the lodge in which my goods were stored, very kindly invited me to board with him during my stay in camp. Whitford and I took watch about over the outfit in the council lodge. On the third day the carousal ceased with the supply of firewater, and we resumed trading till we received more than we could carry away as cargo, although there was still plenty of goods left.

After closing the trade and packing up the outfit, I left them for the night in the care of the now sober warriors and went to sleep in Fisher's tent. Everything in it was beautifully clean and tidy, the meals well cooked and served; the family were good Catholics and had family worship morning and evening, and were truly kind, hospitable and courteous. Fisher was a most cheerful and entertaining companion, and took pleasure in teaching me the French language in use in the country. In fact, I feel bound to say here that wherever I travelled among this class of hunters and traders of the Metis on the plains I ever found the same conditions and met with kindness and hospitality that I can never forget.

THE SERENADERS.

After we had gone to bed our rest was interrupted by a sudden wailing of many voices around our lodge. Alick announced that "Les Sauvages" had come to serenade us, expecting to be rewarded for their vocal music and dancing in our honor by largess of tea and tobacco. The choir attempting the carol was composed of a ring of young men and maidens alternately surrounding the lodge, and bobbing up and down to some monotonous composition of "Hi Hi Ha Ha Ya Ya," *ad libitum*. We stood it for a little while in token of appreciation of the honor, and then gave the expected tea and tobacco in return. It was the only way to get rid of the nuisance, and another band, encouraged by the success of the first, and possibly composed of some of its members, came along again, and had to be listened to and then got rid of in the same manner. This was kept up every night during the rest of my stay in that camp.

Unfortunately these were not the only performing musicians who rendered night hideous in the encampment. Night and day the booming tom-tom of the warriors or the gamblers resounded to the accompaniment of the appropriate vocal music. One would have thought that hunters wishing to allow the buffalo to approach them would have kept quiet for that purpose. But no such consideration seemed to weigh with these revellers.

And when there was the least lull in these outcries the innumerable hordes of dogs of every breed would take up the interval by barking and howling in chorus. Seemingly music hath charms to soothe the savage breast of the Indian dog of much the same sound to civilized ears as that of his master. The animal precentor might be a cur in camp, or his distrusted and detested cousin the coyote, in the open. Let the whole canine family in camp or trading post be sleeping the sleep of the just, at one shrill yelp from one wakeful animal of the precentor class, the whole pack will join one after the other into a united canine chorus ranging from the high falsetto of the pup to the deep baying bass of the big one. Wherever two or three dog trains are assembled together at ease during the night it is customary for them to unite in this chorus, which, arising in the stilly night, in the solitudes may arouse the deepest sleeper. Wherefore a man, who does not wish to be disturbed after once going to sleep, will take the precaution before retiring to mimic the canine note of the precentor and start the pack in full blast, continuing until they have blown themselves out and music hath lost its charms for them for the rest of the night.

CHAPTER XX.

IN THE MIDST OF ALARMS.

MOVING CAMP.

DURING the time I was there the camp was shifted a few miles on two occasions for sanitary as well as hunting purposes. The Blackfeet around were the source of continual anxiety, and we moved in several parallel columns abreast instead of trailing along in one long line Indian file. In these columns were carts; and travois drawn by dogs as well as by ponies. The Red River cart was one of the wonders of the west in its ability to go anywhere and to do anything—besides its inherent capacity for wailing as it went in dirge-like tones, which men, who were not Scots, were wont to liken to the pibroch.

THE TRAVOIS.

But the travois trailed noiselessly along over rough and steep ground impracticable for even a Red River cart. It consisted of two poles lashed together in the form of an acute triangle, the apex of which was secured to the animal's withers and the ends of the sides, which were kept apart by a cross-bar or bars, trailed along the ground. The cross-bars were far enough behind the heels of the animal to permit of his kicking freely without endangering the load, which was placed on a netting or hide stretched between these cross-bars and the side poles. On this netting the lodge, with its animate and inanimate contents, was carried, including babies and blankets, puppies and pemmican, also the blind, the halt and the lame of the family. The dog-travois was, and is still, in

PRAIRIE INDIAN TRAVOIS.

RED RIVER CARTS AND PONIES.

the forests of the north, a smaller implement of the same model.

The Pack-Dog.

Besides the cart and the travois, pack-ponies were also used; also pack-dogs, the latter bearing frequently burdens mountain high in comparison with their size. These also are still in everyday use amongst the Indians of the woods, where the women, too, are the great burden bearers, while the man in shifting camp goes ahead light and ready to shoot the next meal for the family. If he kill any big game, he, too, will carry a big load into camp, and probably send the women and the dogs to bring in the rest.

On the buffalo plains, however, the necessity which compels the wood Indians to pack things on their own or their women's backs did not exist, and carts, travois and pack-ponies and dogs performed the service, while the lords of creation and the ladies of their lodges rode on horseback or in carts—also on pony travois, presenting in the variety of their modes of motion an infinite and picturesque variety.

Bad Water.

The country through which we "pitched" was very dry, with infrequent pools and ponds of water. It was naturally mostly alkaline and contaminated already by the excretions of buffalo—a wallowing animal. The weather was hot and the dogs drawing and bearing burdens came panting with long, protruding tongues along the trail. On catching scent and sight of water these immediately rushed for it and into it regardless of damage to their loads—which might be partly papoose. Then, frantic mothers would rush to save their babies, and old termagants, while rescuing their property, would vent their wrath on the poor dogs with blows, and, in language as foul as the water being befouled, heap every variety of abuse of which the Indian language is capable upon them. The fuss and fury of some of these females whose papooses and other precious possessions were thus endangered by the dogs rushing into deep water, generally attracted a crowd of amused and jeering spectators.

MARCHING ORDER.

The orders of the day were always made public by criers, who marched through the camp shouting them out in a loud voice. When the order to strike camp and move was given it was executed with remarkable alacrity. In a moment the leather lodges were doused and the camp was under bare poles, which soon fell also, and were either lashed in bundles on the carts or else trailed, travois fashion, by a pony.

The baggage was all packed away in bags—babies included —by the women, and in a few minutes lashed on cart, travois or pack-saddle; while others were yoking the ponies and the dogs simultaneously. Then the motley crowd fell into their order in the parallel processions, each of which was preceded by a mounted man to lead the way. In the intervals between these processions women and children on foot and horseback marched along—many of the ponies bearing two or even three small riders.

And so to the sound of the Red River cart, the yelping of terrorized dogs, and the neighing of ponies, the parallel columns went marching along the undulating plain and crushing, in the vales, sage and mint from which fragrant odors pervaded the air. The sun shone strong and bright on the many vivid colors in which the Indians were arrayed. In front, flank and rear rode the protecting force of mounted braves, the whole surrounded by cordons of widely scattered scouts. Then, on some hillock ahead along the line of route, there would assemble " the headquarters' staff," composed of chiefs and elderly headmen, who, dismounted and holding their ponies' lariats in hand, would in a circle, squatting, or lying in a characteristic attitude on their bellies, watch the march and look out for any signs of danger made by distant scouts. Meanwhile, pipe and story would be going the rounds.

THE FEAR OF THE ENEMY.

With as marvellous celerity as they had broken the old camp, they pitched the new one. On that first occasion it was near a conical hillock, which commanded a splendid view of the surrounding country, including the Cyprè Hills to the south-west. From this splendid watch-tower during the afternoon of the next day after our camping there, the look-outs, ever in fear of the enemy, espied a dark, swiftly-moving mass, sweeping like the shadow of a cloud over the undulations of the prairie from the direction of the Cyprè Hills towards our camp. As this mass approached nearer, and loomed larger, it appeared to be composed of mounted men, and who else might they be but Blackfeet? The alarm " Our enemies are coming in mighty number," was given, and instantly the camp, which had been the scene of children at play, of women laughing at work, and of men gambling with the accompaniment of song and drum, became stricken with terror and confusion.

We who live at home at ease, upon whose soil the foot of ruthless invading enemy has never trod, can have little idea of the feelings of those poor prairie nomads, who had been born and bred, and who lived and moved and had their being, in the midst of such alarms. While the men flew to arms there arose from the lodges the weeping and wailing of women and children, the tum-tum of the drum of the medicine men, accompanying their loud prayers for deliverance, and the war cries and drums of the braves inspiring themselves with courage for battle. Others, to give vent to their agitation, let off spluttering volleys in the air, perhaps in the hope of averting the attack on a camp so well supplied with superfluous ammunition, or possibly in the hope that the Blackfeet, instead of making a boldly planned attack in the open, were blindly running into an unknown danger.

BEAR BAITING.

I happened to be on the lookout hill when the alarming object was first sighted, and it afforded, too, a bird's-eye view of the camp and the transformation scene. Also, I had been watching with interest five or six "young bucks," on foot and armed with spears only, who, having surrounded a two-year-old grizzly bear in a hollow at the foot of the hill outside the camp, were tormenting the brave brute. One would prod him in the rear, upon which the bear, quickly facing about, made after his fleeing foe; but no sooner was he about to overtake that one than another lad would give him a fresh poke behind; and so on the game went merrily till, on the alarm being sounded, they ceased their bear baiting and gave him the happy dispatch from his torments. Cruelty, thy name is man, whose inhumanity to brute has been exercised on countless thousands. But these lads were merely training for war, and, next to a fair fight in the open, man to man, with no other weapon but the knife, the greatest feat a warrior could perform was that of attacking and killing a full-grown grizzly with spear alone. I remember that "Poor Man," the Cree Chief of Touchwood Hills, was one to whom both these proud distinctions were due.

THE SHADOW PASSES.

By the time the threatening shadow had swept nearer several men with their buffalo-running ponies, champing at their bits and pawing the ground and capering in excitement and eager to be off, crowded on the hill. Conspicuous by their fine appearance and equipments were the brothers, Louis and Sousie Racette, the latter being Alick Fisher's son-in-law, and living in his lodge. All at once Sousie yelled: "These are not Blackfeet; they are only a band of La Biche." And, truly so it turned out to be a herd of about a hundred red deer (otherwise elk), bearing magnificent antlers which carried on high, gave them the appearance at a distance, of mounted horsemen. Straightway Sousie and Louis sprang to their saddles, tore down the hill with horses on haunches, and, followed by The Zenith, also well mounted, and two or three other Indians, they headed off the red deer and slew twenty-eight on the run.

TEMPTED OF CONSPIRATORS.

During all the time since we had joined the camp, buffalo were being hunted singly, or in small bands, by individual Indians daily, with occasionally a grizzly bear found among the saskatoon (Juneberry) bushes, quite plentiful in those big sand hills; but no regular big general buffalo run had occurred till the day after the supposed Blackfeet were seen to be real red deer From the lookout hill a big band of buffalo, conveniently near to camp, were discovered. The order was given for a general hunt, and everyone who had a pony capable of taking a place in the charge got ready. The cart horse, which the Company had furnished for my riding, was utterly useless for such a race, and I was anxious to try my prentice hand at it. Hunters were in too high demand for me to be able to borrow one, when a strange Indian came up the hill and most pressingly offered the loan of his animal. Fisher interpreted, but at once warned me not to accept the offer, " for," he said, " this is either an Assiniboine or a Young Dog, and they think they would have a good chance to shoot you without anyone being the wiser if you join in the general run after buffalo. They want to be revenged on you for smashing Yellow Head and refusing to give them presents." The Indian made my refusal difficult by the implied challenge in saying they would like to see how I behaved in the charge after buffalo, where the wonder always was that so few men were shot accidentally or otherwise. Fisher said he would have given me his own pony had he not been afraid I might be shot in the back; so, acting on his friendly advice, I declined the suspicious offer of the stranger, and I lived to have many opportunities of running buffalo without incurring any but the ordinary risks inherent thereto.

A GRAND BUFFALO HUNT.

However, this abstention gave me the best opportunity I ever had of seeing the whole hunt in panorama. Whether brought about by their own volition or beguiled by the skill of Indian professors of the art of decoying, a band of several hundred buffalo was bunched together on a rolling plain within a couple of miles to the south-east of my coign of vantage. There was a light wind from the east at the time; so, upon the criers giving the orders, the hunters left the camp going down-wind first south-west and gradually circling round, till heading north-east for the buffalo they formed line behind and under the concealment of a long ridge. The horses, knowing what was coming, were restive and trembling with excitement and impatience to be off. So were their riders. After having crawled to the crest of the ridge, which was within half a mile of the buffalo, and made his last observation, the chief hunter gave the order to move, and upon the line topping the ridge, shouting the word "Ho!" he gave the signal to charge. The line of two hundred men at once burst into the lope, then the gallop, and last into racing speed, leaving clouds of dust behind, in which the laggards were soon enveloped. The line swept on, becoming more broken as it went, by the fleeter forging ahead of their fellows.

By this time those buffalo on the alert had begun to move up-wind, and the rest, taking the alarm from them, quickly followed, until the whole herd was in ever-quickening motion. through which and over a country full of badger holes the hunters blindly charged. After passing through and emerging from the veil of dust the hunters were at the heels of the herd and commenced firing. The bolder men on the swifter steeds still pressed forward, firing as they went and reloading their flintlocks with almost incredible speed and dexterity. A few fell in the rush, tripped up by badger holes or other mishap; but the majority pursued the now frantic animals, firing shot after shot at the fat cows, seemingly regardless of the presence of their fellows in the line of fire. And the slaughter continued till the ponies became outwinded, and dropped behind the main herd or those cut out and scattered in the chase.

We on the hill were auditors as well as spectators of the charge—the hunters' whoops of excitement and the volleying of their firearms, at intervals could be heard amidst the bellowing of the buffalo and the thunder of thousands of flying hoofs.

It was magnificent and it was war, but not against a foe in flight with rear guard, who could shoot back, for only when wounded and brought to bay did the bison show fight.

Meanwhile the squaws with their carts, travois and pack animals were following up the hunters. How each knew his own "kill" amongst the hundreds on that stricken field is a mystery to a white man. But there seemed to be no disputes, and even the squaws appeared to know the animals which had fallen to the flintlocks of their hunter husbands. And there is one thing to the credit of the Indians which must be recorded—old, helpless men and widow women could go and help themselves freely to the best carcasses on the field and it were shame to say them nay, for to the widows and the weak belonged the spoils according to Indian traditionary custom. It was generally from these widows that the finest marrow fat and tallow and the best dried meat and pemmican were obtained by the traders.

In this race, as always, the Metis who took part far outclassed the thoroughbred Indians. They were better armed and mounted, better shots and more skilful. In this way they had won renown as the victors in every attack made on the Red River hunting camps by the Sioux. And whenever these "Tigers of the Plains" had been repulsed and were in retreat, the Metis buffalo hunters sallied forth and, hunting their foes as they did buffalo, drove them into panic-stricken flight.

It was through their wholesome dread of the warlike prowess of the Metis that the Sioux, though always covetous of territory, afterwards professed friendship to them and the British north of the boundary line.

The Spoils of the Chase.

With the speed of long practice, the carcasses, which strewed the plain, were soon stripped of hide and flesh, and the remains left as a feast—first to the camp dogs, which, when gorged, left their leavings to the birds and beasts of prey.

There were full bellies in the camp during the following days, those of the little naked boys being ludicrously remarkable for their distention like unto tightly blown-up bladders. Neither were they the only gluttons, for many young men ate and ate for the pleasure of eating till they could hold no more, and then emptying their stomachs by artificial vomiting they would begin again.

For several days after " the run " the women were busy drying the meat spread on stages or on the ground without being very precise as to the grass being clean. I saw enough of the process of pemmican making that time to prevent my ever having a hankering for any, unless made by people of known cleanliness. The noise of the scraping of the hair off the hides was incessant, the hide having been first stretched by pegging to the ground, while the adherent fat and flesh were scraped off, and then, so prepared, it was stretched on a wooden frame and set up in a sloping position convenient for scraping off the hair. Then followed the process of Indian tanning.

A Night Attack.

On the second night after the big hunt I was awakened suddenly by Fisher shaking me and shouting in agitation: " The Blackfeet—*Les Pieds Noir*—are upon us." As we slept in all our clothing but our coats and hats, with pistol under pillow and gun under blanket, it did not take me a minute to follow Alick outside. The lodges were outside the pony corral, formed by the carts interlocked in a big circle. The Metis had always used the carts with their ladings to form a barricade, behind which they fought, so I asked Alick where I should take my stand. He said, " Right in front of the warriors' lodge, where your outfit is." So I went and stood there ready to shoot at any sign of an enemy in front. There was furious firing being exchanged between the camp to the right and the open, but I saw nothing within range of my shotgun. Then the balls began to whistle about me in a regular fusillade from behind—the Indians of our own camp being the shooters at a foe invisible to me. Realizing that I was in the line of this useless volley firing, after getting a ball or two through my coat, I took shelter in the now deserted lodge—for not one of its warrior occupants was to be seen. My outfit was piled along the eaves at the back of the lodge, which fronted the open, and I went and sat down, sheltered from the volleys coming from behind by the bales and packs of my outfit and trade. There were a few embers in the fireplace and I sat smoking before it listening to the bullets which went on ripping through the upper works of the lodge, even after those on the right side of the camp had ceased firing upon the Blackfeet retiring.

It did not strike me at the moment that the fire from behind was coming from the Young Dog section of the circle of the camp; but next morning we found too many bullets had found their billets in the lodge, its poles and its contents, to have been merely incidental to the Indian practice of shooting without aim at any particular object for the purpose of warning an enemy that they were there with powder to burn.

As far as experience under fire was concerned I did not find it half so trying as I did once in the old country when amusing myself as a boy behind the butts of the range of rifle volunteers, who, in a squad of twenty, suddenly opened fire at three hundred yards and each fired five rounds—nearly all misses—which sent the Enfield bullets gyrating and whirring above me and ploughing up the ground about a little hollow in which I lay till they ceased firing. I remember the great contempt I had for the poor shooting of that squad; and on the occasion now described I felt more annoyed at seeing no chance to shoot at a Blackfoot than at the bullets whizzing from behind. La Pierre said he had shot a Blackfoot; but the attack was not in force, and they fell back without doing any damage to those in camp.

YELLOW HEAD BEGS A SOLATIUM.

Both Fisher and La Pierre suspected that the stray bullets that came my way might have been designed by the Young Dogs to reach me as well as to scare the Blackfeet, and Loud Voice's men were far from pleased on seeing the number of perforations in their lodge and its poles.

I think it was the next day that, as I was lying in Fisher's lodge talking with him, who should step in but Yellow Head himself, clothed in a white blanket belted round the waist, and with no visible weapons. He spoke for some time with Fisher excusing himself and laying the blame for his conduct on firewater and the instigation of Big Beak and his " young men." He dwelt upon the high position he held as a warrior and a great hunter, and said that people were mocking him for being laid out by a blow of the bare fist of a " boy "—as he called me. He would not have felt degraded had I used a club, knife or gun, but the bare fist had disgraced him entirely.

According to Indian custom, at the option of the injured, any injury could be honorably atoned for by the culprit paying a fine in proportion to the offence. Besides, he had always been a good customer of the Company and would continue to have no truck with other traders if I would pay him the fine he proposed, namely, some tea and tobacco, a common cotton shirt, a pair of leggings, and a blanket.

I lay, watching the fellow, with my hand on my revolver ready to draw while this was being said and translated. Then

I told Fisher that I considered myself the party injured and that Yellow Head had only got what he deserved. Fisher explained this to Yellow Head, who could only plead in reply that his reputation was at stake. Fisher then advised me strongly to settle the affair according to the Young Dog's wish, for, he said, he or his people would be certain to assassinate me and then pillage the Company's property in my charge. It was my duty to the Company, urged Alick, to save these goods from pillage in spite of my having been in the right. I hated to yield, but finally agreed to give the things for the sake of the Company. But I soon was sorry for having given the promise, for as it was made, after offering me his hand, Yellow Head let fall his belted blanket from his shoulders, and there rattled down on the ground a pile of round stones about half the size of my fist. "With these," said he, "I came here to stone you to death if you did not yield. But now it is all right." I felt sorely tempted to shoot him on the spot, but I had given the unbreakable word of a white man to an Indian, and so I went with him to the lodge of Loud Voice, and unpacking the things, gave him one pint measure of tea, one yard of tobacco, one common cotton shirt, two-third yard white cloth for leggings, and a "two-point" white blanket—the smallest size I had and much too small for a man. He bundled the things up in the blanket and Whitford interpreted what he said: "Are you afraid of us now?" With the intended stoning rankling in my mind I was in no humor to take this, and making for him I said, "No, never, damn you." The moment he saw me coming he turned round and dived in most undignified haste through the flap-covered lodge door.

Meanwhile the braves of Loud Voice had witnessed the proceedings in sullen silence; but as soon as Yellow Head's heels had disappeared they began murmuring that he should not have got anything. They were brooding over the ripping up of their lodge and the perforation the new one had received, not by accident they suspected, on the night of the Blackfeet attack.

WE PLAN TO DEPART.

I had traded bigger loads of provisions and leather than my six ox-carts could carry; so I had been hoping that Jerry would return with his big brigade of carts, load up the cargo of goods which Fisher and Loud Voice were carrying for me, and allow me to return to the fort with the laden carts. However, there was no sign of him, the oxen were in good travelling trim, La Pierre had carts laden ready to send in to Touchwood Hills, and some of the freemen belonging to that place and to Fort Pelly were also fully laden. So I quietly resolved on the return journey.

This was easier to plan than to put in practice; for, in their desire to keep the camp strong, and to prevent the buffalo from being disturbed in migrating to the country of the Crees to the east, the councils of the camp would permit no one to leave it, unless they were each paid a heavy " export duty." This we were determined not to pay.

The record of how we effected our escape and of our adventures on the return journey are reserved for the next chapter.

CHAPTER XXI.

THE RETURN TRIP TO THE FORT.

WE BREAK BOUNDS.

I ARRANGED with Loud Voice, Little Black Bear and Pasqua, all of whom were good reliable Indians, to carry about in their carts the remaining unbroken original packages of goods—"whole pieces" as we called them—and with Fisher to take the things that had been opened and repacked in buffalo leather; all to be delivered to Jerry upon his arrival. There were also some provisions more than my six oxen could draw to the fort, and these were similarly distributed.

The halfbreeds, as has been mentioned before, were all separated from each other in the circle of lodges, and continually spied upon. But we managed, unknown to the Indians, to agree to break from the bondage of the warriors' lodges upon the next occasion of moving the camp. To our friends in Loud Voice's lodge only, at the last moment, was the plan revealed, accompanied with a satisfactory present.

The Blackfeet were still hovering around, watching the camp, and their proximity spurred on everyone to make haste when the word was given to move, lest those too slow and straggling behind the main body should be cut off by a sudden attack. Our plan was to loiter behind and make a break for liberty as soon as the main body had left us so far in the rear that they would not risk leaving the main body in sufficient numbers to round us up.

Accordingly, on the second morning after our preparations had been made, we allowed the camp to move on without us, and we all made for the crossing of a creek nearby at which we concentrated. Our party consisted of La Pierre's men, composed of Thomas Sinclair, George Gordon and his two

335

sons; of Andrew and Charles McNab and Josiah Pratt,* freemen, all of Touchwood Hills; and a man named Stevenson,
and Peter Brass, of Fort Pelly. Besides Whitford and The
Ten, I hired an English halfbreed named Humphrey Favel,
to assist with my carts.

I rode in front of the carts to the crossing along with Favel,
who had a pony of his own, and found to my disgust that a
party of Indians, under La Pierre's foe, Pee-wah-kay-win-in,
had concealed themselves at the ford for the purpose of stopping us there. Favel interpreted, " They tell us they have
come to stop us." We were man to man, so, without hesitation, I told Favel to order them out of the way, and to say
that I would shoot the first man who tried to stop us. At the
same time I pointed my gun at the leader. "Oh, don't shoot,"
he said, " we did not mean to force you; but there are hundreds of Blackfeet all around who are sure to kill you if you
leave, and the Company will blame us for allowing you to go
into such danger." " Tell him," I replied, " that we would
sooner face an open foe, like the Blackfeet, than remain in a
camp surrounded by Indians amongst whom we could not
tell friend from foe." They then asked for some tea and
tobacco, but, refusing them, we pushed on across the ford;
and they immediately galloped after the moving camp.

STONY REFUGEES FOLLOW.

We had hardly got clear of the creek when we heard several
shots in rapid succession, and saw a number of Indians coming on horseback and with travois after us. I was afraid this
might be a stronger attempt to stop us; but Favel, who had
eyes like a hawk, soon saw that they were fugitives, like ourselves, from the camp, and that they were Assiniboines. Some
of them galloped up and told us the shots we had heard were
those of the keepers of the camp killing the dogs of the Assiniboines to scare them into remaining. They had been within

*Josiah Pratt is now living on an Indian Reserve near Touch-
wood Hills, 16th September, 1913.

an ace of having to fight to get away, and it would have come to that had the Blackfeet not been making demonstrations at the same time.

I think there were about twenty lodges of these Assiniboines who followed our example. They were principally from the North Saskatchewan, with a few of those belonging to Wood Mountain; and they had very few carts, using travois to drag their little goods and gear along. Owing to the killing of so many of their dogs their poor ponies had more than they could well draw and travel to keep up with our carts. One very tall, thin, old and grey-haired man was blind, but to lighten the travois in which he had been wont to travel he was obliged to walk, led by his grandson—a mere child. It was pitiful to see him, with a stick in his hand, hastening, in obvious fear of being left behind to the Blackfeet, with stumbling steps over the trackless prairie.

Humphrey Favel, Renegade.

This rather notorious character was one of the numerous half-caste descendants of Richard Favel, who was master of the Hudson's Bay Company's Henley House on the Albany River in 1775-6. He was a tall, well-built, athletic and handsome man, without any indication of Indian blood but brown eyes and black hair. He spoke first-rate English, sometimes with an American accent, which he had acquired among the miners in the gold fields of Caribou. He was a smart, intelligent fellow, too, but he was distrusted as a renegade who sometimes lived and "married" in the Blackfeet tribe, and then, deserting those of the Blackfeet for a change, he would come and take a couple of wives among the Saskatchewan Crees. Consequently his fellow Red River English halfbreeds were ashamed of him, and he was distrusted by the Company's people.

But when he told me that he was tired of the life he had been leading and wished to return to his relatives in Swan River district and the Red River Settlement again, and offered to work his way to the fort, I was glad to have him, more especially as he spoke good English and could well describe many adventures he had gone through across the mountains and among the Blackfeet.

Scout After Scout.

Our "brigade of carts" had now been overtaken by the train of Assiniboine refugees, and the route chosen by Gordon, who was a first-rate guide, lay in a valley wherein it was hoped we might be concealed from the gaze of the Blackfeet. To keep a lookout for them Favel and I rode along the top of the bank abreast of the train below. We had not gone far when, as we were talking, I saw two black objects ahead which I at first thought were crows. He raised himself high in the saddle, looked a moment, and sunk down. "They are Blackfeet," he said, "and they are watching the carts in the valley. What shall we do? I replied that if they were only two scouts who had just discovered the carts the best way was to kill them before they reported to their main body. A slight roll of the upland now lay between us and them. In the hollow Favel dismounted and prepared himself for the charge we were to make on topping the rise in front. He had a big hunting knife in his belt and a single-barrel flintlock trading gun. This he carefully primed and double shotted. He tied a colored cotton handkerchief tightly round his head and girdled up his loins for the fray by tightening his French belt. He then arranged that I should pick out the scout to the right and he the one to the left: but he warned me most impressively not to fire till he gave the word, as we tried to take them by surprise by rushing upon them at full speed.

We bent over our ponies' necks till, reaching the crest of the swell, we dashed forward about a hundred yards to find not only the two Indians whom we had seen, but to find ourselves surrounded by a scattered score of them. "What shall we do?" said Favel in agitation. "Make straight for the carts," I cried, "and shoot those in the way,"—on which, there were the only two first seen. As we turned towards them, "For God's sake, don't fire," he cried, "for these are Assiniboines, not Blackfeet. They belong to the party." And so it turned out. They had been on the lookout for the Blackfeet also, of whom they had seen a large body in the distance across the valley and approaching it. Of this they had sent warning to the train with word to encamp and make preparations for defence immediately.

A Forced March.

Favel and I at once sped downhill to where the carts had come to a stand in the valley. The Indians were already unhitching, in great agitation, but the halfbreeds had merely stopped to take counsel together. Sinclair said that was no place to make a stand, as there was only a little trickle of water, quite insufficient for man and beast of the party. Gordon knew of a splendid position ahead where the valley terminated at Swift Current Creek. We could reach that by dusk, he said; and once there we could stand off a whole tribe of Blackfeet, for it was a loop of the Swift Current, which formed a high peninsula, commanding full view of the low banks opposite, and the isthmus was so narrow that our carts could securely barricade it. Besides, on the peninsula there was plenty of good grass for our animals. So it was determined to march on for the loop, regardless of the protests of the Assiniboines, and, should they remain behind, we would be relieved of a band who would take every chance to pilfer from us, while they were far more the objects of Blackfeet enmity than we were.

On we went, and were hastily followed by the Assiniboines, who generally had hard work to keep up with our carts. The weather was dry and very hot, and we had a long and wearisome way to go at the slow rate of an ox-cart. Gordon rode ahead picking the path, followed by Acting Aide-de-Camp Favel and myself. Sinclair and another halfbreed and a few of the Indians scouted on the banks on both sides of the valley,

commanding a view of the uplands as well as of our carts. The
drivers were ready to circle round with their carts at a
moment's notice and form a barricade. A few of us had
percussion muzzle loading shotguns, the rest the ordinary
flintlock, all primed and loaded with ball. Every once and
again a scout would bring in a false alarm of the enemy being
about to attack. Sinclair, who was a man of known courage,
came and told me he had seen " The Slavies," as he called
them, coming in a huge black mass of horsemen. But they
did not come, till hot, tired, hungry and very thirsty our
caravan reached the haven of safety, just as described by
Gordon, and just as the sun went down.

A Natural Stronghold.

We immediately took sole possession of the peninsula and
blocked the isthmus with our carts, as well against the Assiniboines, who were quite capable of pillaging us, as against our
open foes of the other tribe. The Stonies then came with
most alarming reports of the Blackfeet being close and preparing to attack, and to defend themselves they wished me
to supply them with ammunition. The halfbreeds who knew
the duplicity of our allies advised me to refuse this request, because they might turn the ammunition against ourselves as soon as they were rid of the fear of the common foe.
So I told them that not till we were certain of attack would
they be allowed to come behind our barrier and ammunition
be served out to them.

Asleep on Guard.

We divided ourselves into watches, and I was to take the
first. So after a much appreciated supper, not having eaten
since early morning, I reclined for a smoke under a cart with
my back against my roll of bedding, gun at hand and pistol
in my belt. It was then getting quite dark. Next thing I
knew was awakening suddenly and raising my head, upon
which I received a crashing blow and saw stars. It flashed

through my mind that here were the Blackfeet in earnest and clubbing me. Again I raised my head quickly, but was again knocked backwards by another heavy blow. Then I remembered I had been under a cart, and projecting downwards through the middle of the axle was a long pin to hold it in its place. Rousing myself again more cautiously, and stooping to avoid the pin, I got out, fully armed, on my feet.

"You are a fine watchman," said the reproachful voice of Josiah Pratt, near me; "you have slept like a log all night."

"What of the Blackfeet?" I asked.

"They did not come, although the Stonies and their dogs gave false alarms twice in the night. But it is now coming dawn and that is the time to look out," he replied.

I felt so ashamed that I, who should have set a good example, had slept at my post, but it was a relief to hear that my keeping awake had been unnecessary.

THE BLACKFEET LET UP.

"Gordon's Loop," when I examined it that morning, was found to be splendidly suitable for defence and for resting and grazing our cattle. There, after the fatigue of the forced march of the previous day, our cattle and ourselves took ease for another day, during which the scouts scoured the neighborhood, and came back with the very pleasing intelligence that the Blackfeet had apparently left us to again turn their attention to the bigger camp.

WOOD MOUNTAINEERS ELOPE.

However, we did not relax our vigilance till, a few days after, having crossed the Couteau de Missouri, we descended its eastern slope and reached the vicinity of the present city of Moose Jaw on the plain beyond. Then on camping no night guards were set, but everyone went to bed with his gun under his blanket as usual. Upon rousing next morning there was a general outcry, for during the night the young buck Assiniboines from Wood Mountain had stolen away, carrying with

341

them two carefully selected women and several ponies belonging to the Saskatchewan tribe, also the flintlocks which the halfbreeds had taken so carefully to bed. They had taken all the best horses, so pursuit was hopeless, and I did not feel it my business to urge it on the losers, for nothing belonging to the Qu'Appelle outfit had been taken.

THE PARTY DISPERSES.

The Saskatchewan Indians being well within the Cree country parted with us at this point, intending to go by Carlton and find their way home up the North Saskatchewan. The Touchwood Hills and Fort Pelly people forked off from us a little later, and after striking the Wood Mountain cart trail where it crossed The River That Turns (generally known now as Moose Jaw Creek), I rode on ahead to Fort Qu'Appelle, where I returned safely after these adventures, on July 16, 1868.

JERRY AND TRAILL HELD UP.

This chapter may be properly concluded by relating that Jerry McKay, having been joined by a party from Touchwood Hills under William Edward Traill, apprentice clerk, reached the big camp within a few days after I had left it. On both his homeward and outward journey he had taken a more southerly route than mine. Their parties united with La Pierre and they had plenty of trouble in that camp divided against itself with the enemy, so to speak, at its gates. Upon leaving after completing the trade, a heavy tribute was demanded of them. This Mr. Traill absolutely refused, and as the cart-train was starting, with Henry Jordan leading the foremost ox, shots were fired "across the bows" of the leading cart and its harness was cut by Assiniboines with the chief, Red Eagle, at their head. While Jerry was parleying with Red Eagle, Traill had the latter covered with his breech-loading Henry rifle (the first ever seen in that country), behind Traill was an Assiniboine with his gun levelled at the former's head, and behind the Assiniboine was a Cree with flintlock ready aimed at the Assiniboine. Had Traill pulled the trigger, and he was within an ace of doing so, the train would have been lit to an explosion of intertribal war in that tumultuous camp.

Fortunately for the future peace of the plains, Jerry, foreseeing the inevitable consequences of refusing, took the responsibility of conceding the demand, and, in spite of Traill's protests, paid to the Warriors' Lodges goods to the value of fifty pounds ($250), and so averted much greater loss.

When I reported to Mr. McDonald (the freetraders and Jerry afterwards did so) I had the satisfaction of being told that I had acted well and "like an old trader," instead of a greenhorn, under trying circumstances.

CHAPTER XXII.*

THE LATE SUMMER OF 1868 AND WINTER 1868-9.

Explanation.

I HAVE now reached the period at which the jottings of dates and incidents in my personal diary ceased to be continuous. As everything of interest and importance was entered by me in the "Journal of Daily Occurrences" of the post, and our supply of paper was strictly limited, I began to use my memorandum book for recording in pencil trading transactions which were duly transferred to the books of the post, kept in pen and ink. These are no longer accessible to me, even if the Company have still preserved them.

A stray entry or two on personal matters and a few of the trade transactions recall to my memory further particulars. These and two drafts of my general reports to headquarters will form the skeleton of the concluding chapters, supplemented by data from other sources.

A Thunderous Summer.

Immediately after my return, as recorded in last chapter, for which he had been waiting, Mr. McDonald left for Fort Garry to bring up the summer brigade of carts with supplies for the district from Fort Garry. It was the season at which all hands and all temporary labor to be had about the post were engaged in haying.

These operations were frequently interrupted by thunderstorms, and the weather was continuously torrid. Nearly

---

* From this place on the matter has never been published before.

every evening a grand storm of thunder and forked lightning arose in the west and swept down the valley.

Every time a storm arose I went out to admire it, until one afternoon about the end of July, 1868, a truly terrific hurricane suddenly swept down the valley, lashing the lake into foam as it approached the fort. The first gust slammed the big front gate and I ran out to secure it, as it threatened to uproot its posts. Just when within a few feet of it, with an awful crash the lightning struck the front stockade and levelled it to the ground. The tempest raged down a narrow, sharply-defined course, sweeping every obstacle before it, and levelling grass and shrub. Getting under two big leather lodges near the fort, it carried them up, poles and all, like umbrellas, until they disappeared in the distance. Flash after flash of lightning followed in quick succession, accompanied by the boom of thunder and the roar of the hurricane. Rain first poured down in spouts, but soon hailstones, ranging in size from that of a trade bullet to that of a hen's egg, took its place and whitened the ground.

Next day the lee shores of the lakes were strewn with ducks and other waterfowl, whose broken heads and bones attested the wholesale slaughter of the downpour of icedrops. From the end of the fishing lakes the hurricane, sweeping in the direction of Fort Pelly, clean cut its way through every bush and cleared as sharply defined a course in the heavy woods of the Swan River valley as if made by a regiment of axemen on a surveyed line.

When the lightning smashed down the stockades it gave me such a shock that for two years after, whenever a thunderstorm was brewing, and long before there was a cloud in the sky foretelling its approach, I commenced to become nervous and fidgetty and could foretell its coming. These effects gradually died away, so that on the third year I neither had any premonition of its coming nor fear when it did come. Similar experiences are not uncommon amongst folk living in the open. Solitary lodges of Indians on the open plain were frequently struck, and certain localities, such as Fort Ellice, where a cow or two was killed by lightning every summer, appear to be peculiarly liable.

The summer of 1868 was unusually hot and sultry throughout the country, and Red River Settlement was ravished by a hurricane on the 3rd of July such as had never been witnessed by the oldest inhabitant.

HAYMAKING AND HORSEKEEPING.

Whilst Mr. McDonald was away Jerry returned with the provisions he had secured in the camp mentioned in last chapter. His men and those who soon afterwards returned from York Factory were set to work cutting hay with the scythe, in which there was keen competition between them. The less skilful were employed in curing and hauling it into the yard at the fort, for the use of our horned cattle.

The "private orders" from York Factory of the regular employees were received at this time, and was one of the great and enjoyable events of the year in their lives. The haymaking was lightsome work, and the voyageurs were all glad to be home again from the toils and privations of the trying trip to the Bay.

Jerry and I rode about every day on the pick of the band of horses, going out to mark the progress of the haymakers, besides doing any shooting that fell in our way. We counted the ponies, and if any were lost, strayed or stolen, arranged for their recovery. To the sick and the many suffering from collar and saddle-galls we, especially Jerry, applied remedies. If the feed were not satisfactory, he directed the horseguards to move to better pasture, and that on which grew "goose-grass" was his special sanitarium for the sick and lean.

A SIOUX CATTLE STAMPEDE.

Affairs were thus going on in their regular course, when one forenoon there came a stray Indian, whose name was

Nee-shoot Kan-ni-wup, meaning "The Twin Kan-ni-wup," (whatever the latter may mean). He was an insignificant fellow and a poor hunter, and we were rather surprised at his air of solemn importance on entering the office. Being a Saulteau he had "the gift of the gab," and made a very flowery and religious preamble, stating that he had always been a poor man but a prayerful one, and now in answer to his prayers the spirit whom he addressed had, after long waiting, vouchsafed to grant his desire, in a wonderful way. Jerry, getting tired of the long harangue, interrupted it to ask what wonder had Nee-shoot's god performed; but he still kept it involved in mysterious and poetic phrases.

While he was rambling on Jerry told me about him. Hitherto he had been fortunate neither as hunter nor horse-thief. Indeed, his get-rich-quick schemes in the latter manner had proven disastrous; for, in an attempt to match the hereditary caste of horse-thieving Stonies in their own game and on their own ground, he had been caught, despitefully abused, and led, ignominiously naked, by a bowstring looped to his person, through the Assiniboine lodges to be pelted with dirt and foul language, spat upon and mocked by the women and children.

Finally he came down to facts and announced that instead of falling in with buffalo he had found, near Old Wives' Lake, a band of white men's cattle roaming masterless over the prairie. At long last the spirit of his dreams had taken pity and compassion upon him, and as he rounded up twelve fat, red and white, young beef steers he anticipated their transformation into buffalo-hunting and cart ponies, and his own elevation into a prosperous and respected hunter and the proprietor of two additional wives. Therefore he had come to the fort to offer the Company the chance of securing at a bargain the valuable animals, which he had driven in to Qu'Appelle.

Jerry and I rode up to the upper lake to see the steers. They were fine cattle without any visible brand, but they had evidently strayed in some way from the American side. It was always customary to pay a person finding stray animals and bringing them to the fort to hold for their owners. So we agreed to give the Twin a buffalo runner, two or three ponies, and some goods for finding them and bringing them in. Sometime after we heard that the Sioux had swooped under the guns of Fort Beaufort and stampeded four hundred head of cattle which were intended for the use of that establishment. Some of these they slaughtered, but many escaped and scattered all over the plains. The circumstance was reported to Governor McTavish by Mr. McDonald, but I presume it would have cost more than the animals were worth to them for the Americans to come and drive them back; so Nee-shoot's steers became draught oxen for Fort Qu'Appelle.

POLICE DUTY.

There were several others of the cattle stampeded found by other Indians and Metis, but only one about which I distinctly remember. Baptiste Robillard, brother of our cartwright, formerly guide of the Cumberland boat brigade, had come to stay on the plains, accompanied by his son-in-law, John Simpson, a natural son of the Arctic explorer, Thomas Simpson, whose pictures, by the way, he very much resembled. Simpson had hired a Saulteau for the season to help him in the buffalo hunt on the plains, where they found one of these fine steers. As he returned too late to make hay to feed the animal for the winter, Simpson made arrangements to have it wintered at the fort. Next spring after the snow had melted off the land, but while the lakes were still icebound, the Saulteau and Simpson had a dispute as to their rights to the animal, and because he was dissatisfied the Saulteau, in passing the Company's herd grazing near the fort, shot the steer. Our watchman, George Sandison, immediately reported this to Mr. McDonald, who ordered me to come with him after the Indian. We set off on good horses and found that he and his people (there were two lodges) had " pitched " off for the lower lake. They had got halfway down and were about the middle of the lake below the fort when we got on the ice and galloped after them. At once one of the party left it on foot and began running towards the bush on the south side of the lake. Telling me to head off the fugitive, Mr. McDonald raced after the party. I made him halt, and kept guard over him with a Sharp's rifle, while he crouched down on the ice with his gun in hand. Whenever he made a move I covered him with my gun, till Mr. McDonald came galloping up. They exchanged some angry, and, I think, very bad language. For a time the Indian looked wicked and ready to shoot. He finally submitted and we took him to the fort where he agreed to pay for the killing of the animal out of his hunt next summer. It was fortunate that I did not have occasion to fire, for on the way back I discovered that the big Enfield percussion cap of my gun had worked off during the gallop.

Our commons were rather low at the time, and Sandison had been busy cutting up the animal for beef while we were away after the butcher; and so we had a rare treat, for to kill a Company's ox for beef in Swan River in those days would have been considered a crime and a shame of the first degree, although we had twenty milch cows and thrice as many other kinds of cattle.

FLEMMAND, A WALKING ADVERTISEMENT.

In the winter of 1868-69 Jerry wintered at " Eagle Quills " and Jacob at Old Wives' Lake. My friend Flemmand, who, during the summer, had been transferred to Fort Ellice, was sent out by Chief Trader McKay to winter in the camp of the Red River and American Metis at Wood Mountain, and to trade with any Fort Ellice people or other Indians within reach. Rumours, which travelled so wonderfully " without visible means of support " about the plains, had become rife regarding the reckless manner in which Flemmand was conducting his trade and himself. These had been largely confirmed by two of his men, Bazil Mougenier and Che-cake, who had been sent to Fort Ellice for further supplies. Mr. McKay, having no one else to send, came to Qu'Appelle, and asked Mr. McDonald to send me out to take account of Flemmand's trade and proceedings.

To provide accommodation for the frequent dances by which the Metis amused themselves in their wintering quarters, each family "in society" built their one-roomed log dwelling large enough to serve as a ballroom as well. If a man were a trader he usually kept his goods in the same apartment, only providing an outbuilding for gunpowder, furs, robes, leather and cured provisions—the frozen fresh meat being piled on a stage outside high above the reach of dogs.

Although he had left his family to winter at Fort Ellice, Flemmand was not the man to be outclassed in floor space for dancing, and incidental room for the goods, which he invariably alluded to as "my property," with strong accent and recurring emphasis on the "r's." He was quite surprised and taken aback when, after I had knocked, or rather drummed, on his clear parchment door, on his permission "*Entre,*" I stepped in. He turned as pale as his complexion permitted, gave a gasp, and then exclaimed, "O, bon jour, mon ami, you just de man I like to see here. De men Monsieur McKay he give me no good, not trustive men. Dam rascals, day lie an' day cheat, an' day steal my prrroperrty. So I glad you come to take de 'cont.'"

Flemmand I knew as certainly a "quick change artist," but he surpassed himself and astonished me as soon as he had uttered the words, for, without the ceremony of knocking, in came Bazil with my baggage, and Flemmand rushed up to him, clapping him on the shoulder, and instantly declared: "Ah, Monsieur, look at dis man, a fine lettle fellow, de only trustive man I got; but dat Che-cake (his partner) a useless trash and dam rascal."

Bazil sullenly shook off his "master's" hand, and only gave him a knowing and contemptuous glance in return for the compliments, and went out to bring in more of his sled-load. As soon as Bazil banged the door behind him, Flemmand's ingratiating smile changed to an expression of hatred, and shaking his fist at the closed door he again commenced, " How can I take care of my prrropérrty w'en de Company give me men like dat?"

Then in came Che-cake, when in like manner I was asked to bear witness to his excellencies and the delinquencies of Bazil, and, the moment his back was turned, of Flemmand's private and confidential official opinion of the kind of men under him. Much to my amusement, this performance was repeated till the men had, coming in alternately, unladen their sleds.

While taking a list of the supplies—furs and pro-visions—" the property of the Hudson's Bay Company on hand at Wood Mountain " that day and date, and making notes of Flemmand's account of his doings, I told him of the accusations against him and his management and asked explanation or denial.

Put on his defence, Flemmand agreed with the ancient saying that all men are liars, but classified those who had spoken ill of him as positive, comparative and superlative liars, who, through envy and jealousy of his brilliant ability as a trader and an advertiser of his wares, also as the favorite he had become in that camp with the ladies, had entered into a campaign of lies and slander to ruin his personal standing and the local trade of the Company at the same time.

Early in the winter he had known that the trade with the few Indians and freemen attached to Fort Ellice and winter-ing out there would be too small to pay expenses. The Metis winterers had several traders among their number, and, of course, opposed to him. These Metis were mostly from the American side, and only a minority from the Red River Settlement and accustomed to deal with the Company there. As none of these classes had much need and as little desire to patronize Le Magazin de Flemmand, he was obliged to initiate methods to secure their trade, which he was well aware were not sanctioned by the ordinary rules and methods of the Company.

But he knew his fellow Metis were as fond of dress, dancing and gambling as he was himself, likewise were they in love of display and envious of those who made it. So instead of defending himself against the charges of having freshly arrayed himself daily and gone out to visit with new clothing and finery from his store, he told me to report to Mr. McKay that he had done so for the purpose of advertising his business, and at the same time to put the fellows from the American side, in their shoddy clothes, completely in the shade, while he, in brilliant array, basked in the smiles of the fair sex. The end had amply justified the means, for these hunters, envious of him, and desirous to eclipse him, one after another began to give up the furs and robes which they had previously refused to trade with him, for fine blue cloth capotes with brass buttons, fine cloth trousers, broad L'Assomption belts, fine colored flannel shirts, black silk neckerchiefs, and foxtail plumes, anointments of pomatum and scented hair oil, besides silver finger rings and gilt earrings.

The dances he gave were also for advertising purposes, and well repaid their cost. Gambling was a besetting amusement, which so often led to loss of life and property as to be most strictly forbidden by the Company. But in its arts and mysteries Flemmand was too expert to fear loss, besides his popularity and position as leader of the fast and fashionable set would have been untenable had he refrained from it. So when a man with furs was not to be tempted to part with them in exchange for the bright raiment which Flemmand advertised on his back, nor, by expressing admiration of them, compel Flemmand, according to the fashion of the country, to immediately disrobe and make a present of the desirable garment to its admirer, who was equally bound by the law of honor prevailing amongst the gay cavaliers of the prairies to double the gift in return, this modern disciple of the versatile Radisson, the father of the fur trade, would challenge

the trader or hunter to a gambling game from which Flemmand generally arose triumphant, and the stakes were paid
by him in goods, while those of his opponents were discharged
in furs.

Flemmand's flirtations with the belles of the camp, he
asserted, had been grossly misrepresented by the malice of
envious male and female competitors. While acknowledging,
without undue modesty, his success as a ladies' man, even in
that delightful pastime he had had the gathering of furs for
the Company as his main aim and object. "It is de women
dat do de bes' trade," he sagely said. "Plaze dem and dey
bring de furs."

In fine, he had made a good trade, and Mr. McKay would
receive ample and profitable returns for the "prroperrty"
committed to the charge of Flemmand, whose zeal in the
service of the Company had led him into many temptations
and transgressions of their rules and regulations.

CAUGHT IN A PRAIRIE BLIZZARD.

That winter I made two other trips with dogs. One was
out to Old Wives' Lake with Jacob Bear and a lad named
Unide Gardupuis, on which we had the unpleasant experience
of being caught by a blizzard on the bare prairie. Scraping
the snow away down to the grass with our snowshoes, we laid
down with robes and blankets under and over us, and let the
snowdrift cover us up. After spending forty-eight hours
huddled together for warmth in this decidedly uncomfortable
" camp," nibbling a morsel of pemmican and trying to thaw
snow for drinking in the covered copper teakettle we put
to warm in our bosoms, Jacob thrust his head up, and, seeing
it was clear, said we must get up and run for the nearest
woods.

Though clear, the north-west wind was strong and piercingly
cold. The dogs were all covered up under the snow around
us. Feeling for them with our feet, and pulling them out of
their comparatively warm lairs, we, with great difficulty and

distress, with hands and fingers already benumbed in lashing the bedding on the sleds, hitched them in and set off. Jacob ran ahead of his train to give a lead, for there was no trail and the wind was blowing hard slantingly ahead and across our course over the Couteau. The two trains of dogs, Jacob's and my own, which I was driving after him, constantly edged away from the slanting head wind, and I had all I could do to keep them on the course. We had eaten little and drunk less while under the snow, and it was forenoon with no chance of reaching the woods on Old Wives' Creek till sundown.

Suddenly Jacob began running harder than ever, and then stopped and began scooping a hole in the snow. When we came nearer he shouted, " We'll boil the kettle here," for he had found sticking out of a badger hole the larger half of a broken pine tent pole, than which nothing could be better to kindle a smudgy fire of buffalo dung. We willingly " rooted " with our feet for the precious buffalo chips, and had a pile high as a haycock by the time Jacob had knifed enough shavings to kindle it. The storm being violent, we covered Jacob with a robe while he struck a light with flint and steel. The fuel soon smouldered into red, and the kettle was boiled for a long longed-for drink of tea, after we had first slaked our thirst by melting snow in the frying-pan. But although it boiled the kettle, that smouldering fire gave out no warmth to us around it. Poor young Unide, thinly-clad in cotton shirt and white cloth capote, with his blanket over all for a shawl, had to keep on the run round and round about the fire, nibbling at a lump of frozen pemmican as he went, and stopping for a moment occasionally to take a drink of tea. Jacob and I were able to keep from freezing, being better clad, and sat down with our robes over our backs and heads on the weather side of the fire, more to protect it from being blown away than for any warmth we could possibly derive from it.

As soon as we got the fire going the dogs were given a little pemmican, enough to keep up their strength without impeding their travelling till night. So the whole party started with renewed strength and spirit to battle with that biting breeze till we should find rest and safety in the bush on the borders of the Old Wives' Creek. Every few minutes as we ran we had to thaw the frostbites on our noses and faces.

The sun had gone down when we gained the desired haven just in time for Jacob to see well enough to chop the big lot of firewood for the blazing bonfire he intended to enjoy in the comfort of a camp in the shelter of the woods, in contrast with the sufferings we had endured on the wind-swept prairie and under the snow.

Had Unide and I been alone we would never have reached that camp; and it had taxed even the hardiness of Jacob to do so. As soon as he had finished cutting all the firewood he wanted, and came to stand by the fire, he discovered that his right ear, on the windward side, had been solidly frozen, and by its commencing to thaw it gave him intense pain, from which he suffered many a day. He bravely bore it and laughingly said, "You will be able to put down my name on the list with marks like a horse with a crop ear, and call me Jacob "Court Oreille."*

The only other trip I made that winter of any consequence was one to Fort Pelly, where, apart from giving me hospitable welcome as a newcomer to Swan River district, I was wanted to extract a troublesome tooth for Chief Factor Campbell's lady.

---

* A few days ago I had the great pleasure of hearing that my good-natured and capable travelling companion is alive and in the enjoyment of fairly good health near Whitewood, Saskatchewan.

CHAPTER XXIII.

HISTORY OF FORT PELLY AND A VISIT TO IT IN 1868-69.

FORT PELLY.

UNDER various names, during their half century of conflict, the North-West and Hudson's Bay companies had maintained more or less permanent posts in the vicinity of the " Fort Pelly" of the United Company. The pious fur trader, Harmon, describes his sojourn at one of these in his published journal.

The earlier fur traders, ascending the Assiniboine from Lake Winnipeg, established posts along the river. From one of these, at Portage la Prairie, access to Lakes Manitoba and Winnipegosis and the Swan River was obtained. Later the Hudson's Bay Company, coming from Lake Winnipeg up the Little Saskatchewan River to Lakes Manitoba and Winnipegosis, found their way up the Swan River and portaged across to the headwaters of the Assiniboine; and on this route the line of posts composing the original Swan River district were established. The posts lower down on the Assiniboine, such as Portage la Prairie and Brandon House, were in a district known as Upper Red River, independent of the Lower Red River district, of which Fort Garry was the headquarters.

In 1831 the Northern Department Council ordered: "That, in order to protect the trade of the Assiniboines and Crees of the Upper Red River district from American opposition on the Missouri, a new post be established at Beaver Creek, to be called Fort Ellice." Next year Fort Ellice was added to Swan River district, and Dr. William Todd, who had previously commanded the " Upper Red River district," from

Brandon House, succeeded the veteran Chief Factor Colin Robertson at Fort Pelly, and in the charge of Swan River district to which Fort Ellice was then added.

Some years after, an outpost of Fort Pelly was placed at the Big Touchwood Hills, forming a supply station on the more direct trail between Fort Ellice and Carlton House than the older route by way of Fort Pelly. The outpost at Touchwood Hills, growing in importance, soon became an independent post, and was in the early sixties moved from the Big to the Little Touchwood Hills, somewhat south of the Saskatchewan trail. Similarly, in the later fifties, Fort Ellice established a wintering post at Long Lake, on the upland prairie rather south-easterly of the site of Fort Qu'Appelle. This outpost was established under the charge of James McKay, who afterwards became known as the Hon. James McKay, of Deer Lodge, Manitoba. Mr. McKay was succeeded by Interpreter Edward Cyr, one of the splendid French-Canadians in the service, and a mighty hunter, too. Of Cyr it is related that, being thrown from his horse in pursuing a young buffalo bull, and losing his gun in the fall, he was charged by the bull, whose horns he seized with his bare hands, and after a long wrestle, which burned and tore the skin off his palms, he succeeded in throwing the animal and killing him with his hunting-knife.* Cyr was followed by William Daniel, an " English " halfbreed of Irish descent, who was born and brought up at or near Moose Factory, where he acquired the Orkney dialect of the English language which formed the common tongue of the natives of British descent throughout the whole of Rupert's Land.

" Big William " Daniel was a great man in strength, in stature and in a dare-devil courage, combined with a cool skill which had carried him triumphant in a York boat, manned only by himself, over the dreaded White Fall on the route to York Factory, and had brought his brigade of boats, cov-

* Related to me by William Daniel and " Gaddie " Birston.

357

ered with tarpaulins, with "hatches batten down," so to speak, under double-reefed sail, across Lake Winnipeg in such a storm as no other guide had ever dared to venture out in.*

Next, Archibald McDonald, then a young apprentice clerk, was in charge of the wintering post and had the good fortune to have such men as Cyr and Daniel with him. He again was succeeded by Postmaster Peter Hourie, who removed the post, which, by that time, had become a permanent one, to the site of the present Fort Qu'Appelle in 1864. Mr. Hourie was a stalwart and intelligent, fine specimen of the native of Orkney origin. Although he had left the Company before I joined it, we often met in pleasant intercourse, and as he became favorably known to the Dominion Government, in

---

* Daniel used to relate with enthusiastic admiration the traditions of deeds of daring which had been handed down to him by older voyageurs. One of these was about a big brigade of one hundred and fifty canoes having been gathered from all parts of the interior at Jack River (afterwards Norway House), to descend to the Bay for the purpose of recapturing a fort taken by the French. The safer Hayes River route was not followed, if known at that time, but that by either the Nelson or the Churchill (which I could not make out, but probably the former), in the descent of which there was a dangerous rapid a mile and a half long, over which the still unthawn ice, in the early season, formed an unbroken roof high enough above the level of the water upon which it had been formed to permit of canoes and their crews passing under it, which they did yearly in the course of their business. In February, 1890, while on a trip to Split Lake, I tried to ascertain the locality of this long rapid with the ice-roof, but it certainly was not between that point and Norway House. However, along the Nelson River, on the dog-train route, there occurred here and there ledges of ice, a few feet wide, clinging to the sheer rocks along rapids, and many feet above the level to which the river had fallen, leaving these projections on which the dog-drivers took the advantage and the risk rather than ascend to the top of the high bank and make a detour to pass the rapid, which had interrupted the easy travel on the ice below and above it. Such ledges and piles of ice, preventing the possibility of landing, occur on many rapids run, "full cargo," by the voyageurs; and possibly the tradition related by Daniel may have simply exaggerated such conditions. However, he firmly believed in the continuous roof, and as he spoke of the feat his kindling eye and glowing features showed that it was one in which he, even then old as he was, would have been delighted to attempt.

whose service he died a few years ago, I need not add my appreciation of a person so well known at Regina.

These bits of the biography of worthy old timers have led me into digressing from what I was going to say about Fort Pelly. Doctor Todd remained as chief trader in charge of Swan River district at Fort Pelly till 1843, when he was succeeded by Chief Trader Cuthbert Cummings, a Highland cousin of Lord Strathcona. Mr. Cummings was followed by other chief traders, Messrs. Alexander and William J. Christie and Alexander A. H. Murray, to whom Chief Factor Campbell succeeded.

Until York Factory ceased to be the depot of the Northern Department from which the trading outfits were received and to which the furs were sent; these were freighted in the district brigades to and from the head of boat navigation on the Swan River, thence carted across land to the fort. The outfit for the "plain posts" of the district ceased to come that way in 1871, but the furs (exclusive of buffalo robes, which went to Montreal by the United States) continued to be sent out to York Factory by the boats sent from the "lake posts" for their outfits till 1874 or 1875. Upon the retirement of Chief Factor Campbell, in 1870, he was succeeded by Chief Trader William McKay, who, after wintering at Fort Pelly, returned to Fort Ellice, which became under him and his successor in the year 1872, Chief Trader Archibald McDonald, headquarters till 1883, when the latter officer, by that time a chief factor, made Fort Qu'Appelle his official residence.

Meanwhile the Hon. David Laird had been appointed resident Lieutenant-Governor of the North-West Territories at Fort Pelly, and the headquarters of the North-West Mounted Police was established near it at "Livingstone Barracks." Shortly after the seat of government was moved to Battleford, and Fort Pelly relapsed into the position of a fur-trading post under the careful management of Mr. Adam McBeath, whose place in charge of the fine post of Shoal River, near the final fall of the Swan River into Lake Winnipegosis, had been taken by his nephew, Mr. Angus McBeath. It is rather remarkable that Adam McBeath was the only one of the original white settlers, brought out under the auspices of the Earl of Selkirk, who, as far as I ever heard, became a fur trader in the Company's service. He entered it under the auspices of Chief Factor Donald Ross, who ruled so wisely and so well and for the greater part of his life at Norway House, and who had the good fortune to take unto himself as wife the sister of Mr. McBeath.

Mr. McBeath had served as postmaster in Mackenzie River District, contemporaneously with Mr. Campbell, and was for many years in charge of Fort Norman there, where his good wife, a daughter of one of the many chief factors named " Roderick " McKenzie, bore him a large family.

Under Mr. Adam McBeath's experienced management the fort, though it had ceased to be the Company's capital of the district and the Canadian capital of the territories, continued to be one of the very best fur-gathering and profitable stations in the whole country, as indeed it had been for the preceding century. Upon Mr. Adam McBeath's retirement, full of age and honor, from the service about 1880, to the beautiful shore of Lac Qu'Appelle, he was succeeded by another member of the family who fully sustained its reputation in the fur trade, Mr. Angus McBeath, who is now living at Edmonton in honorable retirement as a well-pensioned officer of the Company.

One of the reasons for the selection of Fort Pelly as the site of the first establishment of Canadian rule was that of its being upon the government telegraph line from Winnipeg to Edmonton and on the route of the originally projected Canadian Pacific Railway; but when the Canadian Northern Railway took that general direction it passed the site just near enough to destroy the new mixed trade with settlers as well as Indians which the Company's " sale shop " had been profitably engaged in. So, stripped of its ancient and modern sources of profit, Fort Pelly was closed up as a place of business for the Company in June, 1912, some hundred and fifty years after the first permanent establishment of fur trading posts at or near its site.

A Winter Visit to Fort Pelly.

It was, I think, during the still cold winter month of February, 1869, that William Sparrowhawk and I, with a train of dogs each, moderately laden with buffalo tongues and leather for Port Pelly, made a pleasant voyage thereto, and brought back some trading goods as return cargo. It was cold, but one did not feel it in the shelter of the frequent groves of aspen, poplar and willow, which, like islands in the lake, dotted the prairie, through which the trail trended. Passing by the File and Pheasant and Beaver Hills, the latter heavily wooded, on approaching the Assiniboine valley spruce trees began to show among the poplar, and we then added springy couches of spruce boughs to what seemed, by comparison with the hardships of the fireless and shelterless windswept open plains, where the winter trade and travel of Qu'Appelle were carried on, the luxury of easy travel with the comfort of a fire in the cosy protection of the bush whenever we chose to stop, instead of having to make long and rapid traverses between the rare and scattered little patches of firewood, which were the only refuge from the cold blasts and blizzards of the terrible open spaces.

Sparrowhawk was a Saulteau, with possibly a trace of French in him, without, however, any symptom whatever of their volubility, for he was endowed with the golden gift of silence, though not of the sullen sort with which so many Indians are afflicted. He had asked for a trip to vary the monotony of his occupation as assistant cartwright to Robillard. He enjoyed the journey and was a good, handy and active voyageur, besides being of unusually thrifty and neat habits. One of the greatest hardships which a man walking and running hard has to endure is the want of means to slake the thirst thereby produced. From the American post on the Missouri where he had spent the previous and several other years, Sparrowhawk had brought one of those tin flasks in which sporting gunpowder was sold there. This he invariably filled before leaving camp with either tea or " bouyon " (bouillon), and placed inside his clothes in his bosom to prevent its freezing till he required a drink on the march. I mention this, as very few thirsty men on the trip ever took this wise precaution.

A Fight for Furs.

Fort Pelly was all bustle and excitement that winter, occasioned by two of the Company's best traders, who had " gone free," having brought in a big supply of the important articles, tea, sugar, and flour, with which the posts of Swan River were generally under-supplied. One of these free-traders was Keche (Big) William Daniel; the other, on a larger scale, was Mr. Peter Hourie.

It was the fixed policy of the Company whenever any of their employees " went free " and then started as " free-traders," more especially in a district where they were known and personally popular with the Indians, to put forth even greater exertions to crush their competition than was the case against any other of their opponents. The fight for furs then assumed all the fierceness of a fratricidal conflict between the men in and those who had gone out of the Company's service. That winter, too, furred animals were abundant in the hunting grounds of the Fort Pelly Indians, and they were most excellent hunters. Indeed, I must say here, that just as the Metis, as hunters of buffalo, far excelled the ordinary Indians, so also did these known as Indians, but with some tincture of white blood, even when derived many generations back, surpass the pure Indians as trappers and hunters in the woods. The Fort Pelly " Indians," as the family names " Cote " and " Sivwright " and others indicated, like the Okanase band about Riding Mountain, were remotely descended from Europeans, but born and brought up with the Indians, trained in woodcraft from infancy, and not handicapped, like not a few of their kind, who, though nearer the European in blood and appearance, had lost much of the Indian hunting faculty while acquiring little of the industry of the European in compensation.*

Tom McKay, Second in Command.

The chief factor could leave his headquarters to inspect the other posts in his district with easy mind as to the trade of Fort Pelly suffering no detriment through his absence, as his second in command in all the arts of trading and travelling was second to none anywhere in the territories; for Mr. Thomas McKay was of "The Little Bearskin" strain of fur traders for generations, being son of the good Chief Trader William McKay, of Fort Ellice, of whom I had the privilege of writing in a previous chapter. Besides being a "real McKay," "Tom," through his mother, was descended from the notable old Hudson's Bay families of Cook and Sinclair. So, good as they were as "free-traders," Hourie and Daniel met their match in the personality of the Company's trader competing with them. And the competition was not one in which he engaged for the benefit of the Company and to win his way in it alone; but, like every other contest in which men with red blood and sporting instincts engage, it was a game in which the wit and skill of both sides were ardently enlisted.

As in a campaign of actual war, each side watched and spied upon the movements of the other, day and night, so like a general directing a battle, McKay was on the alert at all hours, sleeping with one eye open, and up in a moment to hear from spy and courier their reports from the

* The class just referred to is that of the hangers-on about mission and trading stations, who picked up a living by fishing and shooting wildfowl for themselves, and clothed themselves by serving as boatmen in the summer, and occasionally as trippers in the winter, neither trapping furs like the Indians nor attempting to till the soil like the whites.

front. No sooner would one of these arrive, exhausted from a swift running rush to "Thunder Hill," with the news from that quarter than McKay would rouse from his rest another tripper, and while the tripper was hastily preparing himself and his dog trains, "the second" would be having the trade supplies required, by such as Cote at the Crow Stand, packed up. While so engaged another dog train driver would arrive from another quarter, and similar action be taken to anticipate or meet the free-traders there. And so on the exciting game would go and be played by trippers often as full of ardour as the second himself.

When such an attack was made on the preserves of the Company's post the regular complement of men did not suffice, and it became necessary to engage as temporary servants all sorts and conditions of men, in many cases not for their ability to be of service, but to prevent their capability for mischief and annoyance being used by the other side. Among the men composing these "auxiliary forces" at Fort Pelly I caught a short glimpse of the dashing dandy, Donald, who figured as harlequin in the farce with the ferocious Flemmand in Paul Denomie's shanty at "The Turn." Donald had either forsaken or been forsaken by his former free-trade-in-whiskey master, and had with zeal and agility returned to serve under the flag under which he had been born, and now he appeared to be the most enthusiastic dog driver engaged in supplying the wants of the Indians from the fort, glibly palavering to them in camp and bringing back the furs, accompanying the whole transaction with as much fuss and flurry as circumstances permitted.

About 1872 Mr. Thomas McKay retired from the Company's service to become leader among the pioneer agricultural settlers at Prince Albert, which he represented for years in the North-West Council at Regina, and where he took a most prominent and honorable part among the loyalists during the rebellion of 1885. That the rebellion was confined in its scope amongst the natives was largely due to the daring courage and influence of this highly respected old pioneer.

WILLIAM THOMSON SMITH.

The clerk, who was accountant for Swan River district for about two years before and two years after that time, was Mr. William Thomson Smith, a native of St. Andrews, in "the Kingdom of Fife." He, like John Balsillie, of Fort Garry, and John Wilson, of Mackenzie River, was one of the appointees of Mr. Edward Ellice, M.P. for St. Andrews, the influential proprietor of much Company's stock, and, I think, always on the directorate. Mr. Smith had not only had the advantage of being educated at "The Madras," but also some good business training before entering the service in 1859.

Mr. Smith, among other useful accomplishments, was a good gardener, and he astonished me by declaring that the capabilities of the country at large were splendidly adapted for farming, if practised in a way suitable to the climate, and good seed were used. He had had great success with vegetables at Fort Pelly; from fresh seed which he had procured from St. Paul, Minnesota, because the "assortment of garden seed" supplied with the regular outfit from York Factory was nearly as old as the Company itself, and originally not of suitable sort. This was rank heresy and denial of the doctrine that the country was no good for anything but hunting and would ever so remain, which article of belief, like the Shorter Catechism in Scotland, was in and out of season impressed upon newcomers by their masters and those in authority over them in the Company. It was years, however, before I realized that Mr. Smith was right, and even that the opponents of the Company were not falsifying facts in this respect, for during my first ten years in the country the plague of grasshoppers recurred almost annually, and if they did not, something else in the shape of drouth or frost or hail spoiled the crops, always excepting the ever-hardy potato, which I have never known to be a complete failure from any cause whatever.

Mr. Smith retired from the Company's service in 1872, and found an opening and reward for his abilities in banking and financial affairs in Ontario, retiring from which, for a time he pursued his favorite diversion in an orange grove of California—a far cry from the barren rocks and icy breezes of Great Slave Lake, where he was stationed before coming to Fort Pelly. He now resides in London, Ontario.

ALAN McIVOR.

At that time there was stationed at Fort Pelly, in charge of the farming department and live stock, other than the great band of grade " Melbourne " horses bred there, a very highly-thought-of Highlander, named Alan McIvor, who afterwards settled at Portage la Prairie, and has left a good name and a number of descendants in Manitoba and Saskatchewan. He had seen and performed good service in Mackenzie River district before coming to Fort Pelly.

MECHANICS.

The Company's Council at York Factory in 1830 adopted the policy of taking native-born lads as apprentices to the blacksmiths and boatbuilders and other mechanics employed at their principal posts. The wording of the resolution, which became afterwards a fixed policy, runs:—

" Resolved, that chief factors and chief traders, in charge of districts and posts where regular tradesmen are employed, be authorized to engage strong, healthy, halfbreed lads, not under fourteen years of age, as apprentices, to be employed with these mechanics for the purpose of learning their business, for a term of not less than seven years, at the following wages, which are considered sufficient to provide them with clothes and other personal necessaries, viz.:—The first two years at £8 per annum; the next two years at £10 per annum; the following two years at £12 per annum; and the last year at £15 per annum; making for the seven years' apprenticeship an allowance of £75; such lads not to be employed with their fathers, nor in the district where their fathers or family reside."

From that time on many an apt pupil was trained by these master mechanics, who generally hailed from the Orkney Islands. Of these, while the boatbuilders and carpenters were good, I think the blacksmiths were better, and could turn their hands to and repair anything from an anchor to a watch. Repairing guns was, of course, one of the principal crafts they were called upon to practise; but many of the "non-professional" natives claimed to be able to temper the knives they made for themselves, out of worn-out files, better than any of the blacksmiths. The Indians were all craftsmen in the making of snowshoes and canoes, and many of them wonderful workers in metal without forge or other smithy appliances.

Inheriting the manual dexterity from their maternal stock, the "young halfbreed lads" made good workmen, but more of them were trained as carpenters and boat-builders than as blacksmiths. Their education in other matters was not neglected either, for all such apprentices had a fair knowledge of "the three R's," and quite a number rose to the position of postmasters and clerks in the service.

The blacksmith at Fort Pelly at that time was an Orkney-man named Johnstone, who, I remember gratefully, fixed my open-faced watch, of which the glass had been broken, by inserting a piece of silver, an American coin, in its place. The boat-builder was Jacob Beads, who had served his apprenticeship at Moose Factory, and had accompanied Doctor Rae on one of his Arctic expeditions, and therefore was certified as a first-class travelling man.

The Missionary.

On Sunday service was held in English and Indian by the Rev. Luke Caldwell, a native Indian missionary of the Church of England, in the large office and Indian reception room in the fort.

A Horseguard and Wolf-runner.

The best buffalo hunting horses in the country were those descended from an Irish hunter named "Fireaway," and every descendant, however remote, from this highly prepotent sire showed some of his excellencies. He was the best ever bought by the Company to improve the breed of ponies. A stallion later imported was "Melbourne," which was partly of Clydesdale breed, and whose offspring could be distinguished by the ox-like rump of the strain. There were few really good buffalo runners of the Melbourne breed, but many good, strong saddle and draft animals.

Fort Pelly had been, at least from the time of Chief Factor John Clarke, the predecessor of Colin Robertson, a horse and cattle breeding station, situated as it was amidst the splendid pasturage of a well-watered and wood-sheltered country. Moreover, it was out of the way of the worst tribes of horse thieves. "Melbourne" had been stationed there and a large band of his progeny roamed around the park-like prairies of Fort Pelly, under the watchful care of an Indian horseguard, who did not permit them to range beyond certain limits.

The guard was one Thomas Manitou Keesik, which surname is equivalent in English to "God Above." His Christian name of Thomas was the outward sign of his conversion from the polytheism of his ancestors, but it is said of him that each Monday after receiving communion on a Sunday, administered by the native missionaries—the Rev. James Settee or the Rev. Luke Caldwell—in the fort, Thomas resorted to the forest bearing a strip of red and another of blue cloth, of the kind known as "Hudson's Bay strouds," and offered these up in aboriginal fashion to his ancestral deity or deities. Nor did he make this double profession of opposite faiths in secret, for, said he, "One may be right and the other wrong, or both may be right; so I want to make doubly sure of the future life that both Christians and Indians believe in."

Thomas was not only remarkable for the frank latitude of his views in religion, but also for his pre-eminence as a long-distance runner in a country remarkable for wonderful feats on foot. Besides being of use to the Company as a fur-bearer, the small species of wolf then known as the "Togony" and now as the "Coyote," preyed upon the Company's calves and colts, which ranged at large with the herds about the fort. As a consequence a double reward was given the wolf-slayer there. While not disdaining every other manner of winning the prize, Thomas made a speciality for special reward in the form of rum, which had become a luxury placed quite beyond the reach of an Indian there except under most extraordinary circumstances. By the time I came to Swan River the inter-diction of liquor to Indians had become absolute, and Thomas had to content himself with the less regarded but still beloved tea, of which three pounds (an enormous quantity as com-pared with the one pound only to which an Indian was then restricted, and that at long intervals) was regarded as but a poor substitute for the old allowance of one pint of well-diluted rum. This specialty of Thomas was in running down on foot and clubbing the wolf to death. I am informed by Mr. William Phillips, now a farmer of good repute at Clande-boye, in Manitoba, that when he was stationed at Fort Pelly in 1865 Thomas Keesik (his middle name was generally dropped in conversation) ran a wolf down all the way from Fort Pelly to near Touchwood Hills (a distance of probably one hundred miles), till both the pursued and the pursuer fell down together exhausted, Thomas tripping and falling on the wolf. Both lay as they fell together for some time completely spent, till Thomas, sooner recovering, gave the wolf the final coup, and added it to his long record of such feats.

CHAPTER XXIV.

THE SUMMER OF 1869.

THE NAVIGATION OF QU'APPELLE RIVER.

In the spring and early summer of 1869, Fort Qu'Appelle was the scene of the repetition of the bustle and excitement of the previous season, lacking only the liveliness of the mirthmaking Flemmand, the star *farceur,* who, no doubt, made up to Fort Ellice what Qu'Appelle lost in that respect. In addition to the activities of the previous year, however, the river-bank in front had become the site of an experiment in boat building, and the fort was full of the whole complement of officers and men from Touchwood Hills, with their families.

For it had been decided upon the recommendation of Mr. McDonald that the returns of buffalo robes and provisions of both Touchwood Hills and Qu'Appelle should be sent to Fort Garry by the Qu'Appelle River as far as Fort Ellice, and thence, as usual, down the Assiniboine. Although the Assiniboine was not used for the carriage of freight upstream from Fort Ellice to Fort Pelly it afforded good facility, during the high water of the early part of the season, for the descent of York boats, for the construction of which there were the proper timber and builders at Fort Pelly. But the posts at Touchwood Hills and Qu'Appelle were in the unusual situation of being permanent trading establishments not getting their principal freight in and out by the waterways.

Besides it had been found that the business affairs of the two posts, which were situated at the unusually short distance of only fifty miles apart, overlapped and interfered with each other out on the plains, where the Indians belonging to the separate establishments were continually being mixed up in the same camps in following their common quarry, which no longer covered the whole country. For these reasons it had been decided to abandon Touchwood Hills as a permanent and independent post and to place it and its trade under the direction of the officer-in-charge of Qu'Appelle.

Therefore had Mr. and Mrs. Finlayson with their fine little girls, and Interpreter Peter La Pierre, also all hands and their families come down that spring to Qu'Appelle, bringing the " Returns of Trade " and all supplies and movables with them. Previously to this general migration, all the available transport of the two posts had been busily engaged in hauling the poplar (there being no spruce at hand) planks and boards, which had been prepared at Touchwood Hills for the construction of the fleet of batteaux, to the bank of the Qu'Appelle River, where they were being built that spring.

For years Mr. McDonald had been persistently advocating the construction of a canal across the short height-of-land between the headwaters of the Qu'Appelle and their ancient source in the South Branch of the Saskatchewan, and as a preliminary to that project he had obtained permission to test the natural availability of the Qu'Appelle for flat-bottomed batteaux as far down as Fort Ellice, from which point they had been regularly used to Fort Garry ever since fur-trading began.

His experiment failed. The poplar boards and planks were of soft, spongy quality, no tar was to be had, spruce gum, melted with buffalo grease, only was used on the seams, which were caulked with old leather and rags for want of oakum, and no iron nails, only wooden pins were used in construction. So the batteaux absorbed the water like sponges and leaked like sieves, requiring the crews to be constantly bailing instead of propelling the craft, when it was not compulsory to land the cargo and haul up the boat for repairs. When the " brigade " started the water was at a fairly high stage, and it made fair progress under lodge-leather sails, over the lakes; but the intervening streams were so crooked and offered so many impediments that it was a whole week before they reached the outlet of the second lake below the fort. " Baffled but not beaten " by all these difficulties, by daily desertion of the men hired for the trip, by the discontent of the dispirited " regulars," and by the interminable sinuosities of the stream, the determination of Mr. McDonald finally forced the batteaux to Fort Ellice after a period of six weeks' continual driving. Unavoidably, under such circumstances, a great part of the cargo was spoilt; so this experimental voyage ended any further attempts in that direction.

Deserting Boatmen.

Almost daily, during the three weeks which the fleet remained within ready radius overland of the fort, we received bulletins from the commander, ordering supplies and reinforcements and the punishment of the deserters. Most of these, however, gave us a wide berth, for they did not wish to be stripped of the clothing which they had received as advances on account of the voyage. But one of them openly came back and took up his abode in a lodge on the adjoining plain. He was a big, powerful Ojibway, originally from Red Lake, a place of ill repute for the power of its bad medicine, in the art of using which this man, Pascal, posed as an expert. He was dreaded also as a wanderer from his tribe for the good of it, and by the whites he was looked upon with suspicion as an Indian who deigned to talk a little French and English, and professed Christianity without ceasing to practise paganism. Moreover, as the only one who had escaped sudden death by lightning in a large lodge crowded with Chippeways in council, he was supposed by the Indians to possess a charmed life.

The women's report of Pascal's return was quickly followed by a messenger from Mr. McDonald ordering us to make a special example of him if he came within range of the fort. So Jerry and I armed ourselves and went over to

372

the lodge, where he had taken lodgings, and stripping him of his voyageur raiment (already too unclean to be used by others) and taking his bag and blanket, left him arrayed solely in the strip of blanket which served as breechclout. He had been lolling at ease in the lodge, bragging that he cared nothing for either McDonald or Jerry or "the young doctor" (as they called me) to the fear and admiration of the women, when we took him so by surprise that he had no time to offer the resistance which we had fully expected and were prepared to overcome. Pascal was the last of the Indian deserters from that brigade.

BUFFALO CLOSE.

Soon after this Jerry resumed his usual duty of conducting the trade and hunt for provisions on the plains. He was still away when, after the return of Mr. McDonald from Fort Garry, we received the welcome news that the buffalo in great numbers had come in close to Touchwood Hills and the Last Mountain, from a runner who had been sent by the Indians, who had highly profited by the opportunity and were anxious for supplies of trading goods.

So again, in Jerry's absence with the main cart train, a scratch outfit of old oxen and convalescent ponies was gathered up for me, but on this occasion I was reinforced by procuring Andrew McNab, of Touchwood Hills, as my interpreter and adviser, whose assistance was specially valuable also, because the Indians we were going to were nearly all of those who had traded at Touchwood Hills.

MOVING MILLIONS.

We followed the trail leading to Touchwood Hills for about half a day and then headed northwesterly towards the north end of Last Mountain Lake, round which we went and then fell in with buffalo innumerable. They blackened the whole country, the compact, moving masses covering it so that not a glimpse of green grass could be seen. Our route took us into

the midst of the herd, which opened in front and closed behind
the train of carts like water round a ship, but always leaving
an open space about the width of the range of an Indian gun
in our front, rear and flanks. The earth trembled, day and
night, as they moved in billow-like battalions over the undulations of the plain. Every drop of water on our way was foul
and yellow with their wallowings and excretions. So we
travelled among the multitude for several days, save when we
shot a fat cow for food or a bull made a charge and perhaps
upset a cart before he was shot down, neither molesting nor
molested.

A LONE HUNT.

As soon as we reached the scattered fringe of the mass
through which we had journeyed, marvelling at its myriads
and their passive indifference to us, I thought it worth while
to try my 'prentice hand at running a small band on horseback.
So, mounted on a well-trained roan, down as " Candrie Bonhomme " on the horse roll at the fort, I left the carts and set
off alone. Before I came up to them the band had started to
run and in charging through the cloud of dust, which they
left behind them, " Candrie " dropped right down into the
bed of a narrow, dry watercourse, about ten feet below the level
of the prairie and with such steep banks that he could neither
scramble nor leap out of it. As I was looking up and down the
fissure, in which our race had been so abruptly arrested, for a
way to get out of it, several stray buffalo, apparently following those we had chased, came leaping one after the other
across it. They reminded me of a string of birds on the wing,
and instinctively I let fly at the second and third as they passed
in front, almost overhead. I think each ball took effect, but,
not being gifted like the natives, whose unerring faculty
directed them to every animal they brought down on a run, I
did not find them at the end of my hunt, and we unhitched
that evening too far for my men to think it worth while to
make search.

When, after following up the coulee a bit, we got on the level again the band was far off, but there was a year-old calf at hand, which I set off after. Such youngsters were often the swiftest, but Candrie was taking me within gunshot when he, which before had been quite as eager to close in on the others and to enjoy the hunt as myself, began to edge off to the right, either in alarm or maybe pity of the swift and gamey yellow calf, which kept on with unabated speed till that of Candrie slackened. As I did not get near enough to make a sure shot before Candrie showed distress, I stopped the race and turned, at a walk and occasionally a gentle jog, after the carts. And then the pony which had never made a stumble in racing and chasing began to do so, but most excusably, for the whole plain was honeycombed with badger holes so closely that it was a miracle how we had passed over it without a fall. There must have been a sweet little cherub up aloft who took care of the lives and limbs of both human and equine buffalo runners, for nearly every part of the prairie over which they hunted was more or less closely perforated with badger holes, and yet mar-vellously few casualties occurred.

A CAMP OF PLENTY.

A day or two afterwards we came to the small camp of Mis-cow-pe-tung, consisting of a few Crees and Saulteaux, on a branch of the Arm River, where they had many stages heavily laden with pemmican, dried meat and grease. There were enough men, including Day Star, who considered themselves warriors and chiefs in the camp to fill a council lodge. They were determined to trade in the old style " skin way," not in the new fangled " money way," the pounds, shillings and pence and the avoirdupois weights of which " were mere fool-ishness," they said, and tortured their brains. In the " made beaver" or "skin way" there were no complex mathematics, for a bag of pemmican was valued by the bag at a uniform price, whether it was larger or smaller than the average, and so was a bale of dried meat or a bladder of rendered tallow or one of fine marrow fat. But the orders of Mr. McDonald to stick at all costs to the " money way " could not be departed from by me; and so a whole day was wasted in argument and in impressing upon me the evil of the " money way." At last as they could not prevail upon me, one old beast of a troublesome fellow, generally and appropriately known as " Blackskin," who was one of the bad breed of " Young Dogs," declared " It is no use trying to make a youth like this clerk understand reason. We are all thirsty for tea and can't get any, for he does not have the politeness to give us a present of it as used to be the way in the ' skin way.' So let us begin trading his way."

The women, who had all this time been eagerly waiting to put on their teakettles, at once rushed to our trading lodge, and offered their choicest marrow fat and dried meat and tongues in exchange for the tea to brew the cup which cheered them, and, when they could get all they asked for, also inebriated, especially when a stick of nigger-head tobacco was decocted with it.

Andrew McNab, my faithful friend and interpreter, presided over the steelyards by which the weight of each parcel of provisions was carefully ascertained, while the eager customers waited in disgust at what they considered the irrational delay—especially when their offerings were below the old standard. Then came the tug-of-war to make them understand the values in sterling. While the others were impatiently waiting their turn, the complexities of the new system of finance had to be expounded to each one as they came, at whose elbow sat the villainous Blackskin, continually undoing our teachings and openly accusing us of being as great cheats as he knew himself to be.

Every now and again that wretch himself came with a bladder of marrow fat, in exchanging which for tea or tobacco or vermilion the mathematical problem had to be solved by the use of trading bullets, dinted to represent L., S., D., respectively. For the sake of peace, as he told me afterwards,

Andrew refrained from rendering in full the highly insulting remarks with which Blackskin punctuated his contentions. But now and again, as our trade was brought to a standstill by his tender of a cake or bladder of grease, Andrew would say, " I wonder where the old brute is getting it from; for he is no hunter, and he has been at his old habit again of murdering his wives."

TOTAL ECLIPSE OF THE SUN.

It was during the afternoon of the 7th of August, 1869, while this retarded trade was going on, that suddenly the bright sunshine began to fail, and a horrible noise and wild commotion arose in camp. Looking up at the sun we saw the beginning of an eclipse. The warriors and chiefs rushed to arms and tom-toms and medicine rattles, and furiously delivering volley after volley from their flintlocks, or wildly pounding their tom-toms and shaking their rattles, sought with fierce and blood-curdling war whoops, too, to frighten "the monster which was swallowing the sun." Simultaneously the women and children raised their voices in wailings and shrieks of terror, while, in some scant interval amid the tumultuous din, the deep tone prayer of some medicine man to his familiar spirit or deity imploring deliverance from a world of everlasting darkness might be heard.

The " monster " continued, regardlessly, to " eat up " the sun till it entirely disappeared and complete darkness brooded over the face of the earth. Then, as if in answer to the cry of the despairing, the fury of the firing party, the boom of the tom-tom or the incantations of the medicine man, slowly the thin edge of the sun's disc reappeared. Thereupon the tumult, which had been dying out in despair, was hopefully resumed and gradually as the kind god of light emerged from his conflict with the Mitche Manitou—the devil of darkness— bright and triumphant, the volleyings of the guns be- came a *feu de joie,* and the boom of drums punctuated the glad chorus of thanksgiving which then arose from every voice.

BLACKSKIN—ECLIPSE BREAKER.

Mrs. Peter Hourie had come out with her parents, named Richards, from Fort Pelly, for the pleasure and profit of making the provisions for their winter use for themselves, while doing a little trading, too. She was a smart, intelligent woman, and as we saw the eclipse beginning she exclaimed in vexation, " Now, what a pity I did not look at an almanac this year. Would not I have given these Indians a surprise by predicting it?" However, it was too late for us after the event to increase the prestige of the whites in that manner. Neither would the Indians believe that such a great event could have been predicted.

Blackskin, who upon the first alarm had rushed for his medicine rattle in a state of abject trembling terror, and had frantically accompanied his howling for help from the devils to whose service he had devoted himself, now emerged from obscurity and insolently demanded tribute from the company for having by powerful incantations terrorized the monster into disgorging the sun. Without his strong medicine every other effort in the camp, he declared, would have been without avail. " And what," he asked, " would or could the Company do then?" At this Andrew at last turned loose upon him, telling him he had been the biggest coward in the camp, but now when all was over he was the biggest boasting liar. He persisted, notwithstanding, in his huge self-glorification and the enormity of his demand for reward. I, of course, refused point blank, and laughed at his absurd effrontery. Finding the case was hopeless, addressing the audience, who were eagerly waiting by this time to resume their trading, he scornfully said, " What fools the chief men of the Company must be to send a young fellow like this to deal with us, the wisest and most numerous people on earth!" Then, turning to me, he exclaimed venomously, " You ought to go home, for you are too young to understand reason." " I am too old for you, Blackskin," I retorted through Andrew, accompanying the words with a mocking laugh, in which the audience joining, sent him off in high dudgeon, while we once more proceeded to business.

The Indians kept coming with the provisions so eagerly that we had no time to do other than throw them in a pile indiscriminately. This was quite high towards evening, when Blackskin again arrived from behind it with yet another fine bladder of marrow fat. Andrew looked at it in surprise as he weighed it, and announced the weight. " How," I asked, " is it that he has brought so many of these of exactly the same weight?" Andrew went round the pile of provisions, and, coming back, indignantly replied, " The old thief has been stealing and selling the same marrow fat, time about, again and again." Straightway he sprang at the old rascal, who, at once seeing he had been detected and that the good-tempered but powerful interpreter was at last roused to wrath, darted off with surprising speed and departed never to return again to annoy us. The venomous reptile had no stomach for a fair fight, he was only the murderous ravisher of unprotected little girls and the sneaking assassin of better men by a foul blow in the back.

MY FIRST BUFFALO BULL.

Lest others might be tempted to follow this bad example, a watchman was set behind the pile and others were employed in securing in them all our carts could hold. These were soon fully laden, and in the end we had to build stages for the greater quantity, which was left under the care of one of the good, honest Indians till carts came and took it to Touchwood Hills, for in that year of plenty the storage at Qu'Appelle was far too scanty for the provisions.

Being within the rather indefinite limits of their own hunting grounds, where attack by the Blackfeet was unlikely, the Indians of both posts had scattered about in small camps, each with abundant herds of buffalo about them. So, having supplied the wants of the first band, we went on to the next with just enough carts to carry the goods. There as we were doing a " roaring trade," Jerry joined us with many carts laden with a full trading outfit.

This soon gave me leisure to begin running buffalo again, and that in company with and under the skilful instruction of Jerry. On the first of these sallies from camp we went after a big bull, which he told me, as we were getting near enough, to shoot so that the ball might enter from behind at the end of the right short ribs and, passing through the diaphragm (itself a deadly wound), slantingly pass through the heart.* I made the mark, but the bull did not fall, only stopped and faced us. Candrie, full of excitement, was dancing so violently that I could not make sure enough to shoot again, so I asked Jerry to hold my horse while I got off to do so. " For heaven's sake don't get off, for the bull will charge you at once you are on foot," he cried. " Now," said he, " as soon as he turns shoot him behind the ear." I obeyed and down went my first buffalo. He was a fine fat animal, and Jerry took no time, with his hunting knife only, to skin and dissect him with astonishing deftness. We took the tongue, the boss and the backfat and rode back to camp, whence a cart was sent to bring in the rest.

SMALLPOX ON THE MISSOURI.

The coming of the buffalo in such numbers and so well within their own country gave our Indians plenty and peace that summer. But as the season advanced rumors of the dread disease of smallpox, which had decimated these people about

---

* Jerry had become newly possessed of one of the very first Henry repeating rifles which reached the Qu'Appelle country. With his usual kindness he lent it me on that occasion. The first wound, if made by a trading bullet from a shotgun, would have been instantly fatal. In this way the new repeating arms were found inferior to the old flintlock. A bull, for instance, might become so infuriated by a wound, which in the end would be mortal but not immediately so, as to stand up and show fight after receiving several, sometimes many, such wounds; that is in case he had time " to get mad " ere the first mortal wound brought him down. I have witnessed this in the case of bears and savage dogs as well as in buffalo bulls.—I. C.

ten years before, being rife among the Assiniboines along the Missouri were confirmed. That it would spread northward, as it had always done before, was to be apprehended, and we had no means of enforcing any effectual quarantine. Neither had we any of the vaccine by means of which the Company had minimized the former epidemic.

Towards fall the word of the nearer approach of the disease came in by the southern hunters, and then, providentially, two leading gentlemen of the Metis rode in one day to visit the fort. These were Messrs. Pascal Breland and Salomon Amlin, Members of the Council of Assiniboia and Magistrates for the Red River Settlement under the government of the Hudson's Bay Company. These gentlemen, having heard of the abundance of buffalo near Qu'Appelle, longing to engage once more in the joys of the chase, and unwilling to remain in the settlement over which trouble was brooding, had decided to buy outfits of trading goods and come out to winter on the plains. If it were true that arrangements had been made for the transfer of the government of the country to Canada and the people of the settlement were not to be consulted, there was great trouble brewing. They were both connected by ties of blood and business as well as friendship with people who were likely to divide in politics and in religion on any action taken by the Governments of Britain and Canada and the Company without the inhabitants of the country being asked to consent. " I am afraid," said Mr. Breland to Mr. McDonald, " that, as Bishop Tache said to me, " *nous bons jours sont parti.*"

The Qu'Appelle Indians are Vaccinated.

Further on the great part these gentlemen took in preserving peace on the plains will be duly recorded, and I must return to the subject of the dire disease which threatened to spread from the border. The rumors of it reached Red River before Mr. Breland's departure, and in consequence he had caused one of his grandchildren to be vaccinated before leaving about two weeks before. As I had assisted my father and brother in vaccinating hundreds of children at home, I at once asked Mr. Breland to allow me to take the lymph from his grandchild's arm, and he gladly gave the permission.

Jerry and I rode out to their camp with them that afternoon, and from a fine healthy child I secured, on bits of window glass, enough vaccine to protect every one requiring it in the fort, from whom the supply was increased sufficiently to vaccinate all the people about the lakes and the Indians visiting them that fall. With the fear of the former visitation before them, those who had been vaccinated at the fort took it out to the plains and spread it so thoroughly there among the Qu'Appelle and Touchwood Hills Indians that not one single case of smallpox was ever heard of among them, while sweeping up the Missouri from the Assiniboines, it decimated the Blackfeet, from whose dead bodies a war party of Edmonton Crees caught it. Then the plague and pestilence spread down the North Saskatchewan, carrying off hundreds of helpless natives. That it stopped at the South Saskatchewan and neither invaded Swan River District nor reached Red River was due to the providential visit of Mr. Breland to Fort Qu'Appelle that autumn day in 1869.

The truth and wisdom of the old proverb, that " prevention is better than cure," was well brought home to us in Swan River District, which remained scathless during those two years in which the dire pestilence walked abroad on its southern, western and northern borders, leaving a wide trail of death as it travelled. Of the dreadful devastation wrought along the North Saskatchewan, Butler speaks feelingly in his famous " Great Lone Land," wherein also is recorded his tribute to the self-denying heroism of the brave, good missionaries and of mine honored friend William Edward Traill, of the Hudson's Bay Company, who relieved the chief trader in charge of Carlton, and held the post of danger, made more so by the efforts of the poor, stricken Indians, to whom he ministered so devoutly, to communicate the dread disease to him, his equally devoted and heroic wife and their infant child.

W. E. TRAILL.

Shortly after his marriage to the eldest daughter of Chief Trader McKay, at Fort Ellice, in 1869, Traill had accompanied Mr. W. H. Watt, who had been transferred from Portage la Prairie to Fort Pitt. While engaged in packing the furs, in the spring of 1870, Traill had occasion to chastise a Metis employee, and turning round after doing so to resume the work, was felled by an axe in the hands of the delinquent. The blow in the back of the neck nearly decapitated poor Traill. His life was despaired of; but the devoted nursing of his good wife saved him.

He had been moved from Fort Pitt to start a farm for the Company at Prince Albert, being fond of farming and having practised it in the backwoods of Ontario. The chief trader in charge of Carlton having gone on furlough, Traill had come up from the farm to take his place at the time of the epidemic of smallpox.

Messrs. Watt and Traill, while at Fort Pitt, had the very unpleasant duty of trying to evolve order and discipline among the numerous employees and Indians, who had been allowed by the laxity of native officers to have everything their own way previously. But the current of native opinion and the " peace at any price " policy then prevalent on the Upper Saskatchewan, were so much against the vigorous measures these gentlemen were obliged to adopt, that Traill was sent to Prince Albert and Watt was transferred to Pembina, with the intimation: " We want no fighting men in the Saskatchewan."

CHAPTER XXV.

LAST MOUNTAIN HOUSE, WINTER 1869-70.

ON HORSEBACK " LIGHT."

MR. JOSEPH MCKAY, postmaster (the younger brother of Jerry), who had served a year under Mr. Finlayson, at Touchwood Hills, was sent in the fall of 1869 to build an outpost, under Qu'Appelle, to accommodate the Indians previously trading at or attached to the former post. The site selected was near the southern end of Last Mountain Lake, on the prairie upland overlooking the valley from the east.

It had been arranged that, while Mr. McKay made the post the base for his excursions to the plains in carrying on the trade in the Indian camps, I should take charge of the post itself during the winter. While he was completing the buildings and until the time approached for his going out after the buffalo to secure frozen meat for the winter—the fall hunt —I remained doing the writing at Qu'Appelle. Then after breakfast on the 6th of November,—" the rimy month " of the Indian calendar—when each blade of grass and twig and tree was glistening in bright sunshine, as if bedecked with sparkling gems, mounting Candrie Bonhomme, I took the hard frozen but still snowless trail leading to the new post, sixty or seventy miles to the westwards. My baggage had been sent ahead, and so, intending to make the long ride before dark, I set out " light," without food and only the saddle blanket.

NATIVE ANTISEPTIC SURGERY.

Considering the nature of the ground, strewn with the pitfalls made by badgers and occasionally boulders of all shapes and sizes, as the hunters charged, uphill and down dale, blindly, too, through the cloud of dust left in the

384

rear of the flying buffalo, it was wonderful how few
hunters met mishap by falling. There was scarcely
a man among the old hunters who did not bear on his
left hand the marks left by the bursting of his gun, due to
the bullet not having gone home on the powder in re-
charging it, without use of ramrod, on the run. At other
times one who had fallen and failed to notice that the muzzle
had been closed with mud or frozen snow, had the misfortune
to produce the same result. One of the best of the good
McKay family, named Alexander, had been the victim of
such an accident, in which he lost all the fingers and had
shattered the other bones of his left hand, during the close
of the summer hunt. On his coming to the fort a week or
two after the accident, with his hand wrapped in the anti-
septic herbs which so wonderfully prevented gangrene and
aided healing, I had advised his going to Red River to have
the hand amputated. He would not hear of that nor of my
attempting to remove the shattered bones, and pare off the
ends of the others, so as to give the wound a chance of healing,
covered by the remaining flesh. He had suffered for months,
every now and again getting out a bit of splintered bone, and
all the time keeping the wound perfectly free from gangrene
and odor by the use of Indian herbs. That was the way they
all did till at last, all the splinters having wrought out, they
had a healed but more or less useless member for life. If
the hand were so completely shattered as to be hopelessly
past their remedies, it was either chopped off with an axe or
removed by a swift slash of a hunting knife. While on this
subject I may say that one of the best of the
Saulteaux, Cowesses, having had the last joint of his little
finger blown off, suffered from it the whole of one winter,
because the flesh refused to heal over the exposed end of the
bone. He was proud of his knowledge of Indian medicine
and used it to keep the wound clean. At last he came
to me, and within a short time after the end of the bare
bone had been shaved, it healed up, and gave him a well-

padded and useful stump. I don't think he was very grateful
for my demonstrating a little of the superior knowledge of
the whites in surgery, for I never took pay from any "patient"
who allowed me to practise on him, while the members of
the Indian faculty of medicine invariably insisted upon full
payment in advance, otherwise they declared the treatment
would be of no avail, and they viewed with "professional
jealousy" my giving "advice gratis."

ON THE TRAIL AGAIN.

This dissertation on gunshot wounds has already led me
off the trail to Last Mountain Lake, which my visit to my
good friend Alick also did that morning, for by miles the
shorter way was that which crossed the ford at the fort and
led along the north side of the upper lakes, while that to
McKay's, on a flat on the south side of the upper lake, went
over many bonnie banks and braes ere it joined the north
road above the upper lake.

After that the gently undulating path led up the valley
of the winding river, till the faint newly-made cart trail left
it some miles below the "Little Forks," where the stream
from Last Mountain Lake joins the Qu'Appelle. Candrie
was both able and willing to have covered the distance in a
much shorter time, but he had a slight old halt and the
ground was hard frozen, so I spared him, perhaps unneces-
sarily, during the day, and the shades of evening of the short
day were falling when we forked off the well-beaten trail in
the valley and took the faint track leading up a big coulee to
the upland on the north side.

On reaching the upland a strong breeze began from the
north-west, right ahead, and soon darkness and a clouded sky
made it impossible to follow the slight trail longer. Making
the best of it, I unsaddled and picketted Candrie, and started
to collect twigs for a fire. Then I felt for my firebag, which,
in the fashion of the country, was carried by tucking its long
upper end under my sash, and was shocked to find that it

had been lost, with the flint, steel and tinder, which in those "matchless" days were the only means of striking a light, unless during sunshine with a burning-glass.

A Blizzard.

So, using the saddle-blanket to wrap up in, and as usual the saddle for a pillow, I lay down in the lee of that little poplar grove, fireless and supperless and smokeless, and fell asleep. When I awoke next morning, warm and comfortable, there was a covering of six inches of snow over me, the wind was howling from the north-west, accompanied by clouds of falling and driving snow. Candrie had had good feed and was all safe. I mounted and battled against the increasing blizzard and blinding snow for a while. Blindly buffeting against it, I could not see ten yards ahead. The snow kept forming an icy mask, clinging to every hair on my face, which was no sooner rubbed off than it formed again. I was wearing a blanket capote without buttons, only kept wrapped about me by the sash at the waist and a cravat round the neck, between which fastenings the wind and snow entered, and thawing inside, soaked through outside, and at once was frozen stiff. Turning round for a breathing spell and to get rid of the ice mask, I could see in the distance to leeward the woods of the Touchwood Hills, where food and shelter could be found. There was no trace of the newly-made cart track to the new post, the snow having easily covered that up, and I was simply heading in the general direction, without any previous knowledge of that part of the country and the precise site of the new establishment.

It was considered disgraceful to turn back when one had once started on a journey, unless there were some well-recognized necessity, of which a mere blizzard was not considered one. However I saw I could not do any good by battling against it or by taking shelter in a grove without fire or food till the storm might cease. I could easily make the Touchwood Hills before nightfall, scudding before the wind on my good horse. So, giving Candrie his head, away we went in the new direction, and in an hour's time struck the deep ruts of the well-travelled cart track leading from the south-west to the hills.

LAST MOUNTAIN HOUSE.

Towards afternoon, on topping a rise, I saw an Indian lodge along the road in front, where I was received, fed and sheltered with the kindness and hospitality for which the Cree Indians are remarkable. Next morning, the storm having ceased, the old hunter sent his son to guide me straight across the plain to my destination, at which we arrived in the evening. Next day my guide joined his family as they passed on their way out to where were the buffalo.

The buildings of the Last Mountain House were arranged in the usual manner on three sides of a square. The site was near a spring on the top of the bank of the uplands, on a bare spur between two deep-wooded ravines which ran down to the lake. The stores on the south side and the row of men's houses on the north side were finished, but the master's house, which Joe and family and I were to occupy, was roofless and floorless still. He and his men had done a wonderful lot of good work in the short time they had been at it, and our dwelling was soon habitable.

Then, leaving one man to haul firewood to the woodpile, upon which the men, women and children operated for themselves, Joe left with the others to trade and hunt in the west. The buffalo were in scattered bands up along the Qu'Appelle to the Elbow of the South Saskatchewan all that winter; and the Indians dispersed in small camps wherever game and fuel were both convenient. All would have gone well with our trade had not whiskey dealers, some Metis from St. Joe, on the American side, near Pembina, and others outfitted in Red River, besides an American from Fort Peck, on the Missouri, got among the Indians. The camp of the Young Dogs on the Arm River was one particular hell, in which they murdered each other to the number of seven in their recurrent orgies and quarrels. In that camp were Wap-wy-an-ess (Little Blanket) and Piapot (who was well known around Regina years afterwards, in his declining years), also the bestial Blackskin. The two former always posed as warriors and tried to be recognized as chiefs, but they were good hunters, with many wives, and consequently had plenty of pemmican, robes and leather to trade.

Piapot—"Lord of Heaven and Earth."

For years Piapot had striven to secure authoritative testimony to his standing as chief; but had never succeeded in even getting one of those minute slips of paper addressed by a Company's officer to whom it might concern certifying that the bearer (naming him) was a good Indian who had always been friendly to the whites and deserved a present of tobacco from them when met. Even the most easy-going master ever stationed at Touchwood Hills could not conscientiously give such a certificate to Piapot; but as the " mis-en-hi-han " (the written word) in itself was deemed by these heathen to possess magic virtue of great potency, to be an amulet bringing good fortune and giving a good character and protecting the bearer from all enemies, spiritual and temporal, in fact, to be " Keche-Mus-ke-ke " (Big Medicine) in every sense, Piapot never ceased in his endeavours to obtain one.

And that winter, every time Joe visited the camp of Piapot, where, surrounded by his relatives and retainers, he reigned and drank forty-rod whiskey, Joe had a terrible time in refusing the request, having all the effect of a demand, of the potentate for the " Little Writing "—Mis-en-hi-gan-ess. But neither by bullying nor by bribery did Piapot ever succeed in getting the coveted document from any of the Company's officers. He was determined, however, to get something which might serve his purpose, so, a year or so after, upon getting hold of a solitary English halfbreed out on the plains, who could write well, and somehow procuring pen, ink and paper at the same time, he compelled him to write at his dictation: "I am PIAPOT, LORD of the HEAVEN and EARTH." But I am not aware that this certainly immodest and somewhat blasphemous declaration procured for Piapot the results he desired "from any of the Company's men."

The Brute Blackskin.

Though ambitious, and thereby made troublesome, Piapot was an honourable man and a good hunter, but Blackskin had no redeeming quality that he ever exhibited. Like some other people who are no good for anything else, he was a voluble talker, and used the faculty for mischief. In his self-laudatory introductory remarks he claimed the self-conferred name of "Brave-hearted Bear," and spurned that of Blackskin, by which all others knew him. Early that winter he had indulged his cowardly and murderous nature by stabbing a warrior in the back. Having forgotten in this instance that his victim had friends to avenge him, after the foul deed the assassin, in panic, took flight, and was not heard of for a year. Then Mr. McDonald saw him at Wood Mountain in a camp of Assiniboines, and scared him again for a season, across the line. I think, though he never showed himself at the fort while I was stationed there, that he sneaked back after a year or so again to the district in which his atrocities had rendered him infamous.

Metis Festivities.

The winter quarters of the two Metis Counsellors of Assiniboine had been taken up on the west side of Last Mountain Lake, about fifteen miles north-west from ours. I drove with my dog-sled twice to visit them. On one occasion to relieve Madame Amlin of a tormenting tooth, and on some business as well as for pleasure the other time. As befitted persons of their importance, as well as to accommodate their large retinue of relatives and followers and for trading purposes, their winter camp was large, their single-roomed dwellings being especially spacious.

My former travelling companion, Henri Hibert dit Fabian, accompanied me once when we spent the night under Mr. Breland's hospitable roof. Besides his accomplishments as a voyageur, Henri was a vocalist who knew all the chansons of the canoe men, but the song into which he put most fire and fervour was that of Pierre Falcon, "Le bon garcon," made and composed to celebrate the massacre of the wounded at Seven Oaks in 1816, and "La glorie de tous ces Bois-brules," obtained thereby.

After a feast of the best of buffalo meat, as well as cakes, rice and raisins beautifully cooked by Madame Breland, followed by a flowing bowl of rum punch, Mr. Amlin and his following came to join in further festivities. Fiddles were tuned up, and Red River jig and Scotch reel were joyously joined in by the young men and maidens, who were soon followed by their elders. The mirthful dance was later on, as the ladies retired, followed by joyous song and thrilling story of celebrated adventures on the voyage, in the chase, and in the encounters of the Metis with the Sioux. Each admirer extolled the excellencies of his favourite racing and hunting horse, and the speed and endurance of sled-dogs and their drivers. On the relative merits of all these there at once arose loud and lively argument, to allay which a song was opportunely called for. To wet the whistle, every now and again Mr. Breland, whose twinkling eye and amused smile showed the fun he was having quietly out of the excitement of his guests, would judiciously dispense a little liquid refreshment. As the assembly warmed up, the end of each dance, song or story was immediately followed at first by one or other of the more enthusiastic Metis Nationalists calling out, "Vive mon nation." Gradually more and more joined in the cry, till before the festivities ceased, everyone joined in the shout of triumph, with the exception of Mr. Breland himself, whose genial countenance became grave as he thought of the events then occurring in Red River, and the troubles likely to arise therefrom, and in which it was plain to be seen every Metis in that room would take the side of his own people.

"THE NEW NATION."

A long essay would be required to describe the evolution of that mixed race which had come to consider itself a " New Nation." Maternally originally descended as they were from every tribe of Indians found by the French fur traders and rovers of the woods and waters from the Atlantic to the Pacific, from Louisiana to the Arctic Ocean, the strain of good French blood, however slight and attenuated it might be, and often was, was yet the strong bond which united these people in the wilderness, where they were regarded by the aboriginal Indians as interlopers and intruders on their hunting-grounds, yet a people to be envied and feared for the superiority in all the arts of woodcraft and of war which the addition of European blood had conferred upon them.

When the North-West traders entered the country these widely-scattered Metis, nourishing with pride, which often their French progenitors individually did not deserve, the tradition that their forefathers had been French, and also the dim glimmer of Christianity which the Indian mother had handed down as something distinguishing them from her own people, naturally became attached to the traders from Canada rather than to the ancient enemies of the French represented by the English company on Hudson Bay. Thus Metis, who had been far scattered as individuals throughout the wilds of the West, became gathered together as voyageurs and employees of the Canadian traders, and thereby became more and more united in numbers and by intermarriage with each other and the whites.

The Cross and commerce travelled together in the canoes of the early traders from Canada. But a long interval, during which the scattered Metis or Bois-brule, as they then called themselves, had no priests to fully instruct them in the faith of their French forefathers, elapsed ere the bells of the Roman mission, founded by the Rev. Joseph Norbert Provencher, in 1818, at St. Boniface, summoned the boatmen on the river and the hunter on the plain to worship. As Lord Selkirk was probably quite as indifferent to the claims of the Roman Catholics to be provided with religious instruction by a clergyman of their own denomination and tongue as he showed himself in the nonfulfilment of his pledge to supply his Highland Scotch with a Gaelic-speaking Presbyterian minister, he must be credited more for his astuteness as a politician than for his missionary zeal in the aid and encouragement he gave the authorities of the Roman Catholic Church in Canada to resume their missionary enterprise on the liberal land grants which he donated to them on the Red River.

The disasters to his Highland colony of Kildonan had convinced him of the need of conciliating the *Gens du Bois-brule* and bringing them, through the influence of Christian missionaries, under control. In this he, perhaps, builded better than he knew, for the Bois-brule, under the influence of religious instruction, became a more united body, and were even disciplined into a splendidly effective fighting force to defend their hunting camps and the settlement at Red River itself from assault and invasion by the numerous and war-like Sioux. Within the barricade formed by their interlocked carts the Metis over and over again repulsed, with slaughter to their enemies and little loss to themselves, the onslaught of numbers of Sioux, which seemed overwhelming, and in every such occasion the bravest of the brave were the soldiers of the Cross, who, soothing the dying and wounded, also encouraged, animated and led those still engaged in battle. While the hunter-warriors lay prone or stood protected inside the barrier, these brave priests moved about, seeming to bear a charmed life, in the hail of bullets, which, though sparing their persons, riddled their garments.

When Indians were decisively repulsed and compelled to retreat, the retreat soon became a rout, in which every man for himself ran panic-stricken, and divested himself of every-thing, even their knives, that would impede their flight even a trifle. Whenever such a retreat began and there were enough men and horses left to the Metis in camp to avail themselves of the opportunity, they mounted and pursued and slaughtered the fleeing foe as they would have done a band of buffalo, and great was the slaughter.

It was of such triumphs in war that these Metis were proud, especially as compared with the frequent defeats and few victories the Americans had had, to their knowledge, in contending with the Sioux nation.

As for " Les Anglais," as they called the Company's men, the defeat of these men, whom they outnumbered three to one, and the massacre of the wounded which followed at Seven Oaks, had been handed down, magnified and glorified, as triumphant proof of their superiority in battle to the Company's servants from Britain; and tended to an arrogance which the lickings the latter frequently gave them in single fight—often on the mention of Seven Oaks—failed to affect. That nearly every one of the natives of British descent, who were a very small minority among the Metis during their battles with the Sioux, had, on these occasions, shown them-selves the bravest of the brave, was ascribed to these being halfbreeds like themselves, and not to their British blood.

THE RED RIVER REBELLION AGAINST THE COMPANY.

Whenever the Government of Assiniboia was unsupported by the presence of British troops at Fort Garry, the Metis had always had their own way with it as a united body. The English halfbreeds were often related to them in native blood, and at least sympathizers in a common cause; while the Europeans and Kildonan settlers were too few in num-bers by themselves to oppose the united force of the Metis, trained in hunting and in war.

Rejoicing in their strength as practically the standing army of Red River Settlement, and determined to maintain their rights as patriots who had so frequently defended it by defeating the Sioux on the plains, and even preventing, by their mere presence, its invasion; proud of their prowess and deeply resenting the contemptuous remarks alleging their racial inferiority by English-speaking people whom they deemed intruders into the land they claimed as theirs, they had been alarmed and roused to wrath by Canadian surveyors, without their leave, running lines across their property; and next, to cap that climax, they were told that Canada was sending in a Governor and Council of strangers to rule over them in conformity with a sale of their country made by the shareholders of the Hudson's Bay Company in London, without either they or their members in the Council of Assiniboia, or even their priests being consulted in any way.

The roving habits of the Metis took them over the invisible line between the territories which, without consulting the natives, Britain and the United States had parted between them. As freighters to St. Paul and as customers to the American trading posts along the Missouri they were always welcomed by people desirous of their trade and to possess the rich country from which it came. The Americans professed such great friendship that, if there were ever any trouble with the English which they could not settle unaided, the Metis felt certain of every aid and encouragement from the people who boasted that they had, by force of arms, first thrown off the British yoke, and later on had given Britain another licking with the kind assistance of France. Besides the ordinary friendly American, there was a specially good and sympathetic kind of them who were Catholics like themselves, "le bon monde que ils appellent les Fenien," who had, as Irish Catholics, a long record of wrong to avenge. Many of these were veterans, too, of the American Civil War, who were both ready and willing to come to the assistance of the Metis whenever called upon.

Under these circumstances, in the absence of their two most respected leaders, Messrs. Breland and Amlin, on the plains, of their justly revered lord spiritual, the Bishop Tache, and in the state of impotence to which the good Governor McTavish had been reduced by severe bodily illness and the contemptuous disregard of his position displayed alike by the Company and by Canada, in being withheld their confidence, it would have been a miracle had the proud Metis not used their power to prevent the entry of Mr. William McDougall into their country to usurp its government.

I have been told on good authority that the secretary of the Hudson's Bay Company in London alleged, after Governor McTavish's death, that he had been so confident of his personal influence and that of his counsellors, including Bishops Tache and Machray and other highly representative men from different classes of old settlers, that when a detachment of British troops were offered to be stationed at Fort Garry, he refused them, saying he was quite able to complete the transfer peaceably without outside aid. Probably the secretary's information was true as far as it went, for had common sense and a sense of common justice actuated the Company and Canada at the time, instead of troops being required to inaugurate the transfer of the government of the country to Canada, the inhabitants generally would have hailed the change with joy.

It is not my purpose to even attempt to write a history of the rising at Red River in 1869-70, except in its bearing and effect upon us at Qu'Appelle. At the time I regarded it as rank rebellion, took the Canadian side, and felt disgraced by the stronghold of Fort Garry, with its stores of arms and ammunition and all the other supplies required in war, having been suffered to be taken peaceable possession of by Riel and a few men against whom even the ordinary complement of Company's officers and European servants, all of whom were at that time enlisted to perform all military duty required in defence of the Company's establishments and territories, could and would easily have defended it and held it till the loyal settlers had come to their assistance.

If there were sympathy with the rising amongst the Company's people at Fort Garry and not one but Mr. John H. McTavish, a Roman Catholic, was ever believed by us to have been sympathetic, there certainly was none in Swan River and other districts; and I know Mr. McDonald at Qu'Appelle often endangered his life in his furious arguments against the rising that winter. But I anticipate and must return to my narrative.

FROZEN FEET.

On my return from my last visit to Messrs. Breland and Amlin, I was alone, and it being dark and some miles yet from my post, I went in up to my knees in an overflow under the snow on the lake. It was a very cold night, and instead of a cariole I was using a bare sled. My moccasins soon froze stiff and my leggings too, but it was not very far from the post, which I thought might be reached quicker than I could go ashore and up hill to the woods to make a fire. So I ran as far as I could and then laid down prostrate on the sled. The dogs, knowing where they were going went well on the lake, but when they came to the well-beaten track leading up the ravine to the houses, they set off so furiously as to upset me, and jerking the tail line out of my grasp, left me to crawl up the hill on my hands and knees to the door of the house.

Joe was at home, and he at once tore off my shoes and exclaimed that my feet were frozen solid. He then got a tub of ice-water and put my feet in it till the ice formed over the skin, as it does when frozen meat is thawed in water. After they were properly thawed, I dried them and bathing the legs as far as affected and the feet with laudanum, I went to bed, slept soundly, and next morning, to Joe's astonishment, got up without any sign of what he had predicted would be a very bad case, off which the whole skin, at least, would be shed.

THE COMPANY OF ADVENTURERS

Wood Saulteaux go to War.

Shortly after this, Mr. Joseph McKay withdrew to Fort Pelly, and I was left to carry on the business with the assistance of Interpreter Andrew McNab. After a short visit to Fort Qu'Appelle, during which Mr. McDonald, from early morn till late at night, sat in the Indian Hall discussing the news and rumours of the Red River troubles with Metis, who took the side of Riel, and Crees, who took the Company's side, upon my return to the post McNab told me that a number of the Saulteaux of Egg and Nut Lakes, belonging to the Fort Pelly outpost there, had arrived with large quantities of the fine furs of that woodland region. They refused either to deliver up these furs for safe-keeping or to pay out of them the advances they all had at Egg Lake, and to trade the rest. They had been upset by the rumours from Red River, and, filled with the spirit of unrest, had abandoned the rich harvest of fine furs in the bush to start upon a raid to the plains to secure ponies and scalps from the Blackfeet.

They were all expert hunters, but were very unruly and always trying to intimidate the lonely trader who wintered at Egg Lake. Their camp, where their furs and families were left, was quite close to the post. Shortly after the " war party " left the squaws sought solace in the firewater of a Metis trader across the lake, and by the time the "warriors" returned, without a hair of horse or Blackfeet, the furs had been largely dissipated. However, there was enough left to start a general grand carousal, during which the fighting spirit, which had not found satisfaction on the Blackfeet, was vented in fratricidal strife, during which the braves bit off each other's fingers, noses and ears in the most heroic fashion.

Attempt to Break Into the Store.

Their camp was, during this period of uproar, in very unpleasant proximity to our post, which was every now and

398

THE LATE W. F. GARDINER, OF FORT CHIPEWYAN.

HENRY J. MOBERLY, OF FORT VERMILION.

Chief Traders omitted from great group of Hudson's Bay Commissioned Officers in 1881.

THE LATE JOHN WILSON, OF FORT McPHERSON.

ISAAC COWIE, OF FORT McMURRAY.

again visited by some of the celebrants, whom McNab always managed to get rid of somehow, but never by making the presents for which they always asked. At the time the fall of Fort Garry into the hands of Riel without a blow being struck was the theme of contemptuous remarks by the natives, especially in the case of such of them who had been in the habit of trying to levy blackmail on the trading parties of the Company in the big camps on the plains, and of such of these Saulteaux as every winter tried to impose upon the clerk, wintering with a couple of " noncombatant " temporary servants, at Egg Lake. My friends, W. E. Traill, Tom McKay, and Duncan Matheson, all had related to me such experiences at Egg Lake. My henchman, McNab, who was a settler at Touchwood Hills, where the Egg Lakers sometimes came for supplies in summer, knew most of them personally or by evil reputation. Both he and I had been very much annoyed by their refusal to give up their furs to the Company, and their subsequent dissipation of them for whiskey, to the Metis from the American side, who had so unexpectedly obtained such a big lot of the fine furs of the forest instead of the less valuable sorts of the prairies.

Under these circumstances, when one of the younger hunters came over and wanted supplies on credit, I, of course, refused him. It was against the rules to give advances to Indians not belonging to one's post, especially to those of ill-repute. As soon as he saw that he could get nothing from me, he sprang up and said defiantly, " Then I will break open the store and help myself." While he went out to carry out his threat, followed by Andrew, I went to my bedroom to get and load my revolver. By the time I reached the front door the Indian had shouldered a heavy length of firewood and rushing at the store door gave it a battering blow. As he backed off to give a second I covered him with my pistol, intending to shoot to kill if he burst the door. That brief interval gave McNab the chance to intervene in the line of fire, and, first wrenching the log from the Indian's shoulder, he headed him for camp, and set him off our premises well on his way by a series of well-directed and vigorous kicks, as if he were playing football with him.

Had not the depression, consequent on the failure of the trader's liquor after their furs had been squandered on it, prevailed in that camp, and the feuds between former friends still remained, we might have had some trouble over this incident. As it was it served notice on all whom it might concern of the firm determination of the Company's people under Chief Factor Campbell in Swan River District, not to permit any pillage of their property without a struggle.

Shortly after, as the situation in Red River was getting worse instead of better, and it was the chief factor's intention that, if necessary, all reliable hands should concentrate at Fort Pelly, I was ordered by Mr. McDonald to return to Qu'Appelle with all the goods, furs and provisions and all hands, leaving some friendly Cree to look after the buildings and save them from being burnt by the Indians, as was their practice in the case of all the wintering houses on the plains which we left in spring.

CHAPTER XXVI.

THE SPRING AND EARLY SUMMER OF 1870.

THE GATHERING OF THE CLANS.

IN 1868, the Rev. Father Decorby, O.M.I., newly from France, had arrived at the Qu'Appelle Lakes to resume the mission of the Rev. Father Richot. Father Decorby established, at the lower end of the lake below the fort, the mission which has since developed into Lebret. One of the first things he did was to erect a large cross on the hill above the little log dwelling and chapel, and a new cross still occupies the same station. In consequence of the coming of the missionary a number of hitherto entirely nomadic Metis families had taken up their wintering quarters about the lakes. Some of these were traders with customers who dealt not with the Company, and over whom it had no control. Every one of these opposing traders and their friends were decidedly in favour of the Riel movement and against the Company, and did everything in their power to bring their fellow countrymen, both Metis and Indians, to their way of thinking.

News of the troubles in Red River swiftly reached Qu'-Appelle in every form of distortion and contortion, and as it was further spread by rumour all over the plains, produced a state of such unrest and excitement that the business of hunting came almost to a stop. Family after family of Metis came in from the plains to the lakes, to hear the latest news and take part in discussing it, and to be at hand to participate in any action taken in sympathy with, or imitation of their fellows in Red River.

Mr. McDonald had many old and tried friends among the Crees, hereditary allies as these had always been of the Company, too. He "sent tobacco" to their Chiefs Loud Voice

401

and Poor Man, asking them and other head men to come to the fort and hear the true (Company's) version of the events which had occurred at Nees-tow-wy-ak, La Fourche, or The Forks, as the site of Fort Garry was generally called in Cree, French or English by the natives. When I arrived from the outpost, upon entering the Indian hall it was clouded with tobacco smoke and crowded with Crees emitting it, and Mr. McDonald was in the midst expatiating upon the wickedness and ingratitude of Riel and his followers in acting towards the benevolent Company at Fort Garry, in the manner of which a full account had to be repeated to every new arrival. Besides being loyal Indians to the Company, the Crees, as has been stated before, resented the intrusion of the Metis in always increasing numbers into their hunting grounds. Their seizure of the fort, founded with the consent of the Crees at " The Forks," and their virtual imprisonment of the great chief of the Company and his staff therein without consulta- tion with and the consent of the Cree tribe, was a usurpation of authority which they deeply resented. Moreover, none of the pillage of that great emporium of trading goods, arms and ammunition, not to speak of firewater, had been offered to or reserved for them as the original owners of that part of the country.

That the Metis at the lakes and those who were coming as soon as carts could travel from such large wintering camps as Wood Mountain, should be allowed to gain possession of the Cree trading post at Qu'Appelle, with its great store of the arms and ammunition without which the Crees would be helpless against all enemies as well as in their hunting, and, where the Metis, once in possession, would be able to defy and dictate to them, the chiefs of the Crees declared was not to be thought of. So they were ready and willing to guard and defend the fort against all comers as long as food held out.

This was the purport of similar gatherings daily. Every time a fresh rumour arose a fresh meeting took place to discuss it and decide upon its credibility. The disaffected

Metis, meanwhile, by every wile, tried to counteract the influence of the Company and their more influential allies among the Crees. About ten years before smallpox from the Missouri had invaded the camps of the Qu'Appelle Crees, and subsequent fights with the Blackfeet for the buffalo hunting grounds and for ponies had decimated the tribe, so that, even if the whole of them who belonged to the Qu'Appelle and Touchwood Hills establishments of the Company could have been concentrated for the defence of the fort, in number they would not nearly equal that of the Metis, who were expected to gather at the lakes as soon as the snow had disappeared in spring. Of this we had information, for, taking a mean advantage of the Company's accommodation in carrying letters for others in their winter packet, a letter containing an offer to put, in spring, five hundred horsemen on the field to join Riel, was intercepted by Mr. Finlayson at Fort Pelly. Whether these five hundred " horsemen " were all Metis or composed partly of Indians not so well affected as the Crees, the letter did not state distinctly, but we all wondered where five hundred able-bodied Metis could be found in the Qu'Appelle country.

Messrs. Breland and Amlin Counsel Non-Intervention.

Before the great gathering of the French halfbreeds came to the lakes that spring everyone was painfully surprised by intelligence of the killing of Thomas Scott. On an appointed day in April, 1870, a mass-meeting of the Metis was held at the lakes, composed of men from all quarters with their leaders. Messrs. Breland and Amlin were there on their way home to Red River, and everyone looked up to them for advice and leadership. Apart from his own sterling character, Mr. Breland was respected by the Metis as son-in-law of their old captain, and warden of the plains, Mr. Cuthbert Grant. No one of the Metis ever doubted his loyalty to them or his wisdom in representing them in the Council of Assiniboia. It was certain that these two friends and fellow counsellors,

Messrs Breland and Amlin, would act together and wisely in the crisis which now had been reached, and the question was whether the Metis, who had wintered on the plains and had taken no part whatever in the operations conducted by their fellows in Red River, should join with them or abstain therefrom.

The answer to the question meant, to the Company and to the Crees, peace or war with the Metis assembled at the Qu'Appelle Lakes. Mr. McDonald and all his men of British blood were determined not to suffer their post to be pillaged, and we could rely upon a sufficient number of Crees to give us a good fighting chance to defend it. We hoisted the red ensign that morning, and anxiously waited for word from the meeting. It was certain to be an exciting affair, for perhaps the majority of the Metis regarded the matter as affecting their religion quite as much as their race.

All along, in talking with the more rational among them, we had tried to impress upon them the wisdom of abstaining from interfering, and of allowing those, who had benefited themselves by pillage and left themselves liable for punishment, to take the consequences which would follow the certain re-establishment of government under the good Queen, who had sent them her promise of justice, and to all evil-doers her warning, that that same justice would overtake them, in her Proclamation promulgated at Fort Garry, by Commissioner Donald A. Smith.* Copies of this Proclamation had been spread all over the country, and read and re-read and explained over and over again. "To all and every the loyal

---

* The supply of printed copies of this Proclamation having become exhausted at Edmonton, the officer-in-charge there directed his subordinate at the post named Victoria, to make a pen-and-ᵔk copy and transmit it to the next post at White Fish Lake, ᵕhere the post-master was similarly required to make a copy and forward it to Lac la Biche. The post-master at White Fish Lake accordingly copied the proclamation for Lac la Biche and, thinking its heading " Victoria " applied to the post from which he had received his copy, concluded that the proper heading of that for Lac la Biche was "'White Fish Lake.' By the Grace of God, " etc., etc.

subjects of Her Majesty the Queen" residing at or visiting every trading post in the territory. Our interpreters became quite expert in rendering the often-quoted Proclamation into the language of the Indians, upon whose ears and those of British origin it fell with effect; but the others either doubted its authenticity, or would not be convinced by anything, to take side against their brother Metis. Many of the more ignorant alleged that Riel was a man inspired by heaven, and that he had been seen pacing the verandah of the officers' quarters at Fort Garry, in which he had billeted himself, with a supernatural being in the form of a man, whose coming and going were alike invisible, and who spoke to and was answered by Riel in a tongue (which was neither French nor English nor Indian) unknown to the awed spectators and auditors of the interview, who afterwards related what they saw and heard to Dame Rumour, and she was believed, in this mystery, by not a few.

It was no use for us to argue with such men. But when Mr. Breland addressed the mass-meeting which had been waiting for his words, and, without discussing the question as to whether there might not have been a better way than that taken by their fellow Metis in Red River to have their rights acknowledged, said that it was wrong for Canada to seek to impose her rule over the country without first making terms with its people, but men who would have been with Riel heart and hand before, should now refrain from associating themselves with the murderers of a helpless prisoner. Probably the majority who had come to that meeting had come with the expectation that it would endorse Riel and commit them to his support. But the eloquence of Mr. Breland, seconded by a telling speech on the same lines by Mr. Amlin, swayed their countrymen over as a body, leaving only a few of the more bitter partisans and extremists disaffected. Some of these rushed down to Fort Garry to share the spoil, but by the time they reached it the settlement had quieted down, and they returned to the plains disgusted and empty-handed. In fact, one of the loudest agitators amongst them, instead of being received by the " Provisional Government" with open arms, had a warrant issued against him for some old matter, and fled from the settlement to avoid arrest.

So it came about that, in the killing of Scott, Riel had gone farther than those not already implicated in his rising would follow him; and the grave danger of an attack on Fort Qu'-Appelle and a bloody conflict with the Crees in its defence, with the probability of a war which would have spread over the whole plains, were averted by the wise and brave advice of Mr. Breland and his worthy confrere, Mr. Amlin, and by its acceptance by the majority of their naturally good-hearted countrymen in that assembly.

Although most of the people dispersed, there still lingered about the lake a number of wanderers who were sometimes on the American and sometimes on the British side of the line. Most of these were so untrustworthy that no trader would risk advancing them on their hunts. Amongst them, too, were those whose sentiments were entirely in favour of the country being brought under the American flag. The regular frequenters of Qu'Appelle, who had grudges against the Company, also required watching; so the camp of our Cree allies did not break up.

MEASURES TO PREVENT PILLAGE OF OTHER POSTS.

Meanwhile, throughout the Swan River District, measures had been taken to prevent the posts from being pillaged, by the Metis in their vicinity. All outposts were withdrawn. The station at Oak Point, at the south end of Lake Manitoba, belonging to Red River District, had been entered and anything they fancied had been appropriated by the Metis during Mr. William Clark's temporary absence, the venerable chief trader, George Deschambault, who was residing there that winter preparatory to his absolute retirement from the service, having made no active opposition. At the cattle-raising establishment belonging to that post at Swan Creek was Jack Henderson, a Scot who had seen service as a mate at sea and as a forty-niner miner in California. Jack was alone with his trusty revolver when a score of well-armed Metis came and helped themselves to the choicest beef steers under his charge. He protested vehemently, but seeing he would lose his life as well as his cattle had he opened fire, submitted to the fate of the moment, but swore vengeance whenever a better opportunity occurred. For this he had to wait for years, till, when a hangman was required to execute Riel at Regina, Jack, who was then freighting in the vicinity, eagerly offered his services and performed the office.

The next post north of Oak Point was that of Swan River District, near the Narrows of Lake Manitoba, under the command of Mr. Ewan McDonald, and principally manned by " recruits from Europe " named Alexander Murray (who died years ago), Alexander Munro, now of Minitonas, Donald McDonald, now of Fairford, and " Big " Norman McKenzie, now a retired steamboat captain, farming at St. Louis, Saskatchewan. I think Mr. Duncan Matheson, then apprentice clerk, and now a retired factor residing in Inverness; Gilbert Goudie, who died long ago at home, a remarkably handy Shetlander; John Dyer, now blacksmith at Poplar Point, Manitoba; and others whose names I do not know, also formed the Scots guards of Manitoba House, and were assisted by members of the native loyalist families of Inkster, Thomas and Moar.

Like his brother, the chief at Fort Qu'Appelle, Ewan McDonald was of the fighting Highland race, and equally determined with him and Chief Factor Campbell that no Company's post in Swan River should fall into the hands of the Metis without a struggle. Accordingly he recalled all hands from the outposts at Fairford and Waterhen River, and, the establishment amongst the quiet Indians there being unprotected by pickets, he securely barricaded it with walls of cordwood and building logs; sent out spies and vedettes, and prepared a warm reception for any force which might be sent out from Fort Garry by the self-constituted authorities to put down this demonstration against their power and dignity.

Having only a general knowledge of what occurred at Manitoba House during that trying winter, I leave the duty of recording full details of it to the survivors, merely adding that, apart from safeguarding the valuable supplies and furs of the post itself, Manitoba House commanded the boat route between Fort Pelly and Lake Winnipeg, at the outlet of which, on the main route to York Factory, similar and much more extensive arrangements had been made by the warlike Chief Factor Stewart at Norway House.

The only post in Swan River at which the Metis were permitted to help themselves during that winter was that at Shoal River, where the old man in charge, in great alarm at the terrible reports which had been carried to him by rumour, opened the door of the store and allowed a few poor wretches wintering at Duck Bay, who had come to beg relief, much to their astonishment, to help themselves. After which they went back peaceably on their way rejoicing and heavy laden.

SWAN RIVER FURS SENT DIRECT TO ST. PAUL, MINNESOTA.

There was no doubt that the spirited action taken at Manitoba House had incensed the powers that then were at Fort Garry, and it was fully expected that an attack in force would be made on it when the proper time came, which would be when the furs were being sent from Fort Pelly by the lakes *en route* to Norway House. Whatever were the reasons in full for it, after the peaceable dispersion of the assemblage at the Qu'Appelle Lakes in April, it was decided by Mr. Campbell to send out all the furs from Fort Pelly and the posts on the plains across land by carts to St. Paul, Minnesota, under the charge of Mr. Archibald McDonald. Accordingly the rendezvous was to be made at Fort Ellice, and Mr. McDonald, taking Mrs. McDonald and their two little sons,

John and Donald, with their nurse-girl, started from Qu'-Appelle. With him went Mr. James McKinlay, a mere boy, who, as an apprentice clerk, had arrived from Scotland in 1869. The Shetlanders, Gowdie Harper and George Pottinger, and a Highlander, whose name I forget, besides Nepapeness and other natives, who would have otherwise gone in the boats to York Factory, accompanied the carts.

The party from Fort Pelly, which met that from Fort Qu'Appelle at Fort Ellice, was under Mr. William Thomson Smith, who was retiring from the district, with Mrs. Campbell and her small boy, Glenlyon, and baby girl, as passengers under his protection. These, augmented by that made up at Fort Ellice under Mr. Walter J. S. Traill, made a strong brigade, capable of defending themselves from any hostiles whom they were likely to meet before arriving, *via* Fort Totten, Devil's Lake, at Grand Forks, on the Red River. At Grand Forks they fell in with a cart-train from Fort Garry, under Mr. William Clark, and travelled in company with it to what was the rail-head at that time.

WE HOLD THE FORT.

As Mr. McDonald was leaving I asked him for instructions as to what was to be done in case of attack. He replied, " Act according to circumstances on your own judgment after consulting Jerry." As fully half of the business of that post was in summer provision trade and the principal requirements for it were arms and ammunition, our store contained a large supply of these essentials, and I determined to blow the place up sooner than that they should fall into the hands of any attacking force. Jerry was of the same mind, and in his constant palavers with the Indians urged upon them the necessity of protecting themselves against famine and other foes by protecting the fort, of which the garrison left by Mr. McDonald consisted of himself, young Kennedy, Jacob Bear, George Sandison, George Thorne, with Henry

Jordan as my cook, and myself. All the families, except that of Mr. McDonald, remained in the fort.

The Crees, under Loud Voice, in lodges placed at long intervals, camped in a circle round the fort, ever on the watch, and ably aided by the dogs belonging to them and to us. It was against surprise we had to guard, till the Indians could enter and take position behind the pickets.

Nearly the whole month of June did the Metis belonging to the lakes, and others, principally malcontents from the border, linger round the lakes. They outnumbered us and our allies, but not sufficiently so to encourage them to make an attack, if so minded, for which we were prepared. We all anxiously awaited news from Red River, which might possibly come by a party sent out to augment the malcontents at Qu'Appelle and lead them in an attack on the fort. Rumours to that effect freely circulated, announcing the virtuous indignation of the Provisional Government at the slur cast upon them by the Swan River furs having been sent direct across the plains to evade capture by them. For they alleged that the authorities of the Company in Red River had come to an amicable understanding with them. But whatever the alleged arrangement might have been, it was not recognized by Chief Factor Campbell nor his gallant friend, Chief Factor Stewart, who was making aggressive preparations to recapture Fort Garry, as brigade after brigade from the interior arrived at Norway House. I know not whether or not the determination of these two Highland officers to resist any aggression on their districts and redeem the credit of the Company from the reproach of having permitted Fort Garry to fall into the hands of the malcontents without resistance, had anything to do with their being both " permitted to retire " when the " reorganization " of the Company's arrangement with the furtrade officers was carried out through the diplomatic medium of Mr. Donald A. Smith; but that seemingly was their reward for valour.

COMING OF COLONEL WOLSELEY

The Reception of the Troops.

Daily as the hunters came to visit the fort, we urged them to mind their own business and set out after the buffalo on the plains; but it was not till the end of June that we saw the last of the reluctant brigade. As soon as they were well off on the way our friends, the Crees, followed them, and we were left to our own resources, with only the very few Metis, who had bits of gardens and eked out a living by fishing, left scattered along the lakes. The coming of Colonel Wolseley and his force was now the engrossing topic. Antoine La Roque, a considerable trader, arrived from Red River, and when I asked news of Wolseley's advance he asked me "In what were his troops clad?" "In cloth, of course," I answered. "Then," said he triumphantly, "they will never reach Fort Garry; for the mosquitoes are so bad this year that draught oxen coming from St. Paul have been smothered by swarms; and no man living, unless he be iron-clad is able to get over the route from Lake Superior this season."

Other reports came, saying that Riel was preparing, with the assistance of the Ojibways along the route, to waylay and ambuscade the troops, on portages and other coigns of vantage. Even did they get to Red River, with the bursting shells, which they understood described a visible flight like a bird rising and falling in the air, " Le Metis," declared old Poitras, " are such expert shots that as the shells fly, before they can reach us we will fire at them like ducks and burst harmlessly in the air!" Anyhow, even should the expedition overcome all other obstacles, "Les Americains " (meaning Fenians with the collusion of the American authorities,) will attack it with overwhelming force.

" The Protection " of the Provisional Government Spurned.

The Metis, who had gone out so late after the buffalo, reached the nearer hunting grounds to find the herds had departed for parts unknown. So they split up into small parties and scattered in the search. The summer hunt of the Qu'Appelle hunters and Indians that year was a total failure. The near coming of Colonel Wolseley, too, had lessened our danger of attack from Red River, when, one day, there rode into the fort a solitary horseman, who announced himself as Patrice Breland, son of the worthy Pascal, but now captain in the service of "The Provisional Government," which had sent him to declare to all whom it concerned, that the Hudson's Bay Company were now under the protection of that government, and that no people nor post of the Company's was to be attacked by anyone without incurring their sovereign displeasure. The herald evidently expected to be received with joy and thanks as our deliverer from the fear of the enemy, but he was both surprised and shocked as I at once burst out into mocking laughter and rudely exclaimed: "To hell with the Provisional Government! We have been able to hold our own here in spite of their supporters, and now, when the troops are coming, it is too late for them to pretend friendship."

As the son of so worthy a father we, of course, treated Mr. Patrice Breland with all respect personally, but as the official representative of the Provisional Government, and their very fluent advocate, his "mission of peace" completely failed.

Brown Bess Bellows.

Only a few impotent malcontents remained about the lakes, and his mission destroyed their last hopes of sharing in any pillage others might provide. These now began to fear reprisals for the insulting abuse they had taken every safe occasion to give vent to against the Company's people and the even more hated men from Ontario. So, to encourage them, and at the same time to experiment with an old army Brown Bess as a scatter gun when loaded half up with powder and trading bullets, I had one mounted on a pair of cart wheels, and choosing a calm day began practising with it as a field-piece, taking the precaution to use a long line attached to the trigger to set it off. As a target, and to observe the spread of the bullets, we used the side of the ice-house. Jacob Bear, who had taken great delight in operating it while we were firing this dreadfully overcharged gun for nothing but the noise, when it had been filled to the muzzle with probably a bursting charge, took shelter to one side of the line of fire round a corner of the stockades. Simultaneously with the roar of the gun there came a yell of alarm from Jacob: " It shoots round the corner," yelled he, for he declared that bullets had whizzed past him in his retreat. It certainly was a scatter-gun, and seemed to be absolutely proof against bursting.

The echoes of the loud bellowings of this good old Brown Bess, careering down the valley for miles, aroused alarm along the shores of the lakes. " The soldiers have come to the fort," was the cry. Next day one of the most malignant came up cautiously to find out who had come and brought the big cannon. He saw neither newcomers nor cannon, but we all looked quite consequential. So he went back mystified, to be again alarmed by the rousing echoes next calm day. We had some fun out of it, and we had found that the old blunderbuss might be a very effective weapon at close range to guard our gates.

CHAPTER XXVII.

FALL OF 1870, AND WINTER 1870-1.

Last Mountain Post—The Hunters Return.

AFTER delivering his furs and passengers safely at St. Paul, Minnesota, Chief Trader McDonald returned *via* Fort Garry, then already in possession of the Canadian Volunteers, to Qu'Appelle; and I, shortly after, resumed my charge at Last Mountain post. There the news came in of a big battle at Belly River, in which the Crees and the Young Dogs belonging to Touchwood Hills, with other Crees from Saskatchewan, and Assiniboines from Wood Mountain, had been defeated, with a loss of one hundred and thirty-five killed by the Blackfeet. About twenty of the slain had book debts at Touchwood Hills, which I had to write off to profit and loss, with the explanation "Killed by Blackfeet."

Next there came two of the Metis who had been in the spring the biggest agitators for the sack of Fort Qu'Appelle, and for giving its master what they then declared were his deserts for opposing the Rielites, by pushing him into a waterhole and drowning him in the lake. I had not seen Louison since, after very hot words with me in March, he had rushed down to offer his services to those in occupation of Fort Garry, to lead in an attack of Fort Ellice and Qu'-Appelle. To his disgust his claim to share in the spoils of Fort Garry had been rejected; nay more, he had been chased by the sheriff out of the settlement, and now he came humbly into my office from a long and solitary tour on the plains, asking "What is the news at La Fourche?" With great pleasure I informed him of Wolseley's coming and Riel's going. Whereupon he had the brazen-faced impudence to

414

CHIEF FACTOR ROBERT CAMPBELL,
Discoverer of the Southern Headwaters of the Pelly-Yukon.

CHIEF FACTOR WILSON, OF YORK
FACTORY.

GOVERNOR McTAVISH.

JUDGE BLACK,
Recorder of Rupert's Land.

say: "Ah, Mr. Coue, I take you for my witness that I always been a loyal man. I never join de rebels!" "No," said I, "it was lucky for you they would not have you." Whereat he cast on me a look intended for innocent reproach, and we proceeded to business, in which I was fortunate in securing ten bags of pemmican, being the first lot that had come from the plains that year.

FAILURE OF THE SUMMER HUNT.

At Qu'Appelle there was scarcely a bag of pemmican brought in that fall and only fifty came in to Last Mountain, with the news that the summer hunt had been a failure, and that in the fall and winter sure to be likewise, for the buffalo had gone far off and to parts of the country our people did not dare to follow them, scattered as they were.

The supply of fat was always too small to enable us to convert all the lean pounded or powdered meat into pemmican, for which equal weights were required. Consequently we always had been obliged to buy, at low price, however, quantities of this "pelly" meat that no one except a very hungry person or animal would touch without being mixed with fat. It was indeed fortunate that the summer of 1869 had been one of such abundance that notwithstanding the huge drain upon us in feeding our Cree friends for so many months on pemmican and dried meat, there still remained when the hunt failed in the fall of 1870, a great stock of this dried pounded meat in store at Fort Qu'Appelle.

And to the Lakes that fall and winter there came the Metis, many of whom had come to join in the pillage of the fort in the previous spring had their leaders so decided. The little provisions brought with them from the plains were soon used up, and the lake fishing, with hooks under the ice, was too scanty. There was no other resource but the pounded meat in the Company's store, which was, of course, for sale, but in exchange for furs only. Customers with furs were always welcome, but those who had neither these nor anything but their horses had to bargain with Mr. McDonald. So it came about (just as he had warned them in the winter before when they, thinking that the old Company had fallen, never to rise again, had reviled it and threatened him with drowning) that they had to run to the Company for food to carry them over the winter and to obtain it, too, on credit or charity. And, while he sent none away empty, he certainly took into consideration the conduct of the person during the previous year in the limiting of credit and in the valuation of the horses offered for sale.

The dearth of pemmican was general that fall, and during the winter Mr. William McKay, who had succeeded Mr. Campbell in charge of the district, came to Qu'Appelle saying that the whole transport for the northern districts of Mackenzie River and Athabasca, between Norway House and Portage la Loche, would be impossible if Swan River could not provide pemmican and send it over to Cumberland House during the winter. In spite of my warning that no more provisions could be expected from the plains before spring, when all we had would be needed for our own brigades, Mr. McKay considered that the Northern Transport was of greater importance, and so all we had procured at Last Mountain was sent to Fort Pelly for the purpose during the winter.

With me at Last Mountain that winter there were my good reliable interpreter, Andrew McNab, who, with John Beads and Charles Favel, looked after the trade on the plains; also my old travelling companion, Henri Hibbert, bowsman, for general tripping, and at the post, Samuel McKay, a smart young fellow, who could act as clerk and interpreter and hunter, and was good in all capacities. George Pottinger, an A1 bowsman on the York voyage, who could recite all Sir Walter Scott's poems by heart, staid at the post for general service.

A METIS "MEDICINE MAN."

Among the freemen wintering about the lake was one of the wide-spread Disgarlais families, but decidedly more

Saulteau than French in tongue and tone. The father, named Wah-ween-shee-cap-po, was a giant in size and ancient in days and devilment. When one of his grandchildren had died during the previous summer, in his grief and rage old Disgarlais, arming himself with his long flintlock, with powder-horn and ball-pouch slung over his shoulders, commenced blazing away at the sun, challenging the power up there " to come down and fight him like a man instead of killing innocent children." As a professor of Indian medicine and black art in general he was dreaded, and he appeared to have the faculty of either hypnotizing or putting himself in a trance, lying so long in that state that during that winter his sons twice thought he was really dead, and came to the post for material to bury him. On both these occasions he came to life again after two or three days, during which he said he had visited spirit-land, of which he related his experiences to his fascinated and awestruck family and audience. By the time he fell into the third trance, or actually died that winter, his sons had no occasion to come to the post for winding sheet or coffin nails. The grave had also been dug ready; so, when he once more became apparently dead, his sons lost no time in nailing him down in the coffin and sinking him in a deep grave and covering him with earth. Then they poured water thereon so as to freeze him down in case he should come to life once more to terrorize his panic-stricken and superstitious descendants.

CIVILIZED SOCIETY.

Another of the winterers was William Birston, commonly known as " Gaddie." He was a son of one of those old reliable Orkneymen of the Company, Magnus Birston, for many years postmaster at Oxford House. Gaddie was a great, big, genial fellow, who could turn his tongue and his hand to anything, and we became great friends. There was trading there, on a small scale, an American named Oswald Brodie Nevin, a native of Ogdensburg, who, after serving as a cavalryman in the Civil War, had drifted west as a miner, then becoming a "wolfer," that is a poisoner of wolves, on the Upper Missouri, had found his way with Louison, or some other Metis frequenter of the posts on that river, to the north. Nevin went by the name of "Dick," as evidence of his deserved popularity. He used to go down to Red River to draw funds from home, with which he financed the rather leisurely trade he did in partnership with James N. Mulligan, son of the Chief of Police at Fort Garry in that period.

Besides being cheered at the post by calls from Gaddie, Dick and Jim Mulligan, we were occasionally favoured by a visit from Doctor Covenant, a French medical man, who had come out to the plains from Red River, fondly anticipating an extensive and profitable practice amongst a people whom he hoped would be suffering from the epidemic of smallpox, which had swept from the Missouri to the Saskatchewan. Doctor Covenant cynically professed great indignation at me for having disappointed him of his practice, by introducing vaccination among our Indians. But he forgave me sufficiently to become rather a frequent visitor, and he was welcome for the lively entertainment he afforded us in relating his remarkable adventures and in general conversation.

A Burglar, His Arrest and Attempted Revenge.

There was much distress among the Indians that winter owing to the disappearance of buffalo. Band after band made their way to Fort Qu'Appelle for the relief which was always afforded them free under the heading of the provision store-book of "Charity to Starving Indians." While Mr. McDonald acompanied the winter packet to attend the district council at Fort Pelly, I took his place at Qu'Appelle, and one night Bartle Harper (brother of Gowdie), who was mess-cook, came in and reported there was someone in the ice-house, where our whitefish were stored. McKinley, Kennedy and I at once went out. It was black darkness inside the ice-house and we had no lantern, while it was bright moonlight outside. I went to the outer of the double doors and ordered whoever was within to come forth. Kennedy yelled, " Keep to one side of the door, for he may shoot." Obeying the warning, McKinley and I posted ourselves one on each side of it, prepared to seize the depredator as he came forth. As he rushed out we caught him, and twisting his arms behind his back, we made him come into the office, where Jerry soon joined us. He had been stealing whitefish, as the load which dropped from his blanket, above where it was belted, disclosed when we caught him.

He was one of the Egg Lake Saulteaux, and had distinguished himself during the summer before by selling a bearskin to McKinlay and Jordan at Touchwood Hills, and after being paid for it defiantly taking it back and walking away with it and the goods he had received as well. So he required correction, which McKinley alone had not been able to give, for Jordan was scared of Indians. When I asked him why he had not come and asked for food, which we invariably gave to starving Indians, he replied insolently that the fish belonged to the Indians, who had a right to take what was their own from the whites, who were mere intruders in the country. He gave some more insolence, and, losing my temper, I went up and slapped his mouth. Instantly he drew a big knife from under his blanket, and as he was bringing down his hand—round arm, for the Indians did not thrust— to stab me, Jerry jumped and wrested the knife from him. I then opened the door, and heading him for it kicked him outside, and then right through to the front gate, whence he departed, vowing the vengeance of his numerous relations against me. I told him to bring them along at any time to get their deserts. I kept his big knife as a souvenir, but soon forgot him; in fact, I don't remember exactly his name, but I think it was either " Mus-toos " or " Mou-kees." Anyhow, he was brother of a good hunter, named Tay-taw-pus-as-sung, and Almighty Voice, who gave so much trouble to the Mounted Police some years after (when he killed several, and my gallant friend, Lieutenant-Colonel Jack Allan, was severely wounded by him), was one of the same family.

About two months after, being the only man left at Last Mountain Post at the time, I was out looking at the poison I had set for wolves, when I saw a string of three men on snowshoes making for the post, to which I returned. There was a blazing March sun shining on the snow, and as the party came nearer I noticed they were holding their heads down and were rather wobbly in their walk. I had no idea whom the visitors might be, but prepared to receive them as foes, if not friends. Instead of opening the door of the office and walking in as usual without the ceremony of knocking, they tapped at the door, and, in response to my "Phe-to-gay" (come in) Tay-taw-pus-as-sung, Mustoos and their brother, whom Andrew McNab had kicked off the premises in March, 1870, walked in humbly with bowed heads and streaming eyes, and armed to the teeth. They were suffering all the agonies of snowblindness, with which, fortunately for me, they had been stricken while on the warpath against me.

I immediately metaphorically heaped coals of fire on their heads by dropping soothing laudanum into their burning eyes. Then, after putting flyblisters behind each ear and the napes of their necks, I administered to each a big dose of Epsom salts to cool their blood. They bought some tea and tobacco with a marten skin, and departed, cured, and in peace, next day, without referring to the original object of their visit, and I do not recollect ever having any more trouble with them. In fact, Tay-taw-pus-as-sung and I traded pleasantly several times afterwards at Qu'Appelle, but he was a different and a far better man than his brethren, anyhow.

A Spring Trip to the Plains.

In the end of March Mr. McDonald ordered me to go to Wood Mountain to try to buy pemmican, at any price, to enable the boats to be provisioned for the voyage to York Factory. Henri Hibbert and I accordingly set out on horseback. We camped that night at the mouth of Moose Jaw Creek, with some Metis who had wintered there. One of them had a trading outfit, which had included a puncheon of port wine as his share of the pillage of Fort Garry during the previous winter. I bought from Alexander Breland there a splendid saddle horse, and Henri, having another good one, we made a long day over the rapidly-melting snow under a blazing sun. That evening we found the trader, Kis-sis-away Tanner in camp on the Dirt Hills. He was the only person known to have any pemmican, having ten bags, which he esteemed worth their weight in gold. After some haggling, he sold me six bags at two shillings and six pence a pound, payable in cash at Fort Garry.

The blazing reflection of the sun on the melting snow during the ride from Moose Jaw had scorched the skin off my face, leaving it in a state of very painful rawness, which continued until a week afterwards when, on reaching Fort Qu'Appelle, Mrs. McDonald prescribed bathing it in milk, which acted like magic. The natives at Dirt Hills could do nothing for me, but told me that the use of vermilion prevented sunburn, and I afterwards experienced its virtue in preventing my nose from getting sunscorched and peeled.

The Transformation of Flemmand.

The first man to meet and greet us as we rode up to Tanner's camp was my old friend, Flemmand, who came forward with glad hand outstretched. After my business was over with Tanner, I took Flemmand for a little stroll, and to hear his adventures since he had left the Company's service and entered that of " Mister Kisisaway," as he called his employer. " Well, Flemmand," I enquired, " how have you been getting on?" " Stop," he cried, " I don't want dat name no more! My name now is Jackson—' Mister ' Jackson, too, for dat's what de 'Mericans call me at Fort La Roche

Jaune." "Why?" I asked. "I go dare to buy tings for my boss, for he not speak English, an' I hear de 'Mericans always swear by General Jackson. I want dem to t'ink me Englishman, too, no halfbreed, so w'en day ask my name, I say 'Jackson.' Den day say, 'Oh, Mister Jackson, come an' heat wit us,' an day make much of me. Dat's why I don't want dat old name Flemmand no more." I suggested that he should assume the title of General as well as the name of Jackson, and he was delighted at the idea of exchanging the new title of Mister to the still higher one of General; but whether he ever succeeded in attaining the dignity of being so addressed I never heard, and that was the last time I had the pleasure of meeting my lively and amusing friend, Flemmand.

Sitting Bull Robs a Company's Trader.

While we were there next day, Mr. Joseph McKay, who had been wintering at Wood Mountain, trading for Fort Ellice, arrived on his way back there. He reported that a party of his men, under Baptiste Bourassa, when on their way to trade at Milk River with a camp of Sioux, who had sent for them, had been robbed of their whole trading outfit and arms by other Sioux under Sitting Bull. As this notorious chief had no use for the oxen, carts and harness, and did not care to arouse the Metis against him by lifting Bourassa's scalp and those of the other French halfbreeds composing the party, he graciously permitted them to return with these, but unarmed and without food for the journey.

A Man With a Buffalo Tooth.

McKay, with his family, had come on ahead with a light waggon, and next day Bourassa arrived with the cart-train, by which the precious six bags of pemmican were shipped under his trusty care, to Fort Ellice. Accompanying the carts was a very green and peculiar apprentice clerk. He had wintered under Joe at Wood Mountain, and having been taken out to run buffalo, according to his heart's desire, had been thrown and got a tooth knocked out. Joe had come to pick him up in great alarm, to find that nothing was wrong but the tooth, for which the young man made lamentation. Right alongside lay several buffalo teeth, and picking up a huge one Joe handed it to him, saying, " here it is, you'd better keep it as a souvenir." And, whenever a party of Metis came visiting, Joe would relate the incident in Cree or French to them, and then turning to the clerk he would say, " I have just been telling these fellows about your wonderful buffalo hunt, and they would like to see your tooth." Whereupon the poor simple fellow would proudly go to his trunk, take out the immense tooth and hand it round to the grave-faced visitors for inspection.

A Hard Journey to Qu'Appelle.

If there were any reason why Joe McKay was returning by the way of Qu'Appelle, besides wanting to see his relations there, I do not remember. In an evil hour he persuaded me to accompany him and his family ahead of his party, in going directly to the fort, instead of returning with Henri to the Last Mountain by the way we came. The sudden thaw had inundated the whole plain, and we commenced wading through it in the afternoon of the first day. All the creeks were in flood. It was only at rare and long intervals that enough bare ground above water could be found to unhitch on. We waded in water up to the horses' bellies for hours, swam creeks with lines to haul across the waggon-box, wrapped in an oilcloth to serve as a boat, in which to ferry Mrs. McKay and the children over. We had one cart, and Joe quickly converted it also into a raft for freight. The days were warm, and my raw face suffered dreadfully in the heat, but the nights were bitterly cold. We at first made shift to boil the kettle only, but every bit of wood in the outfit was soon used up, and the dry area was too small to afford the dry dung on which all travellers depended. So, night after night, I slept in the open in wet blankets and clothes, which froze hard on the outside during the night. Soon we ran out of all food but a pound or two of flour, which Mrs. McKay had hoarded all winter for sickness or emergencies. For several days we toiled on, till, having passed the thawn and flooded area, we came to the unthawn snow out beyond the bordering woods of the Qu'Appelle Valley. There, at the edge of the snow, Joe found some buffalo bones, and by cutting up part of the cart he kindled a kind of fire of them, and at the same time selected others for the kettle to make "bouillon." We had some of this, slightly thickened with a little flour, and then went on. In our despite, the weather became cold and the snow was hard, but not sufficiently so to bear the wheels, which sank to the axles. To beat a path for the wheels we tied our riding-horses by the tail to the cart-trams and rode ahead of the horse in the cart, sticking every now and again in big drifts, where, after trampling the snow down, we pulled and hauled and put our shoulders in every way to the wheel. It was only after seven days of this incessant toil and hardship that we struck a beaten trail leading to the lakes. We arrived at the fort on the eighth day after leaving Dirt Hills, to find that Henri had come through by Moose Jaw and Last Mountain post five days before, after an easy trip.

CHAPTER XXVIII.

THE SUMMER AND FALL OF 1871.

Starvation on the Plains.

When Jerry and Jacob and the men who had wintered with them at Eagle Quills arrived that spring they brought harrowing tales of starvation, instead of the usual supply of provisions. Some of them had gone without food for three days at a stretch; they had eaten the buffalo sinews, of which thread was made for sewing leather, and feasted upon any wolf which they had the good luck to poison. On the way in their chief dependence had been gophers, caught by pouring water in their holes and forcing them out to snares set at the openings. The only food which was abundant that spring was suckers, which swarmed the creeks, and these fish of many bones and poor eating, became, with a little milk, barley and potatoes, the only rations at the fort. So when we were packing the furs and robes there was little skylarking and laughter, neither was there any merry-maker, like Flemmand—or rather Jackson—to cheer them up.

Oxen Sacred—Starvation a Frivolous Excuse.

At last the time to start for Fort Pelly on the way to York Factory arrived, and the discontent of the poor fellows, who declared that the diet of suckers had weakened instead of strengthened them, broke out in murmurings and questionings as to why the master did not make beef of some of the Company's cattle. But Archie McDonald was not the man to bring down disgrace upon himself by a proceeding which would have been regarded as highly revolutionary in the Company's service, for year after year the majestic minutes of Council enacted that officers in charge of Swan River

425

and Saskatchewan districts be instructed to use every effort to increase the number of live stock. In fact, the slaughter of a domestic animal was regarded as inexcusable in any event, in testimony of which I may be excused for mentioning the complaint of a chief factor to Governor Simpson against Chief Trader Deschambault for slaughtering cattle on the " frivolous " excuse of starvation at Portage la Loche!

A Surprise Packet of Pemmican.

The boatmen strongly objected to start for Fort Pelly with only the abominated dried suckers for rations, and, in that season of scarcity of game, only ammunition and snaring-twine to secure what they could on the way. " They are not going to catch me in that way," boasted the boss. " Come along with me, Cowie, and I'll show them." We went together up to the loft of the store, and there, under a pile of buffalo leather, he unveiled a big bag of pemmican, which he threw down the hatch to the ration store, where Jerry had meanwhile assembled the voyageurs. They were most agreeably surprised, and the master smiled triumphantly at the big fat bag. Taking the meat-axe out of Jerry's hands he made a blow at the bag to divide it in half, but instead of the blade sinking deep into a rich mixture of fat and meat it struck fire, and the edge was broken. Furiously he again attacked the bag, but the blow brought the same astonishing result. Then Jerry seized a scalping-knife and, ripping the hide off the package, disclosed a mixture of hard mud and gravel, in which, in still more mockery, the manufacturer had placed an old pair of moleskin trousers, a ragged capote and a pair of worn-out moccasins. The scene and outcry which followed can be more easily imagined than described. I, for one, burst out in loud laughter, in which the poor men who had been on the verge of mutiny, soon joined. They saw that their master had been careful to make a cache to provide for them, but that he had been deceived by some rare rascal—the like of whom had previously been unknown in that quarter. Mr.

McDonald at once declared: " No Indian ever made up that dirty bag of tricks, it was a French halfbreed, for look at his cast-off clothes!"

The Indians had always made honest pemmican, well mixed with fat, but after the halfbreeds became our chief purveyors there it became necessary to mark each bag as we bought it with the name of the vendor to put a check upon similar, though rare, forms of fraud.

A Starving Trip Down the Assiniboine.

That spring I had the long-longed-for pleasure of getting a trip to Fort Garry, taking charge of the batteaux going down the Assiniboine from Fort Ellice with the buffalo robes. At Fort Ellice, Mr. Duncan Matheson was, in the absence of Chief Trader McKay, in charge. When the food problem came up for solution also here, Mr. Matheson refused, with horror, my suggestion that one of the Company's old draft oxen might fittingly be sacrificed. " What?" cried Matheson, in horror, " kill a Company's ox! No! never while I am in charge!"

We had good luck in shooting birds and finding their eggs and those of turtles for the first two days. Two of the best hands went ashore and followed the valley after deer or bear, but unsuccessfully. On the third evening I chanced to shoot a big beaver, which afforded a welcome bite to the twelve boatmen, while Bill Moore (an old army pensioner, who was cook at Qu'Appelle) and I finished the last of some dainties which Mrs. McKay had most kindly furnished on our departure. By the time we reached the rapids near which the river was forded by carts (near Brandon), we had nothing to eat; but we saw the fresh tracks of a train of carts which had crossed going north. Hoping to get some food from them I took Henri Hibbert and another man and followed up the trail. Along the way we saw the decomposing bodies of three Sioux who had very shortly before been killed and scalped—by a party of Red Lake Ojibways, as we afterwards learned. The carts turned out to be laden with freight for the Company at Carlton, and the Metis who were taking it were only too pleased to get rid of part of their heavy loads by letting us have four bags of flour, for Henri and his companion to carry with their straps back to the batteaux.

At that time flour was regarded as a luxury at Fort Ellice and Qu'Appelle, only enough for the " winter allowances " of the officers and men being brought in. To use it for any other purpose would have been almost as great a crime as that of slaughtering an ox. So, I could well imagine the indignation of Mr. Duncan Matheson when the freighter, in passing Fort Ellice, called and produced my order for the four bags of flour to be replaced, which, I had been assured by the men, he would be able to do out of the loads of other freighters for Swan River who had preceded them.

Held in Quarantine.

But man cannot live and thrive and ply the labouring oar, from dawn to dark, on flour and water only, and that cooked (the word is too strong) in the most uninviting and indigestible manner. The men all fell ill, of summer complaint. This was relieved by decoctions of oak bark, and finally we arrived at Portage la Prairie on our tenth or twelfth day from Fort Ellice.

By that time the fear of civil war in Red River had been replaced by the fear of the invasion of Manitoba by smallpox from the Saskatchewan. A Board of Health had been formed to enforce a quarantine on all comers from the west, and here was the Hudson's Bay Company, in defiance of the law, trying to evade it by sneaking down the Assiniboine with buffalo robes which *must* have come from the infected district. A provincial constable met us as we put ashore at the old post, and told me he had orders to stop the boats there. In recognition of the majesty of the law, we stopped the boats, but they were too leaky to leave laden with the robes, as the men, of course, could not be depended upon to keep baling while all the attractions of civilization were there to tempt them from duty. Moreover, as they belonged to another district, Mr. George Davis, who presided over the Portage Post, could not be expected to control them during my absence, for I had to go down to Fort Garry to clear the foul aspersions against our cargo. The suspected robes were therefore landed and stored in a building near the bank.

I then set out on horseback with Henri for Fort Garry, where Mr. John H. McTavish took me before Governor Archibald, and before a meeting of the Board of Health, composed of the Bishops, Machray and Tache, Mr. Gerard and the Governor, I was able to convince them of the freedom of our robes from infection, and obtained an order to the authorities at Portage la Prairie to pass them.

AT FORT GARRY.

Whilst at Fort Garry then I had the pleasure of seeing the Canadian Volunteers paraded on the Queen's birthday. They were a remarkably fine body of men physically, as compared with the regulars, with whose appearance I had been familiar in Aberdeen and Edinburgh, and especially as compared with some I had seen in London. Shortly after the parade, a number of the volunteers started in rowboats down the Red River on their return to Ontario.

In the clerks' quarters, which Riel had used to confine his prisoners, I also had the pleasure of making the acquaintance of a number of the volunteer officers, and enjoying with them and my old chum at York Factory, Mr. James S. Ramsay, the society and some of the luxuries of civilization.

RIDE BACK TO FORT ELLICE.

As I was getting ready to start on my return to release the cargo at Portage la Prairie, Mr. Gerard, Provincial Treasurer, came to me gravely to say that very strong evidence had been sent down from there to the effect that the robes had come from infected districts. Another meeting of the Board of Health was held in which I indignantly denied the statements, and reminded them of the great care we had taken in Swan River, which had not only prevented an outbreak of smallpox there, but had also prevented its spreading to Red River. The Board was impressed, but thought it better that I should return myself to Fort Ellice to procure affidavits from others in support of my testimony and that of Henri.

We got under way and then I had the chance of hearing from my companion the reason for his dilapidated appearance. He said that while enjoying himself in a saloon with a few compatriots they had been wantonly attacked by volunteers and beaten up with their belts. He was very bitter against the want of what he considered fair play, and I was naturally indignant at seeing a man who had been my kind and agreeable voyaging companion in the wilds, meeting with such a poor reception in civilization. Still Henri might have indiscreetly, under the impulse of the cheering cup, given vent to " Vive mon Nation !" or, perchance, burst out in chanting " La gloire de tous ces Bois-brulé," at a time and place where they were not in the majority.

Return Again to Fort Garry.

In passing the Portage Mr. Davis informed me that the people were so alarmed that they had been hardly restrained from burning the building in which the robes were stored; and that two of the Highlanders belonging to Swan River had deserted. While there I first made the acquaintance of my friend, Mr. Edward Field, then a clerk under Mr. Davis, and who passed away, much to my sorrow, in 1912.

On my return from Fort Ellice, with the necessary " clearance papers," I fell in for the first time with another, who was to become an old and lasting friend. I was on horseback when I came up with a light buggy on the road between Portage and High Bluff. Its occupant was Mr. Charles Mair, who soon invited me to share the seat with him, so that we might converse more comfortably. We camped that night at House's store at Long Lake, and next day continued the journey and cemented a friendship which has lasted to this day.

FALL OF 1871.

Mr. McDonald went down to Fort Garry that summer and I was left to preside over quite a number of young fellows at Qu'Appelle till the fall when he returned, and I set out to winter at the Cyprè Hills.* While he had been at Fort Garry the Fenian Raid on Manitoba had occurred, when every Hudson's Bay man, from the inspecting chief factors down, " Rallied 'Round the Flag," as per the Lieutenant-Governor's proclamation.

Before I left the fort, we were delighted by the visit of the Rev. Mr. Goldie, then returning from a visit to the Presbyterian Mission of the Rev. Mr. Nesbit, at Prince Albert. Mr. Goldie was a most interesting conversationalist, and a Scot of poetic fire, who loved to quote Scott and Burns and a Canadian Scot named, I think, McLaughlin. On Sunday he preached the very first Presbyterian sermon which ever awoke the echoes of the Qu'Appelle Valley.

* Cyprè, not Cypress, is the correct name, signifying, in French, the Jack Pine after which the Indians named the hills. " Cypress " does not grow in the North-West.

CHAPTER XXIX.

WINTER AT CYPRÈ HILLS, 1871-2.

A NATURAL GAME PRESERVE.

MORE out of charity than for any use the lad might be to him on the trip to Red River, Mr. Goldie had taken one Robert Jackson with him from Prince Albert, whither one of Jackson's tramps had led him. When we spoke of the expedition to Cyprè Hills, where we hoped to be able to open peaceable negotiations with the Blackfeet with the view of establishing a post for them on the Upper South Saskatchewan River, Mr. Goldie mentioned that Jackson spoke the Blackfoot language, being the grandson of old Hugh Munro and a Peigan wife, and might be useful to interpret. Jackson's father was an American and a Methodist, who had taught him good English and his religion, also a good address. So I was very glad when he willingly consented to go with me.

As has been previously mentioned, the Cyprè Hills had been a neutral ground, which the hostile tribes of the surrounding country feared to enter for hunting purposes. Consequently, it had become a natural game preserve, occupied chiefly by red deer and grizzly bears. Our own Indians would not venture to acompany our party to winter there, but the number of Metis frequenting Qu'Appelle had been very largely increased by those who left or ceased to resort to Red River after the establishment of Canadian Government. A strong party of these hunters had been induced by Jerry to join him; and they had gone to the hills in time to put up buildings for the winter. Two of his brothers had also accompanied him, so that for hunting and defensive purposes the number of men was sufficient.

A NARROW ESCAPE

A Blackfoot War Party.

Besides Jackson, John Asham and another Indian formed the party, with horse-sleds, with which I set out for Cyprè Hills. On the first Sunday out we lay all day, suffering dreadfully from the whirling smoke of our green-wood fire in a little ravine on the edge of the next wide open plain on the route. Next morning that plain, which had been vacant the whole day before, was filled by scattered herds of buffalo. We had not gone very far among them when we crossed a trail made the previous day, by a party of over fifty men, evidently—to the Indians—Blackfeet on the war-path. Had we, as usual, travelled on that Sunday, we would certainly have been discovered and probably killed by them.

At the Vermilion Hills we fell in with Benjamin Disgarlais and a few other hunters. After securing their furs and robes, I went on to where our wintering post was situated at the east end of the Cyprè Hills, in a valley in which a small lake, on the height of land between the Missouri and the South Saskatchewan, sent rills in each direction. Frequent Chinook winds during the winter often swept away the snow from the open, leaving only the drifts sheltered in the ravines and woods.

An American Metis Liquor Trader.

Some of our Indians had followed the party under Jerry, but most of the buffalo hunting was done by it, and the Indians all retreated to the east, early in March, to get out of the way of the Blackfeet. There were Metis traders at Wood Mountain, Pinto Horse Butte, and Eagle Quills; but the only one who annoyed us was Antoine Oulette, generally called Irretty, who made several incursions with liquor and delighted in trying to make everyone drunk, and in proclaiming sedition against the Canadian Government and animosity to the Company and their people from the old country. However, as Kennedy, Harper, Jordan and I kept our heads, restrained our feelings and refused to accept his most pressing offers to join in the festivities, by which he opened his trade, we did not become involved in any of the resultant rows amongst his Metis guests on these occasions.

BLACKFEET HOVERING AROUND.

Before we began packing the robes and furs in the spring, the Indians had all cleared off to the east, and shortly after we began to see signs of Blackfeet being about. We tried to open communication with these scouts, by signals, to which they only replied by signs of hostility and derision, mocking us with flashes from their little round mirrors. Even had we been able to secure audience with them, unless one of them could have talked Cree, we should have been confined to signs, for young Jackson had turned out so absolutely unsatisfactory that we had been glad when Oulette, thinking to interfere with our wish to open communication with the Blackfeet, had induced the young scamp to abscond with him to Wood Mountain.

THE METIS RETREAT—ASSINIBOINES KILLED BY BLACKFEET.

Most of the Metis who had wintered with us broke camp and made their way east before we finished packing the returns of trade, which were so large that we were obliged to leave forty fresh buffalo carcasses in store, for want of carts to carry them with us. During all the packing season the Blackfeet increased in number and hovered around watching our movements. We had to carefully herd our horses by day and round them up at night, while they made many attempts to steal them. The Company's buildings were in a row, not in a square, and those of the freemen were similarly arranged in the shelter of scrub at the foot of a hill, which commanded them, and was the watchtower of the Blackfeet prowlers. We were well armed and on the alert day and night, so they made no attack. I was glad, however, when everything had been stowed away in the carts and they got out into the open valley. Gaddie Birston and I remained awhile at the buildings after the carts started to see that nothing of consequence had been left. The Wood Mountain Assiniboines were always prowling about after prey, and nine of them had suddenly appeared around our deserted buildings. They were picking up stray bullets which had leaked out of ragged sacks on to the mud floor of the store and such trifles, while others were helping themselves to the fresh meat we could not carry away. Leaving them, after warning them of the Blackfeet hidden on the hills, Birston and I rode off after the carts. We had not gone, at a lope, more than a quarter of a mile, when we heard a spluttering volley, evidently from a large party, and by the time we reached the carts the smoke, which arose from the site of our wintering houses, proclaimed that the Blackfeet had set them on fire. Not one of the nine Stonies escaped. Their bodies, minus scalps, were found by Metis while hunting deer in the hills next June.

A Hard Trip to Qu'Appelle.

We made a good ring with the carts to protect our ponies that night and for a few nights afterwards, as we journeyed eastward. The snow had disappeared, except in deep coulees; so, as my services were unnecessary with the carts and were required at Qu'Appelle to make up the accounts, I left them, taking Xavier Denomie as my guide, one pack and two saddle ponies, to ride ahead to Qu'Appelle. Our progress was good during the first day, but next morning we struck the snow-line, and from that time on the snow became deeper every day. What was worse, it had been formed in layers by crusts following thaws, and each thaw by a fresh snowfall. The effect of the ponies' feet breaking through these successive crusts was very jarring.

The weather became cold and stormy, too, and our course was over the treeless plains, without even the little kindling wood that might be carried on sleds. Xavier was famous for finding the way, by day or night, across the trackless plains. He was a wiry fellow and was reputed hardy too, but he could not stand the racket of the jarring nor the cold on horseback, without frequently changing his troubles to those of a man struggling in deep snow on foot, when he gave a lead and I drove the ponies after him. I stood the cold and stuck to the saddle better, but the going at a jogtrot, or walk, with the pony making three distinct jars at each footstep, so affected the ligaments and muscles at the back of my neck that they became afflicted with the same agonies as those of the snowshoer with "mal de racquette" in the legs.

Xavier was a first-class hunter and guide, but he was too fond of vaunting himself and "Le Gloire de tous ces Boisbrule," for me to let him suspect that I had "got it in the neck," while he could not conceal his shivering with cold as we lay together in our fireless lairs at night.

We had expected to make the trip in a week easily, but the condition of the snow had made it twice as long, when, after living on one dried buffalo tongue for the last three days, we reached the fort. Xavier went down to his friends at the mission, and related all the hardships of the trip to Father Decorby, who came up next day to congratulate me upon getting through with it, and also upon the way I had stood it to the surprise of Xavier, who never had suspected the continual agony I had endured.

Numerous Grizzlys and Elk.

Incredible numbers of grizzly bears and red deer were killed in the Cyprè Hills that year, of which our share of the skins numbered 750 and 1,500 respectively, and probably the traders and Metis who were not our customers got as many more. Most of these were unprime summer bearskins —mere hides which every hunter was using for cart covers instead of the ordinary buffalo bull hides, for large numbers had been slain off horseback in a run on the prairie. Many of them were of immense size approaching that of a polar bear; one skin measured by me was thirteen feet from tip to tail. This natural reservation of the grizzly and the elk soon ceased to harbour them after the neutrality of the hills had ceased owing to our invasion.

Quite a number of those hunting in the wooded ravines of the hills were shot accidentally by their fellows mistaking men, wearing the red buffalo calfskin jackets, for red deer. I heard of five deaths due to that mistake and the fact that the plain hunters were unskilled in woodcraft. In fact, I may mention that a prairie Indian often lost himself in the woods, as did a wood Indian on the prairie.

By the time next fall that our wintering party would have usually set out to resume operations, many of the Metis, in their discontent at the new order of things in Manitoba, had deserted the settlement and spread themselves in large numbers over parts of the plains into which they had never before ventured. Many of these had leanings towards the Americans, and these, with the American Metis mingled among them, frequently resorted to the posts along the Missouri and found their way to Benton. The American traders were not long in taking advantage of these circumstances, and in 1872 they established whiskey trading-posts at Cyprè Hills and to the west, the steamboating facilities on the Missouri giving them great advantages over us; and their acquaintance among the Blackfeet, some of whom were American "Treaty Indians," by whom the Company's people of Qu'Appelle were regarded as enemies, giving them an added advantage.

CHAPTER XXX.

IN FULL CHARGE OF QU'APPELLE, SUMMER, 1872.

My Apprenticeship Ended.

The five long, weary and lonely and disillusioning years of my apprenticeship were over in June, 1872; but when that fondly-looked-forward-to time came, the sad news of my mother's death at home, and the lure held out at the "Reorganization" of the fur trade in 1871 to the effect that promotion was to be henceforth entirely by merit, not seniority, induced me foolishly to accept the full charge of Fort Qu'Appelle, and engage for another term of three years at the usual advance in pay.

Colonel Robertson Ross Slays a Sacred Ox.

Early in the summer of 1872 Mr. McDonald went as usual to Fort Garry, and having business with Mr. McKay, at Fort Ellice, as I was nearing it he met me on the road to the crossing of the trail to the Carlton, accompanied by Colonel Robertson Ross, Adjutant-General of Canada, who was on his way across the plains on horseback on a tour of investigation. The Colonel stated that the Government intended to form a force for the Territories, and asked me what kind of troops would be most suitable. I told him the men would require to be mounted and good shots with the rifle to be of much use. "Like the Cape Mounted Rifles?" he asked, approvingly. He enquired if I had seen any big game near, and upon my saying indifferently, "Only a bear," he was quite interested.

After bidding him and his son—who accompanied him— "bon voyage across the continent," Mr. McKay and I went on towards the fort. Before reaching it we heard two shots

438

down in the valley, and Mr. McKay, thinking they might be signals, turned back to find out what was the matter, while I went on. About an hour afterwards he came into the office and, with a twinkle in his eye, handed Mr. Matheson, the accountant, a ten-pound note, saying, " Put that in your desk and enter it in the books as the price of one of the Company's draught oxen which the Colonel mistook for a bear and killed." The Colonel was under the good guidance of the factor's son William for the voyage. After crossing the Qu'Appelle a bear was sighted, which took to a bluff of trees in the valley. The colonel rode off in hot pursuit, and as he rounded the bush saw a large animal looking like the grizzly partly concealed in it. Quite naturally he fired and killed it, with two shots. But when they went up to it it was to find an old freighting ox belonging to the fort. Naturally the sportsman was terribly chagrined, and in the meanwhile the bear had departed for parts unknown.

Upon Mr. Factor McKay riding up, the colonel at once tendered payment for the animal, which was accepted, and in consequence of the mistake the mess-table of Fort Ellice was that evening graced by beefsteaks of one of the sacred cattle, which Mr. Matheson had so dutifully defended against me the spring before.

FACTOR McKAY TRANSFERRED TO FORT PITT.

Mr. McKay was then preparing to relinquish the charge of Swan River district and to take his departure for his new appointment at Fort Pitt where the services of a first-rate manager of Indians were very much required in the interests of the Company's safety and business in the Saskatchewan district at large His successor was Mr. McDonald, to whom I in turn succeeded in permanent charge of Fort Qu'Appelle.

NEW PLAN FOR TRADE.

The tried and trusty postmasters, Jerry McKay and William Kennedy, could not be induced by the pay offered to remain longer in the service, and started as free hunters and traders on their own account. The Metis had been flocking to the Qu'Appelle country in increasing numbers, many of them with some articles for trade, and the Company adopted the plan of advancing those who were trustworthy to trade instead of sending out wintering parties of our own men that year.

As these traders scattered about over the plains it was hoped that the Indians in general would be more conveniently supplied than by our sending out parties of our own men to winter in different places As far as the immediate results were concerned the plan worked well and enormously increased the returns of Fort Qu'Appelle. But as the post only got credit in the annual accounts at the tariff fixed in the year 1834 and not at the prices at which the pemmican and robes were actually purchased, it showed a loss of at least six cents on every pound of pemmican and of five dollars on every robe purchased, so that the bigger the trade we did the greater was the "apparent loss" in the balance sheet; whereas the prices at which we bought these things at Qu'Appelle was much more profitable to the Company than the prices current at Fort Garry and Winnipeg by which we were governed.

Moreover, owing to the entire inadequacy of the outfit of goods furnished to meet the increased demand, we were obliged to give orders on Fort Garry in payment, which, whether paid there in cash or goods, were charged against the post as cash. As the returns of trade in 1872 at Fort Qu'Appelle amounted to $100,000 at the old tariff of 1834, the "apparent loss" was very large, and was actually used as an argument (?) by those who had the power to cut down my carefully-prepared requisitions, to do so in the most senseless manner.

ALL ADVANCES TO INDIANS FORBIDDEN.

After the alleged "Reorganization," under Mr. Donald A. Smith, as Chief Commissioner, most stringent orders were issued to officers in charge to cease advancing the Indians on their hunts. In this matter the officers in charge of districts had a certain amount of discretion, but I was ordered to summarily cease to supply the plain Indians with the means of existence which their inherent improvidence and poverty demanded on credit every fall and spring. The omniscient beings composing the London Board had viewed with alarm the annual increase of " Outstanding Indian Debts " placed on inventory, but not valued as assets, every spring. The increase of uncollectable debts was chiefly due to the lack of proper control over native post-masters, interpreters and traders, whose personal sympathy with the Indians and desire to be popular amongst them often led them into being partial at the Company's expense. But instead of taking measures to prevent this indiscriminating practice of sowing the seed broadcast and on barren and unprofitable subjects to obtain the harvest in furs, the Board in its wisdom and justice decreed that the whole system of credit in the Indian trade must cease, forgetting that the universal application of such a principle to any commerce in the world would mean its ceasing to exist.

Great care had always been taken at Fort Qu'Appelle, under Mr. McDonald, in giving advances to deserving Indians at the fort, and he exercised rigorous criticism over any which our people on the plains had been induced, or perhaps, virtually compelled, to give. Only a small proportion of those trading at Qu'Appelle were deemed worthy, and their paying up depended not only on their luck in hunting, but also on their good fortune in preserving their lives from the enemies who encompassed them. For instance, after the defeat of the Crees by the Blackfeet at Belly River, before mentioned, I had to write off the outstanding debts, varying from fifty to a hundred dollars, of a score of the best Indians belonging to Touchwood Hills, who were slain on that occasion.

But in framing the selling prices of goods and fixing those for the purchase of furs and provisions every possible risk had been taken into consideration, thereby providing an insurance fund, which the London Board, in its wisdom, chose to ignore. And so, forgetful also of the loyalty of the Indians and their effective aid in preventing Fort Qu'Appelle from falling ignominiously to be pillaged by the Metis, it was decreed that all advances whatsoever by me to those Indians should be stopped.

They Determine to Help Themselves.

Some of the Indians had, in distress and resentment, left for the plains. The Metis, many of whom were less trustworthy than the Indians, but who might possibly be sued whenever the Canadian Government might afford the protection of law to the plains, had been outfitted and departed for the summer hunt. Only some Indians remained, and among them several splendid hunters as well as warriors of repute. These came to me individually and in parties again and again asking advances, which I was obliged as often to refuse. At last they got together and determined to come in a body to the fort to break into the store and help themselves. They had tried to keep their plan secret and take us by surprise; but we heard of it, and as we had no interpreter then who had the courage to interpret in a war of words, I rode out to the camp of Mr. Edward McKay, a man of education and bold as a lion, and asked him to come to help me next morning.

We saw the band of horsemen coming, all painted and plumed in warlike array, and Messrs. McKay, McKinlay and I were seated in the Indian hall as they trooped in and filled it to within a little space in front of our seats. Every one of them was a walking armory, each with Indian bow and quiver, many with Henry repeating rifles and revolvers, and all the rest with shotguns, besides tomahawks, scalping knives and war clubs. The most highly-decorated and extensively-armed of the bunch was the Saulteau, Tep-is-couch-kees-cou-win-in, that "Man in the Zenith," whose firewater had caused me trouble with the Young Dogs in 1868. He had been the leading spirit in getting up the intended raid, and before anything had been said, for they came in in silence, I addressed him, saying we had heard that he had been trying to get the others to join him in helping themselves out of the store. "There are enough of you to do so, but the first man who attempts to break in I will shoot. Mr. McKinlay and I (we both had Winchesters in our hands) are ready to begin the moment you try to break into the store." Then, pointing at it, I said, "There it is, Zenith, go ahead." As I challenged him Harper was just hoisting the flag, and, pointing to it as its folds flew at the staffhead, I exclaimed: "That is why we are not afraid of you!" The effect was magical. With one accord they denied having come to pillage, but merely to ask again the Company in kindness to enable them to leave for the hunting grounds with ammunition and tobacco. Though I did not believe them, I replied: "You may not have bad intentions, but The Zenith has, and I would like to see him do himself what he tried to incite you to." But he was thoroughly abashed by the turn things had taken, and protested innocence and sincere personal regard to me, which I believed so little that I should have been pleased to have had an excuse to try a shot at him.

WISER COUNSELS.

The wiser Indians then made their plea for advances in very plausible and respectful form. So, as the policy of the Company was always to yield as a favour what the Indians would otherwise take by force, putting all the blame on Zenith for the warlike preparation with which the gathering had been met, I said, while refusing them advances on their personal accounts, that I had authority to present to them as a favour what they had no right to, and let them divide the supplies amongst them acording to need. And so the trouble ended that time.

THE COMPANY OF ADVENTURERS

A Widespread Conspiracy to Raid Manitoba.

The incident was only one sign of the general state of in-quietude and change caused by the bargain between the Company and the government in London for the surrender of the country to Canada without full consideration of the right of its inhabitants to have some say in the matter. Every Metis who had left Manitoba dissatisfied at real or imaginary grievances became a firebrand among the warlike Indians of the prairies. Not content with putting mischief into the heads of the tribes living north of the border, they incited the Assiniboines and Sioux along the Missouri to join in a general conspiracy of Indians and Metis for the purpose of driving every other kind of people out of the old Red River Settlement. The Fenian Raid on Manitoba in the fall of 1871 was a premature performance of part of the programme.

During all the years I had been at Qu'Appelle there was trouble between the Americans and Sioux along the Missouri, and as the power of the United States advanced, the Sioux looked more and more with longing eyes to the country across the line where they would be safe from pursuit. Former defeats which they had sustained at the hands of the Metis buffalo hunters of Red River, and the hereditary enmity between them and the Ojibways of whom the Saulteaux were a tribe, had prevented any general attempt to invade the country. So when the dissatisfaction of the Metis with the Canadian form of government led these to make overtures to the Sioux for an alliance, strong enough to sweep away all opponents from the Qu'Appelle Lakes to Lake Winnipeg, the proposal was favourably considered. Counting the Assiniboines as allies, cognate in language and distinguished for love of plunder, the Sioux in alliance with the Metis would be able to overcome the Saulteaux and their friends, the Crees, and capturing Forts Qu'Appelle and Ellice on the way with the munitions therein, raid the settlement of Portage la Prairie, and massacre the inhabitants of Winnipeg, while besieging Fort Garry.

Aiding and abetting this extensive conspiracy, and in sympathy with the Metis, were American traders and Fenians along the frontier.

The Crees and Saulteaux Refuse to Join it.

The fact that " tobacco " to smoke in council was being sent around by messengers of the malcontents to every chief and influential person among our Indians soon was noised abroad. Our Crees, however, were not to be either cajoled or intimidated by the machinations and magnitude of the alliance. The Saulteaux, while we could not so fully rely on them as the Crees, had from time immemorial been at war with the Sioux, with only armistices intervening, and they as followers of and later intruders than the Crees into the Blackfeet territory, deeply resented the proposal that an asylum should be given, in the hunting grounds so occupied by them, to the new friends and allies of the Metis, who had come in such large numbers, so unwelcomely and with modern repeating rifles, to more speedily exterminate the already woefully depleted numbers of the buffalo. It was our policy and duty to sustain the Crees and Saulteaux in this attitude; yet the orders from the gentlemen in London, who sat at home in ease and considered themselves all-wise, were calculated to destroy our influence over and our ancient alliance for mutual protection with these tribes, by abolishing the " system of Indian debts."

Teton Sioux Send an Armed Delegation.

As the conspiracy between the disaffected Metis and the Assiniboines and Sioux gained strength, the former, instead of concealing, boasted of the movement. " Tobacco " was sent to me by the Teton tribe of Sioux saying that they wished to send a strong delegation to arrange that Fort Qu'Appelle should become their trading post. I replied politely but stated that the Company could not invite or encourage them to come to the Cree and Saulteaux country, against the well-known wishes of these tribes; and that it would be dangerous for them to pay the proposed visit.

My answer did not deter the Tetons from their determination, and a message by a Metis brought me the unwelcome reply that they were coming anyhow, and would not hold the Company responsible for any attack made upon them by our Indians, of whom they expressed defiance. It happened that there were about the lakes a large enough number of Saulteaux at the time to outnumber the Teton delegation, which was reported to consist of only thirty warriors. The Saulteaux head men there were Pus-sung, Oo-soup and Che-Kuk, all good friends of mine and disposed to be reasonable in general; but when I asked them to allow the delegation, which was bound to come, to do so and depart in peace, the hereditary enmity was too strong for them to tie their own hands and those of their "young men" by making any unqualified promise. They had long viewed with resentment the presence of the refugee Yankton Sioux under White Cap and Standing Buffalo, who had been hunting north of the line and trading at Fort Ellice for a number of years, and the recent visit of these to Qu'Appelle, as more convenient than Fort Ellice, had nearly led to a fight at the fort. That these unwelcome intruders, who had been scarcely tolerated, should now be made more formidable by the invasion of the tribe under the notorious depredator Sitting Bull, was not to be thought of.

We had recently renewed the "fortifications" of Qu'-Appelle by a set of high, upright pickets, in place of the original horizontally-placed slabs. There were a number of our old friendly and well-disposed Metis in from the plains; and Alick Fisher enlisted a force of them, who went out and met the Tetons at a day's travel from the fort, and escorted them into it, where they staid during their visit, guarded it, and finally escorted them to a safe distance out on their return journey. During all this time the Saulteaux were warned not to approach the place too near, and they were all the time stripped for fight and ready to take advantage of any opportunity.

The Sioux had sent some of their very best speakers and ablest men to act as ambassadors on this occasion. They went back to ancient history to prove that they had always been the friends of the British against the Americans, and showed a silver medal of King George in evidence. They also mentioned friendly overtures which had been made to them by a great man from Red River after the war of 1814, which I did not understand at the time, and it was only last winter that I discovered in the Selkirk and Bulger papers in the Ottawa Archives that Thomas, Earl of Selkirk, had entered into negotiations with the Sioux for assistance in his conflict with the North-West Company and in another mysterious scheme, in which latter he had employed a man named Dickson of whom Governor Bulger had a very bad opinion.

As evidence of their peaceable intentions towards the Company one of the spokesmen, a most blood-thirsty looking brute he was, stated that they had been for years spying out the land as one they wished to obtain possession of and therein to become good and loyal British Indians, supporting and trading with the Hudson's Bay Company. While engaged in obtaining intelligence in the summer of 1868, he and his fellows had repeatedly stolen into the fort at night and had watched me writing at the desk by "that window," pointing at it, when only two men and I were in the place to guard it and the women and children. All of which was correct, as has been related in a previous chapter.

I told them that we could not encourage them to resort to the Cree country, and that we did not have sufficient supplies to provide for the requirements of our own Indians and the Metis who had been coming in increasing numbers; so that we could not undertake to supply the requirements of so numerous a tribe as theirs. They had better make peace with the Americans on the Missouri, upon which the steamboats could deliver all the trading goods they needed, much more cheaply than we could at Qu'Appelle. Still they boasted that, if the Metis did not go against them, they could soon subdue the Crees and Saulteaux. They would never become friendly with the Americans, and they were bound to find safety on the north side of the boundary line. They were highly pleased with our kindness in trying to prevent any trouble with the Saulteaux, though they felt themselves quite able to defend themselves, and they thanked us for our friendly talk and entertainment; but they could not take our refusal as final. We would hear from them again.

While this delegation had professed nothing but the most friendly sentiments to the British and repudiated any evil intention, as far as I could make out through the Metis interpreters, I was informed by the notorious Shaman Racette afterwards that, like the Blackfeet who were at peace with the Company at Rocky Mountain House and Edmonton while at war with its people at posts supplying the Crees, these Sioux thought they could be at peace and supplied by us at Qu'Appelle and yet take part in joining the projected raid on the new settlers of Manitoba.

Towards fall that same year, 1872, I heard that another delegation of these Sioux visited Fort Garry, where they were highly offended at either their reception or non-reception by the Governor, and departed breathing vengeance. In passing Fort Ellice on their return journey, Mr. McDonald further so offended them, by refusing their demands, that his fort was also marked out for pillage when the raid on Manitoba was passing it.

SHAMAN, THE NOTORIOUS.

This Shaman Racette was the most notorious rowdy and bad man among the Metis hunters who frequented Fort Garry and the incipient town of Winnipeg. A description of him and his deeds would fill a highly sensational Wild West story book, and cannot be given here. But he, too, had been scorned in his attempt to obtain supplies from Mr. McDonald and had arrived at Qu'Appelle more determined than ever to take a leading part in the next raid on the settlement, for, having been run out of Red River to the American wilds before the troubles of 1869-70 started, he had, much to his chagrin, been a non-participant in them and the booty. Mr. McDonald had written me giving Shaman his well-earned bad character, and ordered that no assistance be given him at my post. But my good counsellor and friend, Alick Fisher, came and advised me it would be well for the peace of the lakes to get rid of Shaman by giving him what was absolutely necessary to start him off to the plains to hunt. Alick said that, although Shaman was a bad man and a rascal, yet he "acted square" with those who were not afraid of him and at the same time treated him kindly. So I took the risk of giving him a scaring and then giving him his hunting needs on my own account. He "acted square" with me, and in personally friendly and boastful spirit also revealed much of the plan of campaign being prepared for sweeping Canadian rule out of the Red River country, all of which, as in duty bound, I promptly communicated to headquarters.

THE REV. PERE LESTANC AND THE REBELLION.

During the summer of 1872 the Rev. Father Lestanc, who had been stationed previously at Wood Mountain, took Father Decorby's place for a few months at the Qu'Appelle Mission. He was suffering from ill health and, in doing what I could for his benefit, I had the privilege of having many long talks and discussions with him. Of course, we could not agree on the subjects of religion and the Red River Rebellion against the government of the Hudson's Bay Company; but I gained the advantage of seeing his point of view which led me to investigate the reasons for my opinions upon both subjects. On religion there was a wealth of matter in the British quarterly reviews, including the *Westminster,* for which Mr. McDonald had subscribed for years and carefully preserved. The reviews, however, failed to furnish any light upon the rights of the Hudson's Bay Company, save that admirable article, " The Last Great Monopoly," in the *Westminster Review,* of July, 1867; and the true inwardness of the rising in Red River in 1869-70, of which the reverend gentleman gave me a glimpse then, took many years to evolve itself in my mind, in fact the process is still going on. Still enough is now known to justify, in my mind, the opinion that Canada should have utilized the existing Governor and Council of Assiniboia to tide over the transfer and transition period, with the assistance of a few of her own officials; but, as both he and his Counsellors were ignored by Canada, the proper course for Governor McTavish and the Council of Assiniboine to have taken was to have suppressed the *Nor'- Wester* newspaper for seditious libel against the constituted authorities, to have arrested the surveyors of the Canadian Government as trespassers, and, if "Governor" McDougall and his retinue entered territory as unwarranted invaders, to cast them also in gaol as rebels against the *de facto* Government of the country, as recognized by the Imperial authorities.

Such a manly course would have united the majority of the old inhabitants of the Colony, without distinction of race and creed, and have secured such constitutional recognition of the rights of the people of Rupert's Land as British subjects as to have left no ground for the action taken by the people under Riel. Moreover, instead of becoming the mere " Colony of a Colony "—the status Western Canada occupies in a great measure still to-day—the country would have entered Confederation as the equal partner of Quebec and Ontario and the others which joined them on that basis of justice and self-respect.

Apart from his deplorably unfortunate state of ill-health at this critical period, Governor McTavish was—like all the too faithful servants of the thoroughly selfish and ungrateful London managers of the Company—so obsessed with the idea of doing his best for them, that he could not rise and act on the occasion in the interest of the people over whom he was governor when there arose the troubles, primarily brought on by the policy of secrecy, cupidity and stupidity, which have so often and remarkably characterized the dealings of the "London Board" of the Hudson's Bay Company.

I think now—though in common with those of my kind I was far from thinking so then—that the first intentions of any action taken by the French halfbreeds in resisting the illegal entry of Mr. William McDougall and his party of "carpet baggers" (the first of a subsequent host) was admirable, and, in view of the inaction of Governor McTavish and the Council of Assiniboia, that it was justifiable and even legal. The names of those who took part in the primary movement might have gone down in history as brave patriots but for the subsequent murder of Scott.* For that act, however, the great majority of Riel's followers were not responsible; and, when we consider the passions aroused and their easy access to the rum casks of the Company at Fort Garry, it is truly remarkable how few outrages on person and property were committed in that period of excitement by these wild hunters of the plains. Compared with the Boers of South Africa the Metis of Rupert's Land were gentlemen.

Americans at Cyprè Hills Clean Out a Camp of Assiniboines.

While the shadow of this great conspiracy was brooding over the southern plains, a big cloud of trouble arose in the west around Cyprè Hills, where American traders, chiefly with whiskey from Fort Benton, had commenced operations which deluged that part of the country in firewater and blood, and continued till the North-West Mounted Police put a stop to them two years later. One of the first reports of this American invasion of our territory was that of the slaughter of about eighty Assiniboines near Farwell's post at Cyprè

---

*The only plea I ever heard urged in extenuation of that deed of brutality was to the effect that, while absolutely in their power, Scott, most insanely, used the most highly abusive, insulting and threatening language to his gaolers. It is also said that Riel was personally in mortal terror of Scott for his own life, if he escaped and ever had an opportunity to carry out his threats to kill him.

Hills by half a dozen Americans from Benton, who had come after horses stolen by these Stonies. According to the report of Metis who witnessed the affair, the Assiniboines, in the exercise of their usual calling, had stolen a band of horses from near fort Benton, and brought them to Cyprè Hills, where they concealed them in a coulee, and camped with others of their kind, under the chief Manitou-Potess—the Cree name signifying Little Stony Spirit. Their camp was about a mile from the trading post of Mr. Farwell, across a creek which ran through the valley in which both were situated.

Six white men, one of whom at least was an Englishman, set out from Benton to follow and recover their stolen horses. As soon as they arrived at Farwell's post they sent a messenger to the Stonies demanding the restitution of their property. The demand was met with contempt, the Stonies turning out and making every sign of mockery and challenge towards the post; for what could six white men do against their big numbers? These again sent a friendly Metis to say that if the horses were not returned immediately they would attack the camp. And again the demand was met with derision and a defiance to come and take them.

The creek ran between the post and the camp, but within three hundred yards of the latter, and all was open prairie save a fringe of shrub along its banks. The Stonies, giving the war-whoop and discharging their firearms in the direction of the post, dared the white men to come on. These now accepted the challenge with alacrity and, in rushing across the space between the post and the shelter afforded by the cut bank of the creek, one of them was killed by the Assiniboine fire. As soon as the other five gained shelter they opened fire, with their Henry repeating rifles, at three hundred yards on the camp. Their fire was well aimed, destructive and rapid, quickly turning the yells of defiance and derision to shrieks of panic-stricken terror and the dancing warriors into abject fugitives, who, casting away every arm or other impediment down to the breech-clout, and leaving their wives and children in the hail of bullets, ran for their lives, scattering in all directions for hundreds of miles over the prairies, until they found refuge with some friendly tribe or trader.

The white men continued the slaughter, gathered and made bonfires of everything left in the camp, and left the bodies of eighty slain, with the body of the chief stuck up on the end of a lodge pole, as a warning to evil doers, and an example of the power and lust for blood of the whites, when fully aroused by indignities heaped upon them.

The effect of this bloody lesson on the natives of what a few whites could do was far reaching. The natives had been accustomed to hear from the Assiniboines and Sioux their boastful versions of their murders of stray white men, their ambuscades of American troops and success in fighting them; but the news of this complete rout and slaughter by only five whites, not soldiers but ranchers and wolfers, gave pause to those who so confidently had spoken of sweeping all the newcomers from Canada out of Manitoba and had very much to do with the respect shown to the Mounted Police when they penetrated at first to the Western plains.

A few years afterwards, in order to show the impartiality of British justice, some of the brave men who had, in rescuing their personal property, unconsciously performed this signal service, were arrested by the Mounted Police, whose prestige was so largely founded on this defeat and slaughter of the Stonies, and sent for trial to Winnipeg, when "the ends of justice" were served by their escaping punishment.

THE FALL OF 1872.

In the fall business again took me to Fort Ellice, where I met my friend, Inspecting Chief Factor Christie, then on his way to inspect all along the long route to Fort Simpson, McKenzie River. Apprentice Clerk McRae, who had been stationed at the Qu'Appelle during the summer, was ordered to join Mr. Christie at Touchwood Hills and proceed to Athabasca. With Mr. Christie there had come to hunt buffalo

453

the Hon. Walter Ponsonby, of the Rifle Brigade, an aide-de-camp to the Governor-General, who came with me to Qu'Appelle and made a satisfactory killing of buffalo under the guidance of one of our clerks, Sam. McKay.

By the time Mr. Ponsonby returned from his hunt a party to survey and lay out the 2,500 acres of land, reserved about Qu'Appelle by the Company's surrender to the Imperial Government, had arrived. The party consisted of Messrs. W. S. and Harry Gore and Stewart Mulkins—the latter being a relative of Colonel Dennis and having been in Red River during the troublous winter of 1869-70. Mulkins was a great talker, and cynically confessed that, although not a fighting man himself, he had witnessed with much contentment various attacks by the Canadian volunteers made indiscriminately on Metis whenever opportunity served. Whether the object of the attack had been a Rielite or not seemed immaterial to them. But it was very material indeed in fomenting the general discontent pervading the prairies.

INSPECTING CHIEF FACTOR, THE HON. W. J. CHRISTIE.

I remained at Qu'Appelle during the winter of 1872-73, paying occasional visits to the outposts at Touchwood Hills, under William Daniel, and Last Mountain, under Mr. McKinlay, as indeed I had done during the previous summer. About the beginning of March, Mr. Christie returned from the North and rested a day at the fort with me, hearing all about the state of affairs on the plains, which, in due time, as member of the North-West Council, he laid before the proper authorities. He had rested at Qu'Appelle in March, 1869, when on a journey by dog-train from Edmonton to Fort Garry, accompanied by Mrs. Christie. On both these occasions I greatly profited and was entertained by his conversation, for he was a mine of knowledge on all Hudson's Bay subjects and a most excellent recounter of amusing anecdotes of the old characters in the service. He had been educated in Aberdeen, Scotland, and was one of the cleverest men ever in the Company's service.

CHAPTER XXXI.

SPRING AND SUMMER, 1873.

The Spring Rush.

We had a very busy spring in 1873 when our traders, the hunters and the Indians came in. Besides Mr. McKinlay in the office we had in the stores Henry Jordan and George Drever, both of whom had acquired the Indian tongues and been promoted to the grade of storesmen in consequence. As interpreters and traders my old friend Peter La Pierre and young Alick McKay were usefully employed also. But the biggest job was my own in making all the settlements and general arrangements with the traders and important customers; also in discussing "affairs of state" and obtaining information bearing upon them from the Metis who thronged the office by day and till late at night, during the spring rush.

After that was over, in the interval before the hunters started for the summer hunt, the office became the rendezvous of leading men among the Metis to make business arrangements and hear and give the news of the day. While one would be in my private room arranging his own affairs, those waiting, after perhaps exhausting other interesting subjects, would begin bragging about the merits of their running ponies, generally ending the dispute in a challenge and a race on the track across the valley in full view of the fort. There were also some great tellers of tall stories about hunting and war among them, and the competition between these was keen, and, to the audience, often comical. On the whole, I think, the one who deserved the palm in pulling the long bow was Bonace Davis, who had truly distinguished himself in battle with the Sioux as well as on the hunting field, but, not content with the laurels actually won, was addicted to high romance in detailing other incidents of alleged experiences.

CURRENCY AND BANKING.

There was no money in circulation, and very seldom did one of the Company's sterling notes reach Qu'Appelle. As substitutes for cash the Rev. Father DeCorby used to give those he owed little slips of paper " Bon Pour " various amounts to bearer. Those given in at the fort were charged to his account. Occasionally we had to give similar notes for small amounts; but the chief business in the banking line was effected by making transfers from the account of one customer to another. As the horse-trading and other bargains between the Metis were very numerous, this caused many entries in our books.

THE HON. PASCAL BRELAND AGAIN PEACEMAKER.

After the plain hunters had departed my honored and respected friend, the Hon. Pascal Breland, one of the first members to be appointed to the North-West Council, newly organized in Winnipeg under the Lieutenant-Governor, arrived upon a mission of enquiry into the general political unrest and the conspiracy to attack the settlements in Manitoba. He came to me to get the latest intelligence before going out to visit the different camps on the plains. About a month afterwards he returned, after doing all in his power to quieten the people and assuring them of the good intentions of the Government. He thanked me for what he called the good service I had rendered in trying to prevent an outbreak and in warning the authorities of that danger. "I am witness," said he, "to your good work, and to your good management and influence over these people." In testimony whereof upon his return to Fort Garry, at a meeting of the full council in September, Edward McKay (who had been my able adviser and assistant in trying to prevent an outbreak), and I were appointed Justices of the Peace for the Territories. As I was in February thereafter officially notified that the appointment had been confirmed "By His Excellency the Governor-General in Council under the Great Seal," and as my commission has never been revoked by the same authority, I presume my authority in those parts of the old territory which have not been included in the later formed provinces remains as it has been for the past forty years.

A Canadian Geological Survey Party.

About the end of August, 1873, a party of the Geological Survey of Canada, under Professor Bell, arrived at the fort. The assistant was Mr. George F. Lount, and included J. C. Young, Neil Campbell, John Allen, W. G. Armstrong and T. F. O'Brien. It was a most injudicious thing for the Government to send a surveying party during such an unsettled and dangerous state of native feeling. However, the party were under strict orders to avoid all trouble with Indians, and even go the length of buying back their horses should they be stolen. These orders were certainly not to Mr. Lount's liking, and he said a couple of his men, Campbell and Allen, I think, who had been old plainsmen and Indian fighters on the American side, would be glad of another scrap with Indians. The party went up the Qu'Appelle Valley, but near the Elbow of the South Branch were met by Indians who ordered them back. Mr. Bell explained that they were not surveyors of land for farming purposes, but simply taking the testimony of the rocks. To this the Indians replied, through Mr. Charles Pratt, who had been induced to join the party as guide and interpreter at Qu'Appelle, that such an object was still worse from the native point of view, for they said white men are not so eager about farming land and will not go after it so far as they will for gold. In the consequent retreat on Qu'Appelle, Mr. Bell, with Mr. Pratt, made a cursory side trip to Dirt Hills and Wood Mountain, on horseback by themselves, and rejoined the party before its arrival at the fort. I had the pleasure of meeting Dr. Robert Bell in after years at many widely apart places in the territories which he so well explored, as a member of that noble corps of scientific gentlemen of the Geological Survey of Canada, who "without ostentation" have braved every danger of the wilderness and wrested from it its secrets, and whose names will go down in the history of Canada as the scientific Pioneers of Prince Rupert's Land, who so well followed up the work begun by Richardson, Lefroy and Kennicott in the North, and of Palliser, Hector and Hind in the South.

NEED OF NEW POSTS ON SOUTH SASKATCHEWAN RIVER.

Although the new system of doing a wholesale trade through "the freemen" as middlemen had so enormously increased the returns of Qu'Appelle (my recollection being of 8,000 kit and 5,000 red foxes, 3,000 badgers and the same number of wolves that season), its tendency was to put the Company out of direct touch with and control of the Indians. Moreover, the great influx of Metis from Red River to the West, owing to the curtailment of their range after buffalo in American territory as well as their desire to escape from the new order of things in Manitoba, had greatly accelerated the general tendency, which had been going on for two generations of Indians, of the buffalo herds as they diminished in numbers to roam farther and farther west.

It was evident that, in order to keep in nearer contact with the Indians and carry on the business more economically, a permanent post much further west than either Qu'Appelle or Last Mountain was required, and naturally that post should be established—as, with hardly an exception, every other fur-trading post was—on a navigable waterway, which in this case would be the South Branch of the Saskatchewan River. At that time, before railroads, the Company was preparing to place steamboats on Lake Winnipeg and the Saskatchewan, which latter might as well serve new posts on the South as the old establishments on the North Branch.

So far the scheme appeared in the interest of the Company and the Indians to be wise and proper; but there intervened the jealousy existing between different posts and districts of the same company, which led these rivals for the honor of securing the largest "returns of trade" into competition almost as keen as had they been representing competing and opposing concerns. The dominant factors at Carlton and Edmonton Houses claimed, respectively, the lower and upper countries lying north of the South Saskatchewan as part of their domains, and objected to the establishment of any permanent posts by Swan River District therein. On the other hand Mr. Archibald McDonald was not the man to allow the Indians, among whom he had lived and traded for a great part of his life, to be taken out of his control and to diminish his "returns" incident thereon. The Indians, too, required to be consulted and much preferred to remain attached to the Swan River District.

For years we had been investigating this extension of trade to the west. Our wintering post at Cyprè Hills in 1871-72 had been an experiment, which showed that a single post, at which the ever hostile Blackfeet and Qu'Appelle Indians would meet, was not at all desirable. For the Blackfeet who traded more conveniently with the Americans on the Missouri than at our Company's Rocky Mountain and Edmonton Houses it was necessary to have a post near the head of navigation on the South Saskatchewan, officered by those who were known to them at these posts on the North Branch. At as great a distance farther down stream as was compatible with the object the site of the new post for the Qu'Appelle Indians was to be selected. And I may here anticipate by stating that, under the guidance of "Gaddie" Birston, on the north bank of the river, near the scene of the defeat of the Black-feet in 1866, opposite Vermilion Hills, I selected a point on the river, as far as possible from heights within rifle range, in view of probable attack by Blackfeet, and possibly others.

Again and again I reported on these matters and urged speedy action. Elaborate information was required for transmission to Chief Commissioner Smith on the state of the Indians and the Metis and the country, with suggestions for their benefit. But as Mr. Smith's experience in Labrador and the Southern Department could not guide him in the entirely different circumstances of the Northern Department, especially in the new situation on the plains, he appears to have left the rival chiefs of the Saskatchewan and Swan River Districts to fight out amongst themselves the question of extending the trade on the South Saskatchewan. (See note at end of this chapter.) While they were still engaged in this civil war of words and correspondence, in the absence of any British company's post in the vicinity, the American traders from Fort Benton established themselves in Southern Alberta, using whiskey very largely at the notorious " Whoop-Up " and " Stand-Off," and permitting the formation of the Hudson's Bay Company's first great rival in Alberta, the firm of I. G. Baker & Co. Only when too late to retrieve past error was the post at Calgary established.

Referring those interested in the trade and general state of the country in 1873 to copy of my report to Chief Trader McDonald, and to extracts from my report to Chief Commissioner Smith, which are given in the Appendix, I now go on with my narrative.

CHIEF COMMISSIONER SMITH.

In October, 1873, I went down to Fort Ellice to see Mr. McDonald on business.

Mr. Smith, the Chief Commissioner, was then on a visit to Carlton, and was anxious to make a record trip, so as to attend Parliament in Ottawa, of which he was a member. Relays of horses had to be posted all along the Saskatchewan trail for the purpose, and I was told to take a relay and meet the Chief Commissioner, by taking that road part of the way in returning to my charge at Qu'Appelle. That great run in a buckboard was made from Carlton House to Fort Garry between the 5th and 10th of October, so I suppose it was on the afternoon of the 7th that I met the flying express with the horses. They stopped to change, and while he was drinking a cup of hot tea, I answered Mr. Smith's questions about Qu'Appelle. He expressed himself satisfied with my management and ended by telling me emphatically that place and promotion were no longer by seniority but by merit in the company's service—a theory, which, I may as well say here, I seldom saw put in practice. He then bade me farewell, wished me a successful trade and hurried on his way to Fort Ellice. Such was my first meeting with the gentleman who is now famous as Lord Strathcona.

NOTE.—I do not know of anything having been published of the operations of the early traders on the upper " Bow " River, as they then called the whole South Saskatchewan, except brief references to the old French Post near the present site of Calgary, "Fort La Jonquière," built in 1751; and the incidental mention made by Sir George Simpson, in his " Overland Journey Round the World." Simpson says that attempts to maintain permanent posts had been made from time to time, and that these, as well as several strong expeditions, had invariably resulted in loss of life and property, owing to the hostility of the Indians, and the poverty of the country in valuable furs. At that time heavy buffalo robes and grizzly bear skins were too cheap to stand the enormous cost of exporting them.

CHAPTER XXXII.

WINTER ON THE PLAINS, 1873-74.

Whiskey and Bloodshed.

It had been arranged that Mr. W. J. McLean, who had been transferred to Fort Garry after many years' service in Mackenzie River District, should take charge of the fort during the winter. Upon his arrival, rather late in October, taking Drever and Jordan, I started for the winter camp on the plains, and found the first of the party had decided to stop at Sandy Hills near the Elbow of the South Saskatchewan, 175 miles from Qu'Appelle, instead of going farther west. The reason given for wintering so near in was that whiskey was flowing so freely at the posts the Americans had projected into the Cyprè Hills country that it would be dangerous to go to Red Ochre Hills. The liquor had attracted hostile Indians to that quarter, and the American traders were shooting them down whenever they gave trouble. In the neighborhood of Cyprè Hills it was reported that there were eight hundred tents of Teton Sioux including the band of the notorious Sitting Bull. The band of Assiniboines, to which the party slaughtered by the white horse-hunters at Cyprè Hills in spring belonged, were reported to have left the border and were, in about two hundred lodges, wintering between these hills and the South Saskatchewan, and among them some of our Indians were mingled.

Besides, the freemen and occasionally some of our Indians were procuring liquor from these Americans and bringing it back to their fellows, with the usual result of breaking the peace in camp and preventing them paying attention to hunting. Because of these circumstances and that the buffalo were few within range of our winter quarters, we made a comparatively poor trade on the plains that winter.

A CLOSE SHAVE

A BADGER AT BAY.

Having heard that Antoine Rocheblave, one of the Metis to whom we had given advances, was intending to take his buffalo robes to Fort Benton to buy horses, instead of giving them to us, it was necessary for me to go and see him.   Mr. Jos. McKay was wintering at the Sandy Hills, and consented to guide me to Rocheblave, some distance out on the plains.   We went on horseback, and it soon became cold riding, for a strong head wind arose as we were making the long traverse of a treeless, shelterless plain in order to reach wood before dark. Fortunately there was a slight trace of a trail to guide the horses, and giving these their heads for most of the time we " went it blind," throwing the ends of our saddle blankets over our faces, and lowering them alternately to avoid frost bites and to see if the horses were keeping the trace, for it could not be called a trail.   Each of us had Winchester carbines, with which I was then a good shot, but I had also a small new revolver, which I wanted to try.   Most horses are afraid of bears and badgers, and Candrie Bonhomme, which I was riding, was no exception; so when we saw a badger, going as near as Candrie would be induced to approach— dancing, I emptied the revolver, but only hit the badger once on a paw.   Meanwhile the animal, facing us savagely, had backed off on to a snowdrift formed round a small willow bush.   Joe, who had been watching the performance in amusement, then called out, "Get off your horse, and go and kill him with your whip-handle."   Taking the end of the long line, which was always attached round the neck of our horses in use, in one hand, I advanced on the badger.   The crust of the drift bore me till, on getting within arm's length of the ferociously grinning, strong teeth of the brute, as I made the blow the crust gave way and down I went till my nose was on a level with that of the badger and within half a yard of it.   Instantly I struck out and knocked him dead, saving my face from his powerful jaws and possibly my life.

WHISKEY SEIZED AND A BALL GIVEN.

During the winter I made a trip to the fort, where Mr. McLean, separated from his family and with little to do, for nearly every hunter was away on the plains, was wearying. Mr. McKinlay came in from his outpost at Touchwood Hills at the same time, and to liven things up we gave a ball, at which the principal guests were Messrs. Kavanagh and Kelly, two soldiers retired from the U. S. Army at Fort Totten, Devil's Lake, Dakota. They had married charming daughters of a respectable Metis named Klyne (who was probably a son of one of Lord Selkirk's DeMeuron soldiers), and came as the very first agricultural settlers to attempt farming on the prairie upland, instead of in the valley.

My faithful companion when we broke away from the camp of turmoil in the summer of 1868, Thomas Sinclair, had got hold of a small keg of whiskey, which he was peddling about the lakes. McKinlay suggested that to signalize the honor done me in the grant of a commission as Justice of the Peace and at the same time give manifestation of the majesty of the law, Sinclair's (well watered) grog should be seized and confiscated to the Crown; and instead of being wasted barrenly and unprofitably by being spilt on the ground, our guests at the ball should be qualified as witnesses against Sinclair by sampling the seizure. Two constables were immediately sent in pursuit of Sinclair, and a few hours later returned with the keg and in great good humour.

As the unfortunate man was far from wealthy and had always been a good and loyal subject, who erred in ignorance, and moreover I had no legal instructions or "guide book," no further official action was taken against him. Personally Messrs. McLean and McKinlay and I subscribed the value set on a pony designated "Old Wabby" on the Company's horse list, and as a token of friendship presented the animal to Sinclair, who was also invited to attend the ball, which was a brilliant success and fully enjoyed by all, especially McKinlay.

HAND OVER MY CHARGE

A German Noble Apprentice Clerk.

In the spring of 1874, besides McKinlay, a new apprentice clerk came to assist us, and proved very entertaining. He was going under the name of Frederick William Beneke, but was a son of Count Von Bernstorff, the German Ambassador in London. He was an officer in a crack Prussian regiment, but nevertheless served out his time as a Hudson's Bay apprentice clerk, in New Caledonia, to which by way of Edmonton and the Yellowhead Pass he was sent that summer.

Relinquish My Charge.

As soon as the season's business was wound up I handed over the charge to my amiable friend, Mr. McLean, as my successor. I was anxious to go home to Scotland and was glad to be relieved of a position in which I felt that I had received neither the reward nor the support which I had been led to expect and which I had well earned amid many privations and dangers.

At long last, preparations were then being made by the Dominion Government to police the plains and to make too long deferred arrangements with the Indians who, instead of having been quieted by the establishment of Canadian Dominion at Fort Garry, had been more disquieted than ever thereby. After the Mounted Police arrived on the plains and the Qu'Appelle Treaty was made that summer of 1874, the history of the country is accessible in public documents and numerous other more or less authentic printed papers.

To Fort Garry Again.

Mr. McLean and I journeyed together to Fort Ellice, where we had the pleasure of meeting his good wife and fine family of little children, whose rosy appearance reflected great credit on their place of birth, in McKenzie River. Mrs. McLean was daughter of the genial, talented and highly respected Chief Trader A. H. Murray, the builder of old Fort Yukon, and the designer of that last vestige still standing of old Fort Garry, the Governor's gate on Main Street, Winnipeg.

At Fort Ellice I took shipping for Fort Garry. Instead of the "batteaux" we had rowed laboriously down the Assiniboine in 1871, on this occasion we allowed the current to do the work on three big flat boats. In the bow of one I pitched my tent, and enjoyed my ease on one of the most pleasant voyages I ever made. On landing at Fort Garry I was greeted most warmly by a big bewhiskered gentleman, who had to tell me he was Christie before I saw any resemblance between him and my old chum and shipmate on the "Prince Rupert." He had been transferred as Chief Accountant of the Northern Department, with all the paraphernalia from York Factory, to Fort Garry. Our other shipmate, Armit, was also at Fort Garry; so thus re-united after seven long years we spun many yarns and "fought all our battles o'er again."

The Hon. Donald A. Smith, M.P., had resigned the Chief Commissionership and Chief Factor James Allan Grahame, of Fort Victoria, Vancouver Island, had just arrived to reign in his stead.

———

Should these simple jottings meet with a better reception than I have reason to expect, and encourage me to put on record unwritten memoirs of the districts further north, in which I afterwards served for years, while they remained as much under the dominion of the Hudson's Bay Company as they ever had been before the transfer to Canada, possibly I may attempt to indite another volume.

ISAAC COWIE.

APPENDIX

APPENDIX A.

THE HUDSON'S BAY COMPANY'S EXPLORERS, 1830 TO 1856.

Robert Campbell.

Mr. Campbell was a tall, handsome, dark complexioned man, lithe and strong, hardy and enduring; a pious Presbyterian, and devoted to the service of the Company. A family connection of Chief Factor James McMillan, who had charge of the fur trade experimental farm at Red River, he came out from Perthshire to take charge of a great sheep raising project in connection with that establishment, and was sent with Messrs. Glen Rae and Bourke to Kentucky to fetch the flock, of which a disastrous account is given in Alexander Ross's "Red River Settlement." After the failure of that mismanaged project Mr. Campbell entered the fur trade proper, in which his name first appears as Postmaster serving under Chief Trader McPherson at Fort Simpson, Mackenzie River, in 1835.

The Northern Department Minutes of Council contain from time to time brief and fragmentary records bearing upon Mr. Campbell's career. In 1833, Mr. John McLeod, Clerk in charge of Fort Halkett on the Liard River, was ordered to "be employed with seven men, in the summer of 1834, in discovering the countries situated on the west side of the Rocky Mountains from the sources of the east (?) branch of the Liard River." In 1835, the minutes, after appointing Mr. J. Hutchinson to the command of Fort Halkett, say: "The late discovery of Mr. John McLeod, towards the sources of the East Branch of the Liard River and a large river named Pelly's River falling from the mountains into the Pacific, presenting a field for the extension of trade in that quarter, it is towards that object and with the view of opening communication with our posts and shipping on the Coast, it is resolved that the present establishment of Fort Halkett be removed to Dease's Lake, summer 1836, if possible, and that measures be concerted for the purpose of establishing a new post on the banks of that river at least 200 miles distant in a direct

469

line from the height of land towards the Pacific in the summer of 1837-38." In 1836, the minutes state: "The Governor and Committee being desirous that a post be established as early as possible on the Pelly's (supposed Stikine) River falling into the Pacific, for the purpose of intercepting the valuable trade which now finds its way to the Coast and falls into the hands of the Russians and Americans,

"It is resolved that an officer and six men be forwarded with outfit 1837 in order to enable Chief Trader McPherson to establish a post, to be called Fort Drew, in the summer of 1838, down that river at a distance of at least 200 miles from Dease's Lake." In 1837 the minutes promote Robert Campbell from Postmaster to Clerk at £60 a year, and appoint him to the charge of the post at Dease's Lake, with A. R. McLeod, Jr., apprentice clerk, as his assistant. They also show the reason for his promotion and appointment as follows:—" The extraordinary statement made by Mr. Hutchinson respecting the failure of his mission to the west branch of the Liard River for the purpose of establishing Dease's Lake (post), having been attentively perused and considered to be *founded upon groundless apprehensions*, it is resolved that Chief Trader McPherson take the necessary steps to establish that Post without delay; and that he be instructed to convey to Mr. Robert Campbell the approbation of the Council for his spirited offer to conduct that service." The explanation of the circumstance noted in the minutes which gave Mr. Campbell his chance to distinguish himself is given by Dr. G. M. Dawson, the late distinguished Director of the Geological Survey of Canada, in his report on the Yukon, 1887. Mr. Campbell related to him that Mr. Hutchinson left Fort Halkett early in June, 1836, with a party of men and two large canoes. The appearance or reported appearance of a large force of hostile Indians at Portage Brule, ten miles above Fort Halkett, so alarmed the party that they turned back in great haste, abandoning their goods, and lost no time in running down stream to Fort Simpson, where Mr. Campbell was in temporary charge during Mr. McPherson's voyage with his brigade to Portage la Loche.

As the intention of this book is mainly to record incidents which have not been published, or if so are not generally accessible, and a very good account of Mr. Campbell's achievements is given by Dr. Dawson in the report just quoted, as well as in publications referred to therein and made use of by him, I resist the strong temptation to copy all Dr. Dawson says in full. Even then justice would not be done in full measure to the intrepid and modest discoverer. But, in defiance of the limits set for me by the publisher, I must give in full from Dr. Dawson the honour he gives where honour is due to the fur trade pioneers of the North-West:—

DR. DAWSON'S TRIBUTE TO THE FUR-TRADING PIONEERS.

" The utmost credit must be given to the pioneers of the Hudson's Bay Company for the enterprise displayed by them in carrying their trade into the Yukon basin in the face of difficulties so great and at such an immense distance from their base of supplies. To explorations of this kind performed in the service of commerce, *unostentatiously* and as matters of simple duty, by such men as Mackenzie, Fraser, Thompson and Campbell, we owe the discovery of our great North-West country. Their journeys are not marked by incidents of conflict or bloodshed, but were accomplished, on the contrary, with the friendly assistance and co-operation of the natives. Less resolute men would scarcely have entertained the idea of utilizing, as an avenue of trade, a river so perilous of navigation as the Liard had proved to be when it was explored. So long, however, as this appeared to be the only practical route to the country beyond the mountains, its abandonment was never contemplated. Neither distance nor danger appeared to have been taken into account, and in spite of every obstacle a way was opened and a series of posts was established extending from Fort Simpson to Fort Yukon. Fort Simpson itself may be regarded, even at the present day, as a post very far removed from the borders of civilization, but this further route, which nearly half a century ago became familiar to the Company's voyageurs, stretched out beyond it for over a thousand miles. Mr. James Anderson, in 1853, writes thus of the Liard River: ' You can hardly conceive the intense horror the men have to go up to Frances Lake. They invariably on re-hiring endeavour to be exempted from the West Branch (Liard). The number of deaths which have occurred there is fourteen, viz., three in connection with Dease Lake and eleven in connection with Frances Lake and Pelly Banks; of these last three died from starvation and eight from drowning.' "*

*In the later 1870's while the last fur trader was Chief Commissioner of the Hudson's Bay Company, Mr. James A. Grahame, the good Bishop Bompas wrote to him advocating the bringing in of the supplies for Mackenzie River District from British Columbia by the Liard River. In reply the bluff old voyageur informed his right reverence that on that route there occurred not only a " Devil's Portage," but also " Hell Gates," which the Company's tripmen appeared to dread more than the infernal person and place from which the names were derived.

In this connection, for the information of those who have had little opportunity or previous inclination to enquire into the history of pioneering in the Great West, I must add to the names honourably mentioned by Dr. Dawson those of such other fur-trading pioneers and explorers and discoverers as during the twenty years from 1834 to 1855 decorate the annals of the Hudson's Bay Company by their services in the cause of science and humanity as well as of commerce. The earliest of these was John McLeod, who began in 1834, by the Liard route, the exploration of the headwaters of the Stikine and the main branch of the Liard west of the Rockies, which were utilized in 1838 by Robert Campbell, who, taking up the exploration of the Liard at McLeod's farthest, opposite Simpson Lake, extended it and established posts along the route at Frances Lake, Pelly Banks and the junction of the Pelly and Lewes affluents of the Yukon, which farthest post was named Selkirk in 1848. Outlines of the discoveries made by Messrs. McLeod and Campbell are to be found in Dr. Dawson's report, which also refers to those made by John Bell on the Peel River and the lower Yukon, whose southern headwaters had unknowingly been reached by Campbell at Pelly Banks in the summer of 1840.

In 1828, Sir John Franklin, in returning from his second boat expedition along the Arctic coast, by mistake entered the mouth of a western affluent instead of continuing on the main Mackenzie River. This affluent he named after Sir Robert Peel, and shortly afterwards it was explored by Mr. Bell with the view of establishing a post on it. Bell was for many years in charge of Fort Good Hope, then the Company's farthest north establishment. In 1839 the Northern Council directed "That Chief Trader McPherson take the necessary steps to establish in the summer of 1840 a post on Peel's River, and in 1841 another post on Colvile River*; and, as the recent arrangement made with the Russian-American Fur Company renders it unnecessary to extend the trade down the Stikine River from the east side of the mountains as formerly contemplated, that Mr. Campbell and people intended for that service be employed in assisting Mr. Bell to extend the trade from Peel's River to Colvile River in 1841; and that Hector McKenzie, apprentice postmaster, be sent by the Athabasca brigade to the (Mackenzie) District this season and six recruits next year to enable the gentleman in charge of

---

*The finders of the headwaters of the Yukon in the south and east thought them to be those of the Colvile River, which falls into the Arctic Ocean west of the Mackenzie.

McKenzie's River to carry the projected extension of trade into effect as early as possible."*

JOHN BELL AND ALEXANDER HUNTER MURRAY.

Accordingly Mr. Bell established Fort McPherson on the Peel in 1840. In 1842 he crossed the Rocky Mountains and explored the upper portion of the Porcupine, completing his survey of it to its union with a great river which the Indians called Yukon in 1846. Next year Alexander Hunter Murray built Fort Yukon at the junction of the Porcupine with the Yukon. Three years after, in 1850, Robert Campbell, descending the Pelly from Fort Selkirk to Fort Yukon, rounded off his explorations. Fort Selkirk was thereafter supplied by the much safer and easier route from the Mackenzie by the Peel and Porcupine Rivers, and the terrific traffic by the upper Liard was abandoned.

NICHOL FINLAYSON AND UNGAVA.

Before these efforts for the extension of trade in the Far North West beyond the Rocky Mountains were commenced a similar enterprise had been directed to the Far North East of the Labrador peninsula. Starting by canoe from Moose Factory and coasting along the shores of East Main till a suitable river was discovered, Mr. Nichol Finlayson penetrated the interior of that wild land, crossed the height of land to an also unexplored stream, running into all the dangers of the unknown, he reached the sea on Ungava Bay, on the southern coast of Hudson's Straits, and there established Fort Chimo. The canoe route he followed being absolutely unsuitable for the conveyance of supplies and the resultant fur returns, the Northern Council in 1831 decreed as follows:—

"That the sloop 'Beaver,' under the command of Thomas Duncan, sloopmaster, with a crew of five men, taking Mr. Erlandson as passenger, be transferred to the settlement of Ungava for the purpose of being at the disposal of Mr. Nichol Finlayson, and be dispatched thither as early this season as the navigation admits; and that such supplies in trading goods, provisions and stores be shipped on board of her as are likely to be required until the autumn of 1833, it being intended that she be employed on the coast in trade with the Esquimaux the whole of the next season of open water, and that she may be sent with such returns

*In consequence of this order of Council Mr. Campbell abandoned the post at Dease Lake in the extension towards the Stikine.

473

as may be collected and for such further supplies as may be required to York Factory in the summer of 1833." It was further resolved " That the nine men now at Ungava be retained there and employed as Mr. Nichol Finlayson may consider expedient, and that the servants whose contracts expire in 1833 be brought to York then and be replaced by others if they be unwilling to renew their engagements; and that for further instructions Mr. Finlayson be referred to Governor Simpson's letter of this date."

The Council in 1833 record:—" With regard to the establishment of Ungava, from which no advices have been received since those of date 1831, it is expected that the ' Beaver ' sloop will be forwarded thence to York Factory with the returns and for fresh supplies of goods, provisions, etc., in the course of the present season, in which case it is resolved that Mr. Finlayson's request for men, goods and other supplies be completed by Chief Factor Christie as far as the means at his disposal may permit." "In the meantime Governor Simpson has forwarded communcations to Chief Factors McTavish and Beioley requesting them to concert measures for sending an express to Ungava with the least possible delay, if they have not already heard from Mr. Finlayson, in order to gain some intelligence respecting the state of the settlement, which they are directed to forward to the Governor and Committee, likewise to Governor Simpson in duplicate by the ship and via Canada; and in the event of the ' Beaver ' sloop not having reached Ungava in 1831 or not getting to York (Factory) in the course of the present season, it is resolved that the Governor and Committee be requested to forward the necessary supplies from England or Canada as early in the summer of 1834 as possible; but in the absence of any communication from Ungava either by overland express to the southern department or by the vessel to York (Factory) this season, then in that case it is to be understood that no outfit shall be forwarded either from England or Canada, but that Chief Factors McTavish and Beioley be directed to concert and carry into effect such measures by overland communication towards the protection and safety of the settlement as they may consider expedient under existing circumstances."

The next mention of Ungava in the minutes is in 1836, when it was directed " That the *Esquimaux* brig, which is to be sent from York Factory to Ungava with the outfit and for the returns of that district, be fitted up with deals, bark, and about 50 pieces of flour, grease and pemmican, or such other provisions as can be spared, and any old ironworks or other unsaleable goods at York

Factory which are likely to find a market among the Esquimaux; and with four active servants, under engagements of not less than three years, to fill up the vacancies."

JOHN McLEAN AT UNGAVA.

This was followed in 1837 (after which Ungava was probably provided for by the Council of the Southern Department, as no subsequent mention is made of it in the Northern Minutes) by:—

" Ungava Arrangements.

" Ungava, John McLean, Clerk,
" Erland Erlandson, Clerk.

" Resolved that the brig *Eagle* be dispatched as early as navigation opens with instructions to touch at Ungava, there to land an outfit for that district, and afterwards proceed with the returns that may be shipped on board of her there for England, taking as passengers to Ungava Mr. McLean and six servants, and from thence any servants retiring to Europe."

Those who wish to fill in the wide gaps left between these extracts from the Minutes of Council will find the record of that romantic adventure, furnished by the leader of the expedition, Mr. Nichol Finlayson in Mr. R. M. Ballantyne's fascinating book "Ungava." And here I may be allowed to say that I had the privilege of the personal acquaintanceship of both the hero and the author, through my father's having served the Company for a short time along with both of them. It was through reading Ballantyne's "Hudson's Bay," "The Young Fur Traders" and "Ungava" that I, like other youths, was lured into the service of the Company, and from my later experience in that service I feel bound to warn all boys against reading Ballantyne. Rather let them read, mark and digest the unvarnished account of his life in the Hudson's Bay service, written by the John McLean, Clerk, who was appointed to the charge of Ungava by the Council in 1837,* in which the general reader will find an interesting

*" Notes of Twenty-five Years' Service in the Hudson's Bay Company," by John McLean, London, 1849. " The history of my career may serve as a warning to those who may be disposed to enter the Hudson's Bay Company's service. They may learn that from the moment they embark in the company's canoes at Lachine, or their ships at Gravesend, they bid adieu to all that civilized man most values on earth. They bid adieu to their family and friends probably forever; for if they remain long enough to attain the promotion which allows them the privilege of revisiting their native land—a period of from twenty to twenty-five years—what change does not this life exhibit in a much shorter time? They bid adieu

account of his explorations in the hinterland of Fort Chimo. Reference is also made to him and part of the country he explored is described in a book published a few years ago by an American traveller, Dillon Wallace, on a canoe voyage he made through the wilds of Labrador, entitled, "The Long Labrador Trail."

DEASE, SIMPSON, ANDERSON, STEWART AND RAE.

To the books on the subjects which are accessible in public libraries I beg to refer such readers as are interested for accounts of the services rendered to geographical science by the Hudson's Bay Company's Arctic Exploring Expedition under Messrs. Dease and Simpson; of the assistance rendered to Franklin on his boat voyages, and to British expeditions sent in search of him later by Hudson's Bay officers and men; of the admirably planned and executed searches made for the fate of Franklin by the Hudson's Bay people alone under Anderson and Stewart, and of the discovery of the first traces by Surgeon John Rae on one of the expeditions under his leadership. The deeds of daring and endurance performed "without ostentation," as Dr. Dawson remarks, by these men gloriously illuminate the history of "The Company of Adventurers," and rendered it in their day worthy of the name in its nobler meaning.

OTHER MEN OF MARK AMONG THE ADVENTURERS.

This Appendix, for which the name of the honoured Chief of Swan River District gave me the text on which to start, would be incomplete were I to refrain from brief reference to mighty deeds of daring and endurance done in the ordinary course of every day duty by the officers and men of the Company of Adventurers in the wilds of North America from Labrador to the Pacific across the wide continent, few of which were considered important enough at the time to be reported in writing to the Governor and Committee in London, where the few so recorded appear to have been deemed unworthy of preservation, and, like the wealth of oral traditions which were handed down from one generation of fur traders to another, have perished and been lost sight of

to all the comforts and conveniences of civilized life, to vegetate at some desolate, solitary post, hundreds of miles, perhaps, from any other human habitation save the wigwam of the savage; without any society but that of their own thoughts, or of the two or three humble individuals who share their exile. They bid adieu to all the refinement and cultivation of civilized life, not infrequently becoming semi-barbarians—so altered in habits and sentiments that they not only become attached to savage life, but eventually lose all relish for any other." (Vol. II, page 260.)

forever. It was for the purpose of putting in print some of these continually perishing recollections of the past that I felt justified in attempting to write this book. But the limits imposed by the publisher, as well as the intention of recording only such matter as is not to be found in books accessible to the general public which have a bearing on my personal recollections, only permit of mere mention of the names of such men of talent as Chief Trader Alexander Hunter Murray, whose notes on the Loucheaux Indians and beautiful drawings of them and their works adorn the pages of Sir John Richardson's narrative; of Chief Trader Bernard R. Ross, that distinguished contributor and collector in ethnology and natural history to the Smithsonian Institution at Washington; of Chief Factor MacFarlane, who assisted Mr. Ross and for many years after continued and extended the work and its field of operations in ornithology, as his section of the book, "Through the Mackenzie Basin" (Briggs, Toronto, 1908), bears ample testimony; and of Chief Trader Joseph James Hargrave, author of that text-book of history, "Red River" (John Lovell, Montreal, 1869). All these but the still virile and active Mr. MacFarlane have long ago departed, but not without records which will long survive.

The Hudson's Bay men who served in the old "Columbia Department" on both sides of the international boundary now fixed and in New Caledonia occupied territories and coasts under circumstances which brought them under the notice of numerous writers, and of such historians as Bancroft and the Rev. Father Morrice, now of Winnipeg. Moreover, many of their private journals and papers have been preserved by the patriotic pride and intelligent action taken by the Government of British Columbia in the past history of the country before it became a Canadian Province.

No such active interest in and efficient financial aid to securing the private papers of the fur traders, who retired to the Red River Settlement from the far-flung "Hudson's Bay Territories," has ever been given by the Government of Manitoba. Besides public documents, not trade papers but really Government records, have been either kept, concealed or destroyed by the commercial representatives of the company, in whose custody remained many records of the Government of Assiniboia at the time of the transfer to Canada. The loss has been to some extent minimized by the praiseworthy diligence and research which for some years characterized the Historical Society of Manitoba, and of such writers and collectors as Mr. Charles N. Bell, F.R.G.S., the

Rev. Dr. Bryce of Winnipeg, Mr. Justice Archer Martin of British Columbia, while he resided in Winnipeg, and of other members of and contributors to that society.

Fortunately for the data of North West history the efforts of the Dominion Archives at Ottawa have been indefatigable, persistent and wonderfully successful in rescuing them from oblivion. Those of the Archivist of British Columbia at Victoria have been also largely resultant in acquiring documents bearing upon the history of that Province when it was, in the days of the fur trade, under the direction of the Council of the Northern Department of Rupert's Land. The activity of the Historical Society of North Dakota, the early history of which coalesces so largely with that of Red River settlement, has also been most praiseworthy and worthy of imitation in Manitoba.

APPENDIX B.

REPORT ON THE TRADE OF FORT QU'APPELLE.

FORT QU'APPELLE, *March*, 1873.

Sir,—For the future and further development of the trade, I beg to submit for your consideration and approval the following remarks thereon:

It is surprising that hitherto no active steps have been taken to establish a chain of posts on the South Branch, similar to that on the North Branch of the Saskatchewan River. The country through which the South Saskatchewan flows is stocked with the usual prairie fur-bearing animals, and is hunted over by Crees, Saulteaux and halfbreeds, trading principally at Qu'-Appelle and Red River Settlement, as far up as the Swift Current Creek, a small stream which rises in the Cyprè Hills and flows in a north-easterly direction into the South Saskatchewan.

Along the upper waters of the South Saskatchewan and those of its tributaries—the Red Deer, the Bow and the Belly Rivers—live and roam the Blood, Piegan and Blackfeet Indians, who are poorly supplied at present and have to make long journeys to Edmonton and Rocky Mountain House or to the American posts on the Missouri for the purpose of trade.

I would strongly recommend that two posts be established on the South Saskatchewan River. The site of the lower post should be near the Red Ochre Hills at a spot already examined and found suitable. From it all the Qu'Appelle plain trade could be conducted from a much more central position than at present. The upper post, I think, should be placed somewhere near the site of old Chesterfield House, at the mouth of the Red Deer River, for the benefit and convenience of the Blackfeet and their kindred tribes only, so as to prevent conflict with their enemies the Crees, and their allies; for whom the lower post would be used exclusively.

The South Saskatchewan is said to be much deeper and freer from obstructions than the North Branch as far up as the Red Deer River at least. So the steamboat now being put on the Saskatchewan could take up the outfits, and the returns could

31 479

be sent down at any time by boat. No such long trips nor new wintering posts as are required at present would be necessary from the proposed posts, for years to come.

Such a post in their hunting grounds for the Blackfeet would prevent their visiting and getting into trouble with the Crees at Edmonton, while also stopping to a large extent their trade with the Americans on the Missouri.

But, as American whiskey traders have been, and now are wintering in the Blackfeet country, it may not be expedient to establish a post there without some protective force. However, it appears to me that the place proposed for the upper post of the Company would be equally suitable for a Government military station to keep the traders and the Blackfeet and Crees in order; and it is surely the duty of the Canadian Government to exercise their authority in that distracted part of the country. A gunboat to act and keep up communication and to carry supplies for the military posts along the river might be found both economical and effective.

I would strongly commend this proposal for your approval, and I hope that something may be done towards establishing the lower post at least during the coming summer. In establishing such a post it is false economy to begin on a small scale and gradually make additions and improvements instead of at once completing it in a permanent and well planned form. Half the amount spent in driblets in payment of unskilled labour would complete a good substantial establishment by competent hands. I think such men could put up by contract, in the course of the summer, a suitable establishment, with the outer walls of some of the buildings serving in place of stockades, for about two thousand pounds. The expense of trying to erect it with the unskilled, unruly and lazy day labourers, to be occasionally induced to work out here, would be more than double, and have to be paid for in the best selling trade goods of which we are always under-supplied.

Of the sites recommended, that of the lower post is about eight days' travel with laden carts in a south-westerly direction from Carlton; while the upper post would be about ten days' travel south of Edmonton, and eight days west of the lower post proposed.

All the buildings at Qu'Appelle, except the new trading store, require to be thoroughly repaired next summer if the post is still to remain the focus of trade for this quarter. These repairs cannot be done at a cost of less than several hundred pounds, which would be thrown away if the post at Red Ochre Hills were subsequently established. The need of immediate decision is therefore apparent.

NEW SYSTEM OF TRADE.

The summer trade in provisions at this post was conducted on a new system. No trading parties of employees were sent out to trade on the plains as heretofore; selling at a reduced tariff and advancing goods at the fort to competent freemen to do the trade in the hunters' camps being resorted to instead. The result was that only a few Indians came in to the fort with their hunts, and the main business was done at it with halfbreed hunters and traders.

It would be premature to make any exact assertion as to the greater economy and profit made by this radical change, as our accounts have not yet been closed. But there is no doubt whatever that the provision trade has been more profitable than usual, and besides the new system has had the effect of drawing to this post a large number of new customers who previously took their hunts to Red River and sold them to other merchants than the Company. The same plan to secure their buffalo robes and furs has been attempted, and from the plentifulness of buffalo there is no doubt of its being equally successful.

The great drawback to opening a large trade with the halfbreeds is the lack here of sufficient goods, which compels them to make the long journey to Red River, and compels us to pay their credit balances on their trade here in orders on Fort Garry for cash, or partly cash and partly goods which are charged us at the selling price there.

The mistakes made in indenting for and the delays attending the transmission of the trading outfits are simply disgraceful to a business corporation.

I remain, Sir,

Your obedient servant,

ISAAC COWIE.

Archibald McDonald, Esq., Chief Trader, Hudson's Bay Company, Fort Ellice, Swan River District.

APPENDIX C.

SUMMARY OF REPORT ON THE BUFFALO PLAINS TRIBUTARY TO FORT QU'APPELLE.

By Isaac Cowie, Clerk in Charge, to Chief Commissioner Smith, of the Hudson's Bay Company.

Farming along the Qu'Appelle Lakes has been tried with varying success; crops of wheat, barley, Indian corn, potatoes and common kitchen vegetables, in good seasons, turning out fair returns. Abundant water, pasture and hay and an open country make stock-raising profitable and easy.

On the Fishing Lakes, above and below the fort, some twenty-five families of French halfbreeds have established themselves as "habitans" on a small scale; but depend more on buffalo hunting in summer and fishing in fall and winter, than on their crops. This comparatively fixed community, in a land of nomadic hunters, is the result of the efforts of the Roman Catholic missionary, Rev. Father DeCorby, who has been stationed since 1868 on the lake below the fort. Both he and his colleague, the Rev. Father Lestanc, who has spent some years amongst the Metis, who winter at Wood Mountain, and for a while at Qu'-Appelle, have used every effort to induce the Metis, former habitans of Red River and St. Joe (U.S.), to resume settled occupancy of land near the lakes and to cease from intruding on the Qu'-Appelle Indians' hunting grounds, in which the buffalo are so rapidly decreasing. Father Lestanc has declared to me that those who have forsaken farming in Red River for hunting on the plains "should be compelled to farm;" for which purpose the Government might lend some assistance to start. Besides the twenty-five resident families before mentioned, it is estimated that there is a population of one thousand roving Metis who more or less frequently resort to the fort and mission.

The Indians belonging to Qu'Appelle number approximately 320 lodges, or 2,000 persons, divided into the heathen tribes of Crees, Saulteaux and Young Dogs—the latter being a cross between the Crees and Assiniboines. The Wood Mountain Assiniboines seldom visit the fort, and never in large numbers, but trade frequently with our travelling or wintering parties on the plains. But the majority of them trade at the American posts on the Missouri, where treaties have been made with them by the United States Government. Owing to the severe punishmnt for horse stealing given a camp of Assiniboines at Cyprè Hills last spring, by half-a-dozen of the owners of the horses, who had followed the thieves from Benton, a number of the tribe, consisting of two hundred lodges, are now encamped between Swift Current and Cyprè Hills, instead of along the American boundary.

The Sioux bands, under Standing Buffalo and White Cap, who took refuge about Portage la Prairie and Fort Ellice, after the Massacre of Minnesota about ten years ago, occasionally come in to trade at Qu'Appelle or are met by our traders on the Qu'Appelle hunting grounds. They are very well behaved Indians here; but their intrusion, like that of the Red River halfbreeds, is deeply resented by the Qu'Appelle Indians, who are yearly compelled to seek the buffalo farther west and thereby invade the territory of their enemies of the Blackfeet tribes.

Besides these friendly Sioux refugees of the Yankton tribe, the numerous and warlike Tetons, under the notorious Sitting Bull, and that ilk, are sometimes either driven by United States troops or for food to follow the buffalo across the boundary. From these spies have scoured the Qu'Appelle country and messages and messengers have been sent to me to see if the whole tribe could find refuge in it from the American troops. Our own Indians are very wroth at these efforts, and we have had much difficulty in preventing them from attacking these messengers of "peace." But, in spite of our dissuasions and the threats of our Indians, these troublesome and powerful Tetons seem determined to obtain a footing north of the 49th parallel, and eight hundred lodges of them are reported to be now in the vicinity of Cyprè Hills.

As to the condition of the Indians and Metis who are customers of the Company at Qu'Appelle, it is estimated that on an average each Indian family owns three horses and each Metis five, and, besides their food and much of their clothing, obtained from the buffalo, they barter for other supplies with the Company and the traders yearly about $250 per family. The Indians make less in the summer and more in the winter than the Metis, because the Metis are better equipped for the summer hunt, but do not continue constantly after the buffalo during winter as the Indians do.

REPORT ON THE BUFFALO PLAINS COUNTRY

Our party out from Qu'Appelle this season intended to have wintered several days' journey further west; but, on reaching the Elbow of the South Saskatchewan, the number of American traders, with whiskey from Benton, was reported to be so large in the Cyprè Hills country, and the murders among the different tribes, many of them hostile to people from Qu'Appelle, so frequent, that it was considered only prudent to stop here, which greatly lengthens the distance we travel to the buffalo and our Indians who follow them. A party going out late in the fall, and merely putting up a rough shelter, must go without the protection of the pickets and stockades of a regular post.

It is very galling to see the furs and robes, which should be ours, going to these desperado trespassers on British territory. As the Canadian Government has now assumed responsibility it would appear high time that they should take some means to quieting the minds of the Indians who have hitherto been friendly, of confounding the plots to raid the new Province of Manitoba, which have been hatching for sometime along the boundary, and of ridding the Cvprè Hills country of the bands of outlaws and smugglers who are playing havoc with our Indians and our trade.

The Elbow, South Saskatchewan River,
    16th December, 1873.

INDEX AND EXPLANATION OF
FUR TRADE TERMS.

INDEX AND EXPLANATION OF TERMS

INDEX AND EXPLANATION OF TERMS

INDEX AND EXPLANATION OF TERMS

INDEX AND EXPLANATION OF TERMS

INDEX AND EXPLANATION OF TERMS

INDEX AND EXPLANATION OF TERMS

INDEX AND EXPLANATION OF TERMS

INDEX AND EXPLANATION OF TERMS

INDEX AND EXPLANATION OF TERMS

INDEX AND EXPLANATION OF TERMS

INDEX AND EXPLANATION OF TERMS

INDEX AND EXPLANATION OF TERMS

INDEX AND EXPLANATION OF TERMS

PAGE

INDEX AND EXPLANATION OF TERMS

INDEX AND EXPLANATION OF TERMS

INDEX AND EXPLANATION OF TERMS